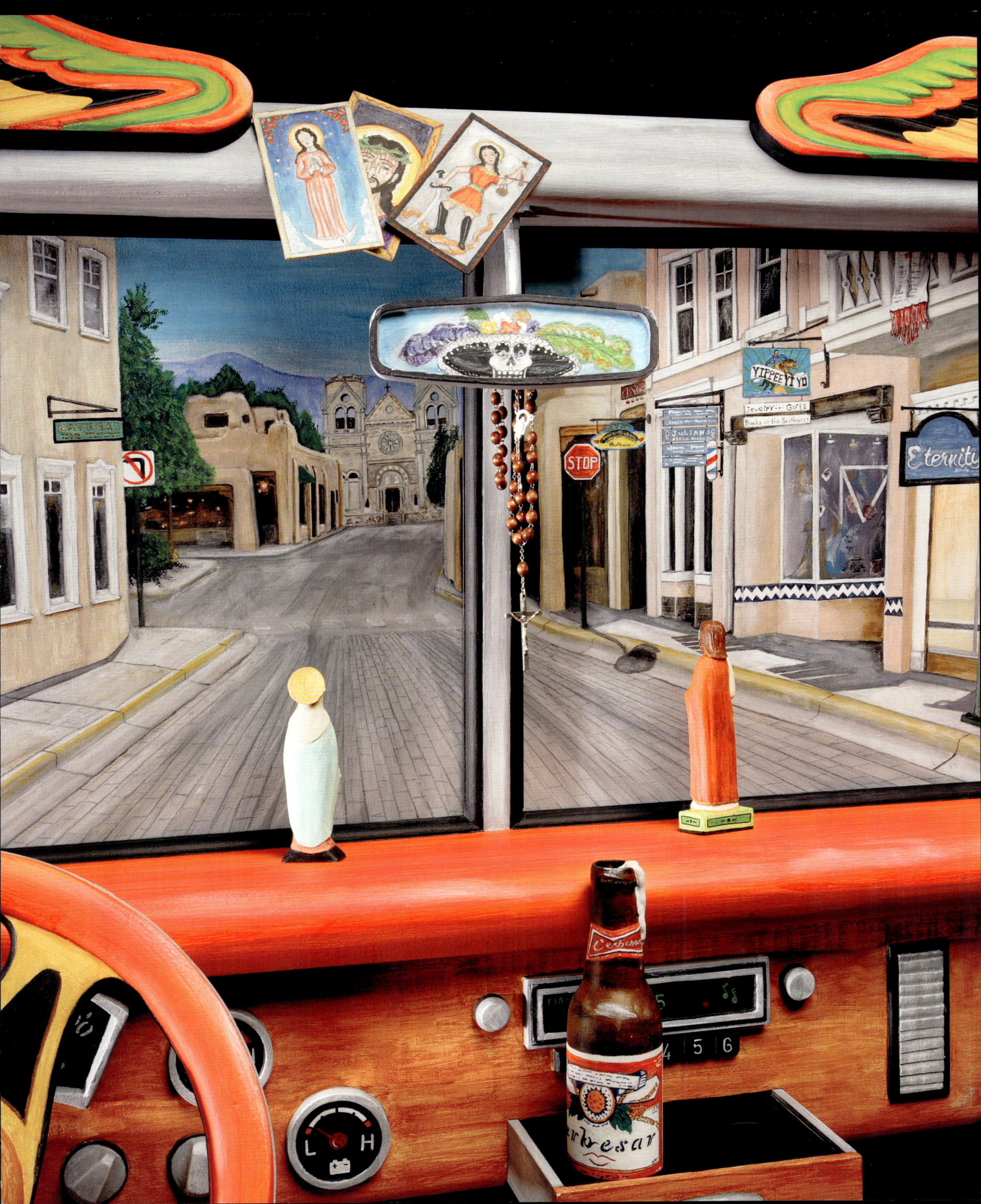

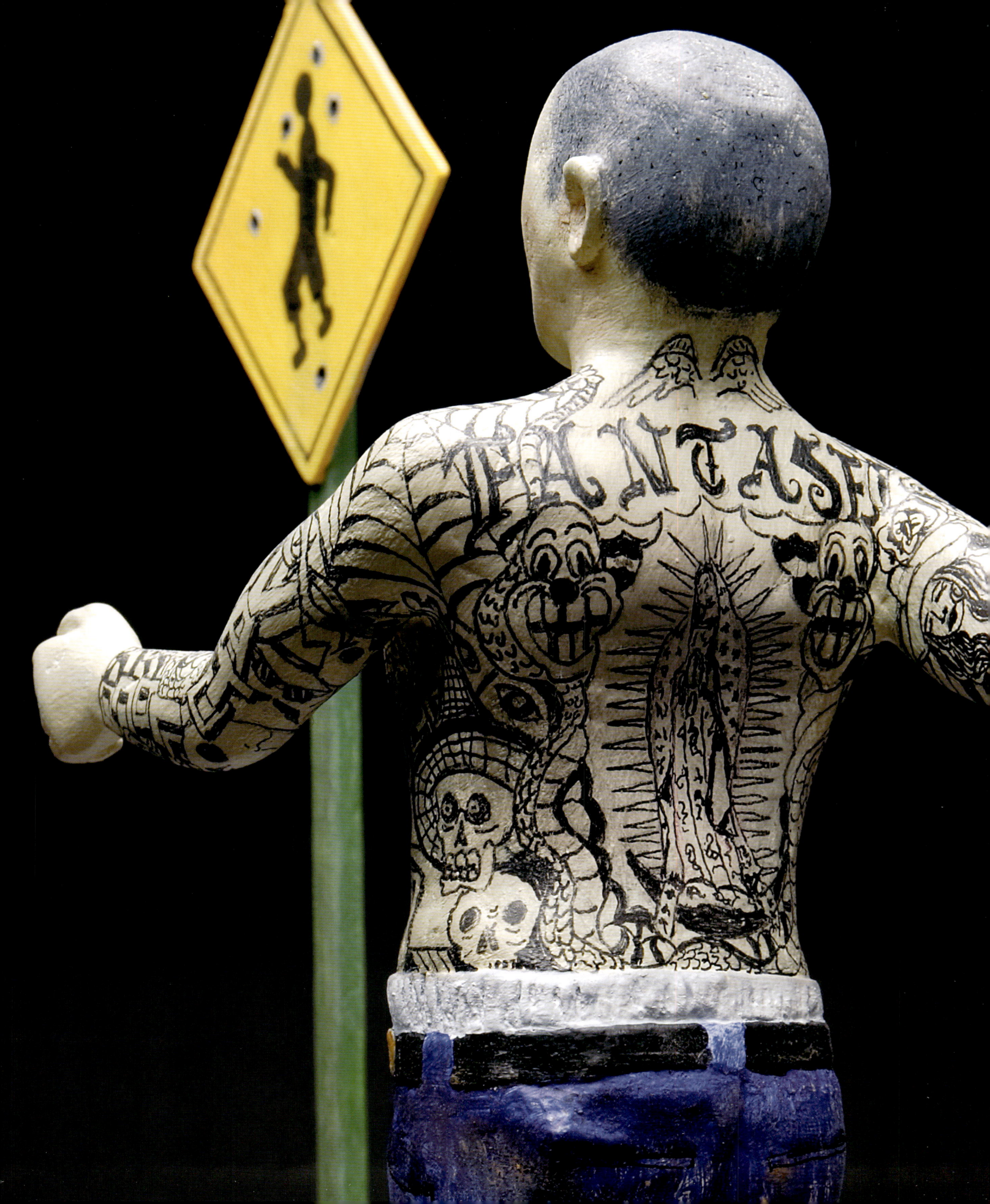

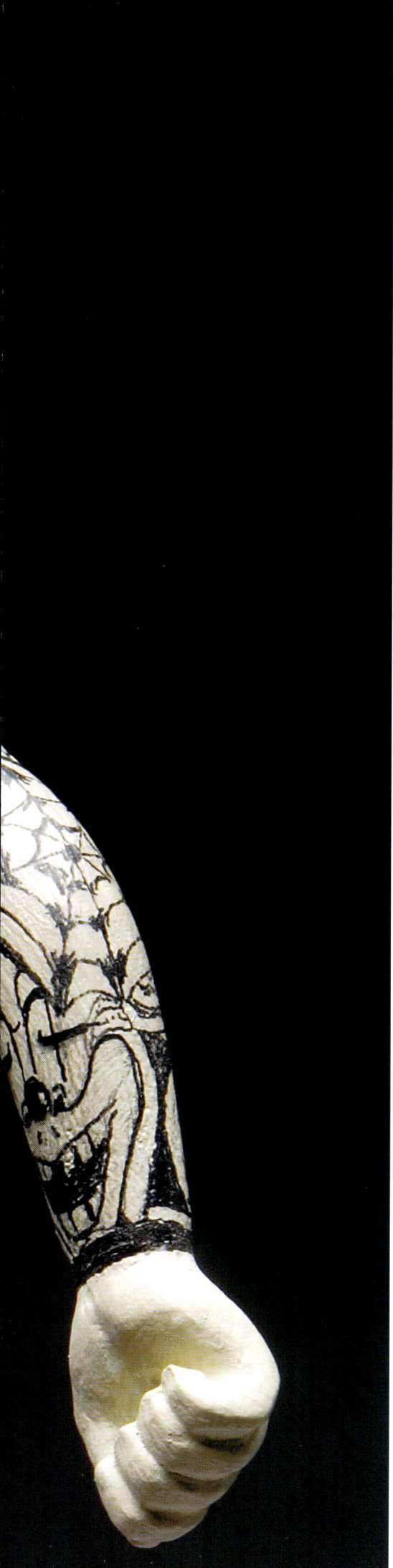

Borderless
The Art of Luis Tapia

Foreword by Dana Gioia
Introduction by Charlene Villaseñor Black

With essays by
Lucy R. Lippard
Tey Marianna Nunn
Denise Chávez
Edward Hayes

Edited by Carmella Padilla

Museum of Latin American Art
Long Beach, California

My THANKS TO The Owings Gallery, formerly Owings-Dewey Fine Art, for more than thirty years of representation, trust, and respect.

To my children, Elena and Sergio, for their faith, understanding, and support, giving me the strength to continue my journey.

To my grandchildren, Andres, Miranda, Annyssa, and the newly presented Paloma, for giving me the will and want to continue.

To my great-grandchildren, Brody Luis and Aleah, for giving vision for the future.

And to the woman with the drive and determination for perfection, without whom this publication would never have been possible, my wife, Carmella. You make me want to be.

Con mucho amor,

Dad. Granpo. Sweetie.

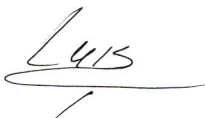

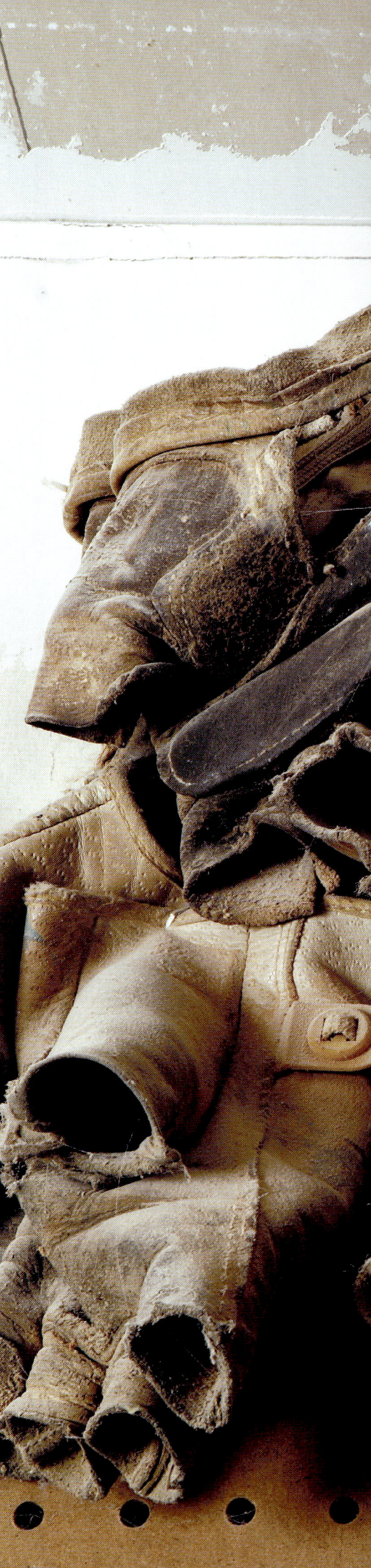

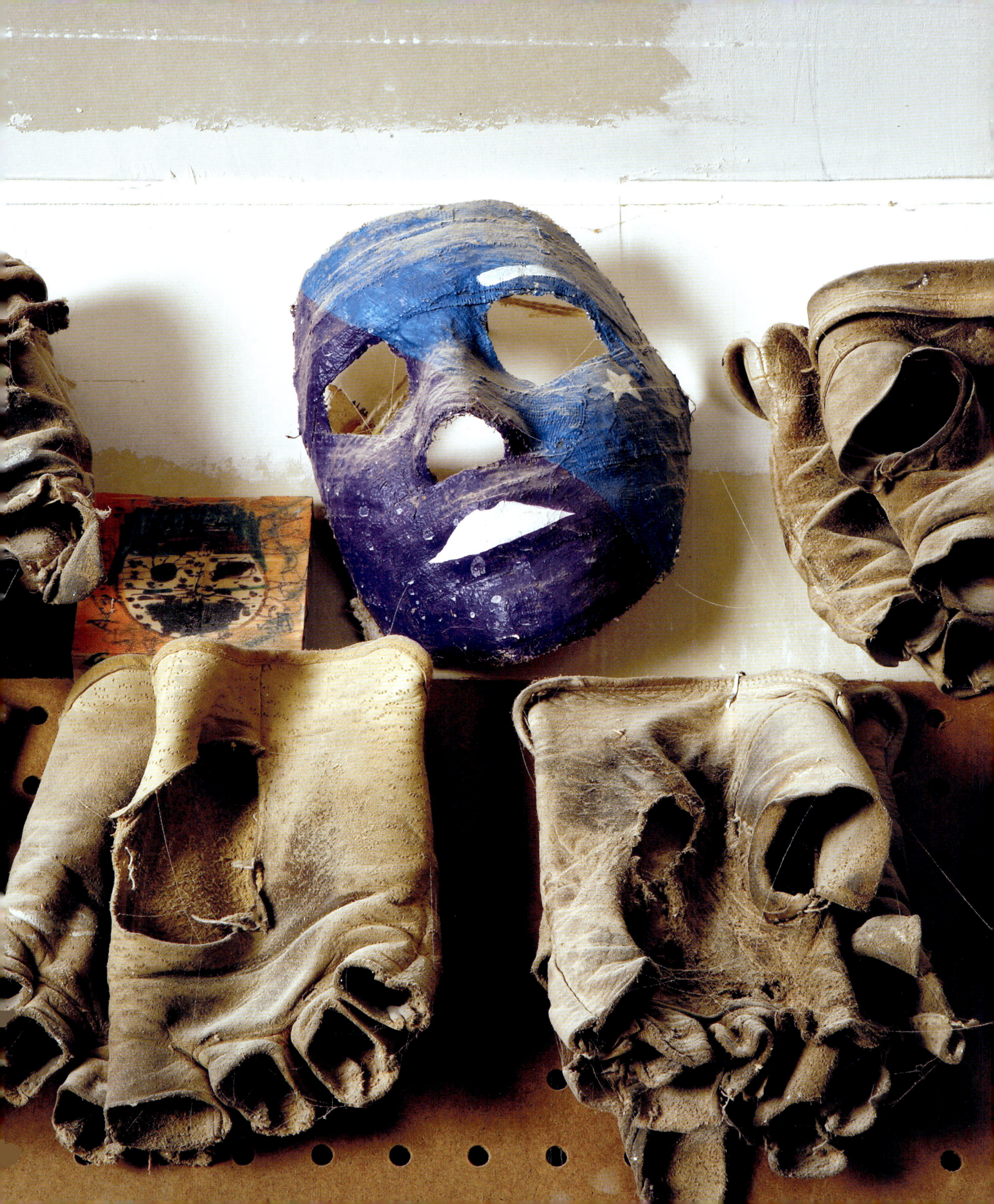

Contents

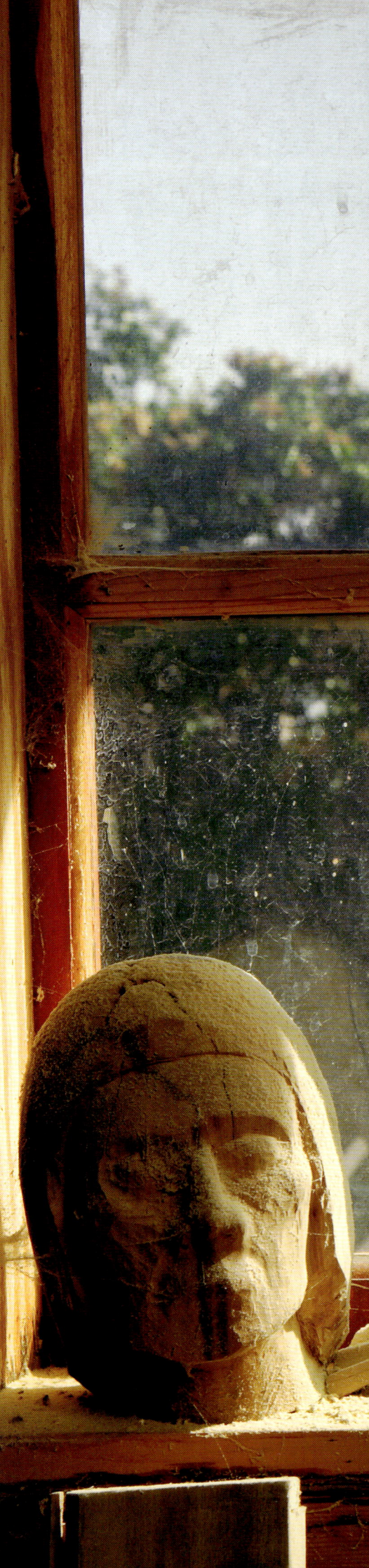

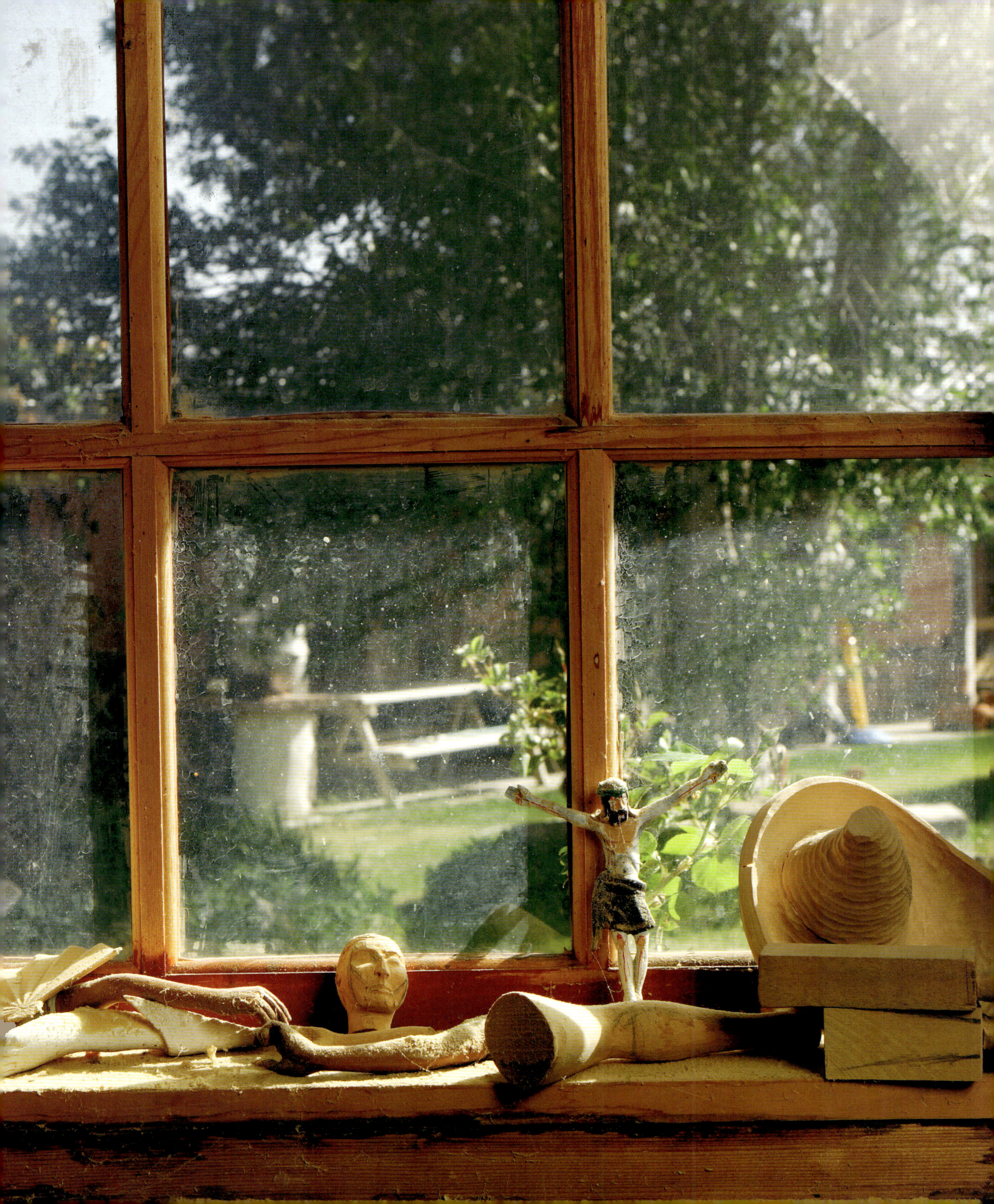

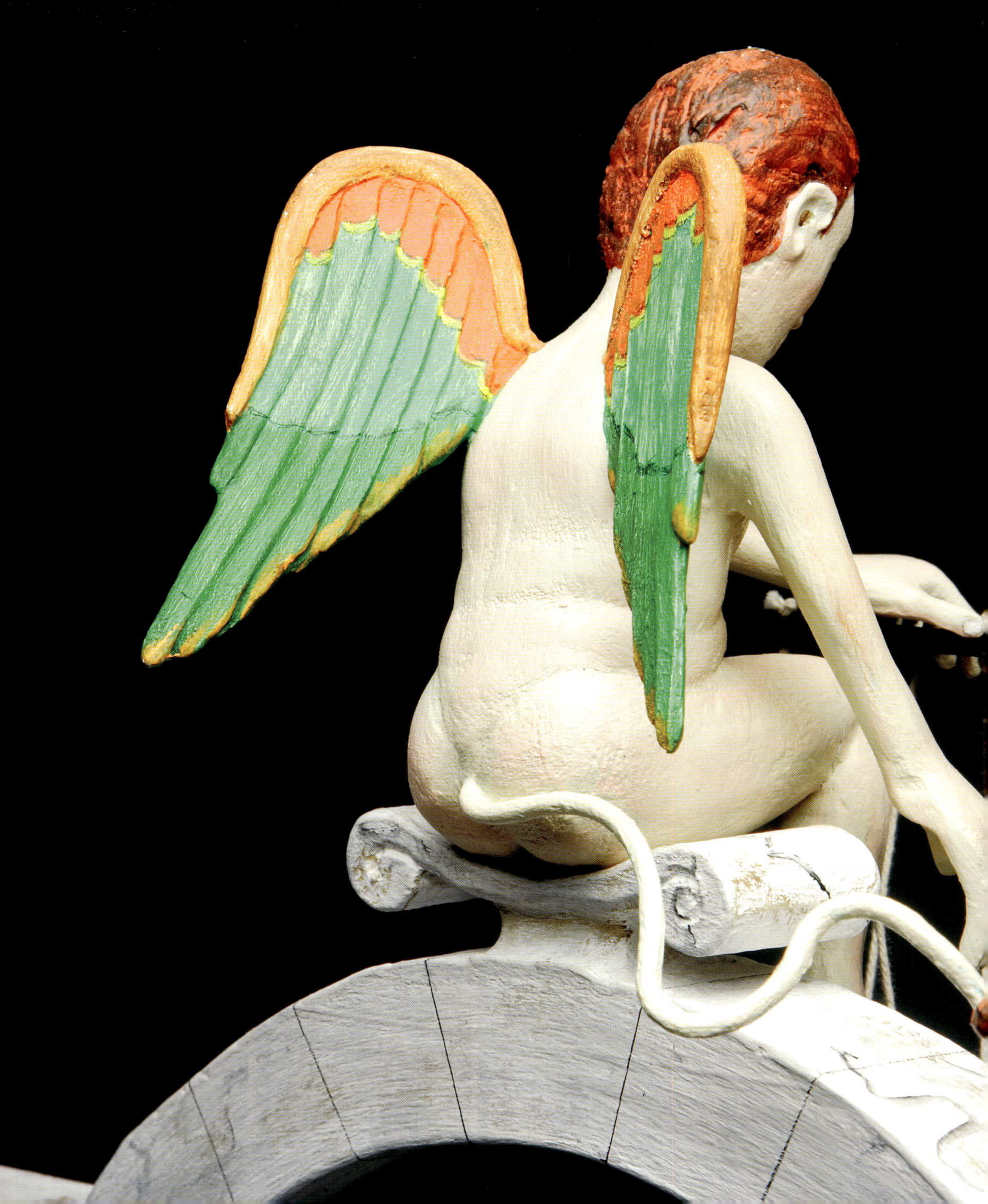

THIS BOOK *es un regalo*, a gift of immeasurable generosity and support for the art of Luis Tapia from the following friends and loved ones who made its publication possible:

Curt, Christina, and Jonah Nonomaque
Museum of Latin American Art
Mr. and Mrs. H. Earl Hoover II
The Owings Gallery
Kathryn Minette and Stan Biderman
Judy and Ray Dewey
Robert and Ellyn Feldman
Nathaniel O. Owings
Laura C. Widmar, Paloma L. Tapia, and Sergio L. Tapia
Edward and Virginia Lujan
Zenaida Padilla
Peter Brill and Wendy Lewis

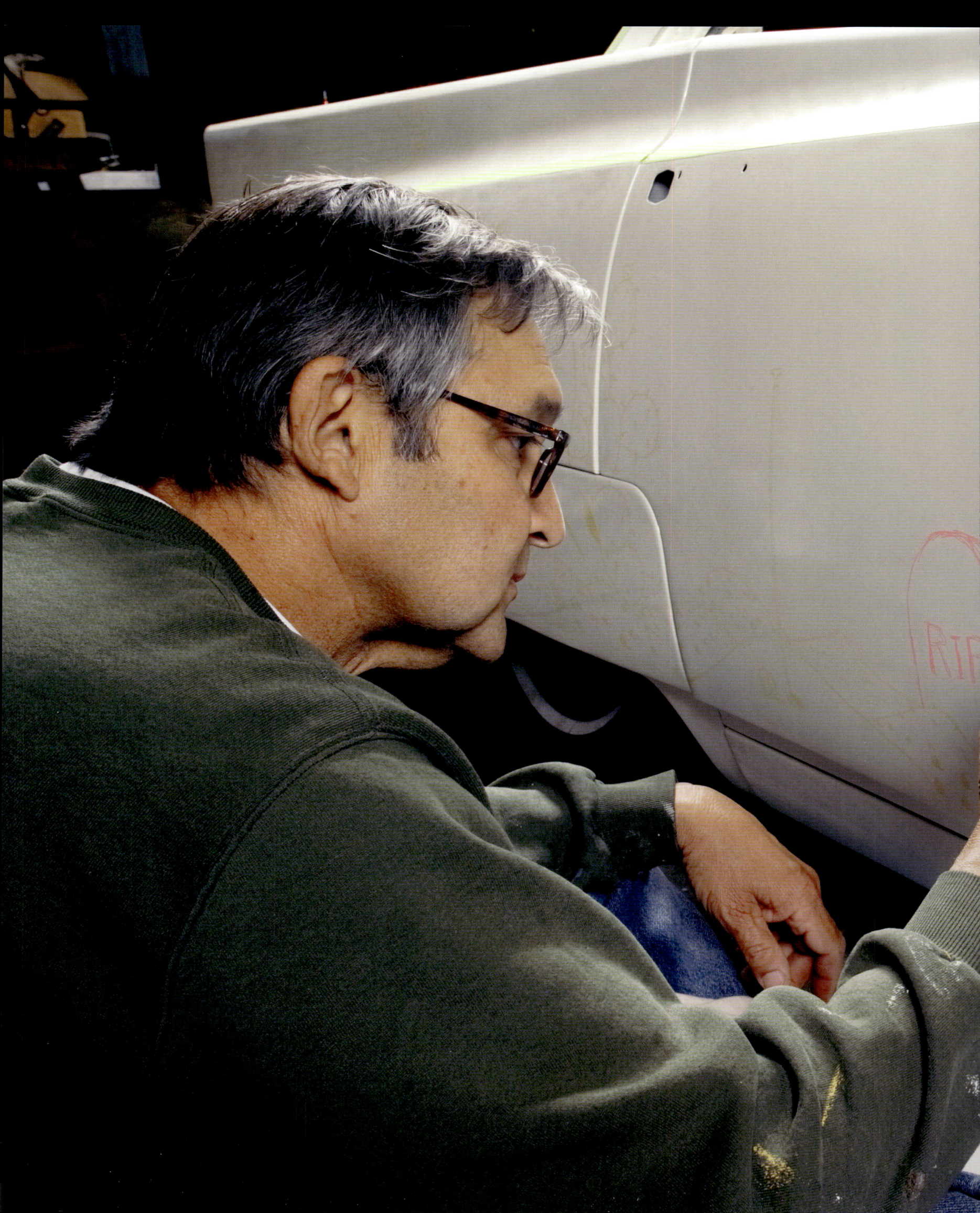

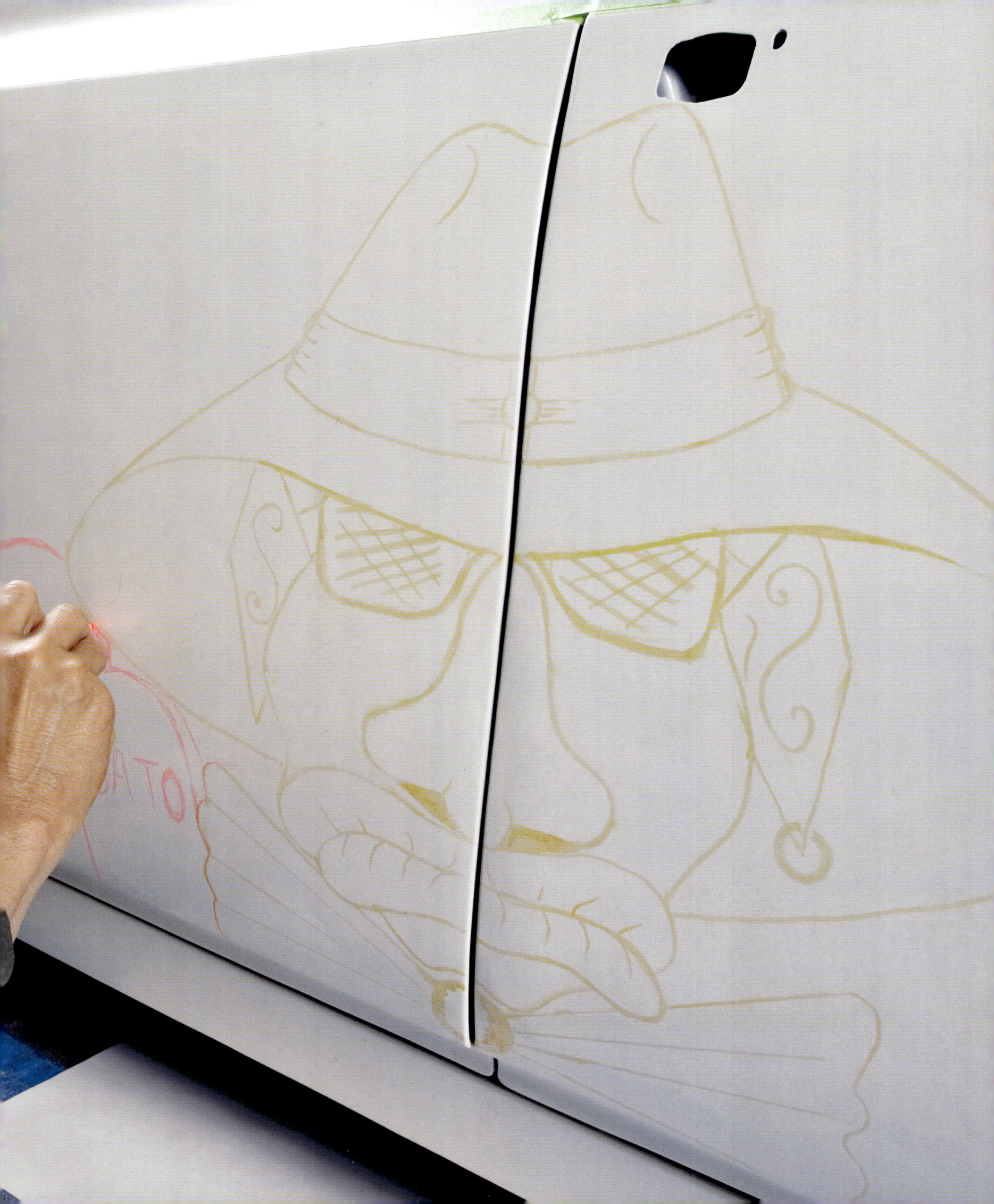

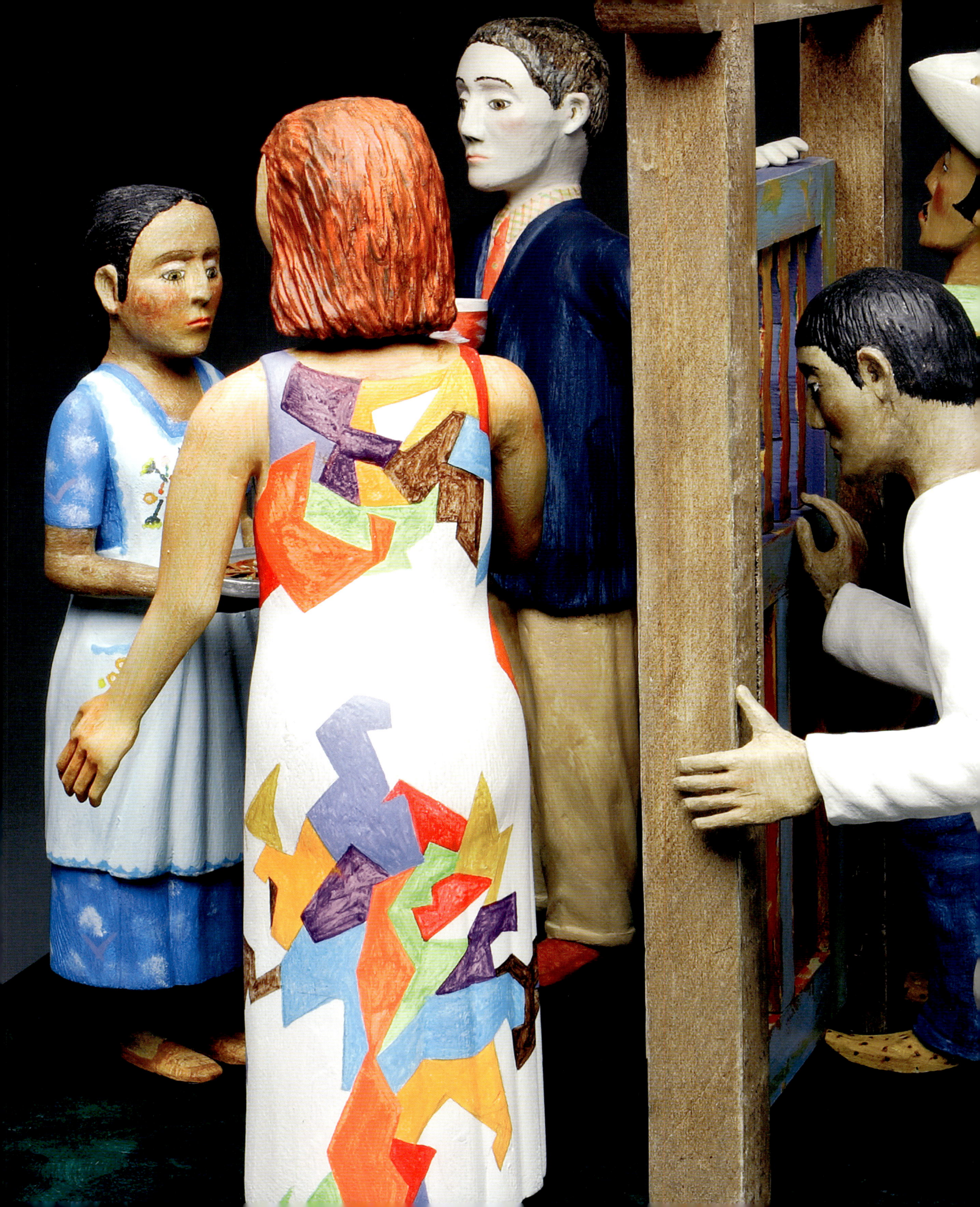

The Cosmopolitan and the Campesino

DANA GIOIA

THERE IS SO MUCH ACTIVITY AND VARIETY in the American visual arts that it is difficult to assess the significance of any individual artist, especially one still productive and unpredictable. Over the last quarter century, however, it has become clear that the sculptor Luis Tapia has accomplished something singular, important, and slightly surprising. He has reconceptualized one of the oldest traditions of Latino and American regional art—the *santero's* craft devotional sculpture—in a way that is both strikingly original and deeply respectful of its origins. In the process, Tapia has not only redeemed this powerful but narrow tradition from the weight of its own past; he has given his personal revision of it an international presence, thereby elevating the distinctively Hispanic form of sculpture beyond its folkloric identity. Without losing his personal connection with the past, Tapia has transformed the restrictive roles of the *santero* and the *santo* into something meaningfully new—more fluent, contemporary, and expansive.

The art world is more accustomed to disruption and transgression than to transformative renewal. (What is more normative in art nowadays than transgression?) It is easier to renounce or mock the past than to master and reshape it to new ends. Assimilating the past, however, allows new work to carry powerful formal and cultural resonance, such as Tapia's adaptations of New Mexican Catholic folk subjects and symbolism into new secular and social contexts. Tapia does not approach the past with the distanced irony and intellectual condescension of artists such as John Currin or Jeff Koons. Tapia remains invested in the forms, themes, and techniques of the New Mexican Latino Catholic tradition. There is irony in his depiction of contemporary economic and racial relations between Anglos and Latinos, rich and poor, but his attitude toward his subject matter is never detached.

The vibrancy of Tapia's ironic and incisive satire seems closer to Goya or Daumier than to his voguish urban contemporaries. If he is ironic, he is also big-hearted and vulnerably human. Tapia gains a particular kind of energy and authenticity in allowing the viewer to feel quite directly his complex and sometimes contradictory emotions. He is angry, amused, affectionate, rude, and reverent—often at the same time. Tapia is a visionary realist who visibly

Fiesta at the Border (detail), 2007; see page 156.

occupies the same daily world as the viewer but also discovers its hidden moral, indeed religious, resonances. He has made the devotional forms of the *santero* profane and political without losing their sacred authority.

Without renouncing his own roots, Tapia has become a significant American artist of unique identity, personal style, and political power. He did not abandon his tradition; he transformed it. Tapia has emerged from the Latino, Catholic, southwestern, rural poor—five varieties of marginalization, all alien to the mostly metropolitan world of contemporary American art. He has made each of those "minor" and frequently patronized categories mean something different from his precursors. He has enlarged his tradition to make it capacious enough to contain his imagination and the complexities of contemporary Latino experience.

To discuss Tapia's artistic identity in cultural and sociological terms is clarifying, but it also risks losing the main reason he is worth discussing in the first place—his excellence and originality. Contemporary art labors under heavy clouds of ideological weather. Latino artists in particular are rarely allowed to exist as individuals; they are abstracted into representations of group consciousness. Tapia's art doesn't matter because it is Latino, culturally marginal, or politically engaged. His art matters because it is so powerfully expressive, memorable, and original on its own individual terms. Studied in depth, his oeuvre reveals itself to be intellectually ambitious, thematically diverse, stylistically inventive, and masterful in technique.

Tapia's particular genius is also refreshingly democratic and inclusive. His sculptures arrest the viewer's attention whether that person is intellectually sophisticated or not. He has developed a visual language, drawn from both the Hispanic vernacular and elite traditions, that engages equally the cosmopolitan and the *campesino*. Significantly, his mostly small works hold the viewer's gaze in ways that are simultaneously pleasurable and painful. Tapia is a conceptual artist. There are always ideas animating both his forms and subjects, but those concepts are not imposed on the works. The meanings emanate from the physical objects themselves. We enter his disturbing and darkly beautiful work not intellectually but intuitively through its iconic images and visual narratives. There is also a conspicuously joyful mastery in his sculptures. They remind us that art, even tragic art, works most potently through pleasure.

I worry that I have taken too many theoretical flights in describing Tapia's very sensuous art. If that has been the case, I blame him. I can't look at Luis Tapia's work without being flooded with ideas and emotions. Whenever I see his work in a gallery or museum, I have the same intense experience—I come, I see; he conquers. Even in a crowded exhibition, Tapia's work arrests my attention, draws me in, and lingers in my memory. If you don't believe me, turn these pages.

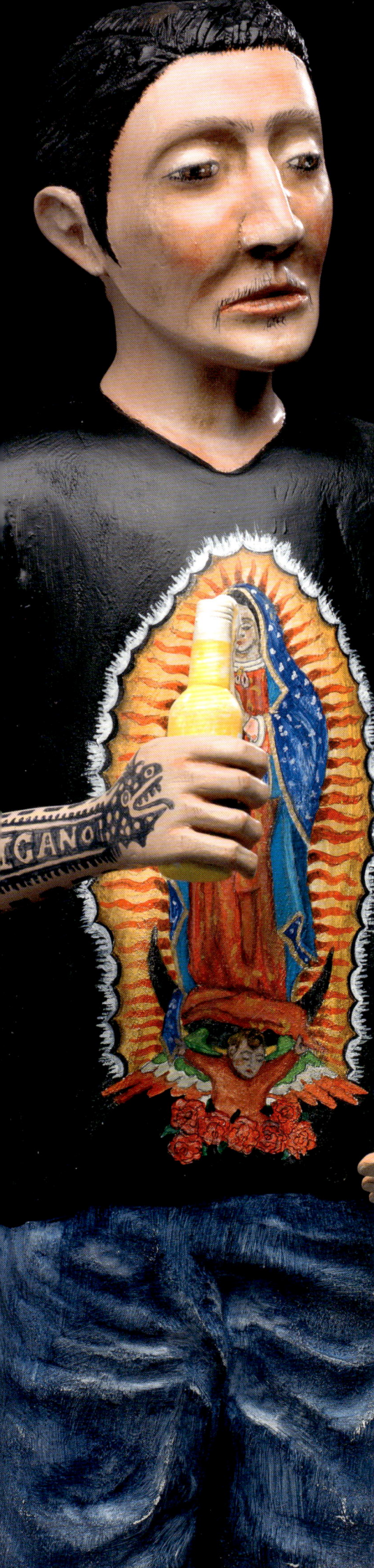

Juan Diego (detail), 2015; see page 164.

Artist in Between

CHARLENE VILLASEÑOR BLACK

SCULPTOR LUIS TAPIA CHANNELS CHICANO and New Mexican Hispano cultures, articulates contemporary political concerns, and resonates historical echoes in his work. As an artist, he is fluent in the language of the New Mexican *santero* tradition, carving Catholic saints, and is equally at home with his peers in the Chicano art scene. His artistic legacy, the subject of this book, extends into both domains.

Many of Tapia's works articulate powerful social commentaries, themes prevalent in Chicano art—racism, classism, migration, the carceral state. He also redresses the invisibility of Latino culture in the fine arts in his depictions of icons such as the Virgin of Guadalupe, in his odes to car culture, and in his support of indigenous American issues. By figuring contemporary Latinos in his works, and suggestively giving them saintly names such as María or Juan Diego, he not only valorizes our humanity but literally makes us visible. His work is multilingual.

Working at the nexus of these various worlds—Chicano, Hispano, Anglo American, indigenous American—Tapia is an artist in *nepantla*, a Náhuatl (Aztec) term meaning "the place in between."[1] The concept was first theorized by noted Mexican anthropologist Miguel León-Portilla as a survival strategy fashioned by indigenous peoples in the colonial period, who in the face of conquest and colonization chose to live "in the middle."[2] The term has been richly elaborated by Chicana theorists, most notably Gloria Anzaldúa, Pat Mora, and Laura Pérez, as well as by artists such as Yreina Cervantez. Anzaldúa likens *nepantla* to the border, a liminal space, "an in-between state."[3] She notes: "Transformations occur in this in-between space, an unstable, unpredictable, precarious, always-in-transition space lacking clear boundaries. Nepantla es tierra desconocida, and living in this liminal zone means being in a constant state of displacement."[4]

Thinking about Tapia's work over the past forty-five years as a manifestation of *nepantla* highlights tensions existing between cultures but also the incredible creative, productive power generated in the face of such displacements. Living in *nepantla* is a survival strategy, but transcultural *neplanteros* such as Tapia possess the power to effect political change. This vantage point of living between cultures offers a fulcrum for political engagement, as we see in his work. In fact, political engagement is one of the distinguishing hallmarks of art produced in the Americas, and Chicano art in particular, in its insistence on confronting political, and not simply aesthetic, concerns.

Tapia's work also challenges existing temporal divisions. Coming from an important contemporary Chicano artist who is deeply knowledgeable about New Mexico's colonial artistic traditions, the work reverberates simultaneously in multiple chronological spaces, calling to mind Argentine theorist Néstor García Canclini's concept of "multi-temporal heterogeneity." According to García Canclini, multi-temporality is characteristic of post-modern Latin America, where ancient, colonial, modern, and postmodern worlds and prac-tices coexist. In contrast to western Europe, modernization "did not replace the traditional or the ancient"[5] in the Americas. Multi-temporality characterizes the work of Latino artists such as Tapia, who are clearly engaged in historicizing projects yet are also positioned on the forefront of the latest aesthetic and cultural debates. Tapia's artistic production takes history seriously, questioning its discursive formation and arguing for the importance of the relationship between our past and our present.

The greatest power of Tapia's works, though, resides in their assured representational strategies, their three-dimensionality, focused compositions, bold color, and reality effects. We see these traits in two 2017 creations: *¡Ay! Qué milagro* (Plate 58) and *Chuy con su carga* (Plate 97). In the first work, a sorrowing female figure, clad in the blue robe of the Virgin Mary, is covered in hundreds of handwrought *milagros*, or offerings of blessing and healing. A closer look reveals these as contemporary *milagros*—guns and gunshot victims, skulls and crossbones, drug paraphernalia and alcohol bottles, and other chilling icons of modern violence, addiction, and suffering. In *Chuy con su carga*, which translates as "Chuy [a shortened form of the name *Jesús* in Spanish] with his load or burden," the figure of a contemporary gardener impels a wheelbarrow, transporting a globe of the earth. The image calls up traditional representations of Christ—for example, as Salvator Mundi, or savior of the world, or depictions of Saint Isidore the Farmer, an important holy person in Hispanic culture. Chuy's T-shirt, emblazoned with "Aztlán" and "505," the artist's area code, reaffirms Tapia's shared identity as a Chicano and a Nuevomexicano.

Existing between temporal divisions as well as between cultural divides, Tapia's sculptures embody what Chicana scholar and cultural critic Laura E. Pérez has described as "visual cultural nepantlism."[6] His work gives visual form to the power of *nepantla*, of being in between, as it combines past and present. From the place in between, Tapia imag-ines a role for artists in creating a more inclusive, more just future.

OPPOSITE
¡Ay! Qué Milagro! (detail), 2017;
see page 184.

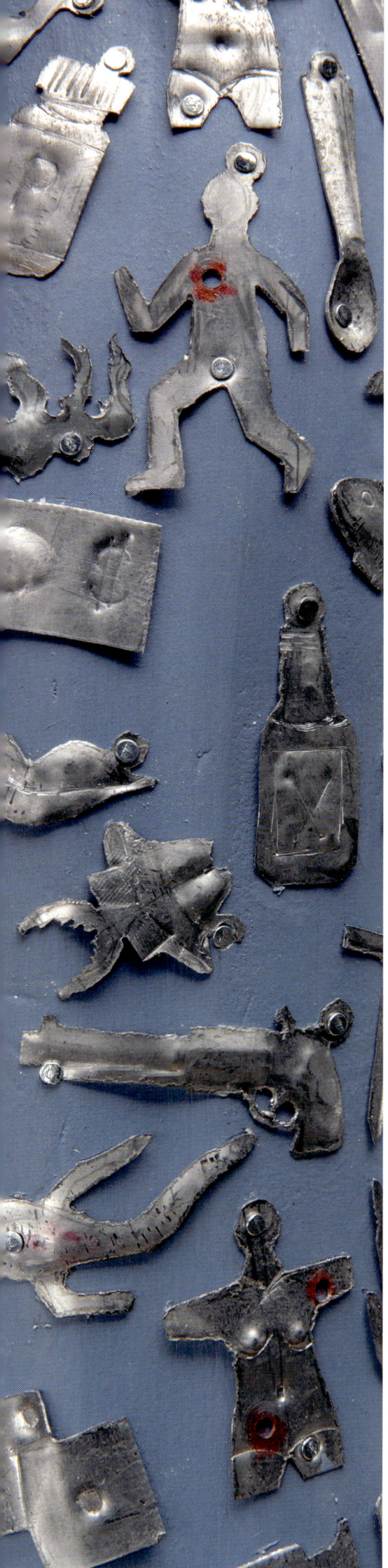

I take the viewer on a *viaje*—a journey.

—LUIS TAPIA

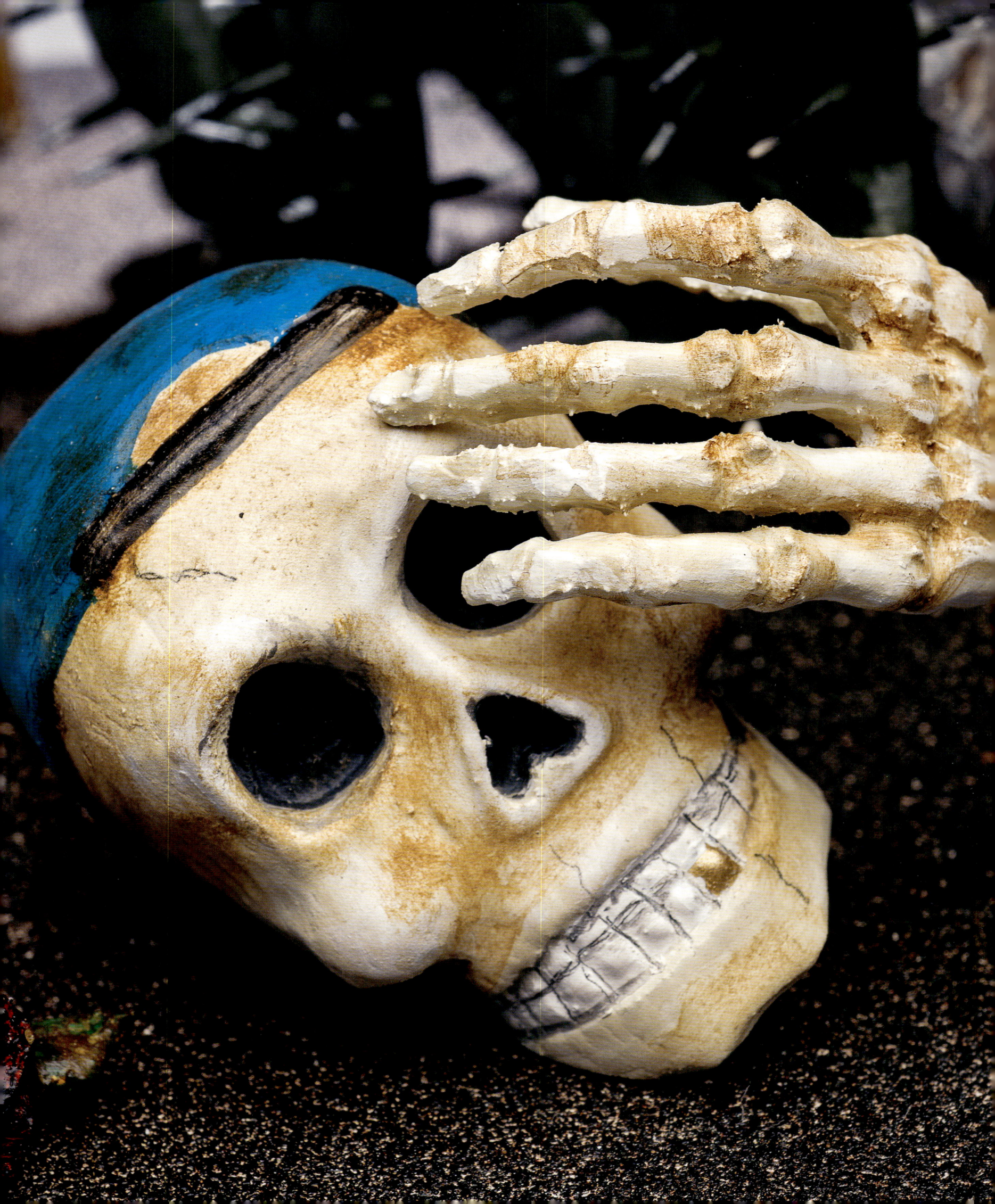

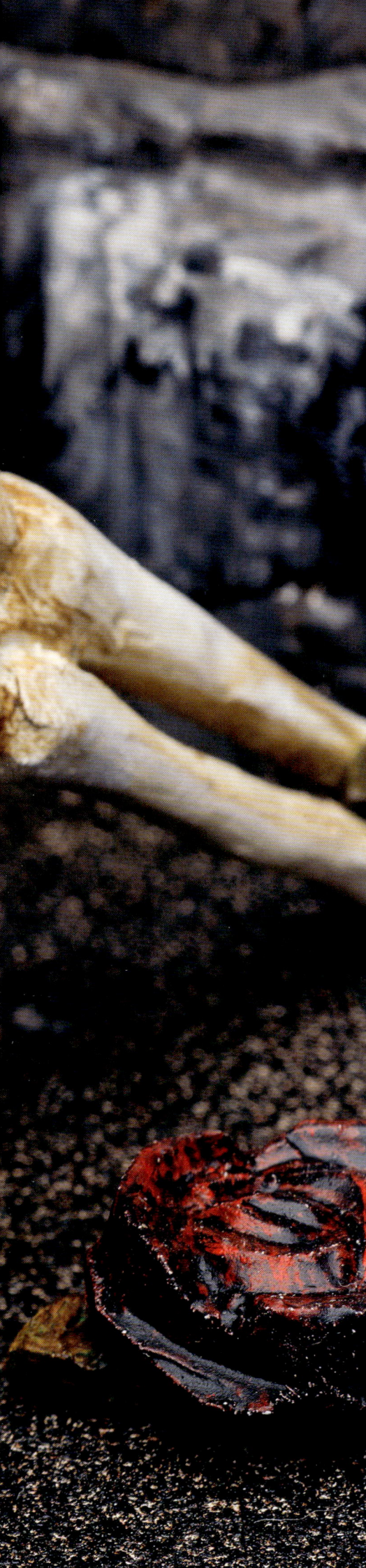

Nobody's Perfect

LUCY R. LIPPARD

LUIS TAPIA'S BRAND OF SOCIAL ACTIVISM is unique to his culture and his place, possibly opaque to those unfamiliar with New Mexico, and profoundly meaningful to those who have internalized the state's complex history and contentious present. Politics and religion and social life are interwoven in Tapia's art, which can be at once aesthetically pleasing, humorous, entertaining, and provocative—even infuriating to some within his own families of peers. He challenges viewers as he challenges himself, constantly abandoning his comfort zones for uneasy sites on various borderlines.

In 1987 John Beardsley wrote: "There seems to be an unwritten presumption that the nearer an artist aspires to the level of high art, the more leached out will become the ethnic content of the work."[1] That was all too true for years, until identity politics revalued inherited cultures. But Tapia was among those who refused to deny his roots all along, maintaining overt "ethnic content" while the art world was catching up. While other Latino artists in New Mexico and beyond confront similar issues, Tapia's deeply centered sense of place makes his work unique.

He began as a traditional *santero* (saint maker), wood carver, furniture maker, and altar screen restorer (at Ranchos de Taos, for example, the church made famous by Georgia O'Keeffe), so his early credentials should have been golden. But as he introduced brighter colors—closer to the originals than the distressed palette of old and faded *santos* (saints) preferred by the Anglo cultural establishment—and began to take tentative steps toward a modernization of the genre, he was evicted from Spanish Market around 1978. The conservative organizers who vetted works for the annual show and sale rejected a Noah's Ark, for instance, because it was "not a traditional subject."[2] Tapia had a wife and two children to support and had just quit his job on the basis of five years of success at the market. Following his ouster, "I had to hustle," he recalls. "My work became better known in Texas, Utah, even Washington, D.C., than it was in New Mexico."

However, everything turned around in 1988 when he joined the prestigious Owings-Dewey Fine Art (now The Owings Gallery) in Santa Fe. He was finally free to do what he wanted—move into social commentary and "add politics to traditional forms."

Virgen del camino de sueños (detail), 2016; see page 176.

Political radicalization led to aesthetic radicalization. Tapia was raised in Agua Fría Village, which shares a border with Santa Fe. He learned belatedly about Mexican arts and his own heritage (the Mexican flag flew over New Mexico from 1821 to 1846) when he was drawn into the Chicano movement of the late 1960s. The movement enlightened young people in New Mexico about the history of land grants and grabs and other cultural losses since the 1848 Treaty of Guadalupe Hidalgo. Today, Tapia and the writer Carmella Padilla, his wife of eighteen years, often travel to Mexico and have accumulated an extraordinary collection of masks, among other objects, the general influence of which is traceable in Tapia's own art. This attraction is in itself a political statement.

The relationship between Mexico and New Mexico, Mexicanos and Nuevomexicanos (or Indo-Hispanos) remains an issue today. Northern New Mexico can feel sufficiently distant from the actual U.S.–Mexican border, but the south side of Santa Fe has become another city, home to many Central American and Mexican immigrants, many of whom are undocumented, living in a "sanctuary city" that is not always so safe. Some native New Mexicans prefer to see themselves as pure Spanish, ignoring their ancestors' sojourn (and often indigenization) in Mexico before they occupied New Mexico as the northern frontier of New Spain in 1598. Immigrants and native New Mexicans have rumbled in the high schools, and a recent theater piece by Santa Fe's Littleglobe collective explored interactions between the two closely related and divided groups. In 2016 Chicana writer Sandra Cisneros said in an interview that she considered moving from Texas to northern New Mexico until she concluded that "residents there don't like Mexicans." (A Tejana neighbor of mine had the same take.)

Tapia addresses this complex identity issue in *Juan Diego* (2015; Plate 48). A young cholo with Indo-Hispano features wears a T-shirt with a popular image of La Virgen de Guadalupe—a "Mexican" saint who appeared to the Indian Juan Diego in the sixteenth century. At the feet of Tapia's twenty-first-century counterpart are the roses by which the original Juan Diego proved his vision to the Catholic Church. He holds a bottle of beer, and the back of his shirt advertises El Azteca Taqueria. One arm bears a tattoo reading "Mexicano" with an Aztecan design twist, and the other arm reads "Zapata." This is not, however, a caricature. It is a compassionate portrait of a vulnerable young man who wears his history on his sleeve, so to speak.

The faces of Tapia's freestanding figures depart from the somber or impassive features of the traditional saints he studied and carved early in his career. His empathetic portraits themselves represent an activist stance in a racist nation. They are imbued with an overwhelming sweetness that is never saccharine. The men portrayed may be saint-adorned sinners or just ordinary *vatos*. *Dos amigos con sus vicios* (2015; Plate 49) shows a pair of pals—a Native man in camouflage and a Chicano man in a Che Guevara T-shirt—both war-weary vets clinging to their beers and to each other. The piece reflects a theme explored by Tapia in the 1997 *Cerbezar* (Figure 1), a title translated by Tapia as "making out with your beer bottle," a playful merger of the Spanish words *cerveza* (beer) and *besar* (to kiss). A bottle of beer is enshrined in a glass reliquary and smothered in flowers—a

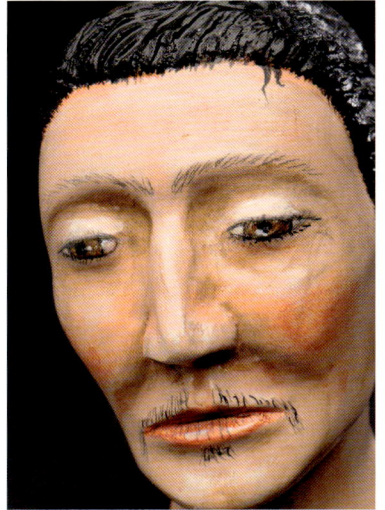

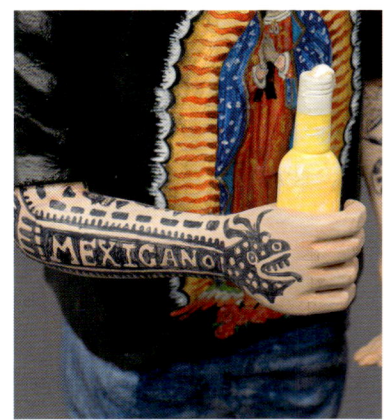

Juan Diego (details), 2015; see page 164.

20

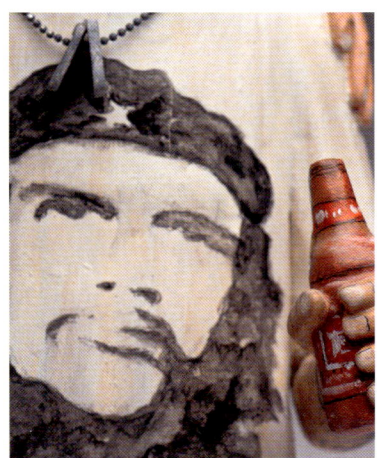

Dos amigos con sus vicios (detail), 2015; see page 166.

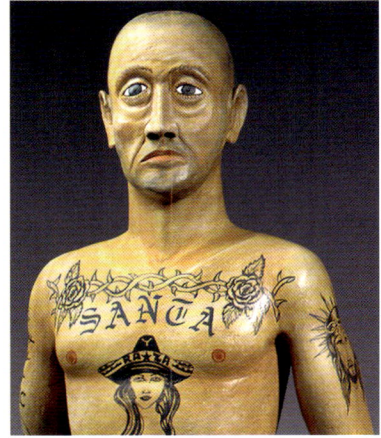

Neighborhood Watchdog (detail), 2004; see page 144.

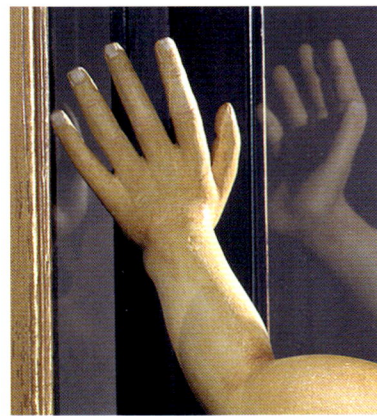

Man Trapped in His Religion (detail), 2004; see page 138.

comment on the contribution of alcohol to cultural stereotypes and the controversies surrounding New Mexico's drunk driving epidemic.

Neighborhood Watchdog (2004; Plate 38) is an older, more saddened version of *Juan Diego,* his harsh life reflected in his face. The tattooed "saint" on his chest is a girl in a sombrero, and on his back Our Lady of Guadalupe and "Zapata" appear again. A hand in his pocket suggests that he might be packing heat as he protects what remains to him and his culture. Two early works suggest the inevitable consequences. In *Dos Pedros sin llaves* (1994; Figure 26), the two "keyless" prisoners are embraced by traditional New Mexican architectural elements that convey a sense of lost home. In the 1999 *Pieta* (Figure 2), a gun lies on the ground behind the mourning mother and her dead son.

Tapia's women are presented with a certain sexy dignity. *Sirena del Río Grande* (2014; Plate 46), a quietly beautiful portrait of an aging nude "temptress" with tattoos, is identified as Eve by an apple on the ground. She is brought home by flanking views of the Río Grande Gorge from north and south. *The Three Graces* (2016; Plate 53) is a virtually feminist back-to-back triple portrait of the Mexicana/Hispana/Chicana across time: the Adelita (a female soldier during the Mexican Revolution) with her long skirt, *bandolera,* rifle, and no religious adornment; La Pachuca with her zoot suit, cropped hair, and gold cross; and a contemporary woman, stylishly dressed and tattooed with roses and the Virgin of Guadalupe nestled in the rise of her back. Their gazes are serious. They stand straight and proud. They have one another's backs.

In 1992 a surge of multiculturalism and historical revisionism grew up around the quincentennial of Columbus's "discovery"—a paradigm shift in how Americans think about America and the Americas. In the following years, Tapia began a new cycle of politically relevant works, triggered by "so many injustices around and in religion. I had to speak out about it," he says. With an increased awareness of himself, his times, and his culture came a desire to update traditional imagery. "What would Christ and Mary look like today? They'd be tattooed in our culture, right?" When he researched the lives of the saints, he was struck by the fact that they always died "because of *political* issues . . . Christ too."

Tapia's take on morality and religion is particularly courageous given the power of the Catholic Church in New Mexico. (In 2001 a furor erupted among Catholic clergy and congregations over California artist Alma Lopez's fond depiction of the Virgin of Guadalupe in a modest two-piece bathing suit, prompting the state-owned museum that exhibited the piece to close the show earlier than planned.) Tapia is critical but not iconoclastic, respecting the beliefs of *la gente,* of the faithful but not faultless, reflected in his T-shirts and tattoos, murals and graffiti. *Man Trapped in His Religion* (2004, Plate 34), a victim of his dogma, is treated with sympathy rather than condemnation. His downcast *indio* features as he pushes futilely against the walls of a golden, reliquary-like cage make this image a historical drama. Even the agonized pedophile cardinal of *Man without a Heart* (2007; Figure 3) is presented as heartless but still human, perhaps more so than the priests and cardinal in *See No Evil, Hear No Evil, Say No Evil* (2011; Figure 4). Above them cocks are crowing, as they did when Jesus

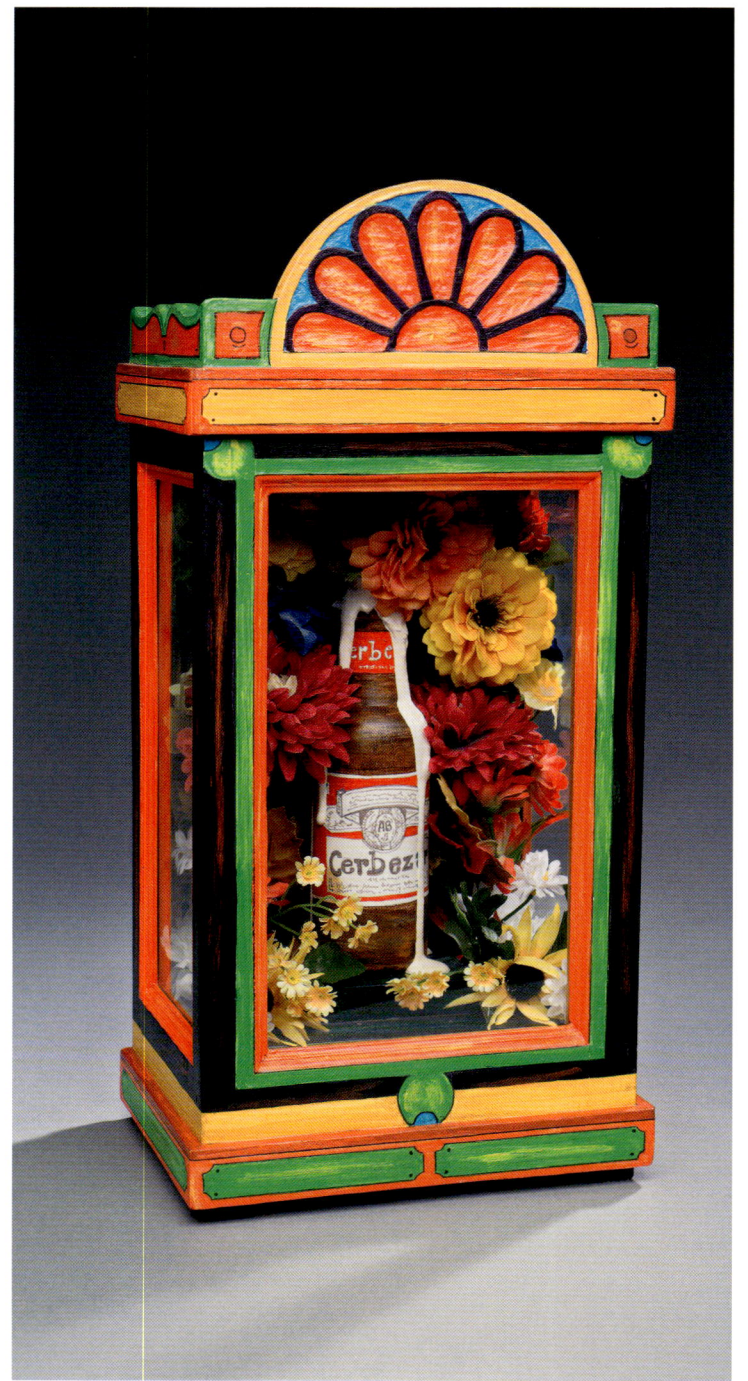 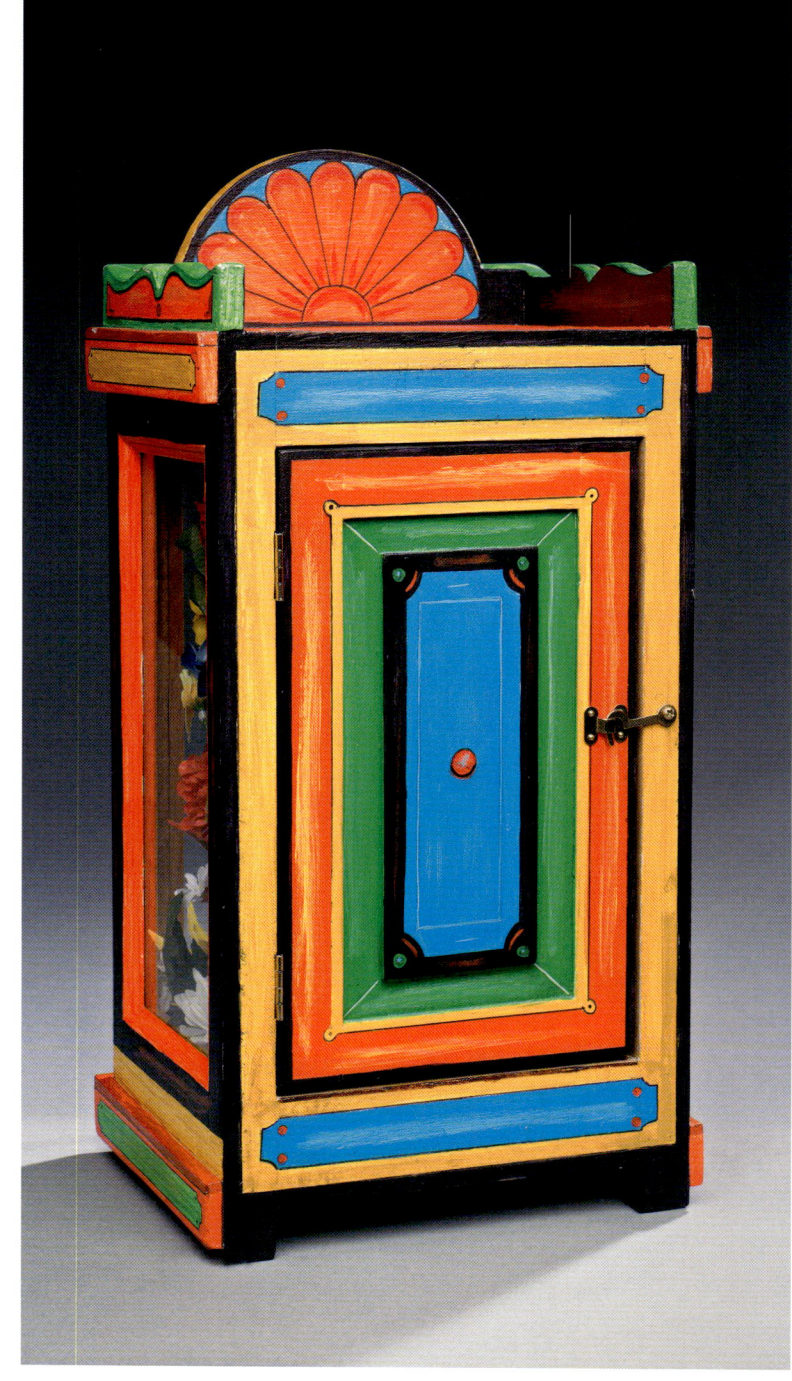

Figure 1. *Cerbezar*, 1997. Carved and painted wood, cloth flowers, 20⅜ x 9¾ x 7⅜ in.
Collection of Mr. and Mrs. H. Earl Hoover II. Photo © Addison Doty.

Figure 2. *Pieta*, 1999. Carved and painted wood, 20¼ x 14½ x 9½ in. Collection of
John Robertshaw. Photo © Dan Morse, courtesy of The Owings Gallery.

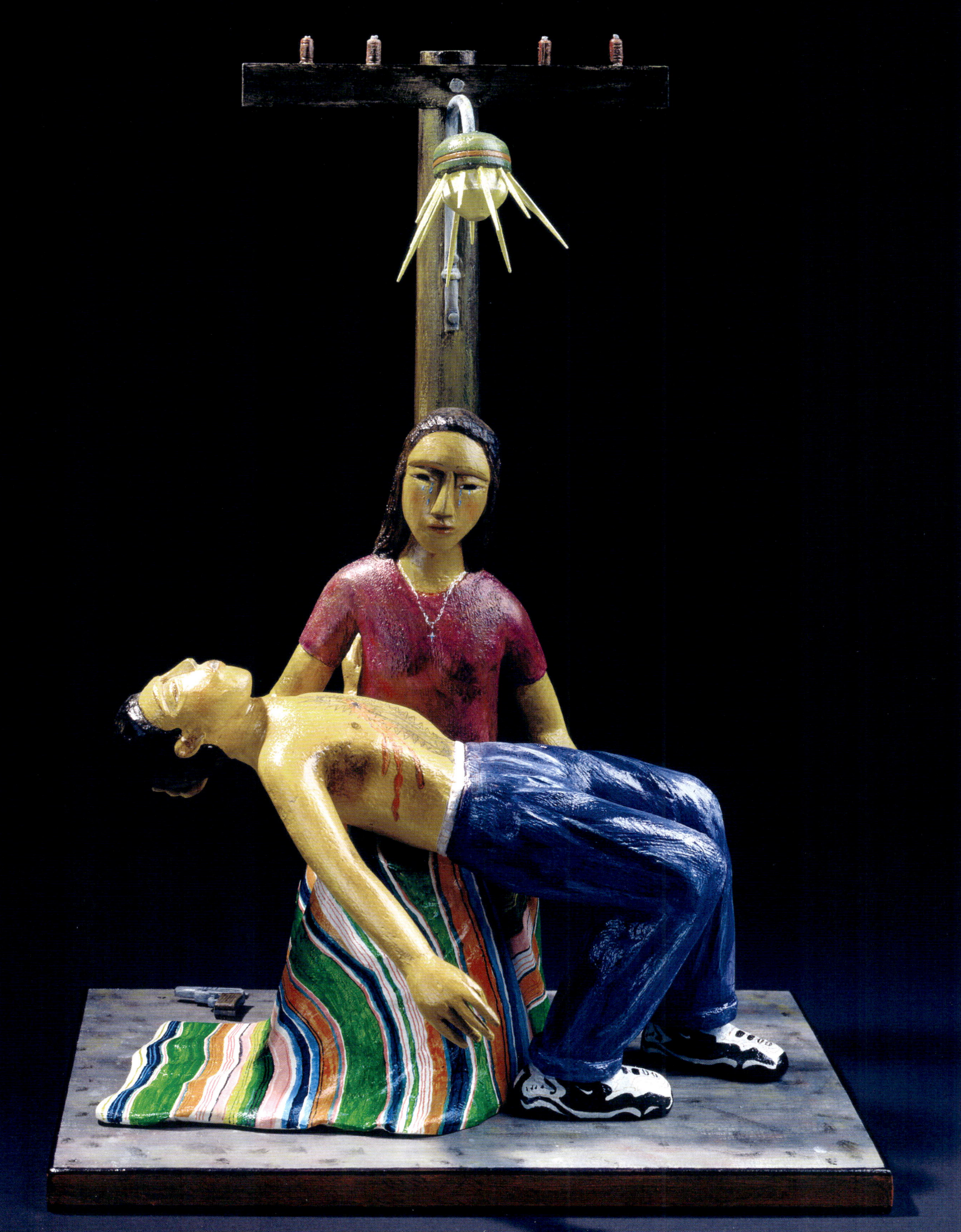

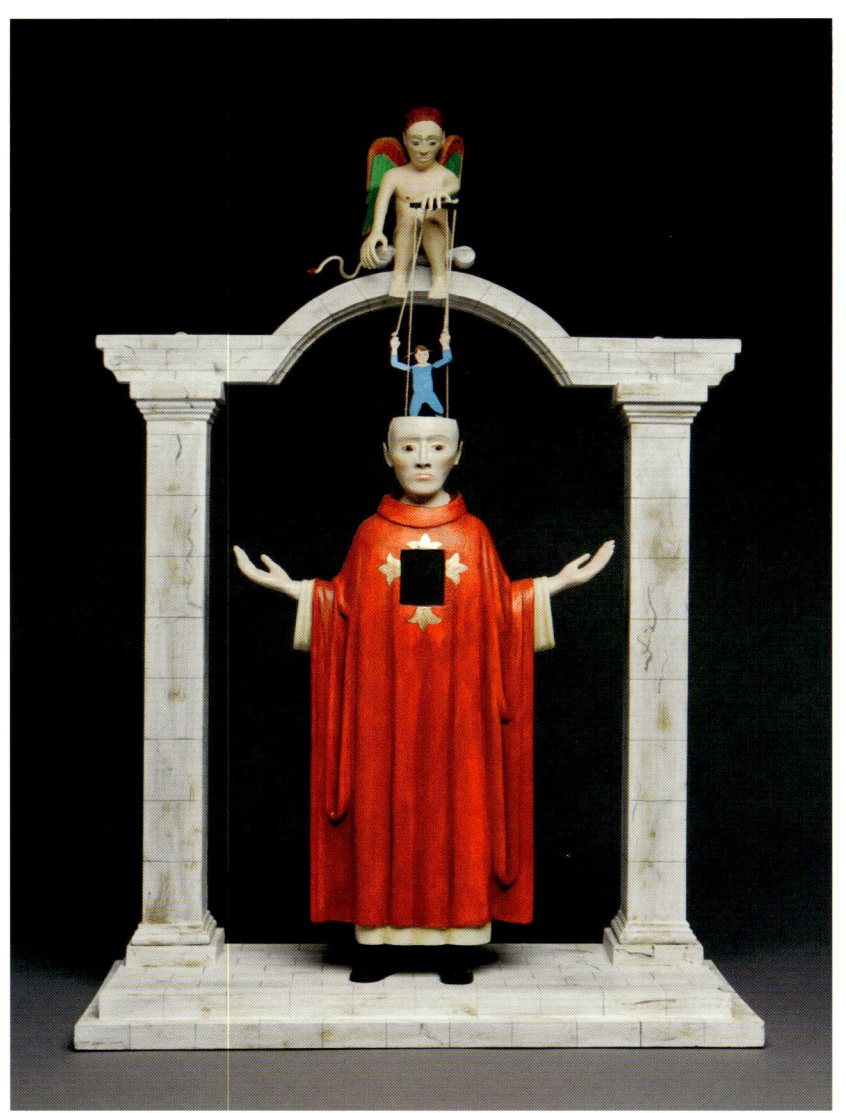
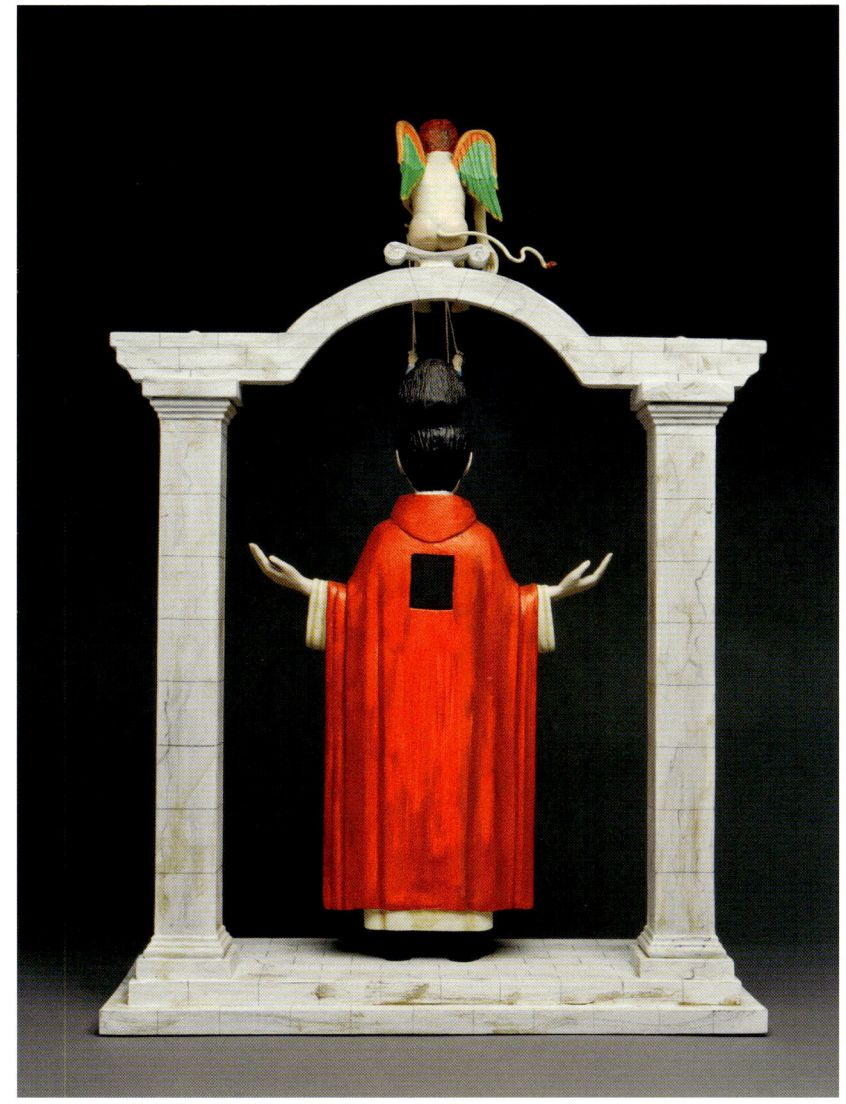

Figure 3. *Man without a Heart*, 2007. Carved and painted wood, 30 x 20½ x 9 in.
Private collection. Photo © Addison Doty, courtesy of The Owings Gallery.

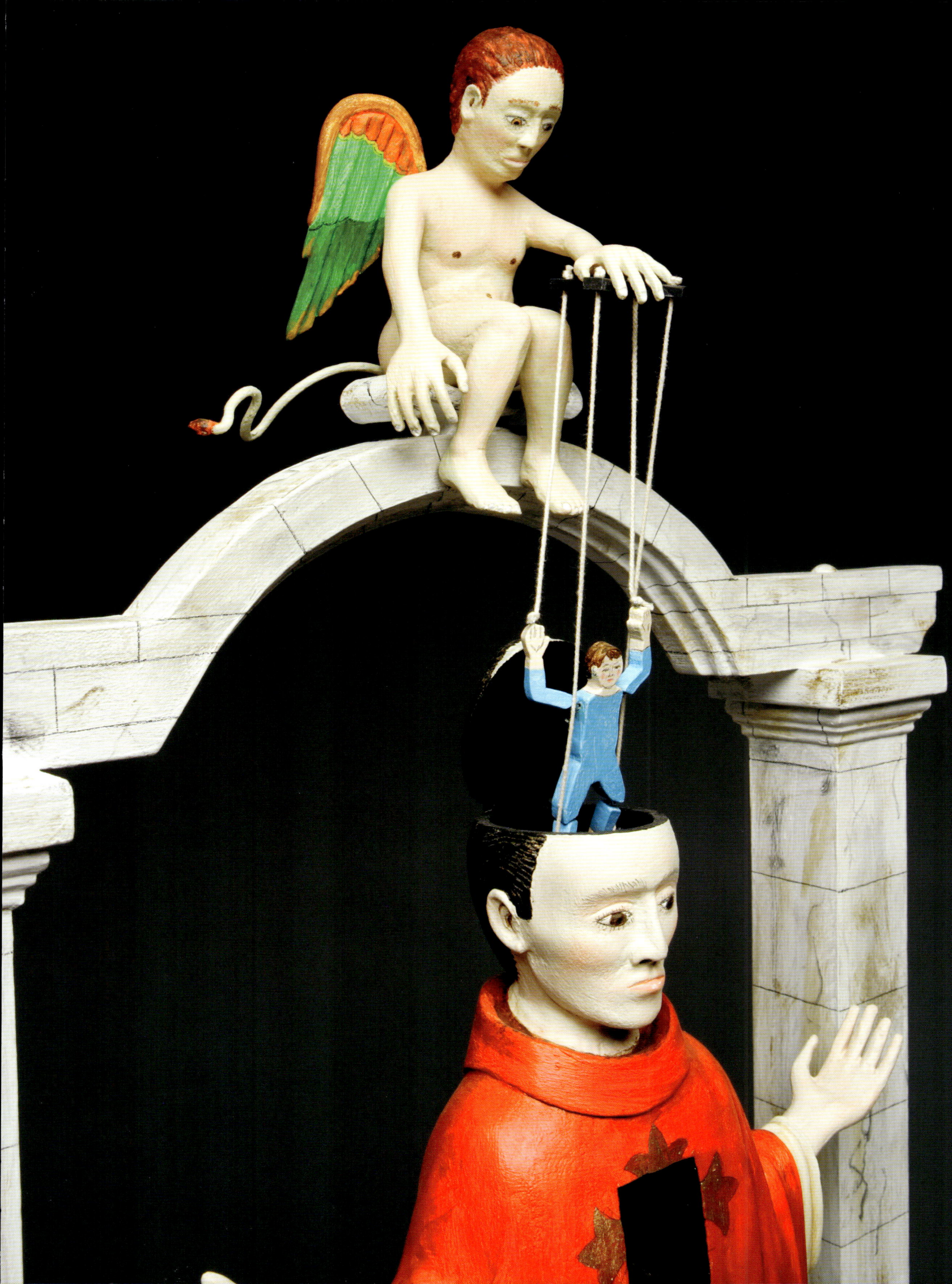

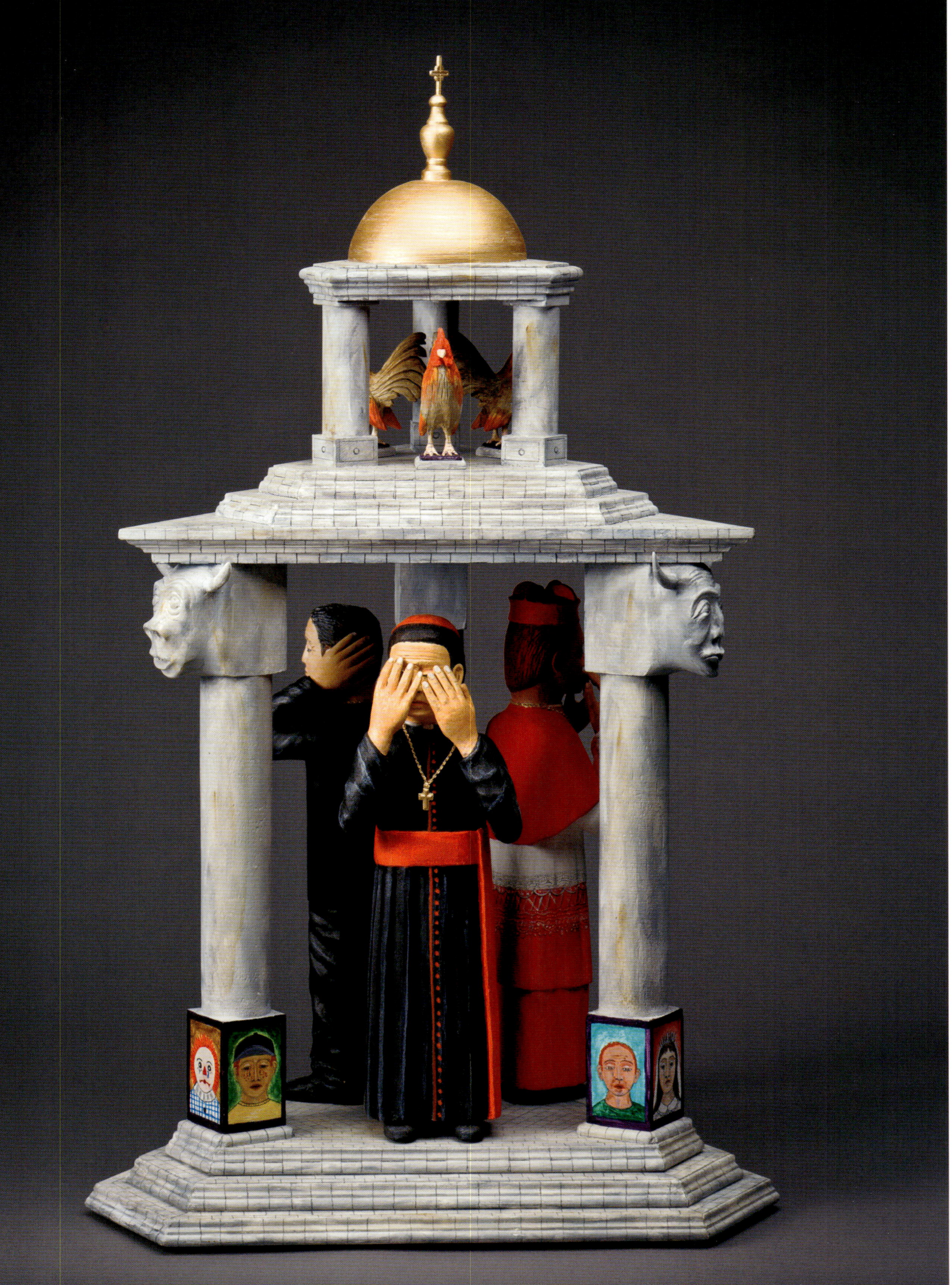

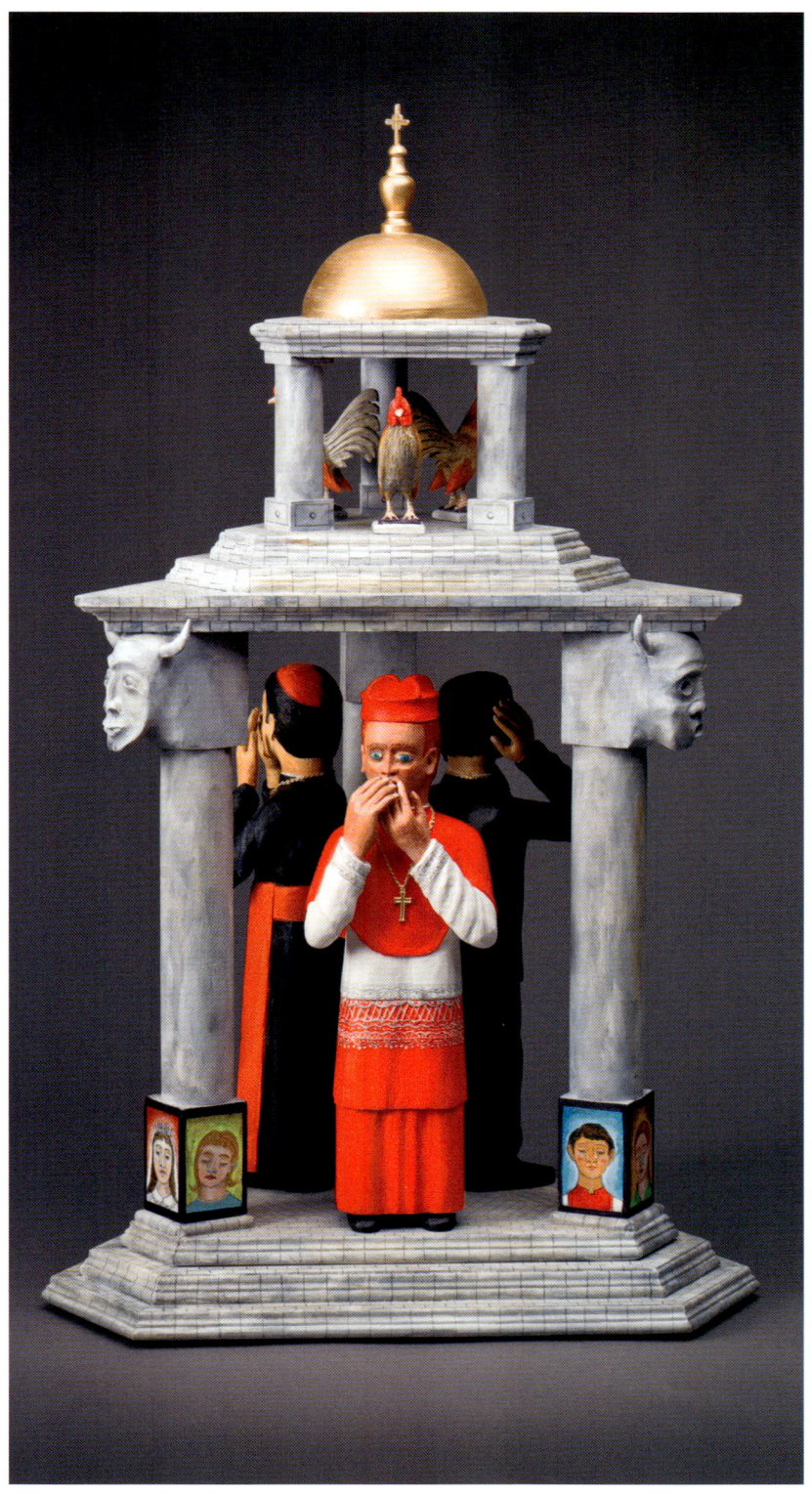 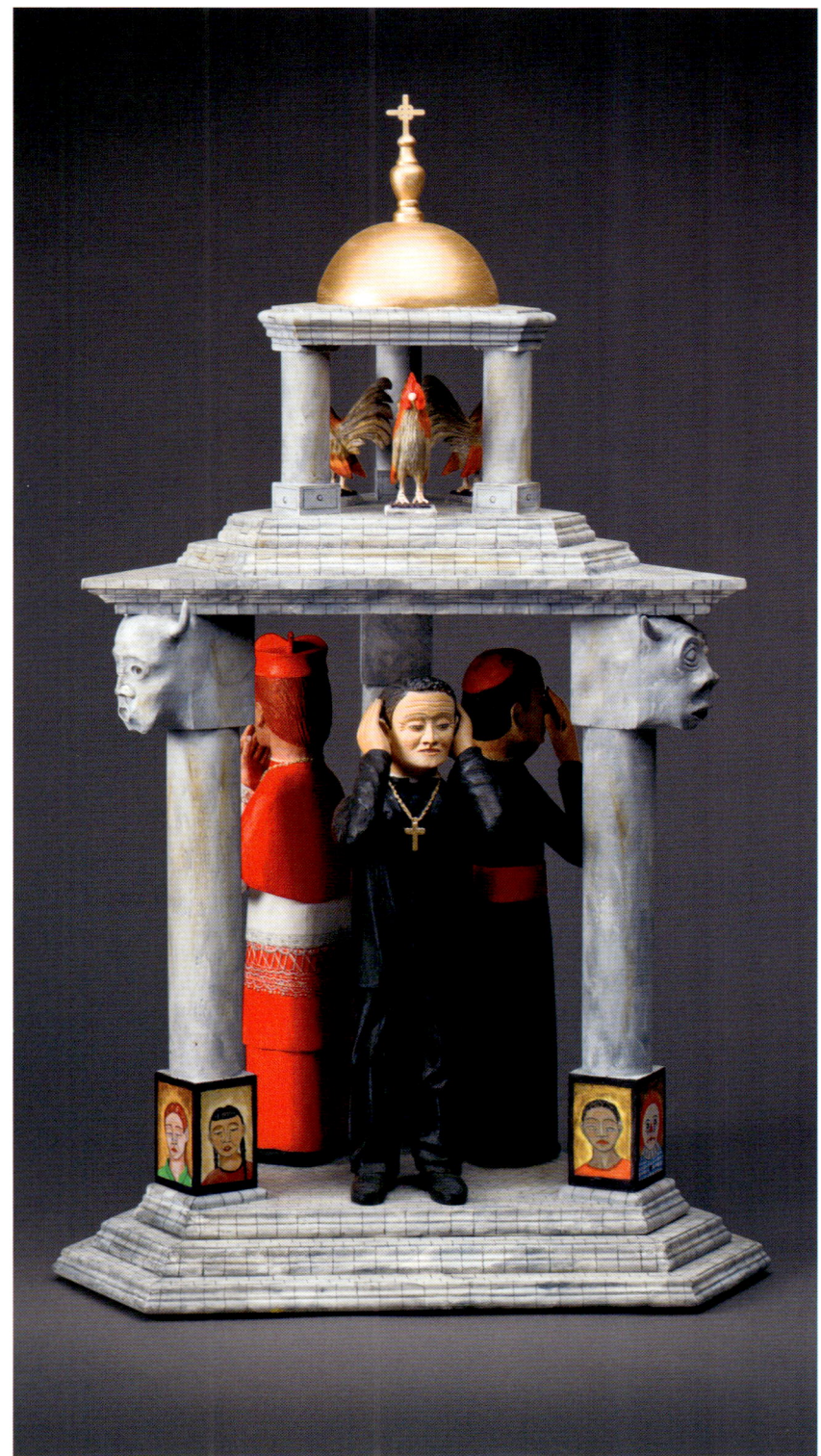

Figure 4. *See No Evil, Hear No Evil, Say No Evil*, 2011. Carved and painted wood, 31 ¼ x 14 x 17 in. Rockwell Museum, Corning, New York (2015.8). Photo © Eric Swanson.

was betrayed. *Corazón negro* (2016; Plate 56) is another heartfelt protest against priestly pedophilia. The heart has horns, and hands and feet, and is baited with a candy bar, a doll, a crucifix. A little girl in a first-communion dress is at the center, and on the hollow back, three children are trapped behind bars.

Nobody's perfect. It is no longer revolutionary to merge sinners and saints, but Tapia paved the way for younger *santeros* to incorporate critical thinking. He has made fewer traditional saints since leaving Spanish Market, which continues to prescribe subjects, materials, and iconography largely based on centuries-old prototypes. When he does take on a traditional subject, as in *Mary Magdalene* (2016; Plate 55), he appropriately casts her as something of a renegade herself. With her fan headdress and beautifully carved overskirt, she is both body and architecture. In *Nativity* (2001; Figure 5), the holy family is homeless, the father a veteran, the manger a cardboard box, with dog, shopping cart, and garbage bag as the attendants. And *Happy Birthday, Jesus* (2016; Plate 50) portrays a youthful Christ, a sadly puzzled look on his face as he contemplates the weapons of destruction (tank, fighter plane, rocket, and cell phone) he has been given by modern society.

The geographical isolation that shaped the beliefs of the early Penitentes (a local lay Catholic brotherhood) and *santeros* who were Tapia's original aesthetic models was altered in 1987. That's when he entered the mainstream art world as one of only thirty painters and sculptors selected for *Hispanic Art in the United States,* a landmark national exhibition at the Museum of Fine Arts, Houston, and the Corcoran Gallery in Washington, D.C. Nevertheless, over the intervening years, Tapia has remained faithful to and politically rooted in his place—a strong move given the increasing globalism and dislocation of the twenty-first-century art world. In the Houston show, his 1986 *Carreta de la muerte* (Figure 11) was a respectful continuation of New Mexican Penitente images of Doña Sebastiana, the fabled female death figure. In his version, she has human teeth and hair, giving her a disturbing new image. He has since made several Doña Sebastianas in which Lady Death is becoming an agent of change, defying the fatalism promulgated by the Catholic Church. In *Doña Sebastiana, la maestra, Will Take Your Requests* (2001; Figure 6) she plays a cello, but the bow is an arrow, a play on the traditional bow and arrow with which she fells her victims. In *State of the Art Sebastiana* (2006; Plate 43), she holds a TV remote and a cell phone ("for talking to God").

Tapia's deep attachment to what we call "nature" or "the environment" is an inseparable element in his devotion to place. Natural resources, especially water, have always been the subjects of pressing political activism in the arid Southwest, all the more so given the property-driven battles across centuries and across cultures. The ancient *acequia* (ditch) system of irrigation, for instance, is pitted against golf courses and upscale development. The "leakage" of water to the highest bidders is the subject of Tapia's *Hole in the Bucket* (1997; Figure 7), showing San Isidro—ubiquitous patron saint of farmers and frequent subject of *santeros*—with a badly leaking bucket of water and a dead corn plant. Beneath him an angel is playing on a well-watered golf course. Tapia again weighed in on this contentious local issue with *Indian Gaming Dance* (1997; Figure 8), in which the dancer, backed by a gaming wheel, wears a Plains Indian headdress made of cards and holds rattles

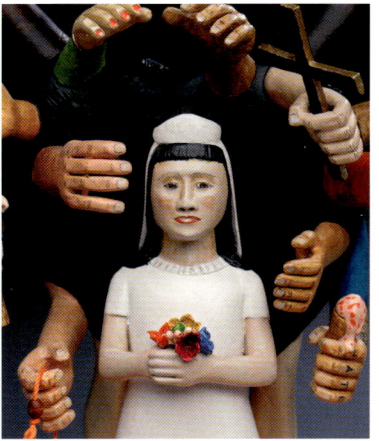

Corazón negro (detail), 2016; see page 180.

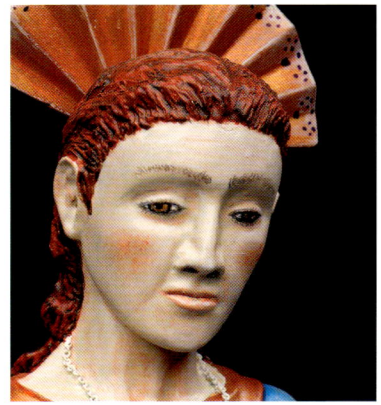

Mary Magdalene (detail), 2016; see page 178.

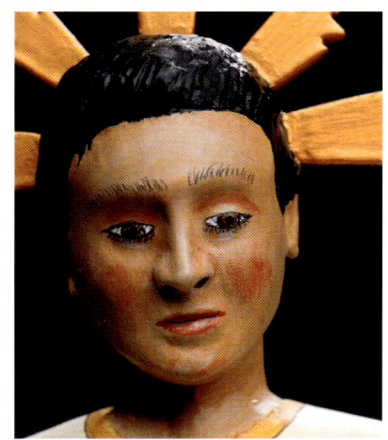

Happy Birthday, Jesus (detail), 2016; see page 168.

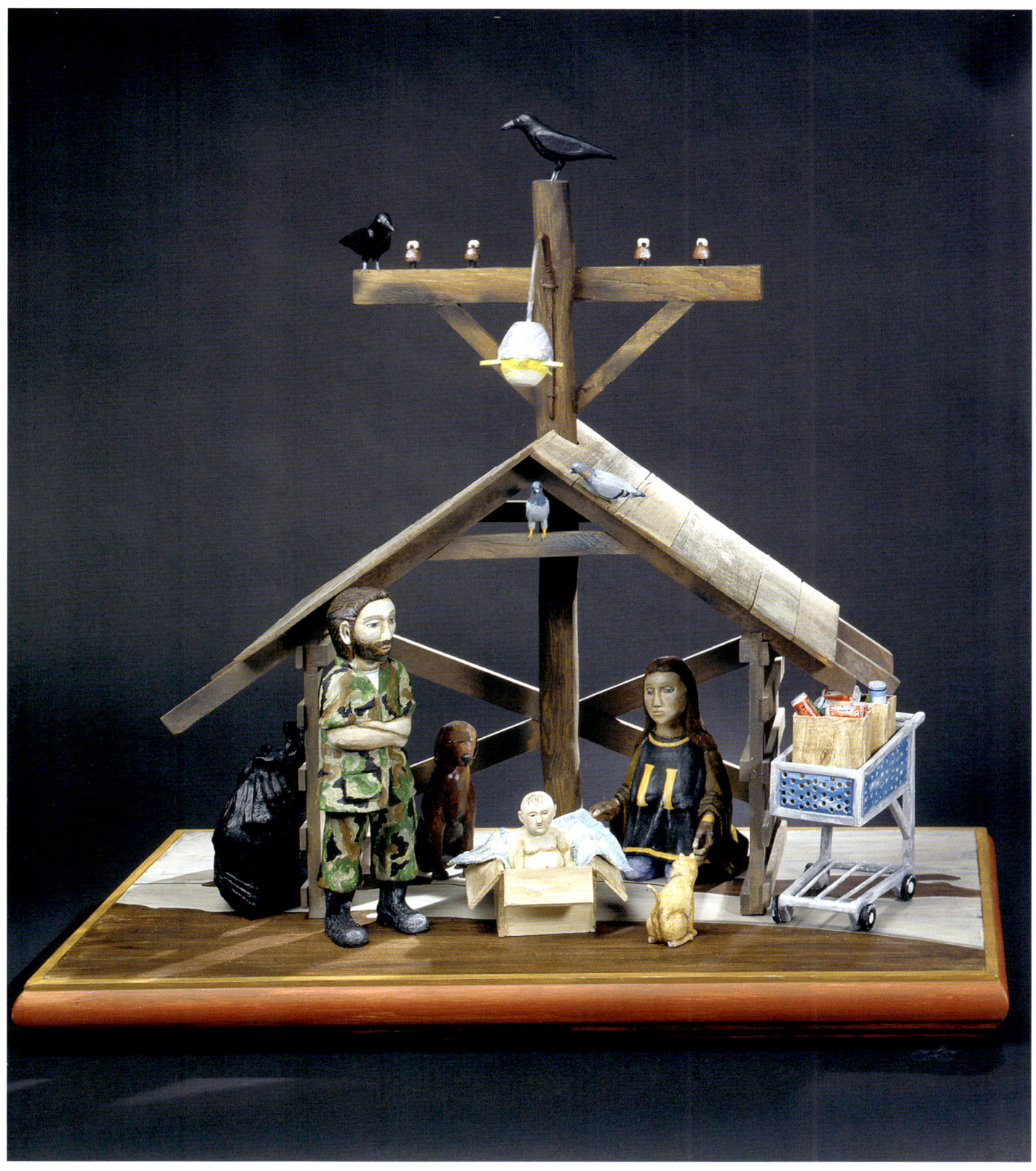

Figure 5. *Nativity*, 2001. Carved and painted wood, 24¾ x 25⅜ x 14⅜ in. Private collection.
Photo © Dan Morse, courtesy of The Owings Gallery.

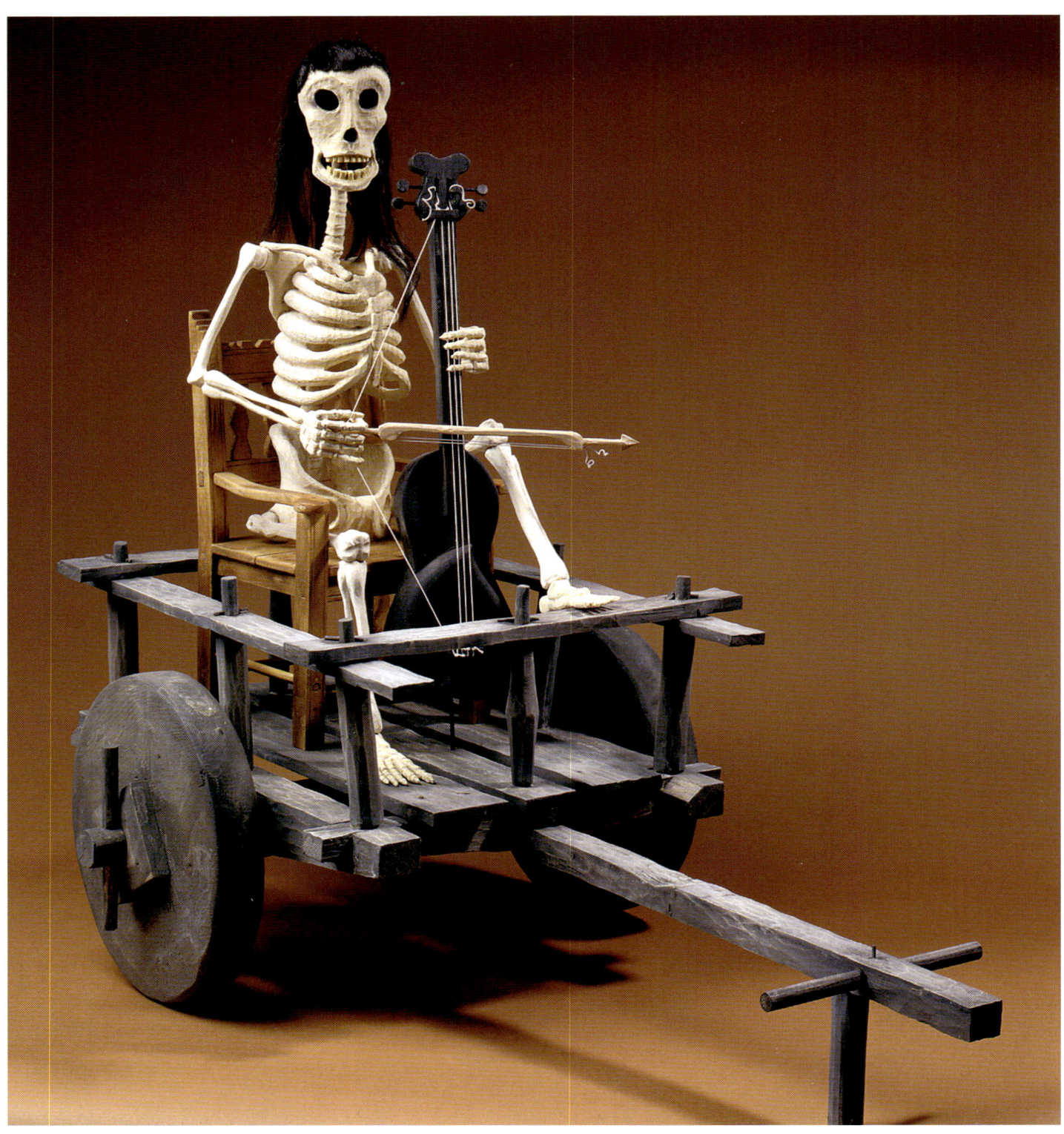

Figure 6. *Doña Sebastiana, la maestra, Will Take Your Requests*, 2001. Carved and painted wood, horse hair, 31¼ x 40¼ x 22½ in. Denver Art Museum Collection; gift of Susan Cosgriff Kirk (2009.483). Photo © Dan Morse, courtesy of The Owings Gallery.

Figure 7. *Hole in the Bucket*, 1997. Carved and painted wood, 17¼ x 11 x 7¼ in. Nancy B. and Howard K. Cohen Collection. Photo © Dan Morse, courtesy of The Owings Gallery.

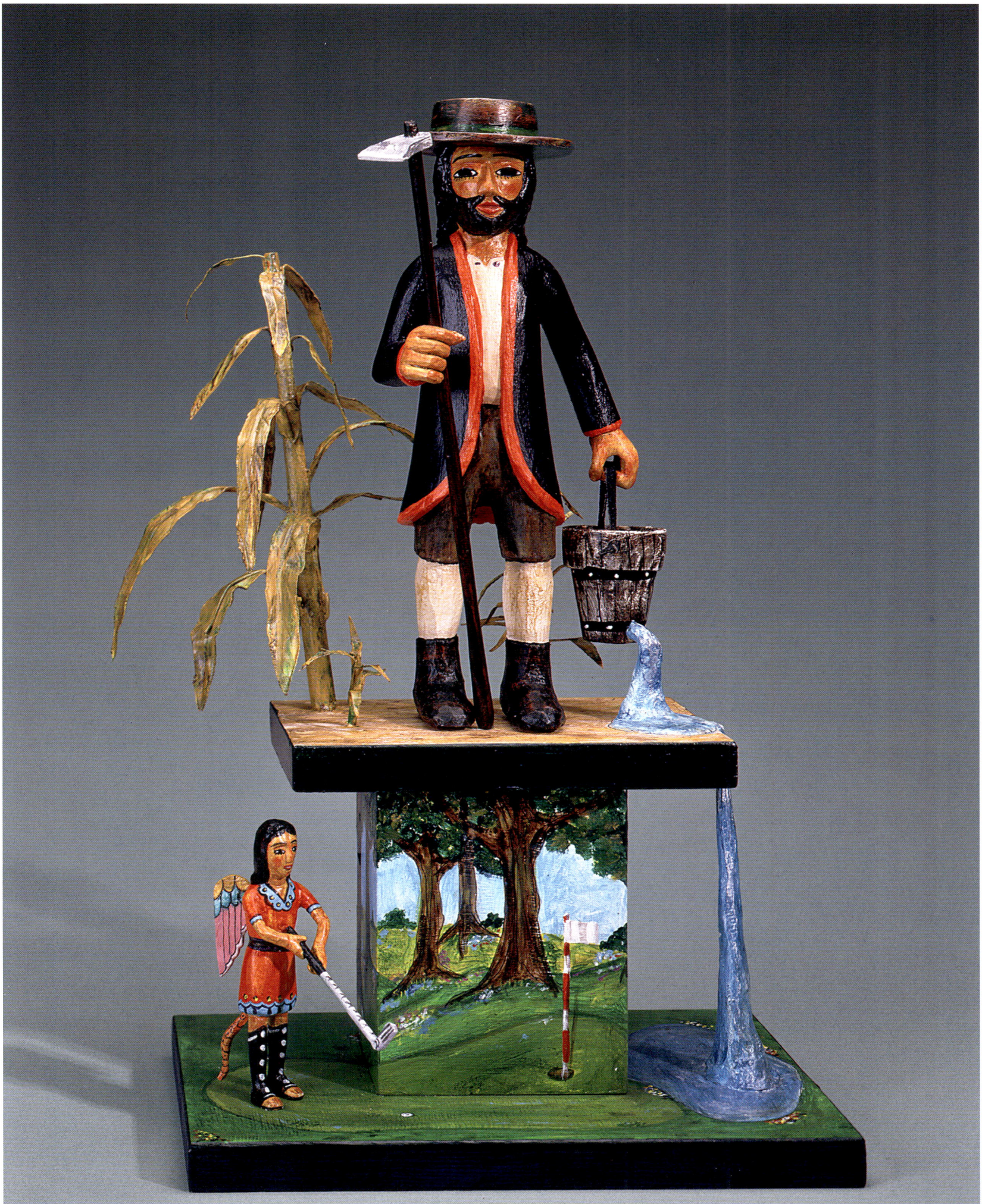

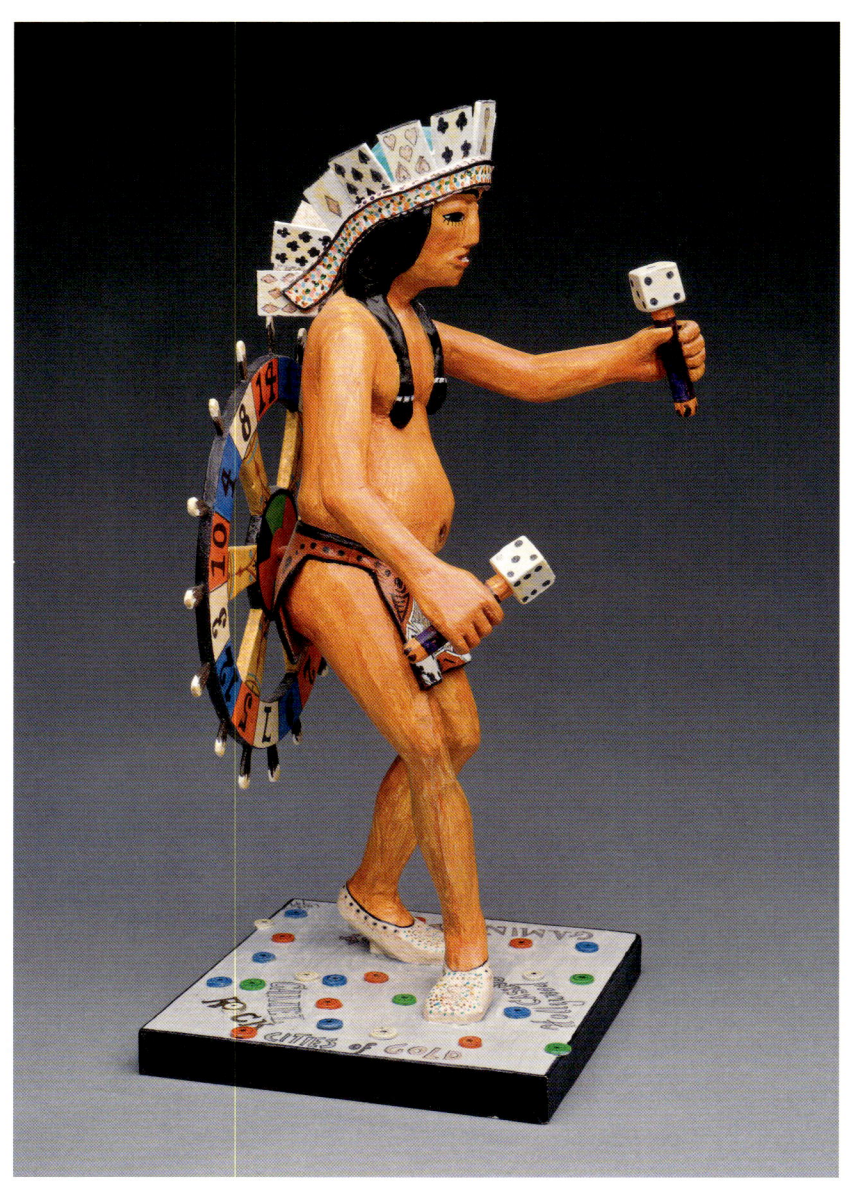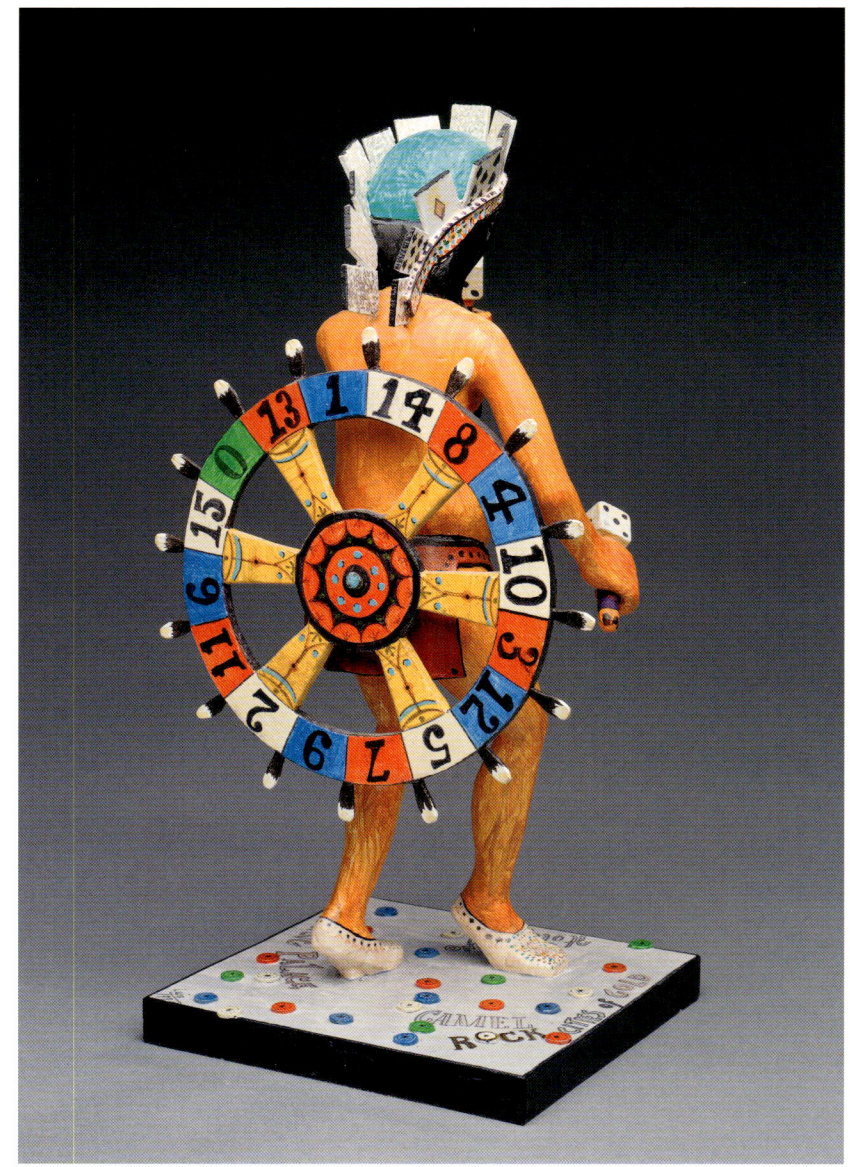

Figure 8. *Indian Gaming Dance*, 1997. Carved and painted wood, 15 ¼ x 7 ⅞ x 7 ¾ in.
Collection of Mr. and Mrs. H. Earl Hoover II. Photo © Addison Doty.

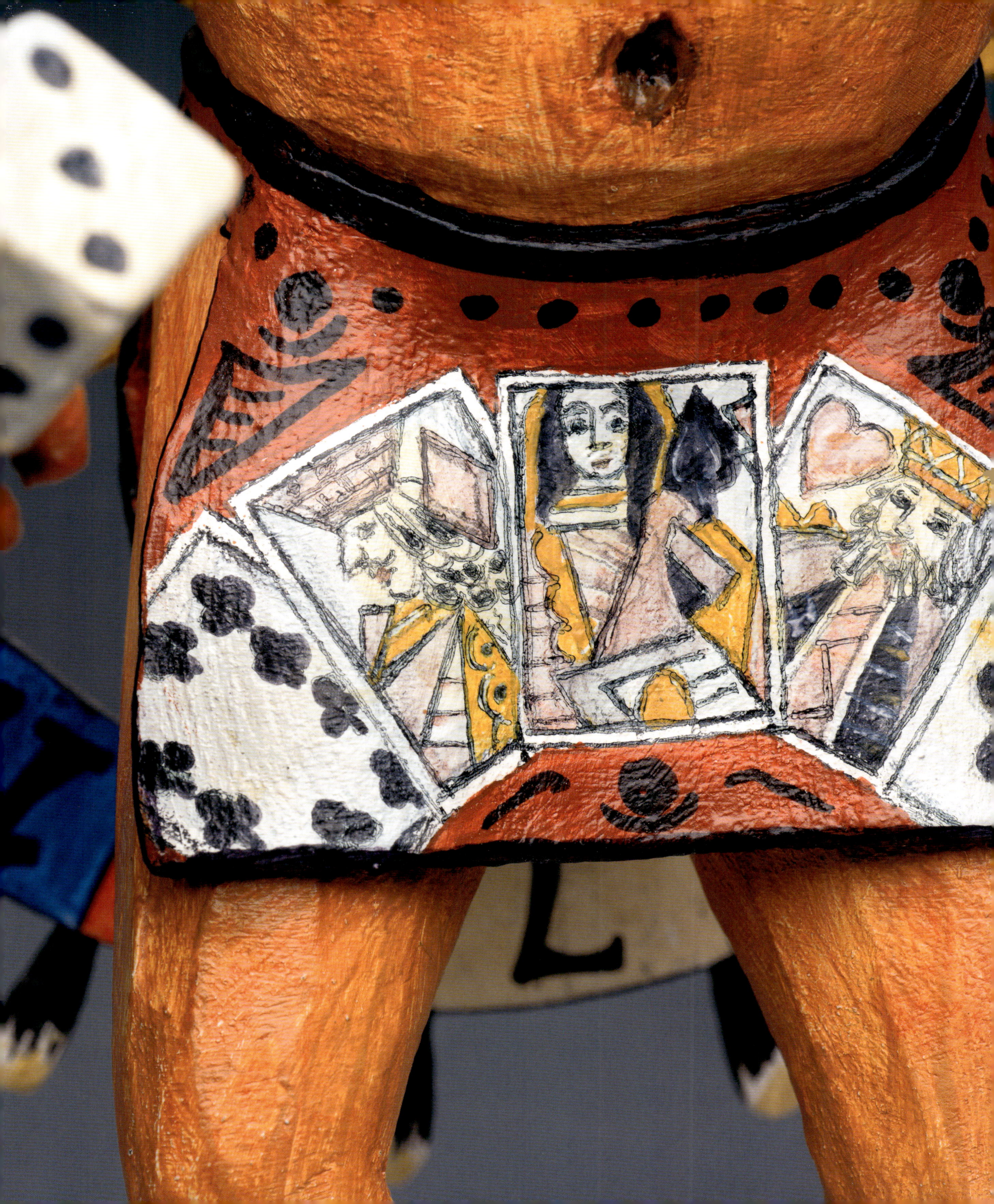

that are dice. The artist says he had always respected Native Americans' devotion to the land, but "it pissed me off" when, suddenly, they were opening casinos and golf courses. Another reading might be a reference to the exploitation of Indian people by the tourism industry, countered by profits that have helped some Native nations out of poverty while flinging too many locals into it.

The long-contested U.S.–Mexican border has become even more politicized as I write after the 2016 presidential elections, with the debate exacerbated by bigotry and threats of mass deportation and an even huger wall. *La frontera* plays a role in several of Tapia's major sculptures. In *Fiesta at the Border* (2007; Plate 44), a Mexican maid serves hors d'oeuvres to a well-dressed couple while *campesinos* peer wistfully through the closed gate to the United States. Two recent works—*Camino de sueños* (2015) and *Virgen del camino de sueños* (2016)—display the subtle detail that is one of Tapia's most effective tools, bearing clues to the meanings of his works. In *Camino de sueños* (Plate 47), a vulture perches on a cross that doubles as a highway sign leading to the "U$A" and overlooks a many-branched cactus (meticulously constructed of a thousand toothpicks) surrounded by frantic footprints. Entangled in the thorns or lying on the ground are abandoned artifacts of hope, flight, fear, and death: a skull, a purse, a shoe, an empty water bottle, a baby bottle, a teddy bear, and a driver's license—referring to the ongoing struggle in New Mexico to keep undocumented immigrants licensed. A bra and panties suggest the all-too-common rapes occurring on these desperate journeys. A scroll attached to the cross is a (fictional) list of names that includes the artist and friends, evoking and identifying with those who have perished in the desert crossing.

Even more poignant is *Virgen del camino de sueños* (Plate 54), flanked by cactuses, crosses, dead roses, and a skull with a skeletal hand over one eye as though blocking unbearable sights. Tears stream down the Virgin's cheeks, and her cloak is decorated with more skulls. On her oval back is a painted horde of individualized and racially diverse faces of those lost, including an Aztec dancer with a towering feathered headdress, calling attention to the fact that this road that has existed for thousands of years is now closed to descendants of its ancient traders and travelers. The cactuses imprison and unite the two sides of the border. The *sueño*, or dream, may be a reference to the Dreamers, those brave young Americans who were brought across without papers as children and are now demanding citizenship. Or perhaps it is simply the dream of a better, less dangerous life.

Tapia's commitment to Chicanismo remains an essential component of all his work. A recent sculpture in his ongoing series of "dashboard altars" is *Cruising Hollywood: Homage to Magu* (2016; Plate 57), a memorial to his now-departed friend Gilbert "Magu" Luján, a well-known L.A. Chicano artist. In the windshield is a painting of a chaotic sign-filled Hollywood Boulevard, traffic ahead, empty of people except for a "sort of portrait" of Magu crossing the street. (In the ashtray is a pipe, in honor of Magu's pot smoking while cruising through Hollywood in the early 1990s, when Tapia lived there and worked out of Magu's studio.) A fluted "shell" crown brings this homage to freedom back to New Mexico, where drivable dashboard altars are common and art activism is quieter, more

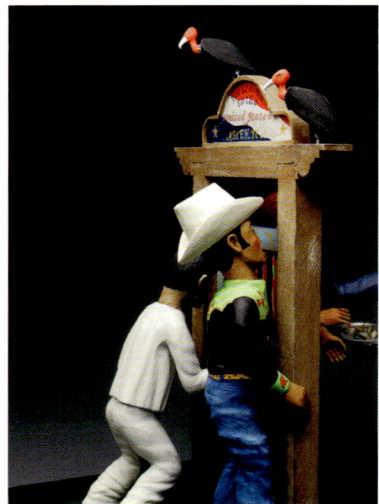

Fiesta at the Border (detail), 2007; see page 156.

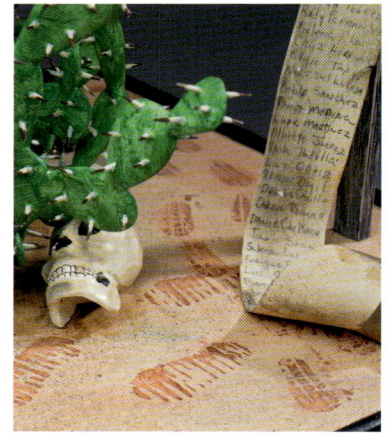

Camino de sueños (detail), 2015;. see page 162.

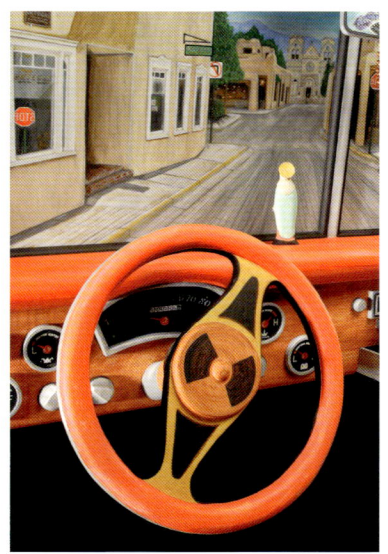

Santa cruz (detail), 2006; see page 106.

embedded in daily life than it is in the noisier and better-known California contingent. A similar earlier image, *Santa cruz* (2006; Plate 10), looks out toward the iconic nineteenth-century cathedral on Santa Fe's San Francisco Street, where upscale shops have replaced local enterprises. Like the lowrider culture of both L.A. and New Mexico, these pieces can be construed as comments on religion in motion, a folk religion that can be an escape, a refuge, and a prison.

Thirty years ago, Tapia explained: "I believe in the tradition. I *am* the tradition. But tradition is not copying. What I do to continue my heritage is to renew it, like a growing plant."[3] Histories and traditions that are allowed to languish unquestioned tend to disappear. Vital art like Tapia's regenerates the images, the stories, the good and the bad, guaranteeing that they remain resilient and significant to future generations.

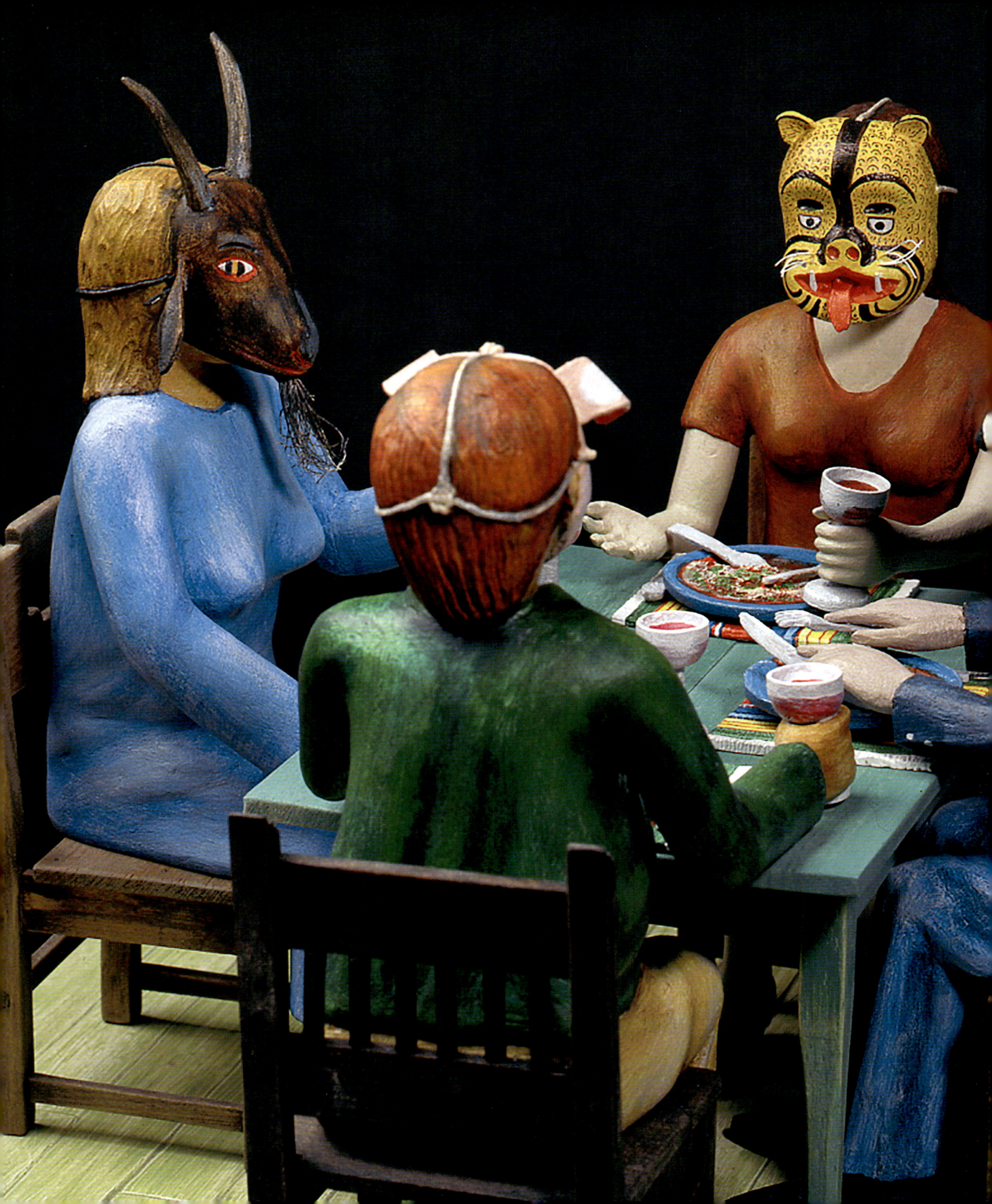

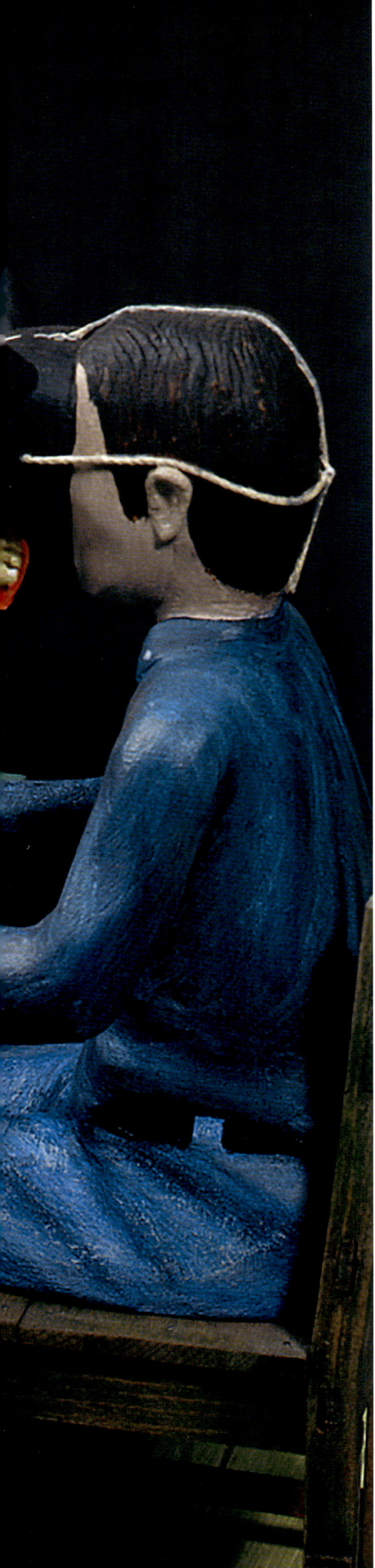

¡Órale!

TEY MARIANNA NUNN

LUIS TAPIA IS NOTED FOR USING THE PHRASE *¡Órale¡* when greeting or meeting someone. This Spanish exclamation has many different definitions and is commonly used in Mexican American and Chicano street lingo. It has powerful meaning for Tapia. "I use *¡Órale!* to identify myself," he says, "to make sure people know who I am."[1]

A self-identified Chicano artist from New Mexico, Tapia produces visual and social commentaries rooted in Nuevomexicano experiences and cultural complexities. Yet he is comfortable in the multifaceted layers of Chicano, Hispano, and Latino identity. As an artist, he merges traditional and contemporary approaches and techniques, addressing universal themes, issues, and constructs. He creates art that is simultaneously local and global in appeal while staying true to his own identity, cultural observations, and opinions.

Tapia has revered stature as a master wood sculptor within his local community. Generations of Nuevomexicano artists have been, and continue to be, influenced by his pathbreaking questioning of artistic and cultural stereotypes, whether they involve subject matter, color choice, or technique. In his passionate and creative (and at times daring and direct) challenges to conventional norms, Tapia has provided a gateway for other artists, including his son, Sergio, a talented sculptor in his own right, to pass through and to express themselves without constraint. For many, Tapia is the one to emulate.

Tapia has also received well-deserved national and international artistic exposure and recognition. However, his visual contributions and cultural critique have for too long been undervalued in the national and international artistic conversation. So it's quite significant that this volume, which accompanies and expands upon a one-person exhibition of works by Tapia at the Museum of Latin American Art in Long Beach—the museum's first one-person exhibition highlighting a Chicano artist from outside California—is the first major monograph about Tapia and his pioneering forty-five-year artistic career.

The importance of recognizing and lauding a non-Californian Chicano artist does not go unnoticed. Indeed, for the most part, twentieth- and twenty-first-century art historians, gallery owners, and museum decision makers have perpetuated a great disservice to the native-born artists of New Mexico. Too few

Guess Who's Coming to Dinner (detail), 2002; see page 116.

have paid attention to the incredible creative production generated within this geographic and cultural locale, which, like California, was once part of greater Latin America. Whether New Mexico artists identify as Spanish, Chicano, Hispano, Hispanic, Latino, or Nuevomexicano is of little concern.[2] What matters most is that the majority have received little critical acclaim, attention, interpretation, and inclusion within the Chicano, Latino, and especially "American" art worlds. The numerous disturbing reasons have to do with race, ethnicity, identity politics, and most of all, perceptions of non-Hispanic cultural gatekeepers about how these artists should be presented and what type of art they should make.

Works by New Mexican Chicano, Hispano, and Latino artists are commonly dismissed as folksy, naive, and rustic in technique and content. The artists themselves are often linked to a direct familial lineage of other artists, especially those described as working in the "folk" and "craft" categories. As a result, a traditional narrative about a New Mexico–born artist like Tapia might read something like this: "Luis Tapia, a Hispanic folk artist from Santa Fe, carves *santos* (saints), a primitive, centuries-old Catholic tradition in this part of the Southwest. *Santeros* (makers of saints) are pious individuals who pray as they carve local woods and paint rustic images, usually working by candlelight as their ancestors did."

Narratives that connect tradition and family run through communities around the world as a way of linking traditional art to artistic identity. Placing an artist inside or outside a community-based tradition, however, is frequently a politically motivated labeling device that may pigeonhole the artist into a quaint or naive category that underestimates his or her creative vision and cultural intent. In Tapia's case, some of the traditional narrative is true. The artist does have relatives who created art, including *santos*, though all were deceased by the time Tapia was born on July 6, 1950. Most notable is Tapia's great-uncle Celso Gallegos (1864–1943), a pivotal early-twentieth-century New Mexican sculptor with a modernist aesthetic. Gallegos was from Agua Fría, the same Santa Fe–area village where Tapia grew up, though it was still on the city's outskirts in the 1930s and 1940s when Gallegos made his career carving "against the grain," so to speak, in a distinctive unpainted style. Two other Tapia uncles, Domingo and Refugio Leyba of Santa Fe, were working artists during the same period. Domingo carved furniture as part of the Works Progress Administration's Federal Art Project in New Mexico. Refugio made and sold weavings at the Native Market in Santa Fe, a private enterprise that promoted works by New Mexican artists practicing traditional arts and design. Tapia's father, Ben Tapia, who died when the artist was thirteen months old, also carved furniture and made toys as a hobby.

As a self-taught artist whose aesthetic foundation is in the centuries-long history of New Mexican wood carving, Tapia is firmly connected to the traditional cultural practices and practitioners of home. But he is equally influenced by the modernist sculptural aesthetic of Henry Moore and the primary colors and freeform sculpture of Alexander Calder. He also finds great inspiration for his work in (old) Mexico, where he feels strong creative forces. "I feel comfortable when I am in Mexico," he says. "I'm fueled by everything around me."

Tapia is not easily pigeonholed. He is a barrio barrier breaker, a blazing border-blurring artist whose broad and intentional combination of "traditional" and "folk" with "contemporary" and "fine" allows viewers of all backgrounds to access his work and connect it to their own experiences. He portrays his—and our—community with all its facets and complexities. He shines a light (and often multiple rays) on its imperfections. Tapia celebrates *mestizaje*, the cultural interchange and combined identities of people in the New World. He acknowledges the multiple and simultaneous layers that make up modern Chicanos, Hispanos, and Latinos. He understands that they are all valid, and all true.

The civil rights and Chicano movements of the 1960s and early 1970s prompted Tapia to critically examine notions of the traditional and contemporary Chicano experience. Galvanized by these movements, all of which were active or began in New Mexico, Tapia felt connected—to the Brown Berets (he wore one in solidarity), to Reies López Tijerina's land grant movement, to the United Farm Workers movement led by César Chávez and Dolores Huerta, also a New Mexico native. Tapia supported these causes at lectures, demonstrations, and protests throughout New Mexico. He recalls: "I saw the injustices that I didn't realize were happening in Santa Fe. You didn't really hear about it in Santa Fe at that time. It was mellow then. Becoming aware of injustices in the world made me want to know more about my culture—even though I was living my culture."

Tapia now recognized artistic expressions of his culture that surrounded him every day. At home there were plaster and plastic saints. At his grandmother's house, where he spent a significant amount of time, there was a collection of *santos* and other artworks made by his uncles during the WPA. And at San Isidro Catholic Church in Agua Fría Village, where as a child Tapia always sat with his mother next to a statue of San Isidro, there was a range of religious art made specifically for its sacred spaces. "I consciously realized that New Mexican *santos* were significant. They were our true art," he says. Tapia also reveled in other vernacular art forms, especially music. He attended weddings in Gallinas and went to bars in Santa Fe where local musicians belted out *corridos* (ballads) and other songs in Spanish. Topics for these songs ranged from accounts of how a young man died en route to Taos to lovers' tragedies to other local lore and *chisme* (gossip).

Tapia was about twenty-one years old when he decided to try his hand at carving. His first works—animals, small-scale nudes, and other secular figures—were unpainted and often abstracted. His interest in works of the early New Mexican *santeros* was encouraged by his wife at the time, Star Tapia, who was also an artist. He was further encouraged by Alan Vedder, a former curator at both the Museum of International Folk Art and the Spanish Colonial Arts Society, who allowed him to study both organizations' important collections of New Mexican–made Spanish colonial–style art. Researching the world's largest collections of historic New Mexican art forms fueled Tapia's creativity and provided inspiration. He saw Moorish, Spanish, and Mexican design elements; hand-hewn furniture; church altar screens; and sculpted and painted *santos*, including three-dimensional *bultos* and two-dimensional *retablos*. Connecting to this visual culture, Tapia connected to his seventeenth-, eighteenth-, and nineteenth-century colleagues and bridged an aesthetic continuum with a markedly Río Grande–inspired sensibility and style.

Tapia quickly transitioned to *santos* painted in the dark, antiquated shades of the prototypes he studied. But he was particularly drawn to the works, and especially the color choices, of Molleno, who made *santos* in New Mexico in the early nineteenth century (circa 1815–1845). "Molleno helped me start my color palette—reds, creamy greens, and yellows," he says.

By the early 1970s, Tapia had juried into Santa Fe's annual Spanish Market, then and now the largest market of New Mexican Spanish colonial–style art in the United States. This culturally significant arts market began in 1926, spearheaded by the Spanish Colonial Arts Society, an organization formed to preserve and revive the traditional arts of the New Mexican colonial period, including wood carving, religious paintings and sculpture, furniture, tinwork, colcha embroidery, and weaving.[3] Most of the society's founders were newly arrived members of the Anglo intelligentsia from outside New Mexico. Their aesthetic sensibilities influenced the core guidelines market artists were required to follow in terms of media, technique, and subject matter. Some more innovative works have recently been allowed into the market, at the artists' insistence, but the question of who decides what is "traditional" or "colonial" New Mexican art has for decades been a source of friction between Anglo patrons and some Nuevomexicano artists, while giving rise to complex and fascinating identity politics. Nonetheless, Spanish Market has provided much-needed revenue for generations of artists, passed along stories and techniques of New Mexican artistic practice, cultivated collectors, and helped position Nuevomexicano art.

Few would deny that Tapia was one of the most influential—and controversial—artists to show at Spanish Market. In the early 1970s, when many market artists were making unpainted *santos*, following an early-twentieth-century convention, he was among the first artists to show painted *bultos* and *retablos*, in the tradition of the early master *santeros*. He also moved beyond *santos*, creating award-winning furniture and paintings on animal hide. And he broke new ground by depicting such religious themes as Adam and Eve, *Noah's Ark* (Figure 9), and the Last Supper, as well as such figures as *Kateri Tekawitha* (Figure 10) and Juan Diego long before they were saints. Though these subjects are now commonplace at Spanish Market, back then they pushed deeply embedded market boundaries and definitions of "traditional" Spanish colonial art.

Tapia kept pushing. Most radical (at the time) was the artist's fondness for brilliant hues, initially created with homemade egg tempera paints and later with commercial acrylic paints. This reflected his research-based belief that Spanish colonial–era colors were originally brighter than the aged museum examples (which conservation scientists later proved true). Tapia's works were popular with market buyers and at other shows around Santa Fe and northern New Mexico. In the early 1970s, he began regular wood carving demonstrations at El Rancho de las Golondrinas, a living history museum in La Ciénega, south of Santa Fe. He was also a featured artist at pivotal regional exhibitions at the Taylor Museum at the Colorado Springs Fine Arts Center (*Hispanic Crafts of the Southwest*, 1977), the Albuquerque Museum (*One Space, Three Visions*, 1978), and the Smithsonian Institution's Festival of American Folklife in Washington, D.C. (1976 and 1977). But

OPPOSITE
Figure 9. *Noah's Ark*, 1991. Carved and painted wood, 19¾ x 27⅞ x 19¾ in. Private collection. Photo © James Hart, courtesy of The Owings Gallery.

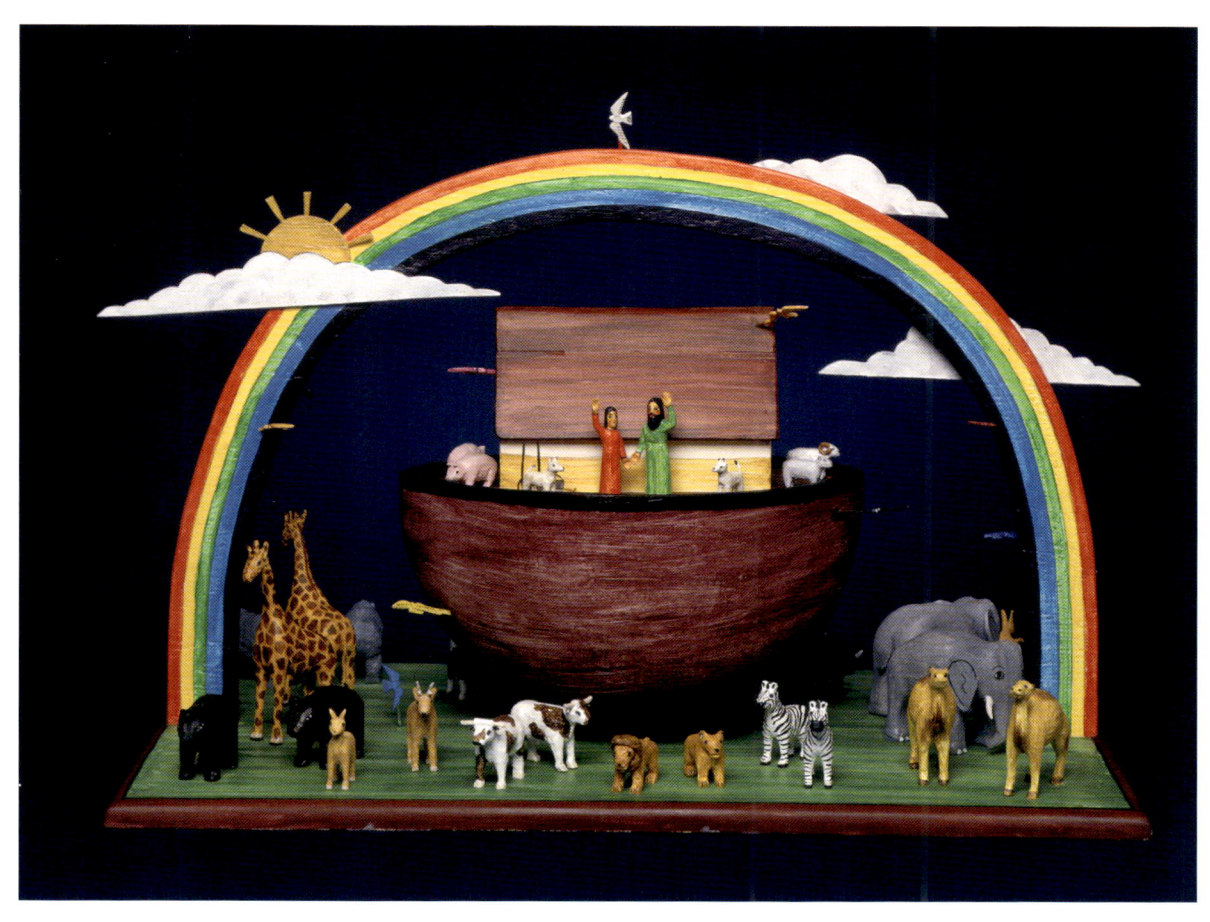

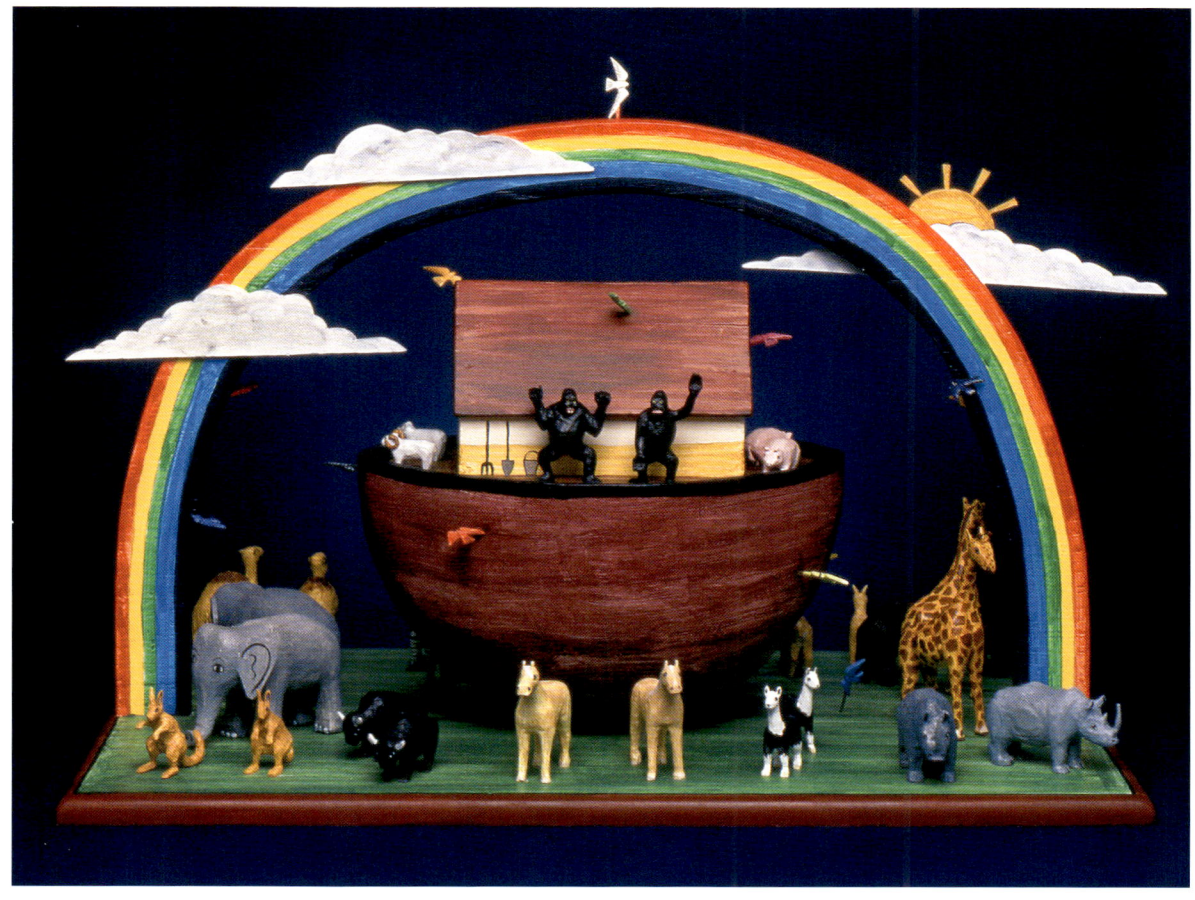

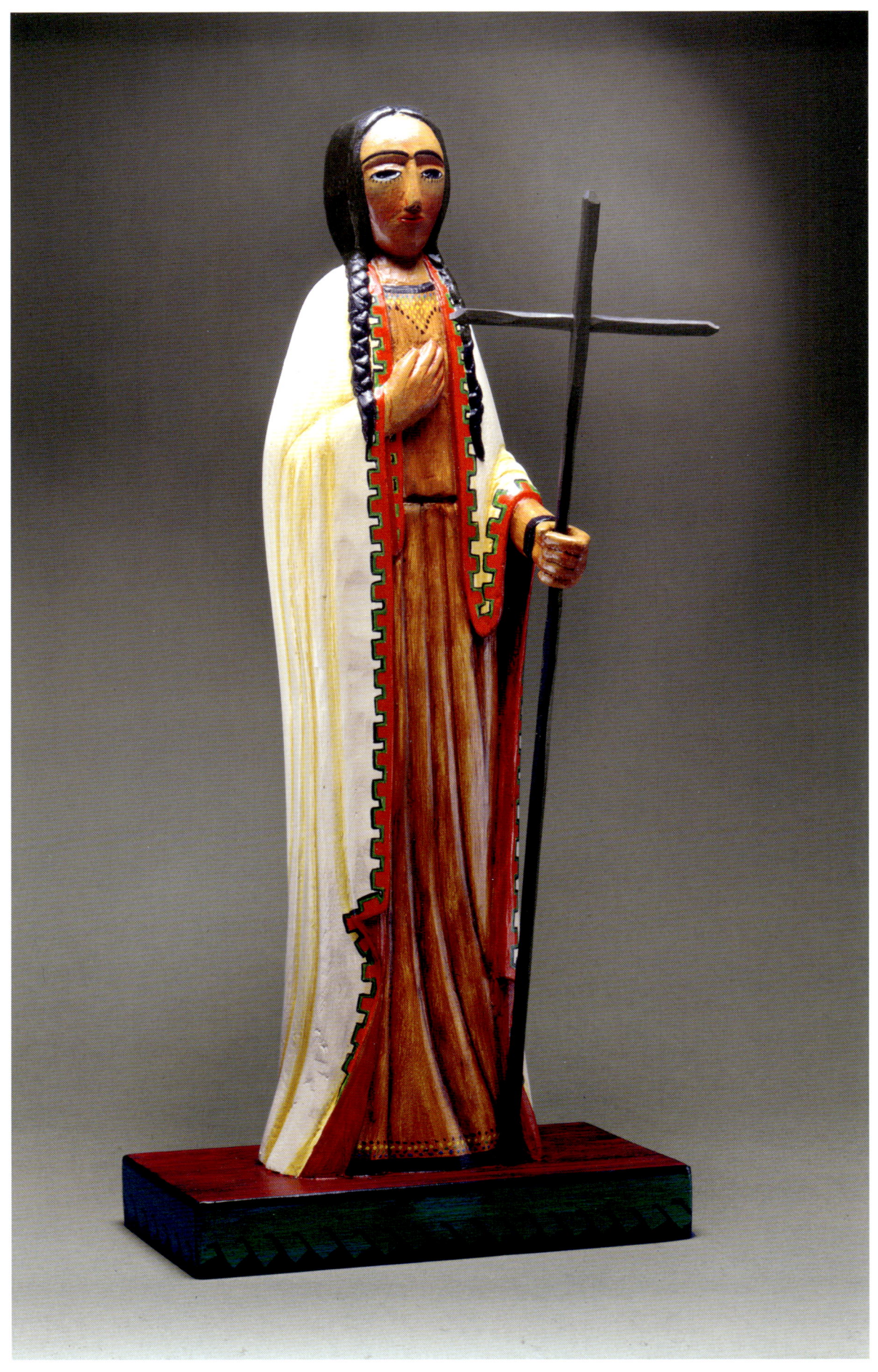

Vedder and other Spanish Market organizers weren't keen on the direction of Tapia's creativity, especially his rich and saturated color choices. "They kept trying to keep me in line," Tapia says. "They only wanted me to do copies of existing works. I wanted to stay with religious subject matter, but I wanted to do *santos* that hadn't been done yet." Around 1978 Tapia was asked to leave Spanish Market. He struck out on his own to pursue his singular vision of New Mexican art—one soundly outside the confines of Anglo-imposed ideas and the enduring New Mexican narrative of what was "authentic," "colonial," "traditional" art.

Meanwhile, during the 1970s, many contemporary Chicano art groups formed in California, Texas, Chicago, and elsewhere. At the time, few of Santa Fe's cultural institutions would even consider exhibiting artworks or hosting performances by Hispano and Chicano artists. Their narrow definitions of what constituted New Mexican Hispano and Chicano art fueled Tapia and many fellow New Mexican artists to form a collaborative *grupo* of their own, La Cofradía de Artes y Artesanos Hispánicos (the Confraternity of Hispanic Arts and Artisans). The *grupo* comprised a range of visual artists, writers, musicians, and other performers who agitated for inclusion of all types of Hispano arts and artists in Santa Fe's museum, gallery, and cultural scenes. In addition to Tapia, the group's Santa Fe cofounders included Star Tapia, Frederico Vigil, Wilberto Miera, and María Luisa Delgado Roybal. Taos residents Vicente and Dorotea Martínez, Juanita Jaramillo Lavadie, and Eduardo Lavadie, as well as Pola López of Las Vegas and others, soon joined them in organizing artists from across the state.

La Cofradía's mission, according to its 1978 articles of incorporation, was to "encourage the survival of traditional and contemporary Hispanic arts and crafts, and promote the social, cultural, economic, and general welfare of the Hispanic artist and craftsman." To achieve this, La Cofradía's card-carrying members subverted the Anglo paradigm and hosted inclusive exhibits in churches, homes, schools, and community spaces throughout northern New Mexico, from a Taos school gymnasium to Highlands University in Las Vegas to the Santuario de Guadalupe in Santa Fe. The *grupo* disbanded in 1982, but the experiences that Tapia and his cohorts created were deeply formative. Many New Mexicans today fondly remember these communal gatherings and especially the power of the artworks the group expressed and exposed.

La Cofradía solidified Tapia's seriousness as a creative rebel committed to going his own way and opened new doors of opportunity. In 1980 he was invited to present a solo exhibition at the Institute of American Indian Arts in Santa Fe. The event was unprecedented and was a nuanced acknowledgment of the artist's Chicano (Indo-Hispano) identity. Tapia also explored the art world beyond Santa Fe, jurying into the Festival of the American West Art Fair in Ogden, Utah. He laughs when he recalls showing his work to mostly Mormon viewers, who didn't understand his Catholic religious art. He didn't sell anything, yet showing there wasn't in vain. An East Coast curator who noticed his work later invited him to participate in an exhibition. And, Tapia jokes, he came home with gifts of eight editions of *The Book of Mormon*.

OPPOSITE
Figure 10. *Kateri Tekawitha*, 1993. Carved and painted wood, 23 ¼ x 10 ⅜ x 4 ⅞ in. Private collection. Photo © Dan Morse, courtesy of The Owings Gallery.

In 1987 Tapia's work was featured in a groundbreaking national traveling exhibition, *Hispanic Art in the United States: Thirty Contemporary Painters and Sculptors*. Organized by the Museum of Fine Arts, Houston, and the Corcoran Gallery of Art in Washington, D.C., the exhibition traveled from Houston to the Los Angeles County Museum of Art and the Brooklyn Museum. The show, and its accompanying catalog, was among the first pre-quincentennial projects to highlight the work of contemporary Hispanic artists across the country.[4] Along with Tapia, notable artists included Rudy Fernandez, Carmen Lomas Garza, Luis Jiménez, Felix López, Gilbert "Magu" Luján, John Valadez, Felipe Archuleta, Rolando Briseño, Martín Ramírez, Frank Romero, Carlos Almaraz, and Glugio "Gronk" Nicandro. During the tour, Tapia became especially close to Magu, Fernandez, and Jiménez. Before they became Chicano cultural icons, these artists forged a multistate Chicano network of support.

Ironically, the museum and gallery environment in Santa Fe during this time remained mostly unwelcoming to Hispano artists, especially those who defied accepted stereotypes. Nonetheless, Tapia was one of the first New Mexican Chicano artists to be represented by a major Santa Fe gallery. Joining Owings-Dewey Fine Art (now The Owings Gallery) in the summer of 1988 was a meaningful moment for Tapia and an important opportunity to fully express himself. Tapia told the gallery, "If I come with you, I want to do what I want." He had his first solo exhibition there on Saint Patrick's Day 1989, a date strategically distant from the July Spanish Market. Opening to a packed audience, it set the tone for decades of successful shows at the gallery for Tapia. Writing in 1994 about a similarly packed opening there in 1991, Heard Museum curator Diana Pardue declared not only that Tapia "broke new ground with a one-man show" but that the overwhelming interest in a show of works by an individual Hispano artist "marked a significant shift in emphasis in a town that is well known for promoting and emphasizing Native American Art."[5]

The late 1980s and early 1990s marked a definitive turning point in Tapia's art and career as his images grew more inspired and expansive in style and his artistry became more refined and innovative. He mastered different stylistic techniques, often within the same subject matter, as evidenced by his *Carreta de la muerte* series, featuring the skeletal image of Doña Sebastiana, a significant figure and symbol of death in the Holy Week rituals and processions of New Mexico's centuries-old Penitente brotherhood. Tapia says that the death cart figures gave him one of the first creative opportunities to explore his individual expression, as his historical research demonstrated that the early makers had also put their personal spins on this particular image.

Most of Tapia's *carretas* are large in scale. One of his first, *Carreta de la muerte* (1986; Figure 11), was featured in the *Hispanic Art in the United States* exhibition and was soon acquired for the collection of the Smithsonian's National Museum of American Art. Carved from aspen, Doña Sebastiana sits regally in a hand-adzed cart. Her long black braid, with a patch of gray hair, hangs past her upper rib cage. The elongated carved aspen wood aptly conveys bleached bones. Sebastiana sticks out her tongue through an open

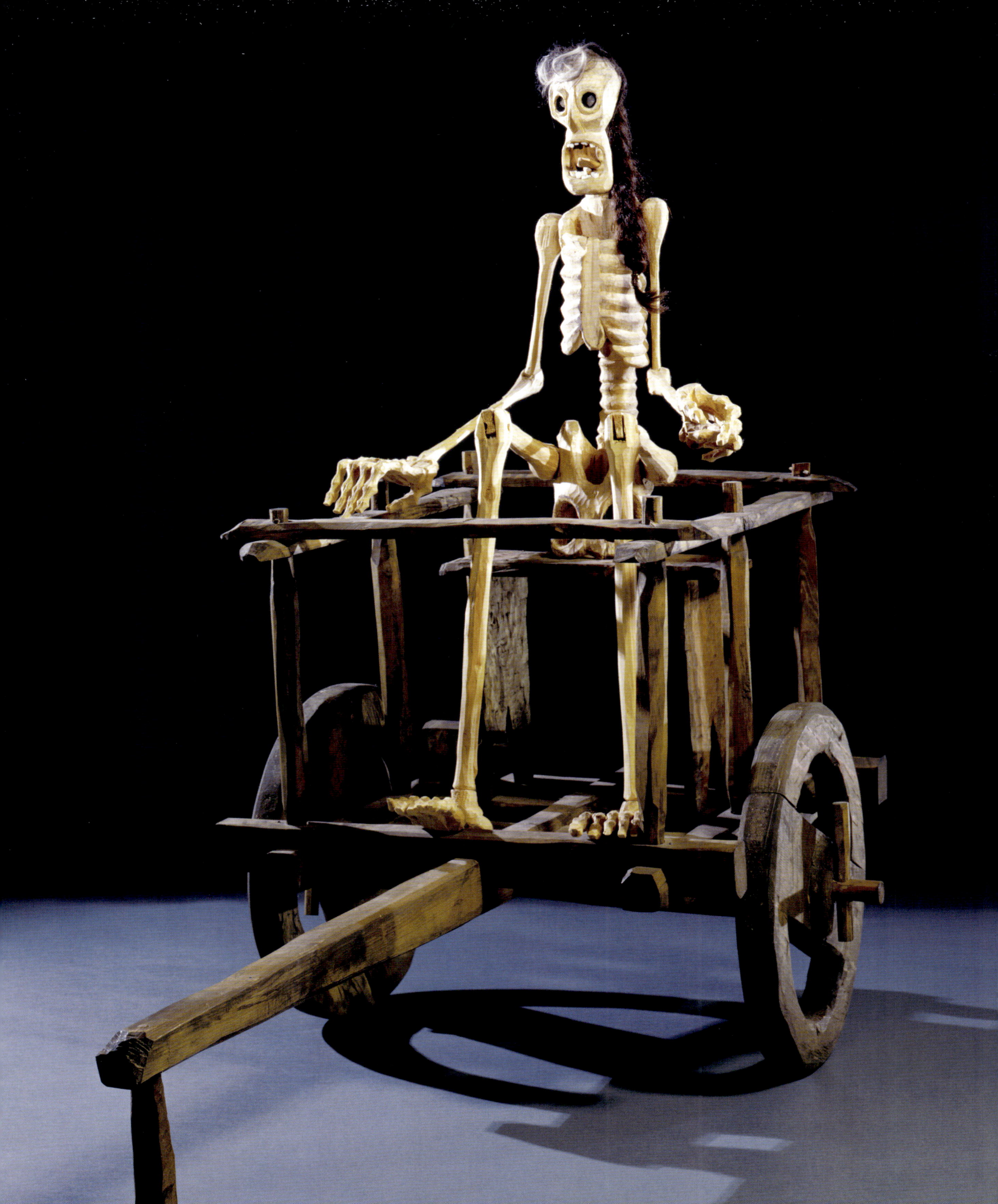

mouth baring carved teeth. Her eyes, made of mica, shine ominously. In contrast, Tapia's *Santa Fe Blue Carreta* (1987; Figure 12) features a tongue-wagging, finger-pointing Death figure without hair. She sits in her cart on a New Mexican–style bench. Small crosses, the color of blue typically seen on doors and window frames in northern New Mexico, adorn the cart's rim. The same color brightens the hubs of its four wheels. Tapia carved the cart handle in the form of a cross, in direct reference to the traditional processional use of *carretas de la muerte* in New Mexico during Holy Week.

Another large death cart, *Doña Sebastiana with Parasol Riding through Purgatory* (1991; Figure 13), is infused with Tapia's signature wry humor mixed with some sarcasm. Doña Sebastiana grips the cart with her right hand and holds a bone-like parasol that is unable to provide shade. She appears to be in motion as the cart lurches ahead, pulled by a companionable skeletal bull. The pedestal below is a painted purgatory of multi-ethnic souls. In Tapia's *Carreta de la muerte con rosas* (1996; Figure 14), Doña Sebastiana sits on a traditional-style New Mexican chair with mortise and tenon joinery—a nod by Tapia to the early *carpinteros* who inspired him. The long-haired figure arches forward with a gap-toothed grimace. Her menacing expression is softened by her crown of bright reddish-pink roses and matching wrist corsage.

Tapia also took aesthetic liberty with other religious subjects, as demonstrated by two important works from the period. *La Santísima Trinidad* (1988; Figure 15) melds the three faces of the Father, Son, and Holy Ghost on one head. The head tops a single figure, brightly dressed and seated in a New Mexican–style chair with a traditional chip-carved design. In this and earlier versions of the subject, Tapia innovated, depicting all three images as one, another departure from his artistic counterparts during that period. The message of the triple visage, though subtle, caused a stir among traditionalists. Ironically, today this version of the Trinity is in the collection of the Spanish Colonial Arts Society, the longtime sponsor of Spanish Market. Eyebrows also were raised by Tapia's early nude renditions of Adam and Eve, as, surprisingly, nude figures in "traditional" New Mexican art were quite uncommon at the time. In *Adam and Eve* (1989; Figure 16), Tapia depicts two anatomically correct figures with their sensitive parts strategically covered by leaves, though they are obviously communicating about a certain symbolic apple. A stark brown tree trunk stands between them. An apple-red snake is wrapped around it, seemingly squeezing the vital essence from the Tree of Life.

Even as Tapia was innovating with traditional subjects, he also undertook a number of strictly traditional church commissions in New Mexico. His 1978 conservation of the late-eighteenth-century altar screen at the San Francisco de Asís Mission Church at Ranchos de Taos led to a 1979 commission to create a new altar screen in the church at San Ildefonso Pueblo (since removed and destroyed by a subsequent tribal government). This was followed by another original altar screen, created in 1986 for the traveling *Hispanic Art* exhibition. This twelve-foot-high altar work (Figure 17) features paintings and sculpture, including images of the crucifixion, La Virgen de Guadalupe, San José, and Saint Francis. Near the bottom, below the Franciscan coat of arms (the extended arms and hands, with stigmata, of Christ and Saint Francis), Tapia signed the work in the tradition of Spanish masters, intentionally using an *s* instead of a *z* to inscribe "Este Altar Hiso Luis Tapia Año 1986" ("This altar was made by Luis Tapia year 1986"). The artist later donated this work, in memory of his father, to his boyhood San Isidro Church in Agua Fría Village, where it stands today. A personal tragedy in 1990 resulted in another traditionally inspired dedication, *Altar Screen, Dedico este altar a la memoria de mi amigo Chris Corriz 1974–1990* (1990; Figure 18). This twelve-foot-high altar screen, carved from aspen and pine, honors a sixteen-year-old Santa Fean whom Tapia had taken on as an apprentice. When the youth died in a car accident, Tapia expressed his massive grief in this massive work. "I've never taken on another student again," Tapia says.

After the *Hispanic Art* exhibition, church commissions came from California. In the early 1990s, he was hired to create a large-scale nativity scene for the Church of the Nativity in Rancho Santa Fe. This led to a commission of New World saints for the San Francisco Solano Catholic Church in Rancho Santa Margarita, for which Tapia combined skills in sculpting, painting, and tinwork. For a year, while working on the Rancho Santa Fe commission, Tapia shared a Hollywood studio with Magu (1940–2011), an influential figure in the 1960s Chicano art movement in Los Angeles and a cofounder of the *grupo* Los Four. Later, Magu lived with Tapia in New Mexico. The two artists shared an interest in car culture, which Tapia refers to as "the root of all urban art," especially the artistic shapes and colors of vintage and lowrider cars and trucks. Their work during and after this time highlighted the influence of popular culture as well as popular and folk art traditions and images from Mexico, Latin America, and the southwestern United States. Among other things, Magu created paintings, prints, and three-dimensional works out of board, featuring local personages, community scenes, and Aztec religious icons. These resembled some popular New Mexican art forms, including religious imagery, and were also painted with a striking and bold color palette. It is no surprise that the two artists drew energy and creativity from each other.

Some of Tapia's most recognizable works are obviously influenced by Chicano car culture. His original series of "dashboard altars," inspired by the *santo*-adorned dash of his mother's '56 Ford, plays on the popular and devotional aspects of cars, expertly reframing these vernacular art forms into fine art. In these *homenajes* (homages) to the dashboard, viewers look out the front windshield to expansive northern New Mexican landscapes or familiar streetscapes. Tapia includes elements found in early New Mexican art and design, such as color palettes, iconography, carving techniques, and architecture. As he combines these bits and pieces, he creates reverent and dedicated sacred spaces that reference not only road culture and road trips watched over by *santos* but also the idea of faith and place. Details include New Mexican–style bucket seats or priest chairs, hand-carved curtains, visors like angel wings, chain-link sacred heart steering wheels, a beer can in a drink holder, *santos* on the dash, and even a Guadalupana gearshift knob. Rosaries and other cultural memories and artifacts hang from rearview mirrors, reflecting apparitions of La Virgen or Doña Sebastiana.

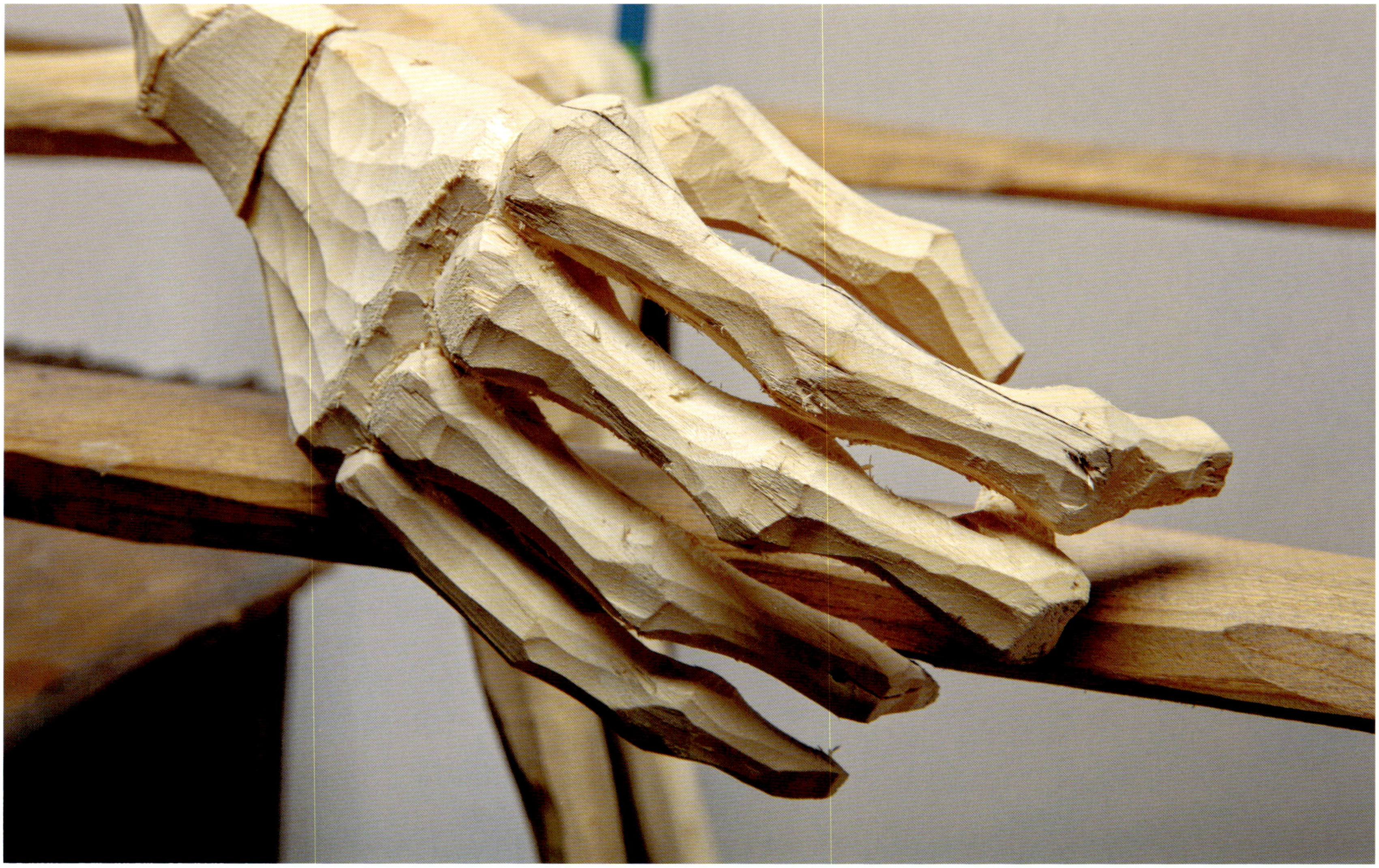

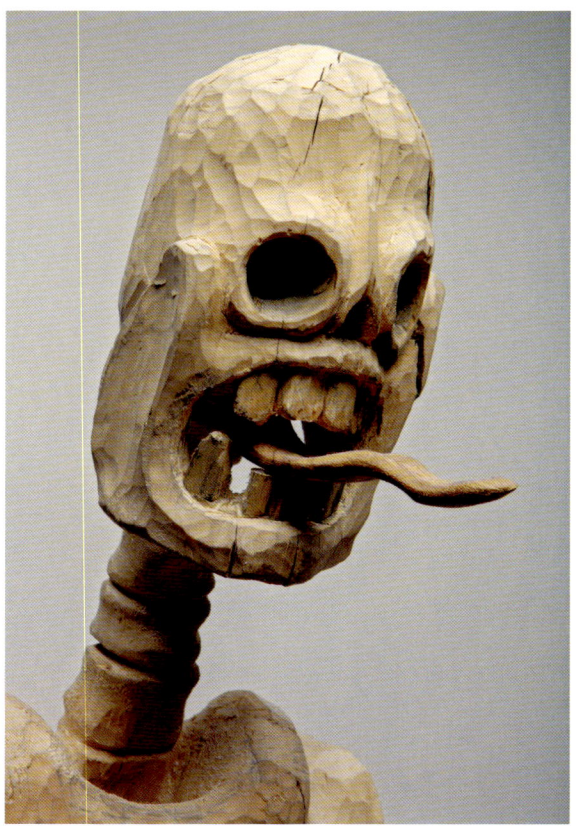

ABOVE, LEFT, AND OPPOSITE

Figure 12. *Santa Fe Blue Carreta*, 1987. Carved and painted wood, 56 ½ x 55 ⁵⁄₁₆ x 27 ⁷⁄₁₆ in. Museum of International Folk Art, Santa Fe, IFAF Collection (FA.1988.1.1). Photo © Addison Doty.

FOLLOWING SPREAD

LEFT

Figure 13. *Doña Sebastiana with Parasol Riding through Purgatory*, 1991. Carved and painted wood, human hair, 43 x 23 x 72 in. Private collection. Photo © James Hart, courtesy of The Owings Gallery.

RIGHT

Figure 14. *Carreta de la muerte con rosas*, 1996. Carved and painted wood, cloth flowers, 52 x 26 x 32½ in. Collection of the National Hispanic Cultural Center, Albuquerque; gift of Pamela McCorduck and Joseph Traub. Photo © Addison Doty.

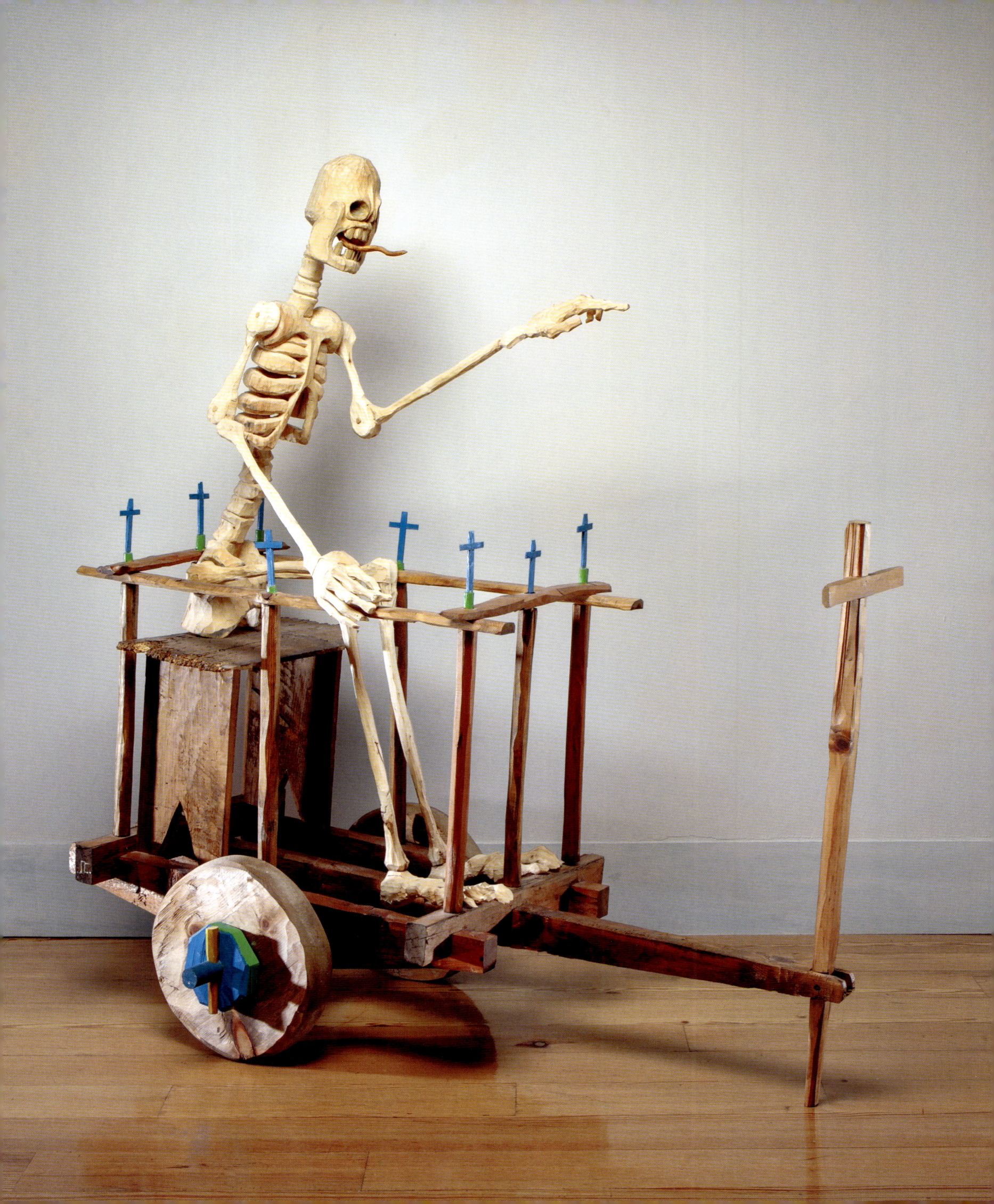

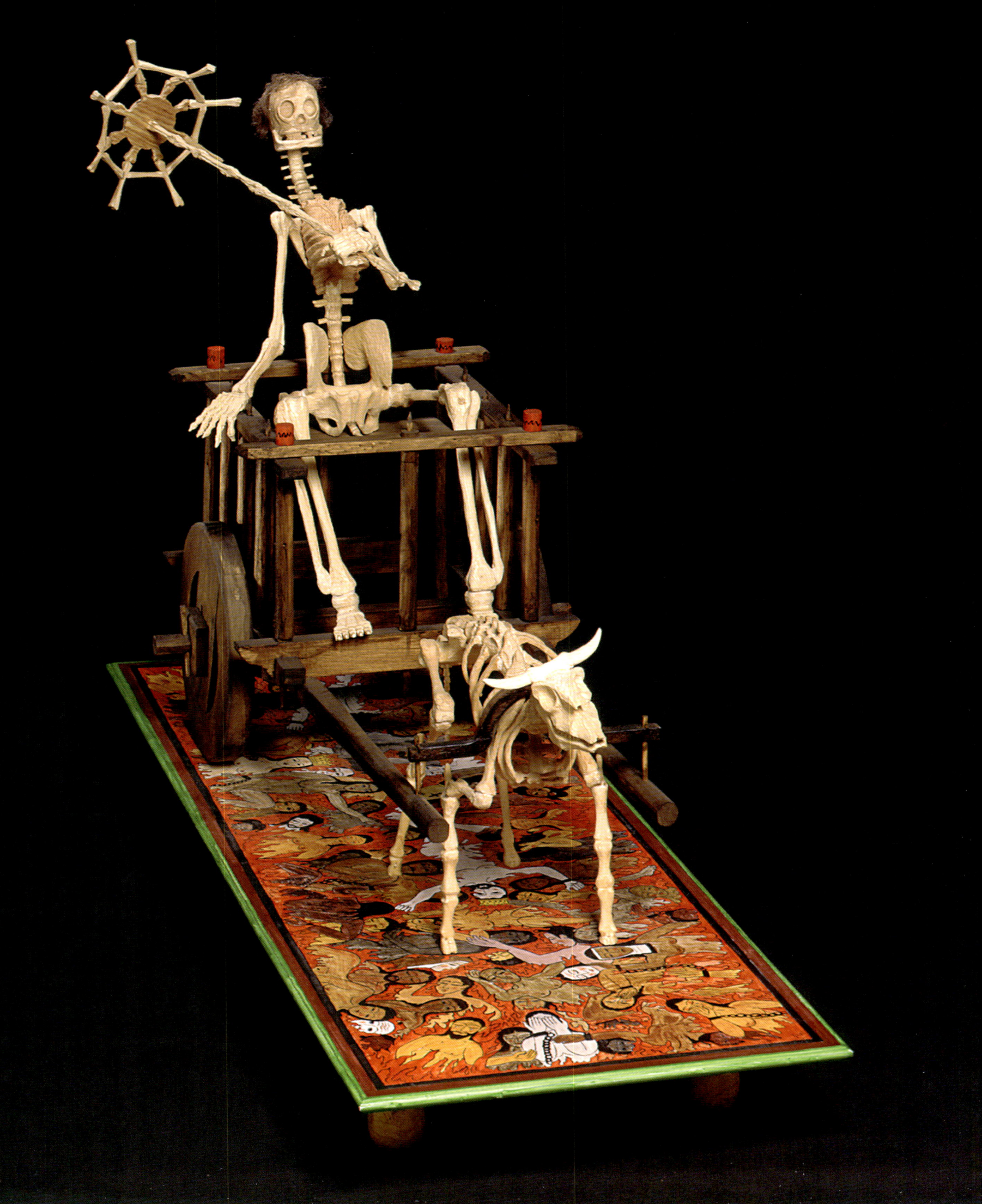

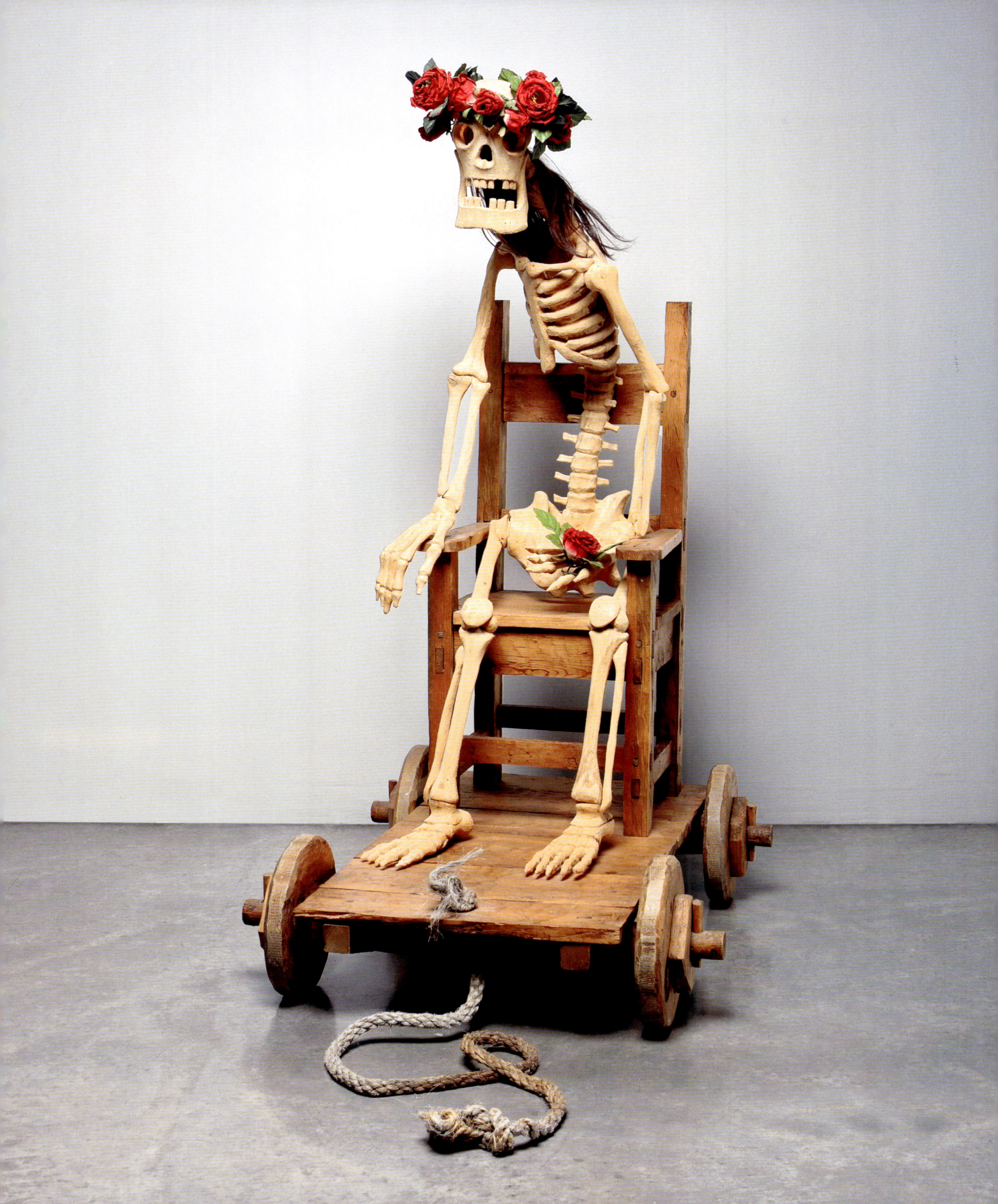

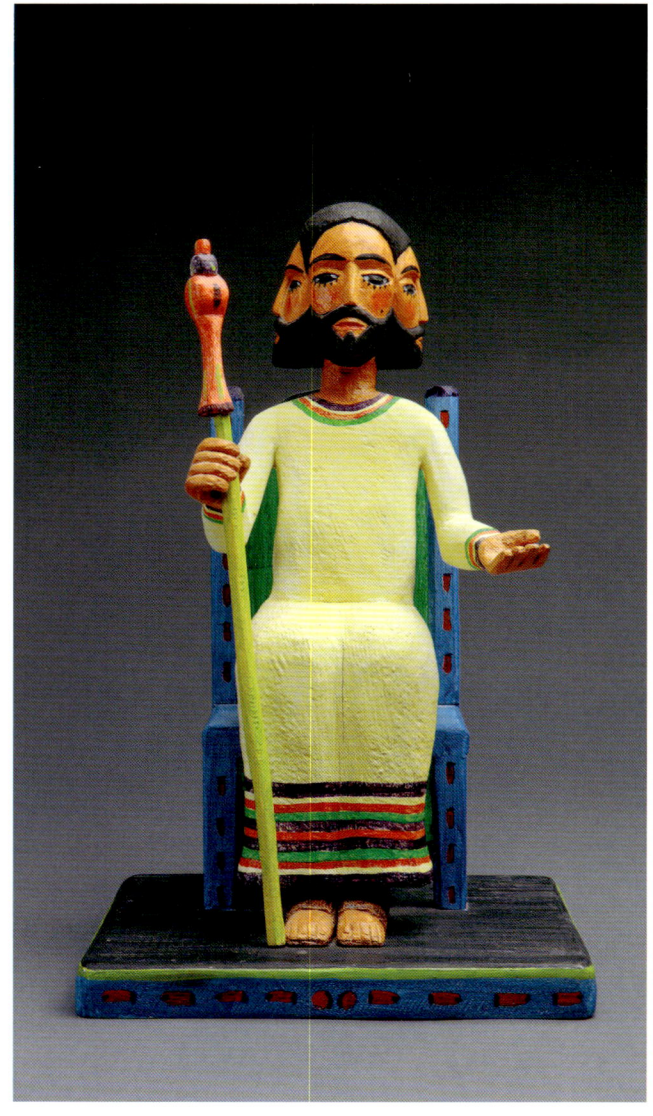

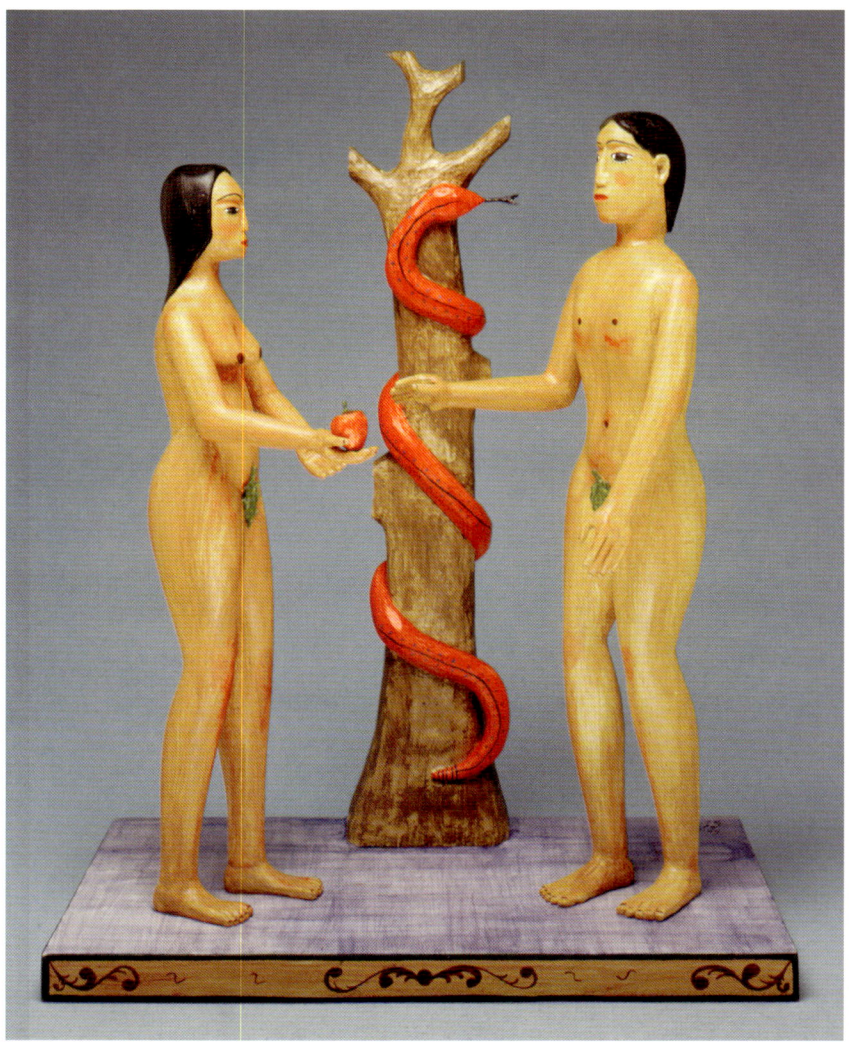

Figure 15. *La Santísima Trinidad*, 1988. Carved and painted wood, 7¾ x 7¼ x 5¾ in. Collection of the Spanish Colonial Arts Society, Museum of Spanish Colonial Art, Santa Fe. Photo © Addison Doty.

Figure 16. *Adam and Eve*, 1989. Carved and painted wood, 26 x 20 x 12 in. S. Millington Collection. Photo courtesy of The Owings Gallery.

Figure 17. Altar Screen, 1986. Carved and painted wood, 146½ x 96 x 26½ in. Collection of San Isidro Catholic Church, Santa Fe. Photo © Addison Doty.

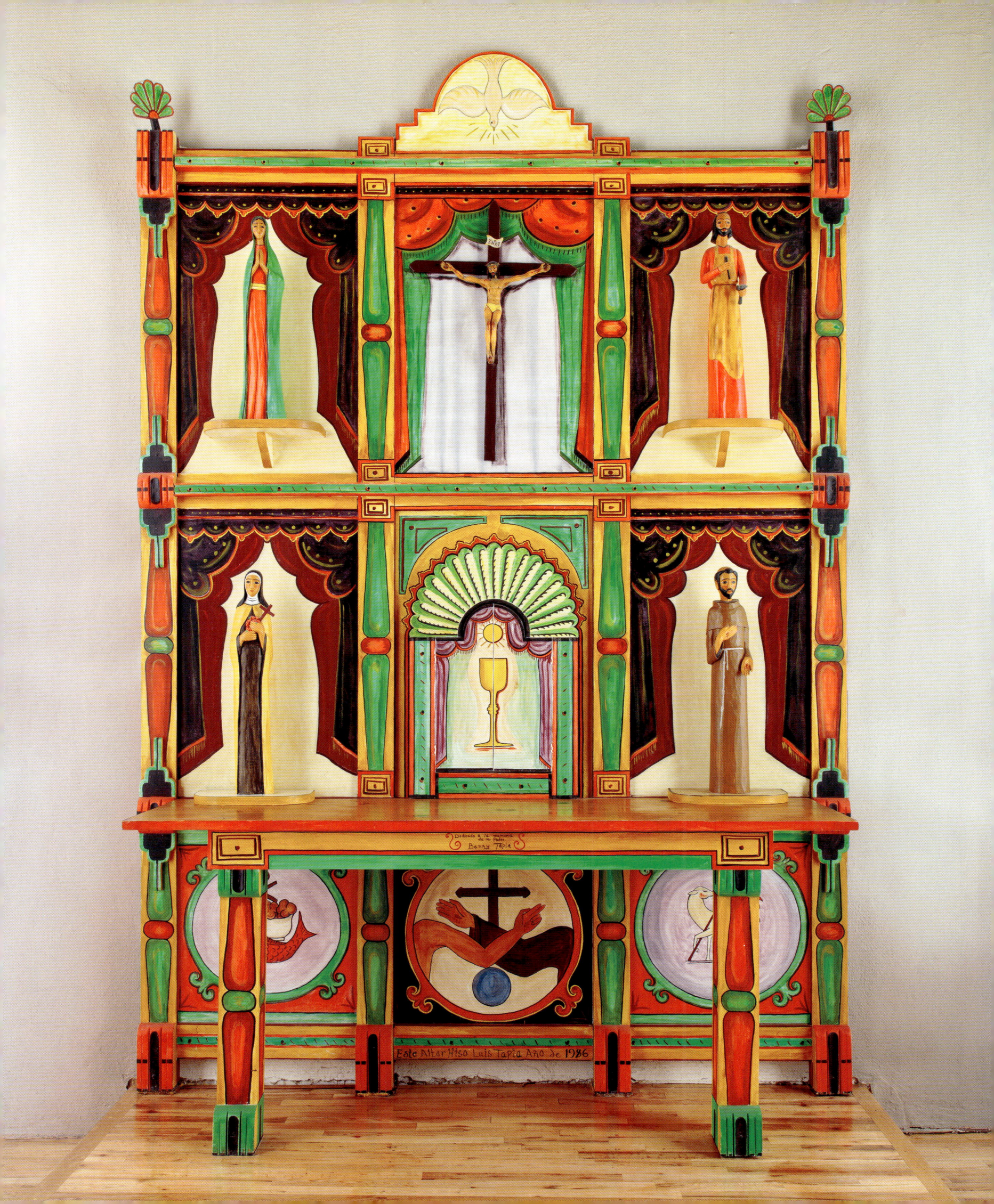

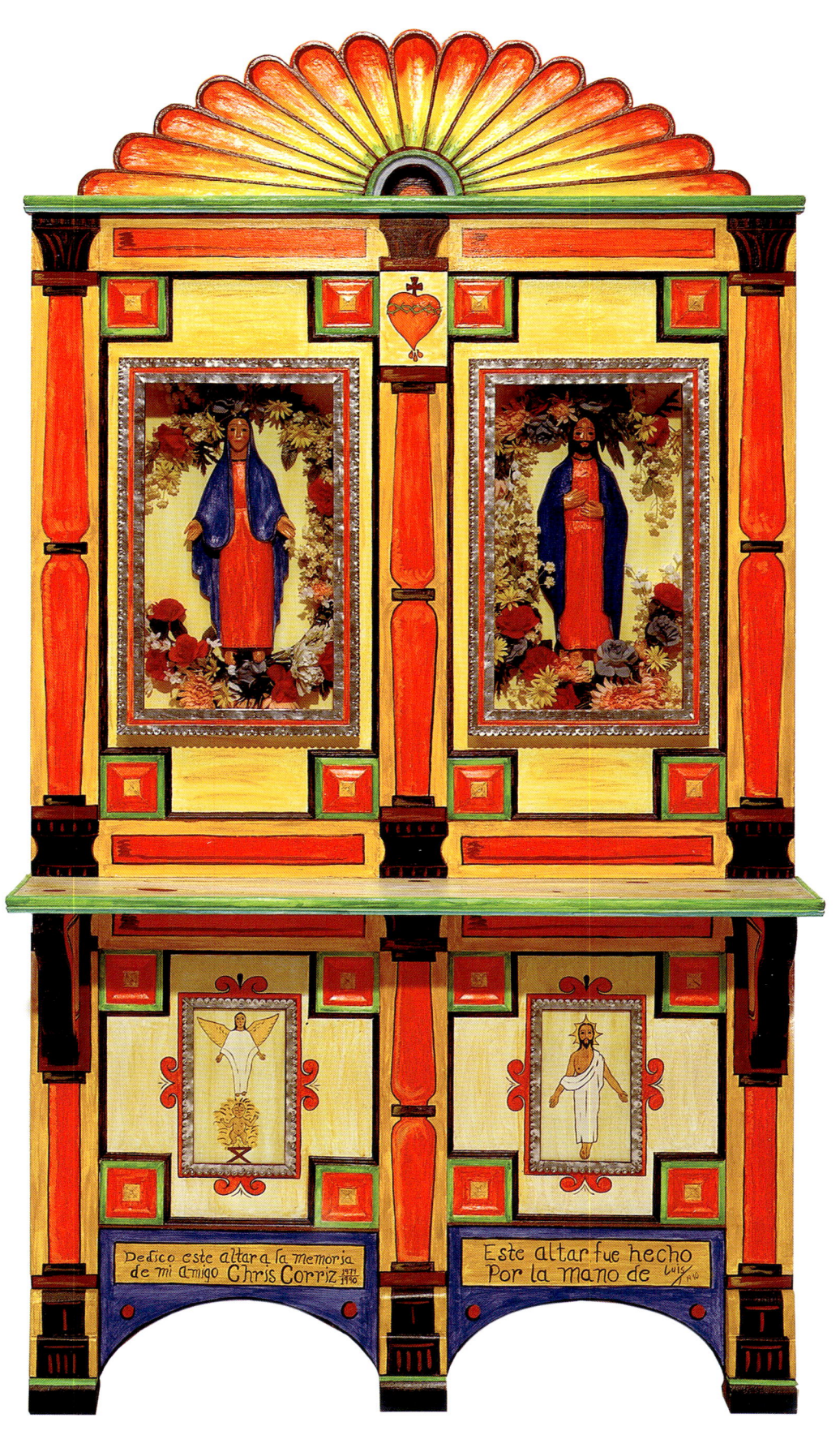

Dedico este altar a la memoria de mi amigo Chris Corriz 1971 1996

Este altar fue hecho por la mano de Luis '96

In his 1992 *Chima Altar II (Bertram's Cruise)* (Figure 19), Tapia uses these details to subtly maximum effect. The gearshift is in reverse while the speedometer is stuck at top speed. Chasing, or perhaps awaiting, the impending disaster is Doña Sebastiana herself, reflected in the rearview mirror in her rickety cart of death. We may be driving in New Mexican high style, looking out the windshield to clear blue skies beyond, but still, we are stuck somewhere in the middle of the road, our mortality imminent at every turn. In *Porfie's Cruze* (1996; Figure 20), we see a full ride, as Tapia depicts a 1960 pink Cadillac owned by a now-deceased compadre from L.A. He "Newmexicanifies" the car by carving the two front seats in a traditional New Mexican furniture style. Each sunshade takes the shape of a lunette, a decorative element reminiscent of the scalloped half shell often seen on traditional New Mexican *retablos,* carved furniture, and tinwork. In *Northern New Mexico Procession* (1999; Figure 21), five lowriders parade bumper to bumper, their colorful exteriors flaunting saints and other religious symbols in varying shades of blue, orange, yellow, black, and brown. Tapia's edgy take on these everyday automobile icons cuts through socioeconomic barriers to become approachable and accessible for all audiences and ages. His portrayal of place in these and other car sculptures leaves little doubt that he is cruising New Mexico.

Tapia's *A Slice of American Pie* (2008; Plate 32) is an auto-inspired masterwork on a different canvas, this time one-half of a real (not carved) 1963 Cadillac. The work, seventeen and a half feet long and seven hundred pounds, illustrates Tapia's acknowledgment of other forms of Chicano, Hispano, and Latino visual art practice, creating something both local and global. The car's mural acknowledges early Spanish colonial artists who created graphic and bold outlines of religious figures. Along with his obvious nod to local lowrider culture (Española, New Mexico, touts itself as the lowrider capital of the world), Tapia gives a stylistic shout out to incarcerated artists known as *pintos.* They practice a form of art reminiscent of tattooing, using a Chicano visual vocabulary of inked images drawn on *paños,* or handkerchiefs. It's perhaps no coincidence that during Tapia's days with La Cofradía, he went into the state penitentiary in Santa Fe and got prisoner-made *paños* to include in group shows.

Whether topically or technically, Tapia's recognition of the major New Mexican artists he looked to as models of success in his early career is meaningful. His *Tribute to María* (1990; Figure 22) honors María Benítez, a native New Mexican who broke Spanish dance barriers to become an international flamenco icon. Technically, Tapia says, Benítez's strong and soulful dance style inspired his first attempt to capture a sense of movement in his sculpture. The dancer in *Tribute to María* wears a flame-red dress and holds her arms high above. In color and form, the work aptly conveys the dancer's fiery charisma and power. *Homage to Patrocino Barela* (1998; Figure 23) is the artist's significant nod to Barela (circa 1900–1964), a Taos sculptor who worked for the Federal Art Project during the Franklin Delano Roosevelt presidency. When Barela's artworks were featured in the 1934 exhibition *New Horizons of American Art* at the Museum of Modern Art in New York, his powerful creations took members of the modernist movement by storm. The first Taos

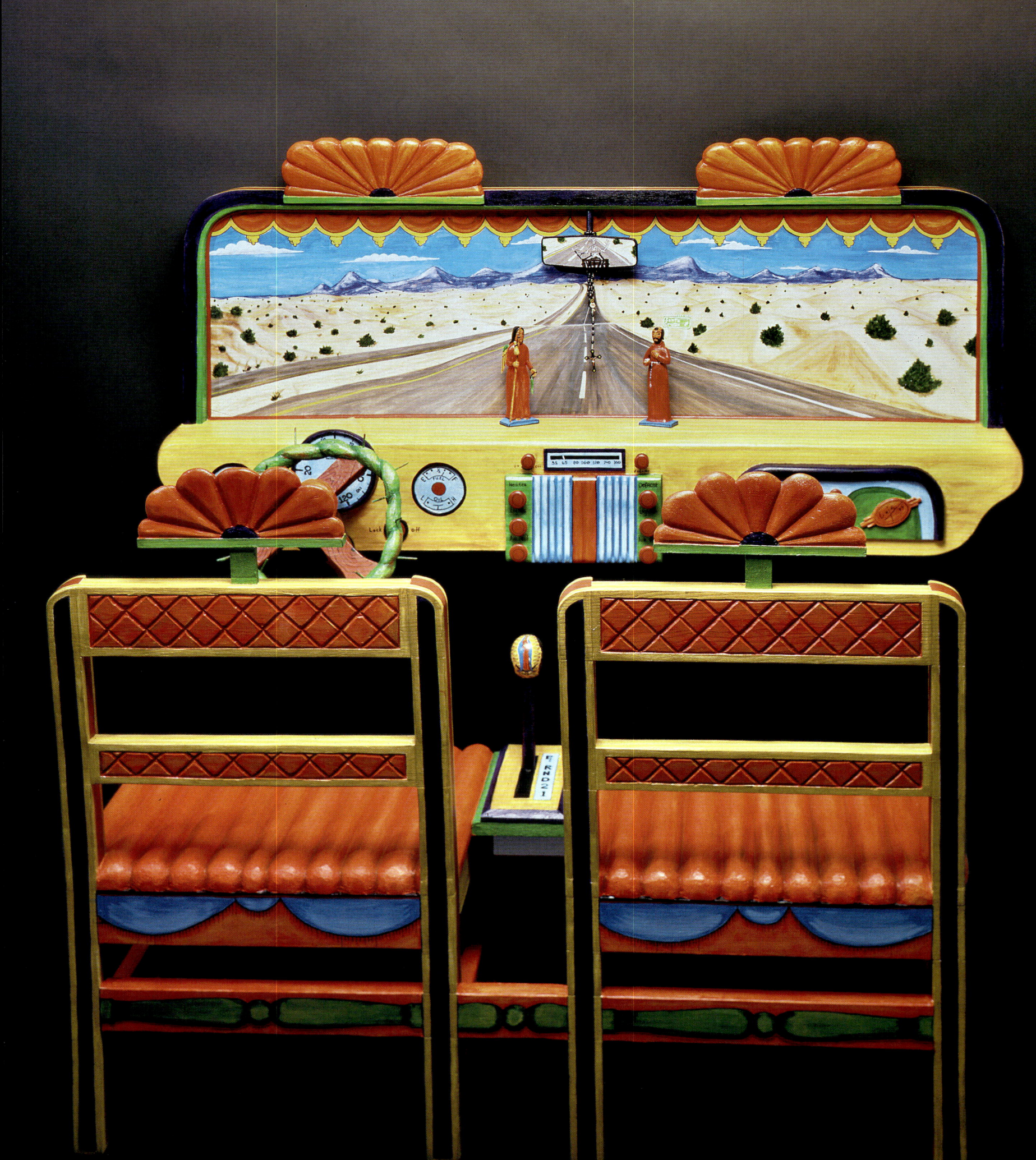

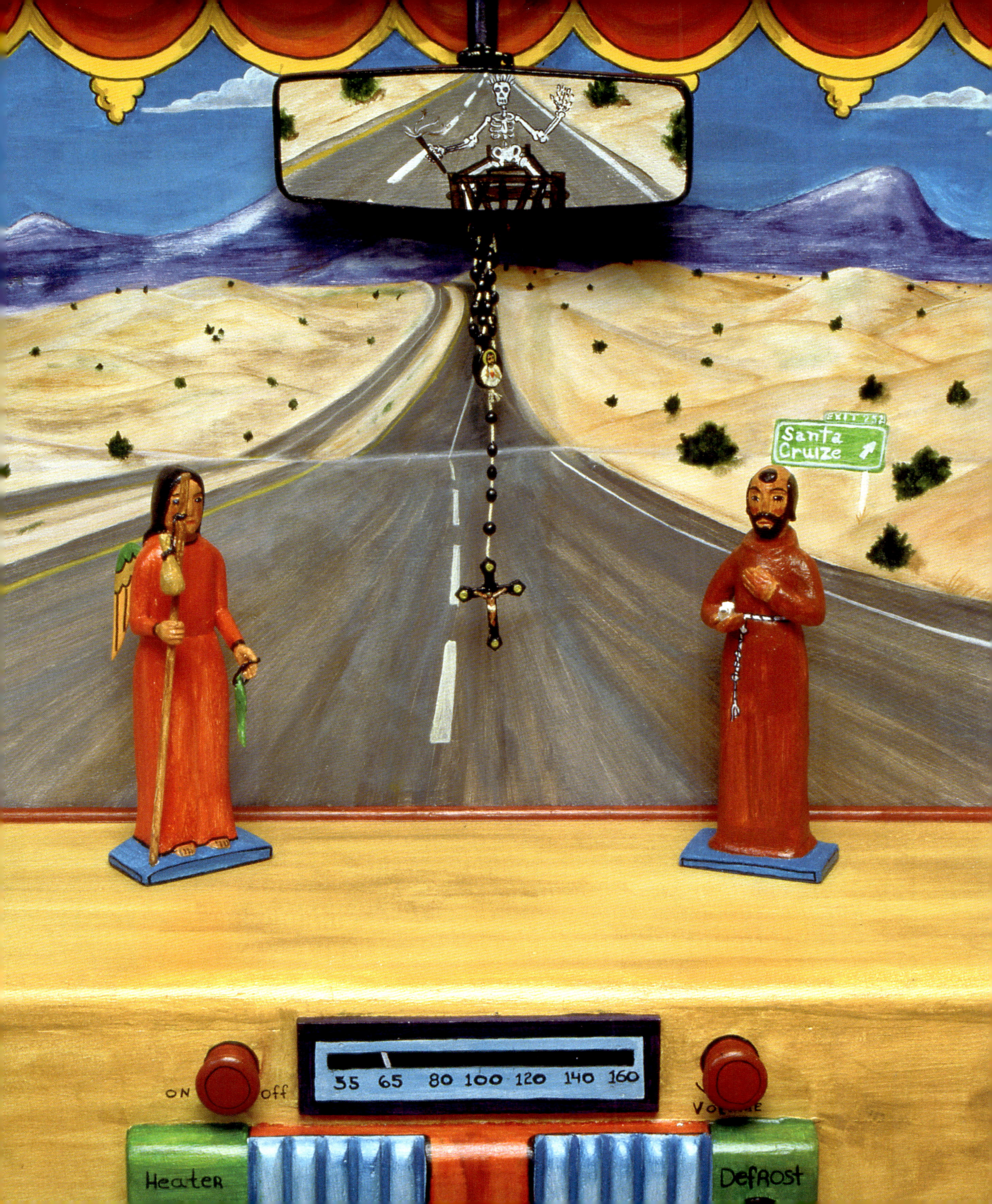

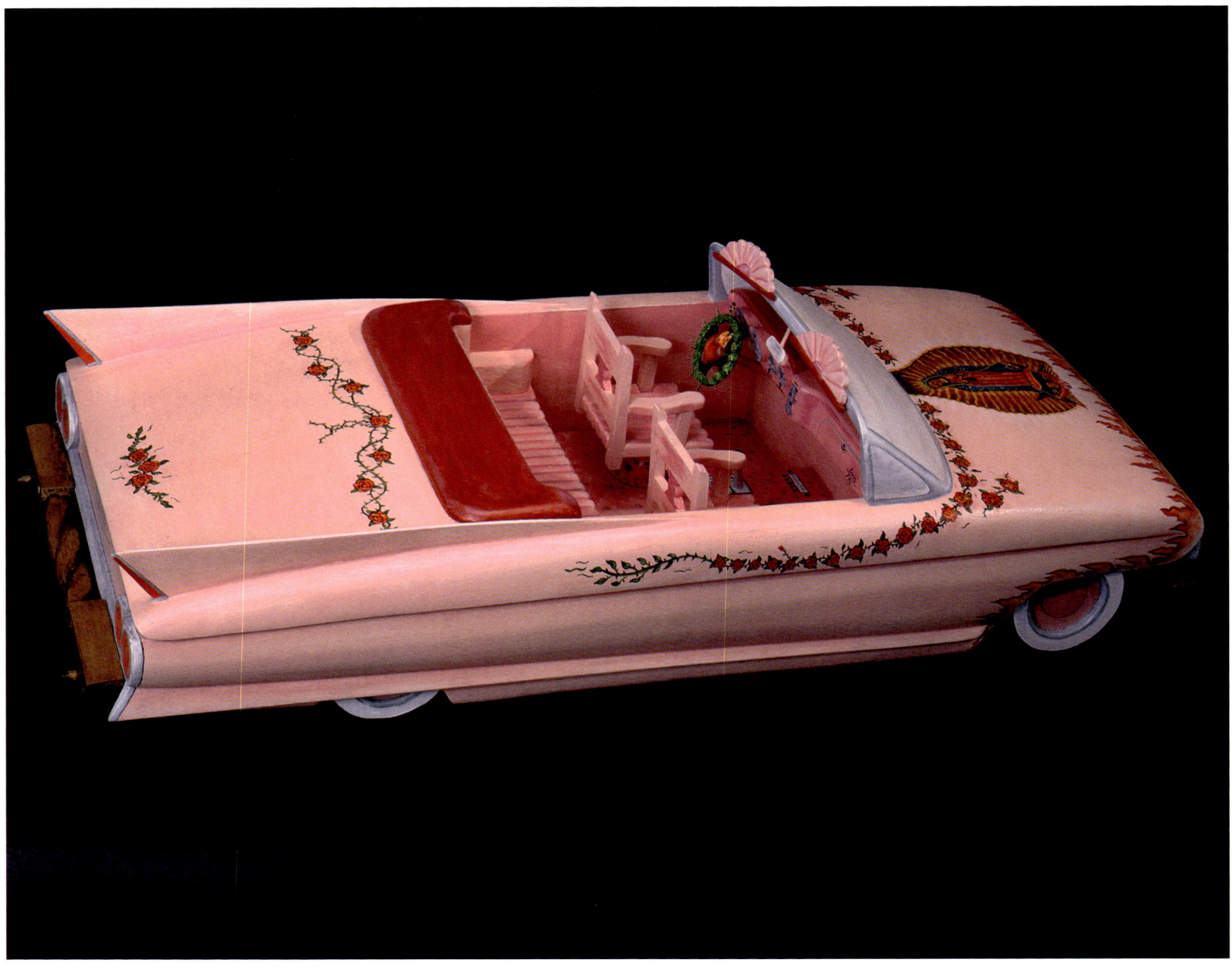

Figure 20. *Porfie's Cruze*, 1996. Carved and painted wood, 11 x 15¼ x 38½ in. Private collection.
Photo © Dan Morse, courtesy of The Owings Gallery.

Figure 21. *Northern New Mexico Procession*, 1999. Carved and painted wood, 4 x 58¾ x 7¼ in.
Collection of Barbara Windom. Photo © Dan Morse, courtesy of The Owings Gallery.

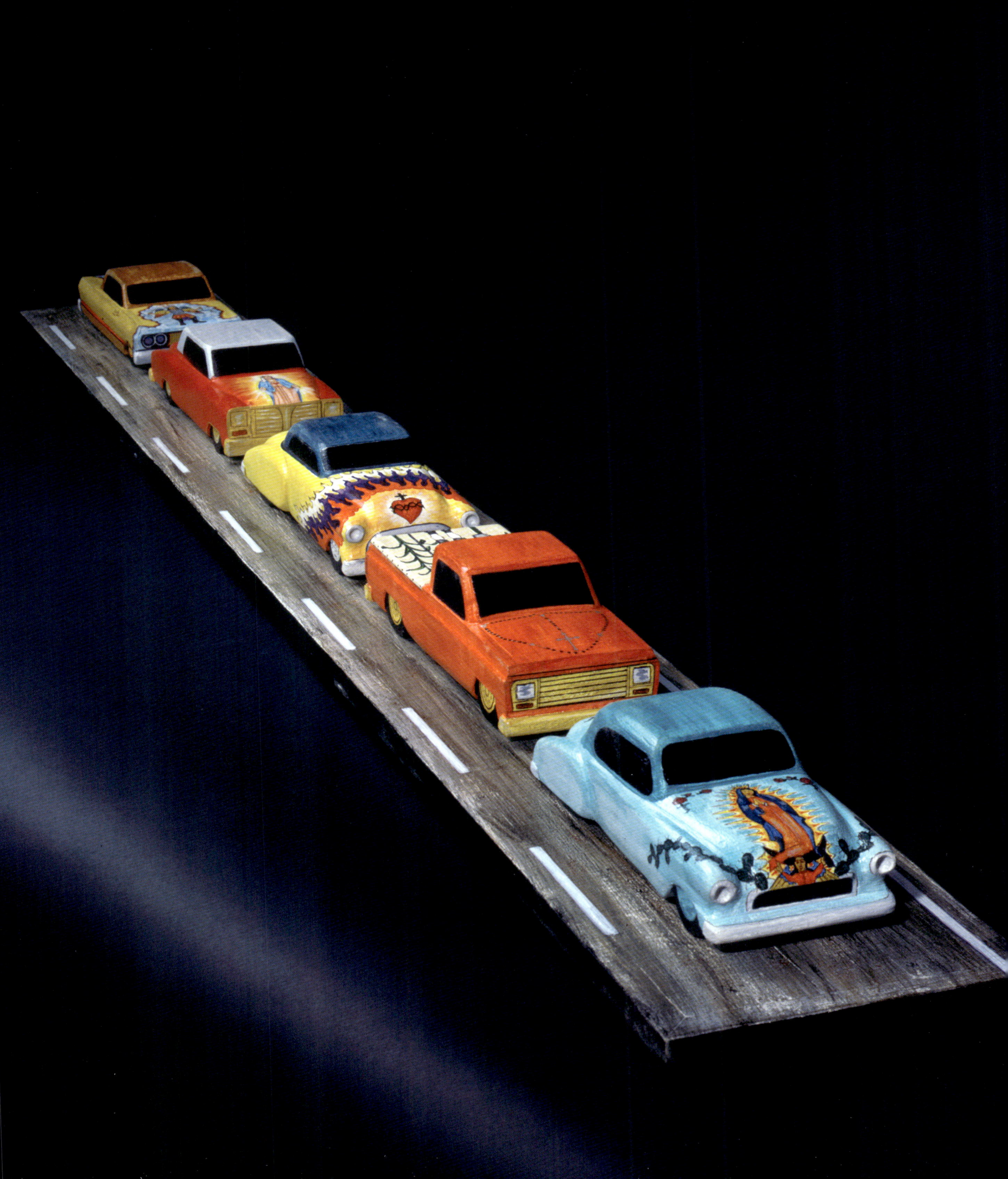

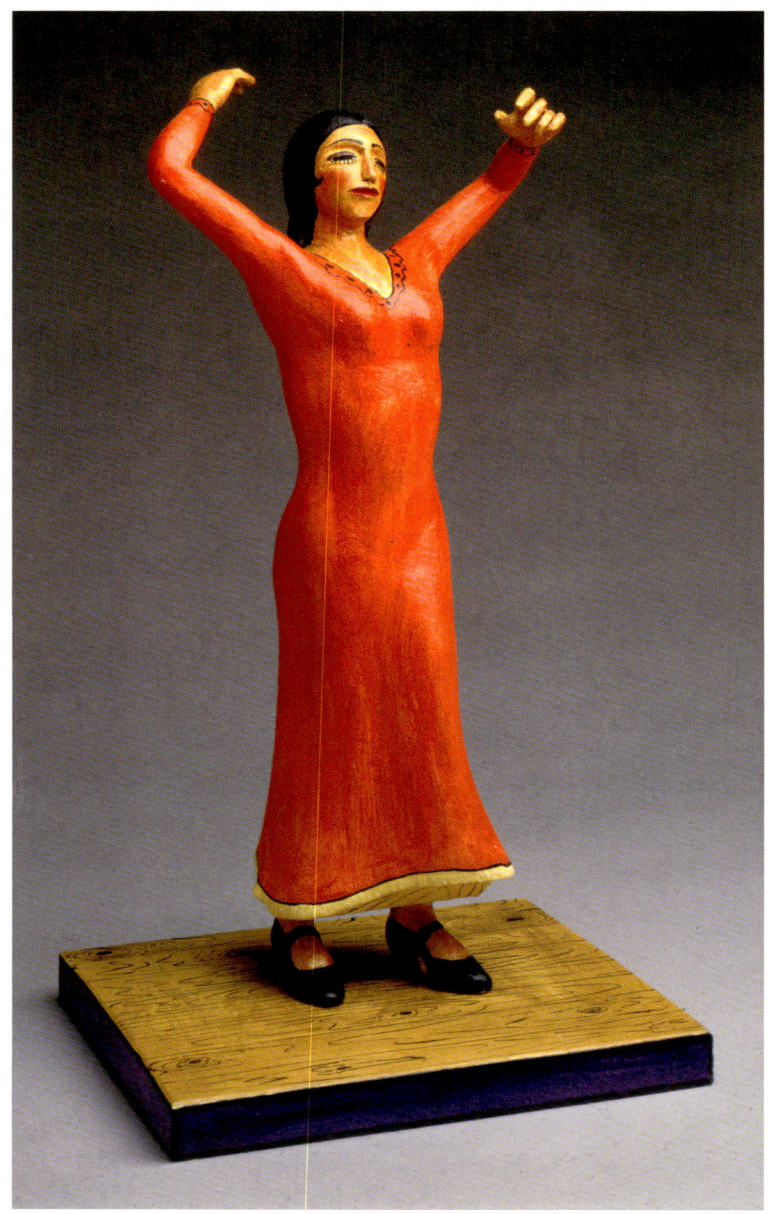

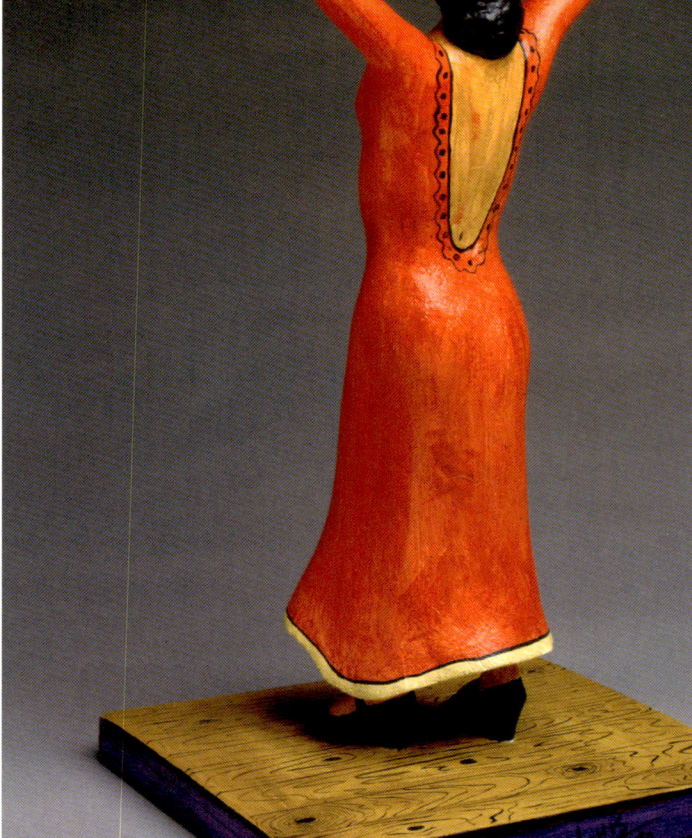

LEFT AND RIGHT

Figure 22. *Tribute to María*. 1990. Carved and painted wood, 21¼ x 11 x 10⅜ in. Collection of the Autry Museum, Los Angeles (90.242.1). Photo courtesy of The Owings Gallery.

OPPOSITE

Figure 23. *Homage to Patrocino Barela*, 1998. Carved and painted wood, 20 x 11¼ x 8½ in. Collection of Curt, Christina, and Jonah Nonomaque. Photo © Dan Morse, courtesy of The Owings Gallery.

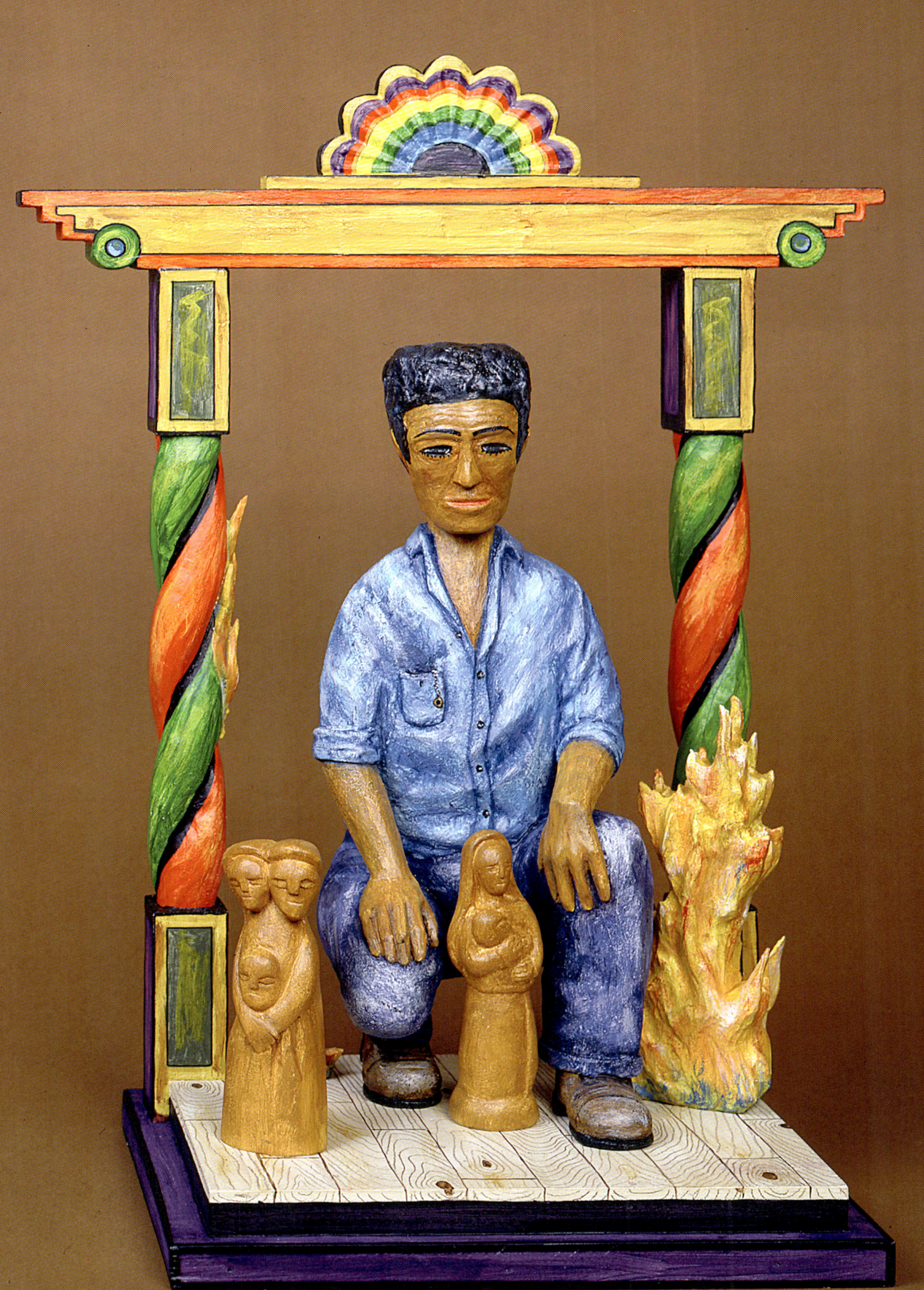

artist of any ethnicity to be shown at the museum, Barela was hailed as a "true primitive" and a "naive genius," and his image was featured on the cover of *Time* magazine. To the modernists, Barela was a genuine creative; they envied his work and wanted their works to be as nonconformist in expression. In Tapia's homage, the artist acknowledges Barela's significance not only for northern New Mexican traditional artists but perhaps more so for Tapia himself. Like Tapia, Barela collapsed categories and pushed the boundaries of contemporary art. He made his name as an artist outside New Mexico, expanding traditional notions of what Spanish colonial art should be by demonstrating what it *could* be.

Tapia masterfully homes in on issues embedded in northern New Mexican culture that connect to a larger worldview. Over time, his thematic narrative and social commentary have become more complex and pointed. In the early 1990s, Tapia began to place saints in a contemporary context and to ground the figures in the everyday, a vital new direction for New Mexican Hispano art.

The Temptations of Saint Anthony (1991; Figure 24) portrays the saint surrounded by all his human urges. A slithering snake's head and a human arm emerge from the base of the sculpture, as if to pull Saint Anthony under. Devilish figures tempt him with money and bottles of alcohol; in the background, a skeletal figure raises an ax over his head. The swirling action of the figures conveys fear, vulnerability, and hopelessness. Created the same year, *San Pedro Apostól* (Figure 25) was one of Tapia's first significant attempts at incorporating New Mexican vernacular architecture into his sculptures. By intentionally situating normally stagnant religious figures in homelike surroundings, and forcing viewers to explore scenes fully in the round, Tapia activates the saints and draws viewers in to connect directly with the image. Often depicting these subjects floating in clouds or heavenly environments, he demystifies traditionally motionless images so often revered as untouchable. In *Dos Pedros sin llaves* (1994; Figure 26), Tapia further transitions the traditional religious figure of Saint Peter, who holds the keys to heaven's gate. Here the saint takes the guise of two everyday Pedros, who contemplate their existence without keys, a commentary on the high rates of Latino imprisonment in the United States. Each figure is adorned with a Guadalupe tattoo on his back; one looks into a cell while the other looks through the gate (in this case, prison bars), perhaps imagining a more heavenly life on the outside. The bars themselves are framed by a Peñasco-style New Mexico door.

An excellent later example of Tapia's interactive approach is *Untitled* (2002; Plate 17). Three male figures convene against a graffitied wall, conversing over beers. Tattooed and dressed in iconic street style—jeans, expensive sneakers, and Guadalupe T-shirts—they appear to visit outside a neighborhood building. Viewed in the round, however, "the hood" is so much more, comprised of multiple angles and scenes. A truck is parked on the street, while a home interior features an altar—a miniature carved table with a *santo* at center. Family photos and other homey touches complete the scene. A crack in the plaster wall that divides the faithful family on the inside from the *vatos* outside hints at a fragile story in between.

OPPOSITE

Figure 24. *The Temptations of Saint Anthony*, 1991. Carved and painted wood, 21⁷⁄₁₆ x 14³⁄₁₆ x 14½ in. Museum of International Folk Art, Santa Fe, IFAF Collection; gift of the Diane and Sandy Besser Collection (FA.2005.44.13). Photo © Polina Smutko.

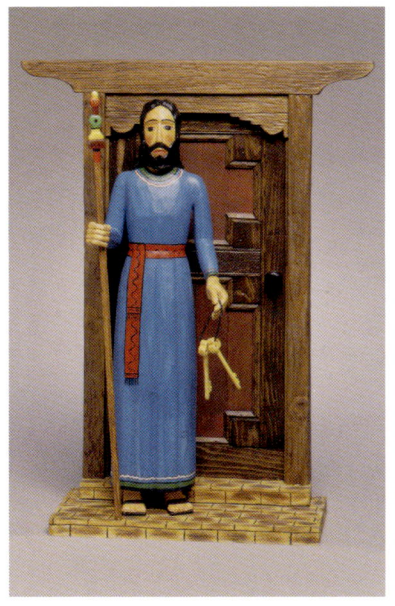

Figure 25. *San Pedro Apostól*, 1991. Carved and painted wood, 24 x 18⅛ x 8½ in. Private collection. Photo © James Hart, courtesy of The Owings Gallery.

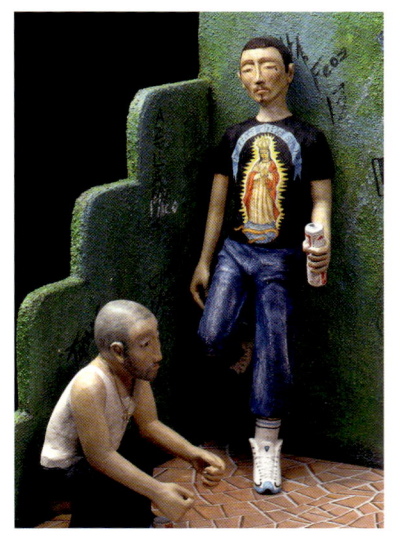

Untitled (detail), 2002; see page 115.

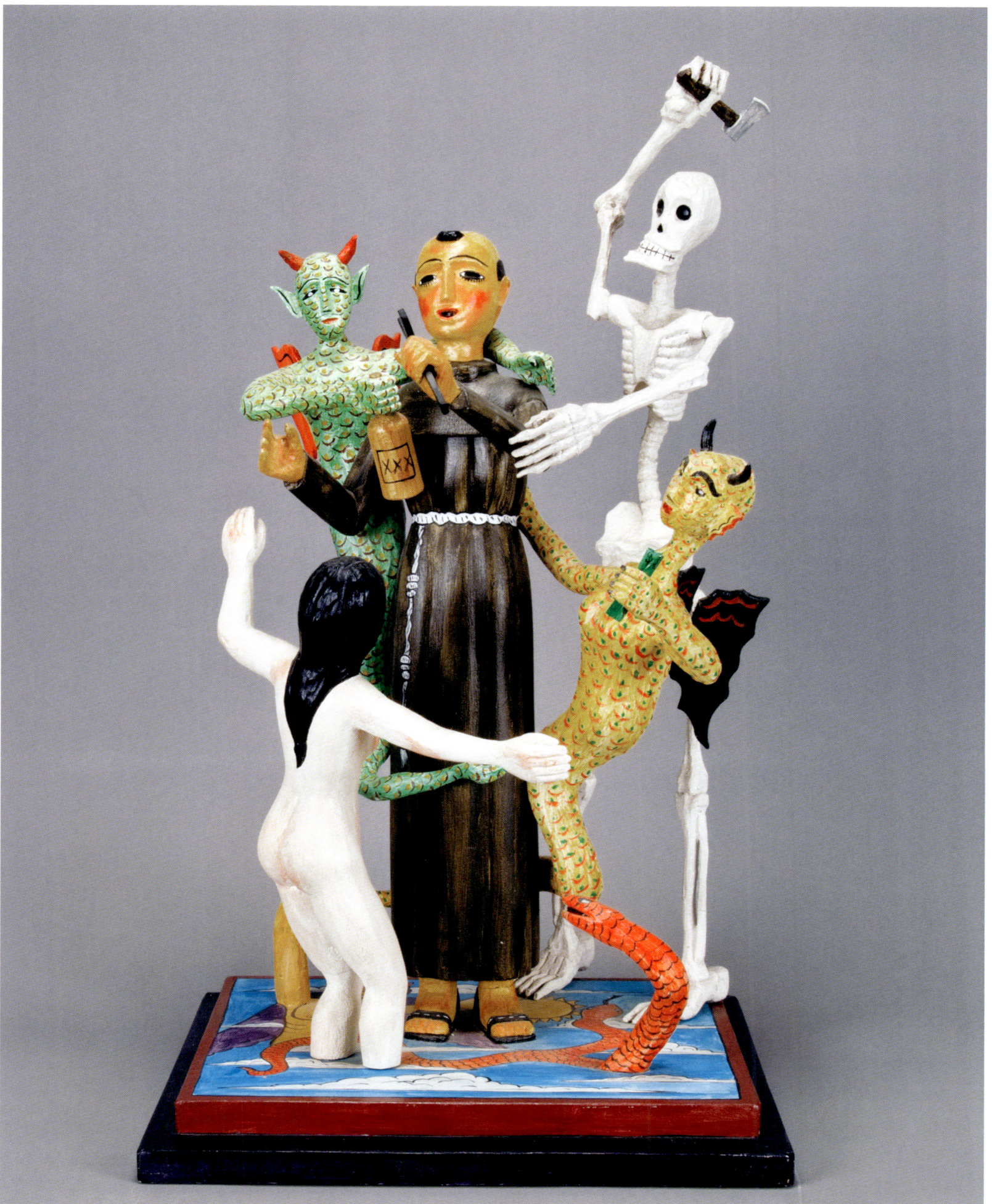

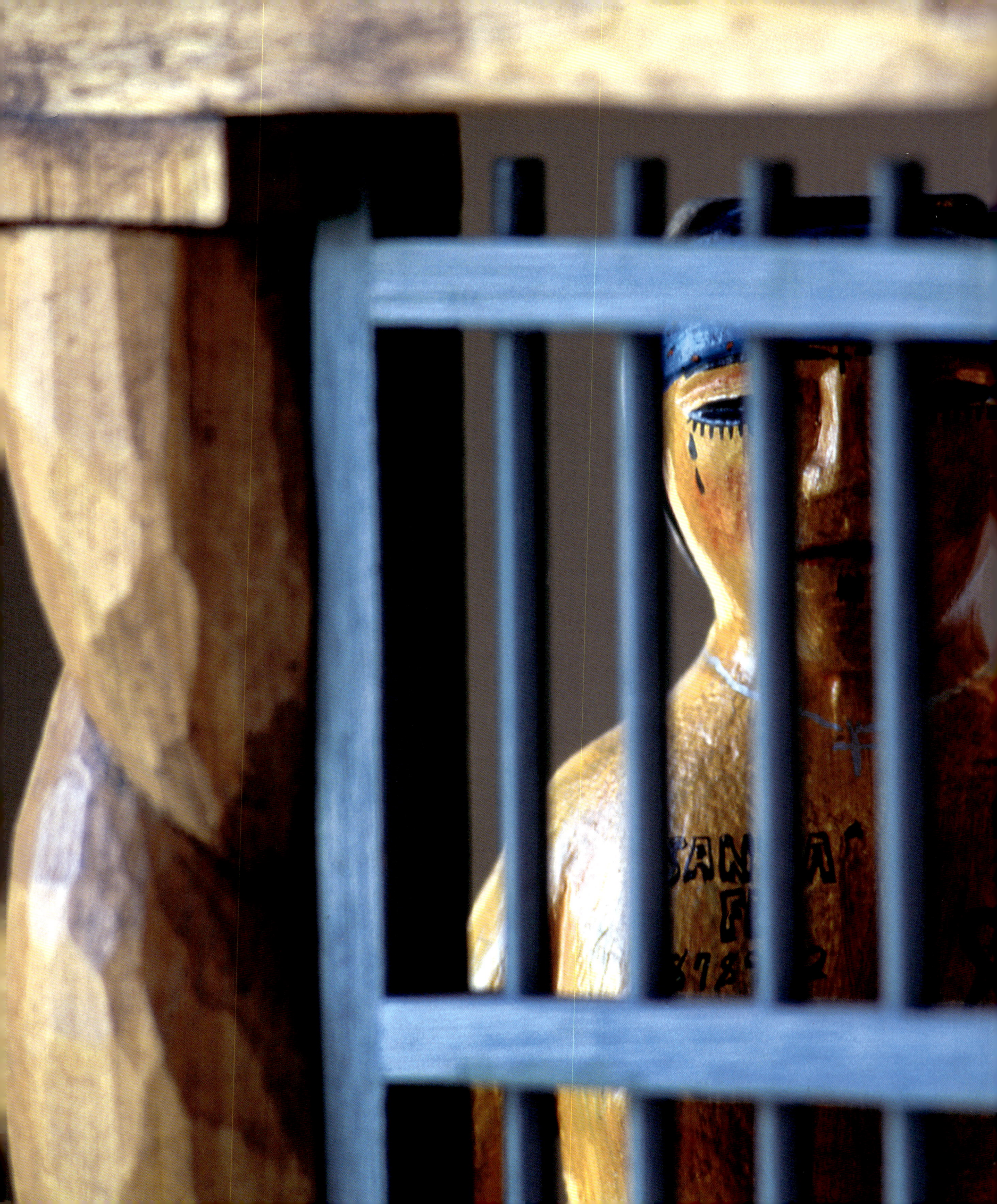

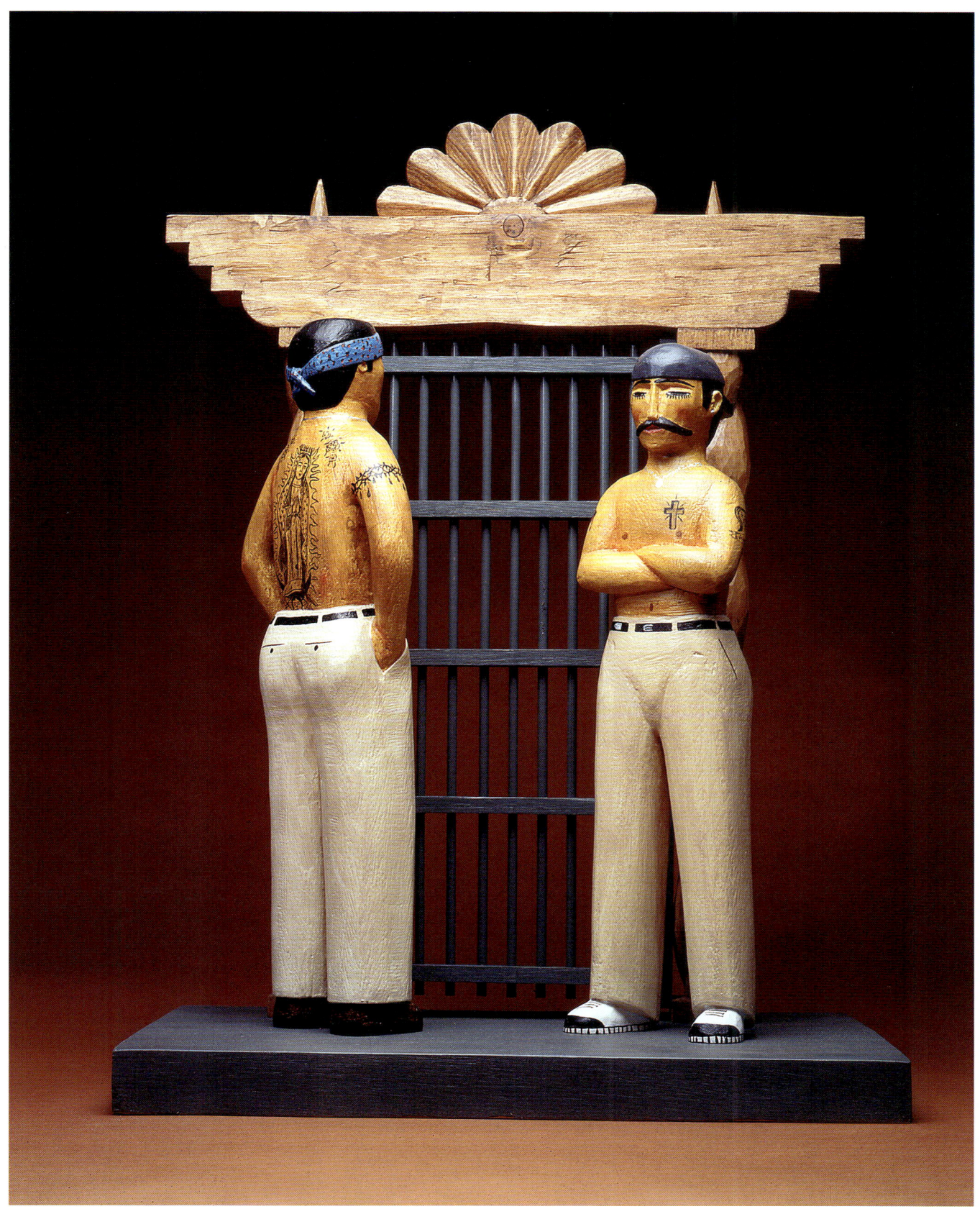

Figure 26. *Dos Pedros sin llaves*, 1994. Carved and painted wood, 25 x 11½ x 7¼ in. Collection of the Maxwell Museum of Anthropology, University of New Mexico. Detail photo (left) © and courtesy Jack Parsons. Photo (right) © Dan Morse, courtesy of The Owings Gallery.

Female saints and other women have long been prominent subjects for Tapia. Over time, he has explored the image of Eve in various ways—as temptress, as earthly mother, as someone to be admired and adored. *Eve the Temptress* (1991; Figure 28) conveys the strength of the legendary Eve in the nude, a continuation of Tapia's first sculptures depicting the nude female body. With her long black hair flowing and a green snake tattoo coiled around her left arm, Eve simultaneously crosses her legs and offers an enticing apple. In 1992's *Eva (The Girl Next Door)* (Figure 29), the artist positions Eve high on a pedestal, her right hand on her hip in an obviously Latina (her name is Eva, after all) power pose. She holds an apple in her left hand with a gesture that says, "Come and get it." Her green dance dress reflects her Garden of Eden. Tapia's *The Three Eves* (1993; Figure 30) depicts a trio of neighborhood women. These barrio babes hold no apples but tempt with well-coiffed hairstyles, sleeveless tops, and tattooed skin.

Tapia's renderings of women in the hood are important to him, but also to women. He elevates the power and beauty of everyday women of all shapes and sizes, infusing strategic cultural references as much as technique. He also updates traditional holy women, giving them stature and relevance for today. *José y María* (1991; Figure 31), for example, portrays the holy couple in contemporary dress. María wears a red dress (a mini strapless number) with matching red high heels. Her sacred heart (referencing the sacred hearts of Mary and Jesus) is tattooed on her chest. José's streetwise, partially undressed look boasts voluminous pants and black suspenders hanging around his hips. On his back is an extraordinary tattoo of La Virgen de Guadalupe wearing a green cloak over a red gown, referencing the *colores nacionales* of the Mexican flag. Tapia's 1992 *Adán y Eva* (Figure 32) looks nothing like *Adam and Eve* from 1988. This scene shows the couple as an everyday *vato y vata* one might normally see chatting or flirting on the street. Eva wears lace-trimmed *chones* (shorts or underwear) and white boots. She taps a shirtless Adán on the left shoulder and offers him an apple. Adán may be tempted, but he appears cool and impassive, his arms crossed tightly over his chest.

Tapia's reverence for women underscores the fact that he was raised by two women—his mother, Pauline Leyba Tapia, and his grandmother Doloritas Leyba—after his father died. Their influence is felt in *A Temple Sacred by Birth Built by Hands Divine* (2004; Plate 35), one of the most technically and visually striking creations in his work in honor of women. The title, taken from a quote by the seventeenth-century English poet John Dryden, references the beauty, grace, and strength of all that is female. Tapia's interpretation details four multigenerational female figures who lift up a celestial woman; her gown depicts the heavens. Not only is this an obvious ode to the women who raised Tapia, but it also pays tribute to the women—the grandmothers, mothers, sisters, *tías*, and others—who have raised us all up with values of strength, patience, and love. Another meaningful take on the interconnected value and vision of women in the history of New Mexico is seen in *Northern New Mexico Bella Living with Her Past* (2002; Figure 33). This *bella* is a fully contemporary beauty who reclines in the nude on a New Mexico–style daybed, a Río Grande weaving spread on the pine floor before her. Outside, holding up the window

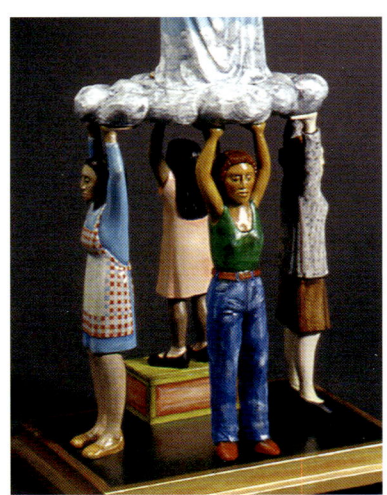

A Temple Sacred by Birth Built by Hands Divine (detail), 2004; see page 140.

frame that presumably divides the *bella*'s past from her present, is a weathered man wearing an Adobe Bros. Construction T-shirt. He literally grows out of the earth to hold the weight of her ancient adobe house on his shoulders. She appears oblivious to his burden, but the *bella* is clearly embedded in her past. She cannot escape her history, and perhaps she does not want to.

Tapia's works are layered in meaning. Whether serious or lighthearted, all provide contemporary commentary through their images as well as their titles. Tapia is deeply observant about his culture and the cultural encounters around him. He can't help but address the underlying messages of tradition and identity that emerge. His keen ability to translate his observations, whether subtly or overtly, only adds to his significance as a creator of visual culture. His jokes, pokes, and wry ironic nuances consistently provide the viewer with aha moments as the messages sink in.

The Folk Art Collectors (1992; Plate 11) is among the cheekiest of his early works. (It makes this author laugh out loud every time she sees it.) Two touristy figures face the viewer. Both hold miniature *bultos*: one of the archangel San Rafael, the other of La Virgen de Guadalupe. The gentleman proudly wears a camera around his neck and a bright yellow New Mexico T-shirt with the red Zia sun symbol. He appears unembarrassed that it clashes with his pink floral "ugly American" shorts. The woman represents "Santa Fe Style" in a long denim dress, Navajo squash blossom necklace, and red cowboy boots. She holds a fistful of green dollar bills and clutches her purchase. Tapia's commentary is both humorous and pointed. The piece directly addresses issues of patronage and the commodification of Hispano spiritual imagery. It bluntly asks: Who is buying our culture?

Santa Fe Carousel (1994; Figure 27) is another commentary on Hispano identity. Four relevant religious figures are situated on the base of a merry-go-round. Santiago (Saint James) and San Gabriel ride the carousel horses with swords at the ready, while San Rafael and San Miguel stand their ground. With typical carved and painted New Mexican design elements, the work alludes to the entertainment value of traditional Hispano culture and comments on the "Adobe Disneyland" image of Santa Fe lamented by many locals. In *El Santero* (1995; Figure 34), the artist pokes fun at himself with a figurative self-portrait that places Tapia in his own "traditional" role as a wood carver. He holds paintbrushes in his left hand and a bottle of beer in his right. His painted pedestal is covered with wood shavings. His jeans, T-shirt, and shoes are a canvas for gesso, paint, and more wood flakes. *Northern New Mexico Clothesline (Two Weeks of Laundry)* (2002; Figure 35) is another self-portrait of sorts that shows some of the apparel you might find on the artist's clothesline. Carved and painted clothing—two pairs of pants, six T-shirts, one pair of *chones*, and socks—hangs from old-fashioned clothespins. Denim overalls, as well as religious and secular T-shirt images (including Veronica's Veil and a bottle of Budweiser), reflect both daily life and societal issues in northern New Mexico. The artist might joke about wearing one pair of *chones* for two weeks, but the icons he chooses are emblematic logos of the blight, plight, and challenges of struggling families within New Mexico's Hispano/Chicano culture.

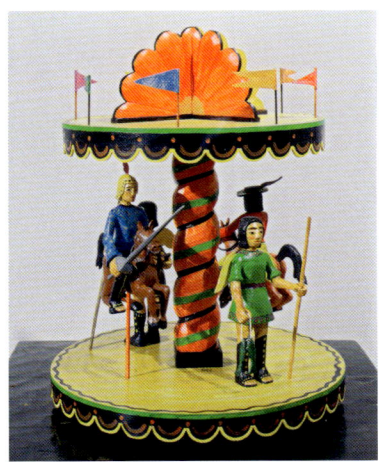

Figure 27. *Santa Fe Carousel*, 1994. Carved and painted wood, 26 x 20¾ x 20¾ in. Private collection. Photo © Dan Morse, courtesy of The Owings Gallery.

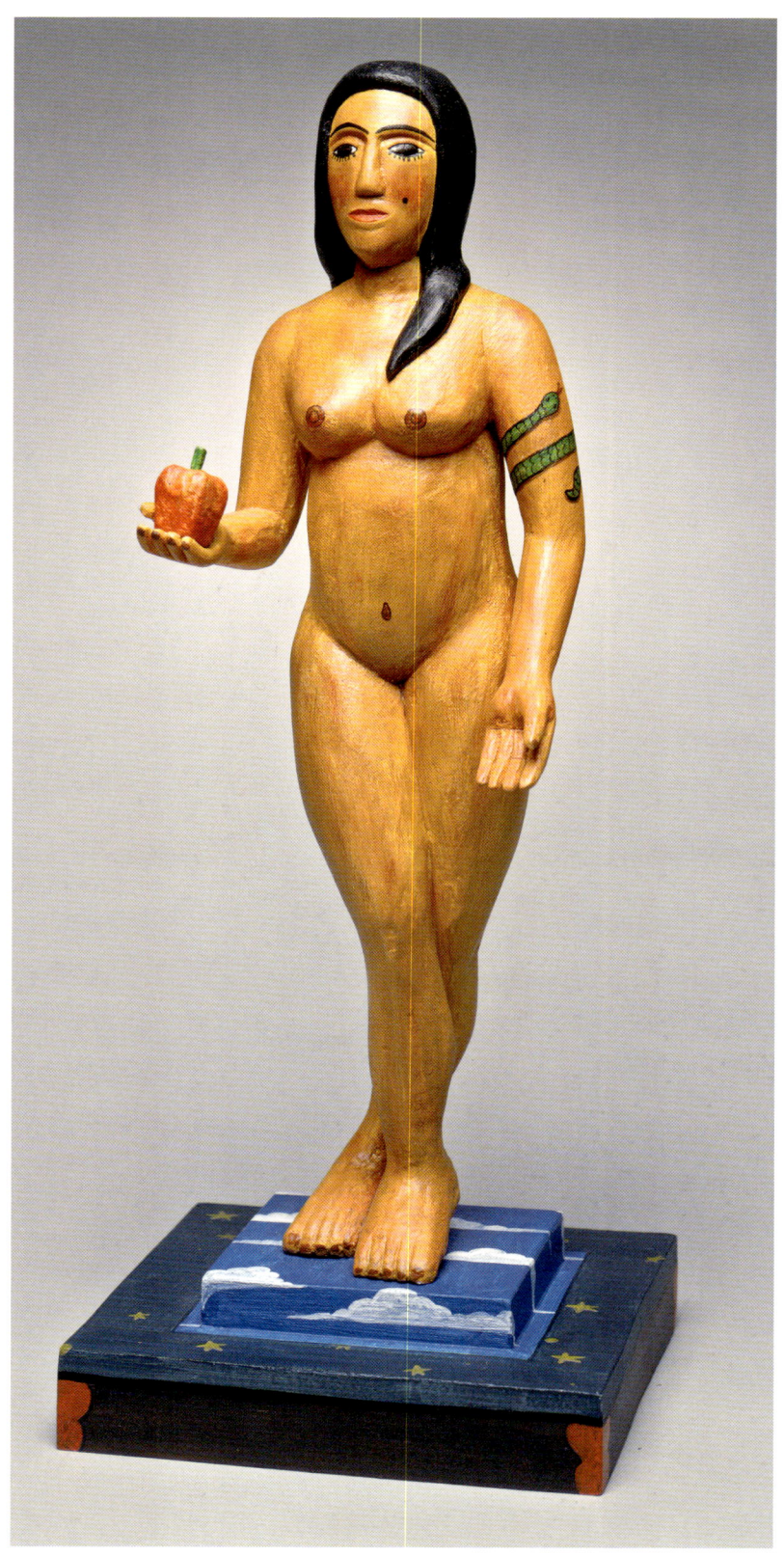

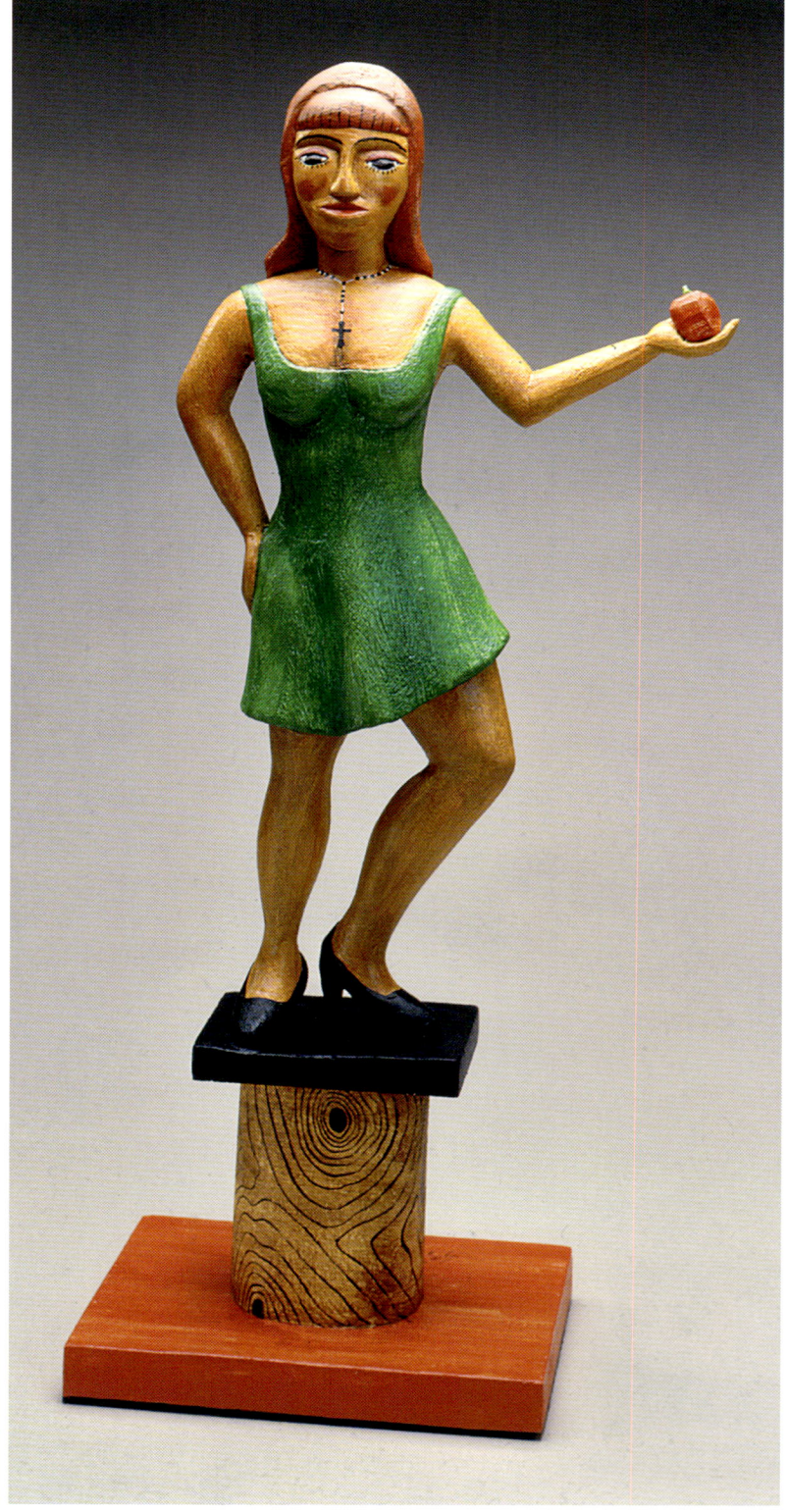

LEFT

Figure 28. *Eve the Temptress*, 1991. Carved and painted wood, 20½ x 7 ¾ x 7 ⅜ in. Private collection. Photo © James Hart, courtesy of The Owings Gallery.

RIGHT

Figure 29. *Eva* (*The Girl Next Door*), 1992. Carved and painted wood, 26 x 10 ½ x 7 in. Collection of Mary and Michael Mahaffey. Photo © Dan Morse, courtesy of The Owings Gallery.

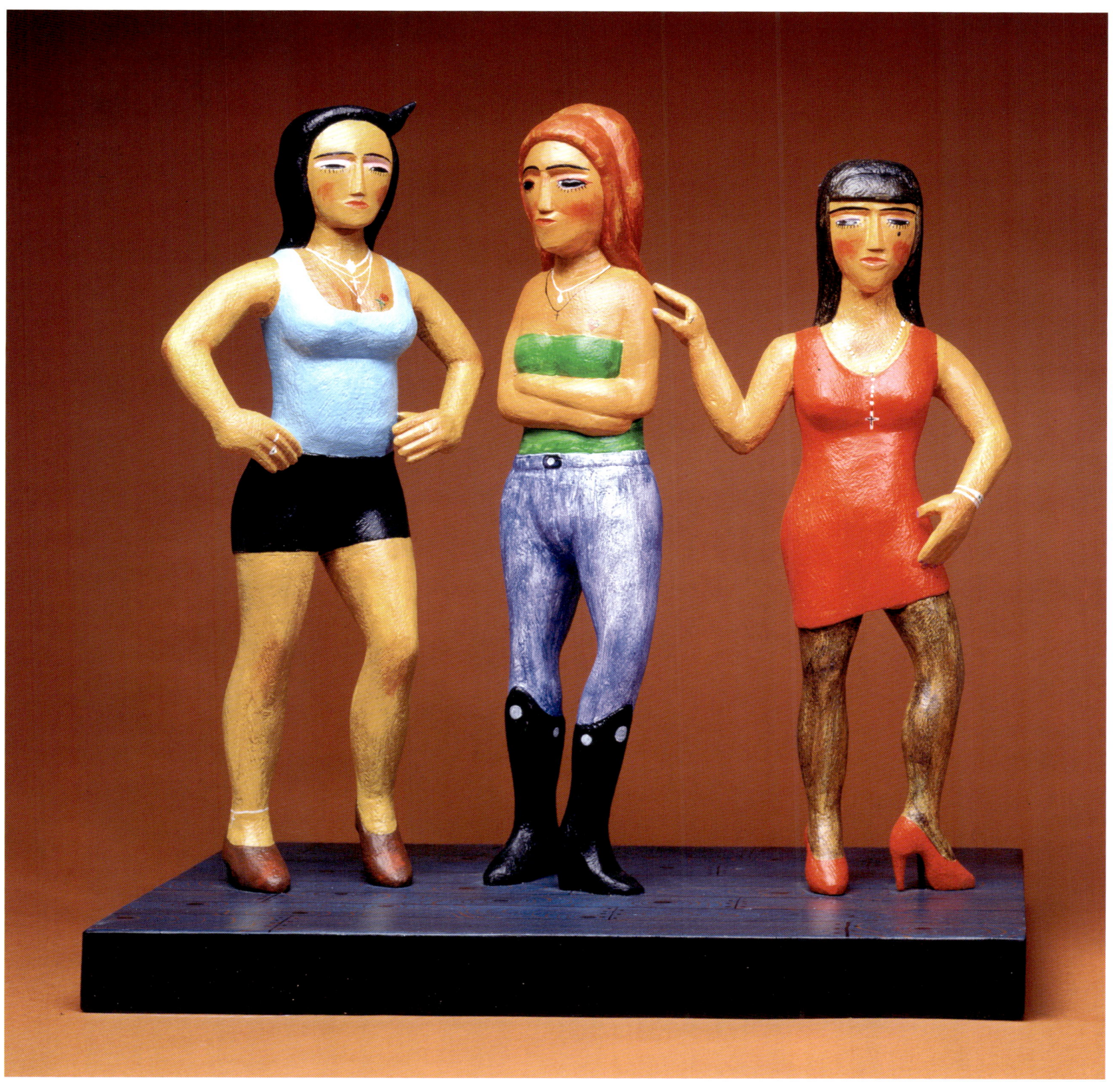

Figure 30. *The Three Eves*, 1993. Carved and painted wood, 17 ½ x 17 x 10 ½ in.
Collection of R. Steven Padilla. Photo © Dan Morse, courtesy of The Owings Gallery.

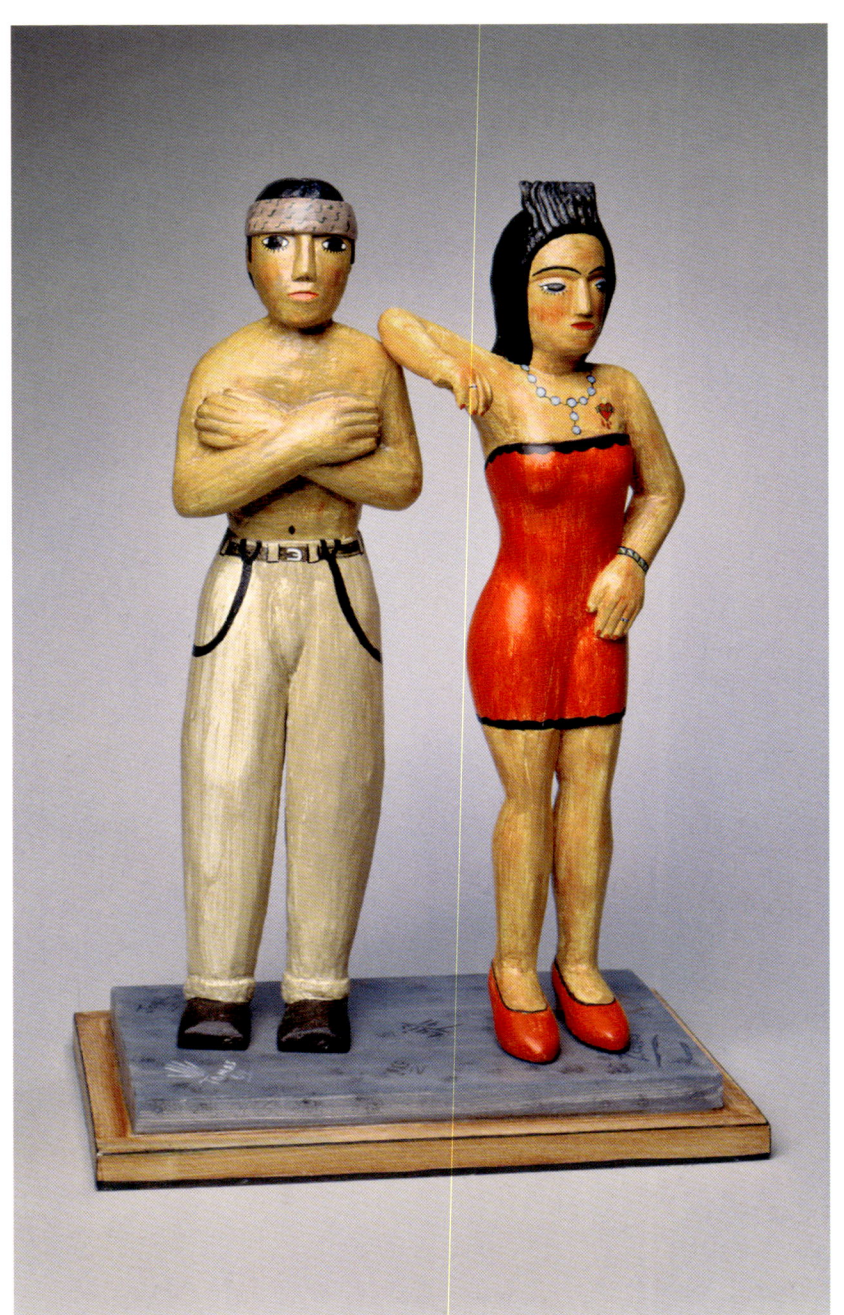
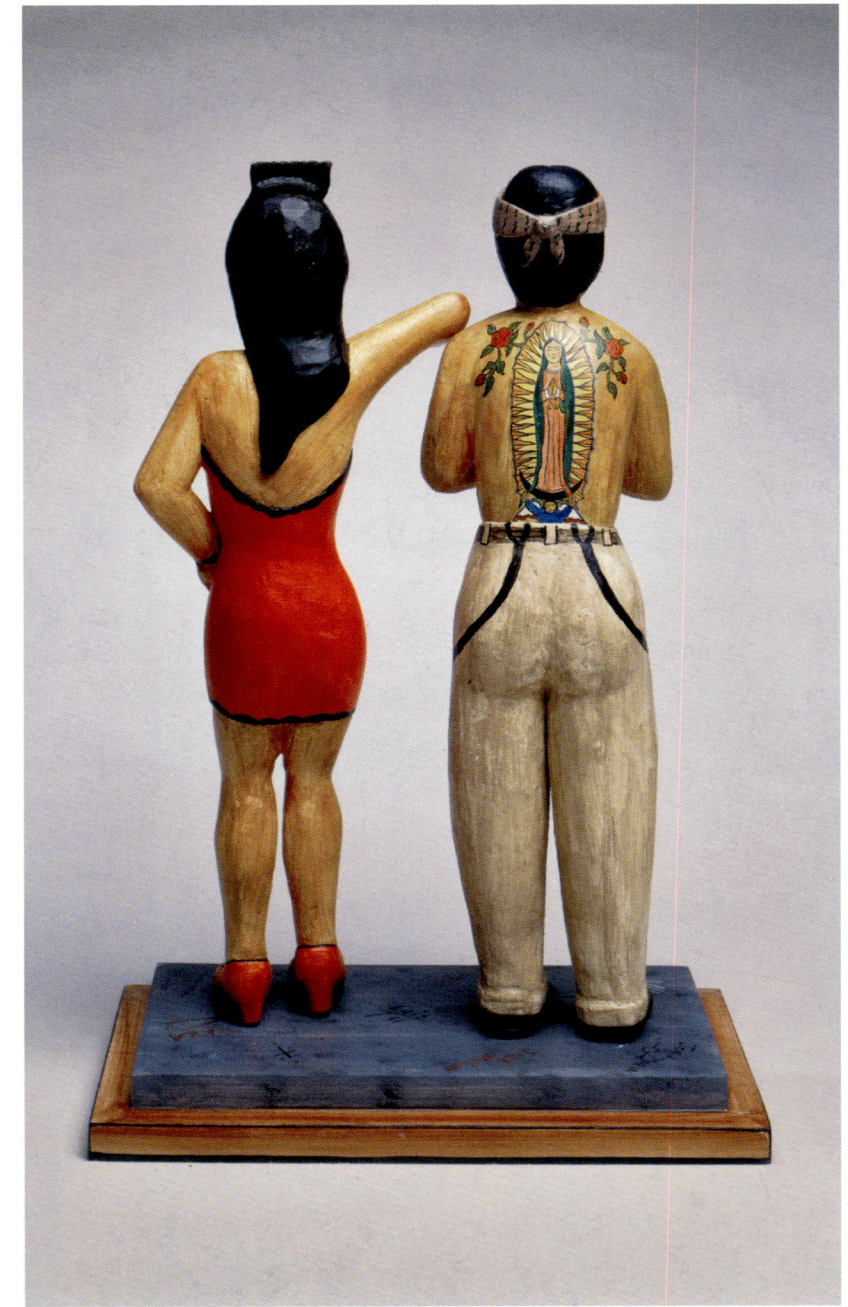

ABOVE
Figure 31. *José y María*, 1991. Carved and painted wood, 19¾ x 13 x 8⅜. Collection of Barbara Windom.
Photo © James Hart, courtesy of The Owings Gallery.

OPPOSITE
Figure 32. *Adán y Eva*, 1992. Carved and painted wood, 16⅛ x 14⅞ x 8⅛ in. Collection of Barbara and Ted Flicker.
Photo © Dan Morse, courtesy of The Owings Gallery.

FOLLOWING SPREAD
Figure 33. *Northern New Mexico Bella Living with Her Past*, 2002. Carved and painted wood, 24 x 18½ x 20 in.
Collection of the Museum of International Folk Art, Santa Fe; gift of Paul Pletka and Nancy Benkof (A.2008.73.1).
Photo © Dan Morse, courtesy of The Owings Gallery.

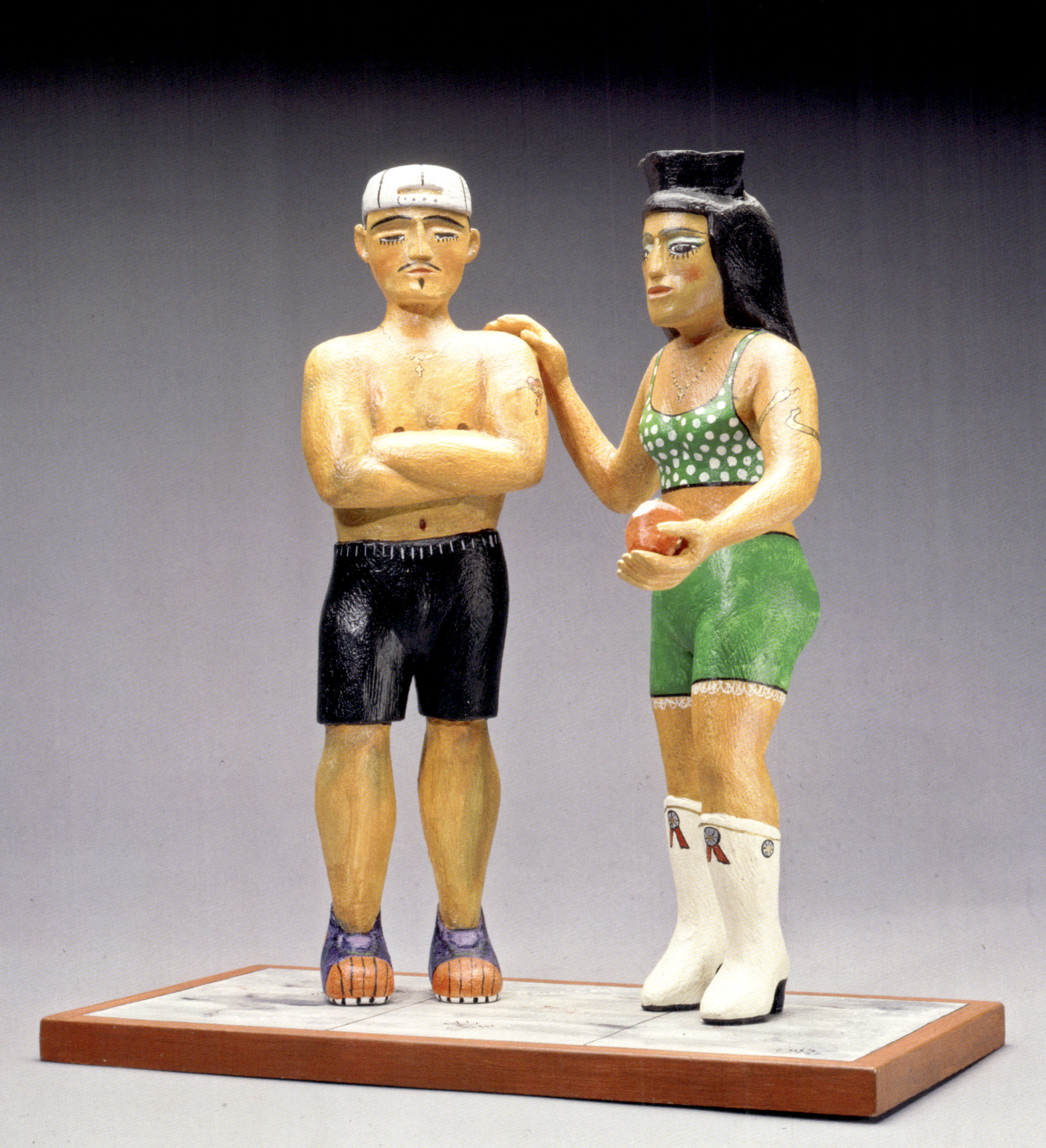

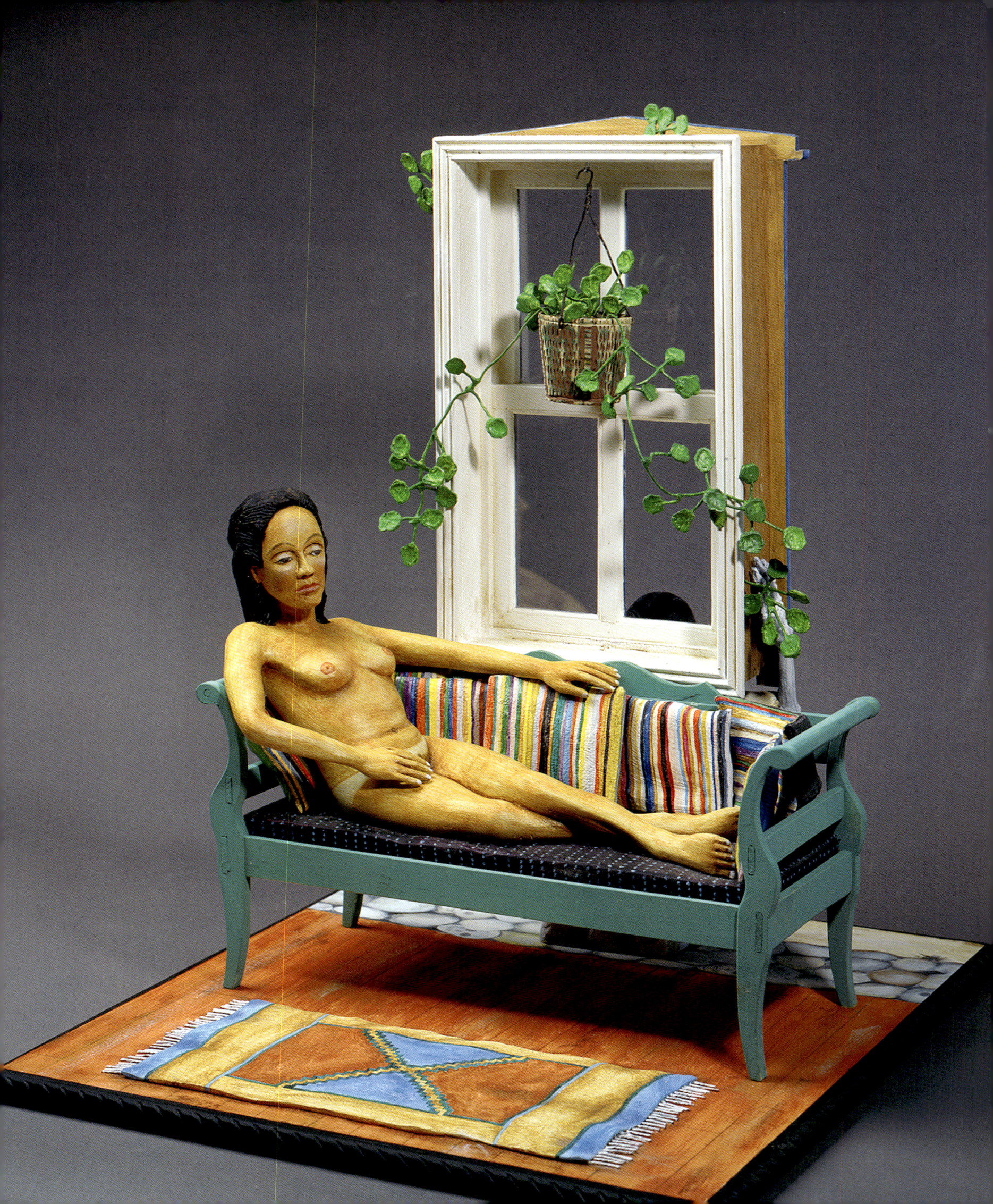

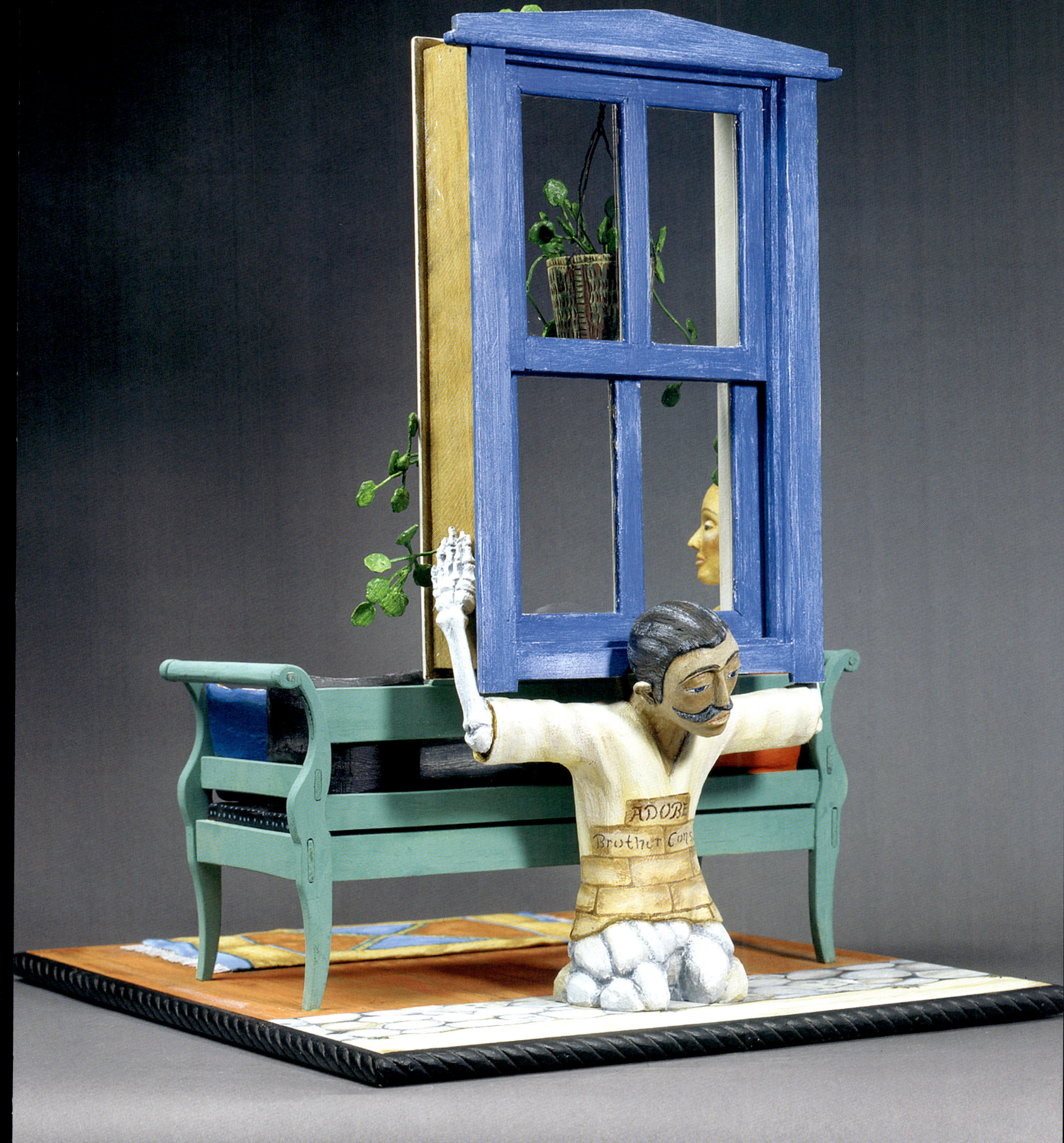

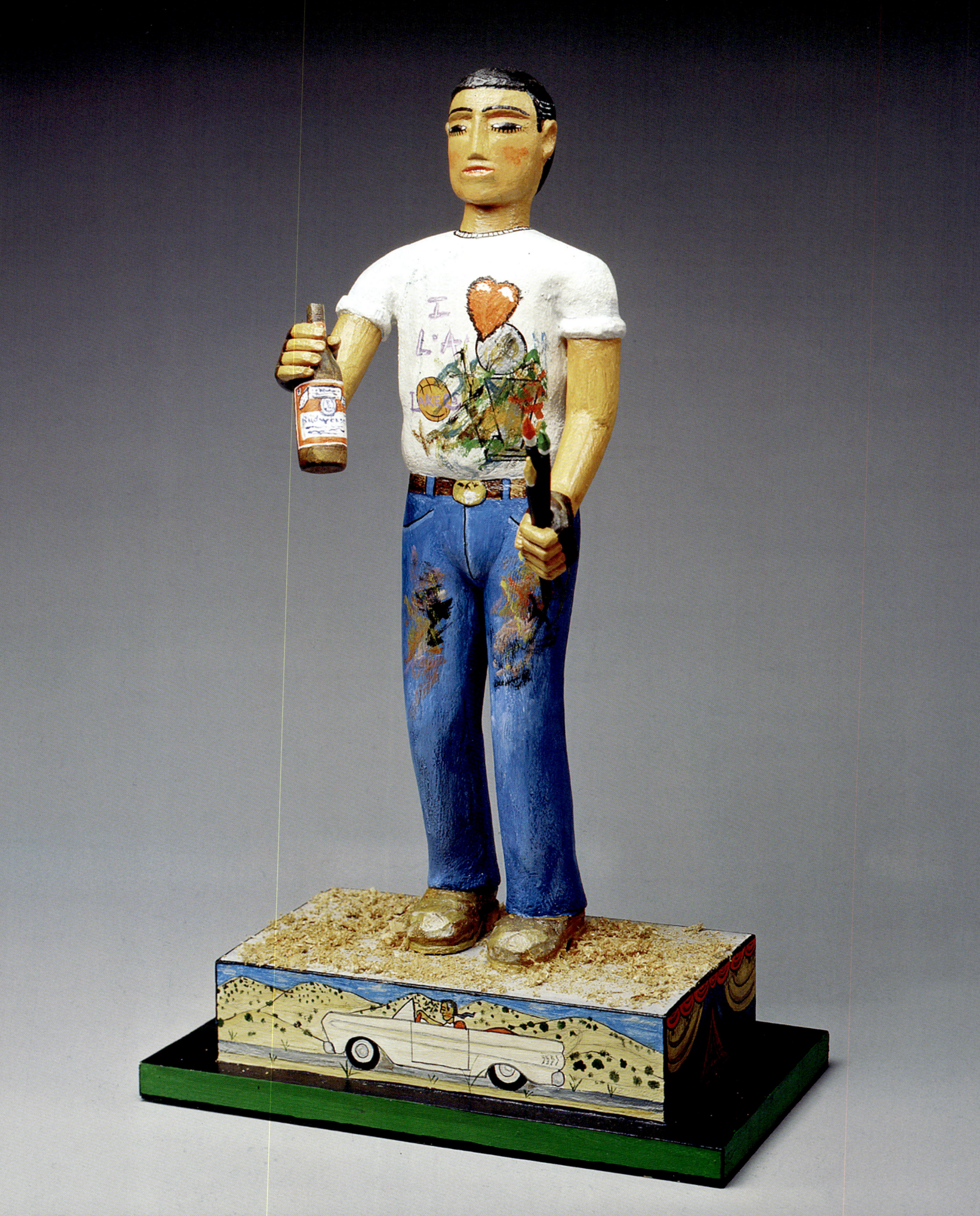

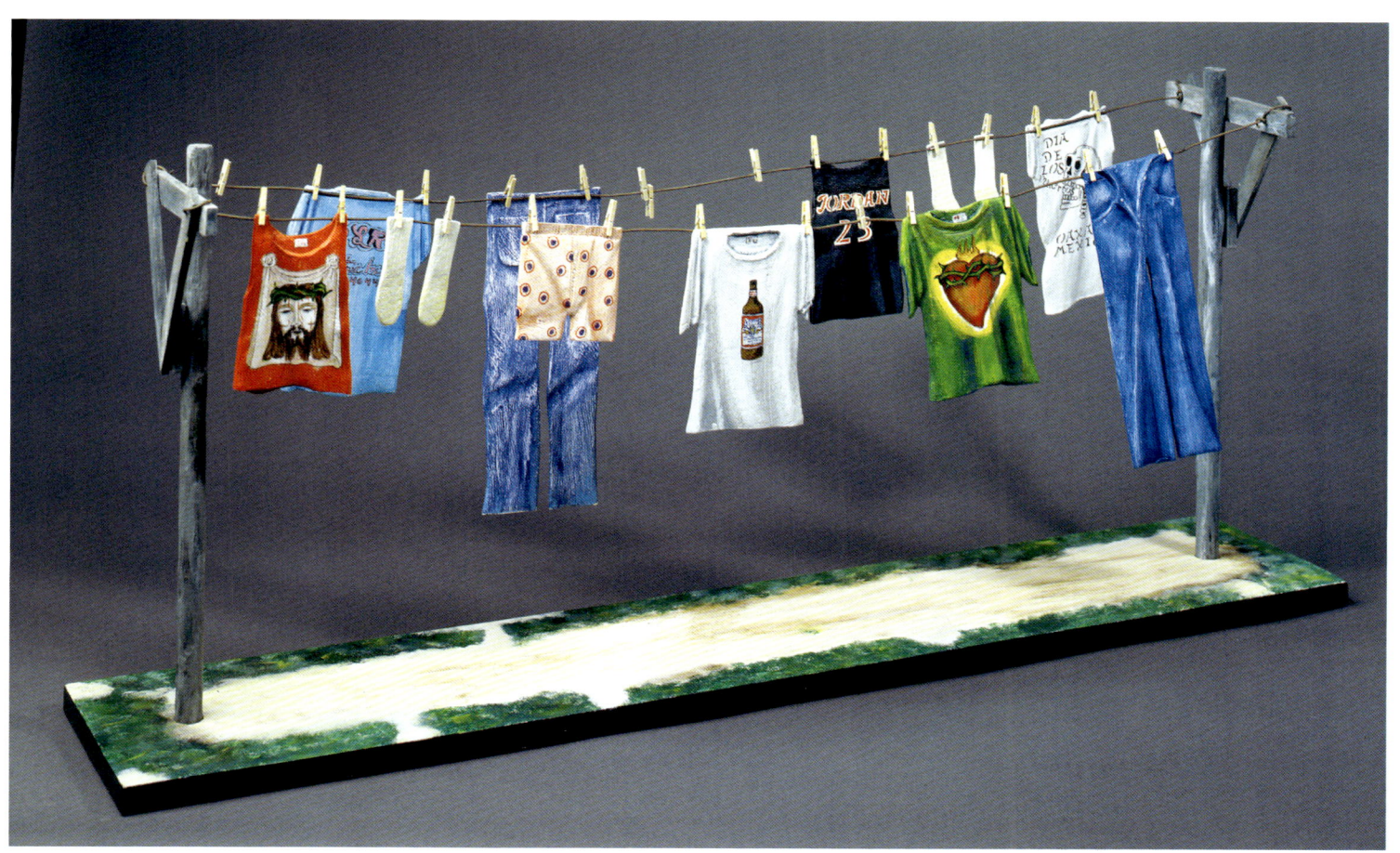

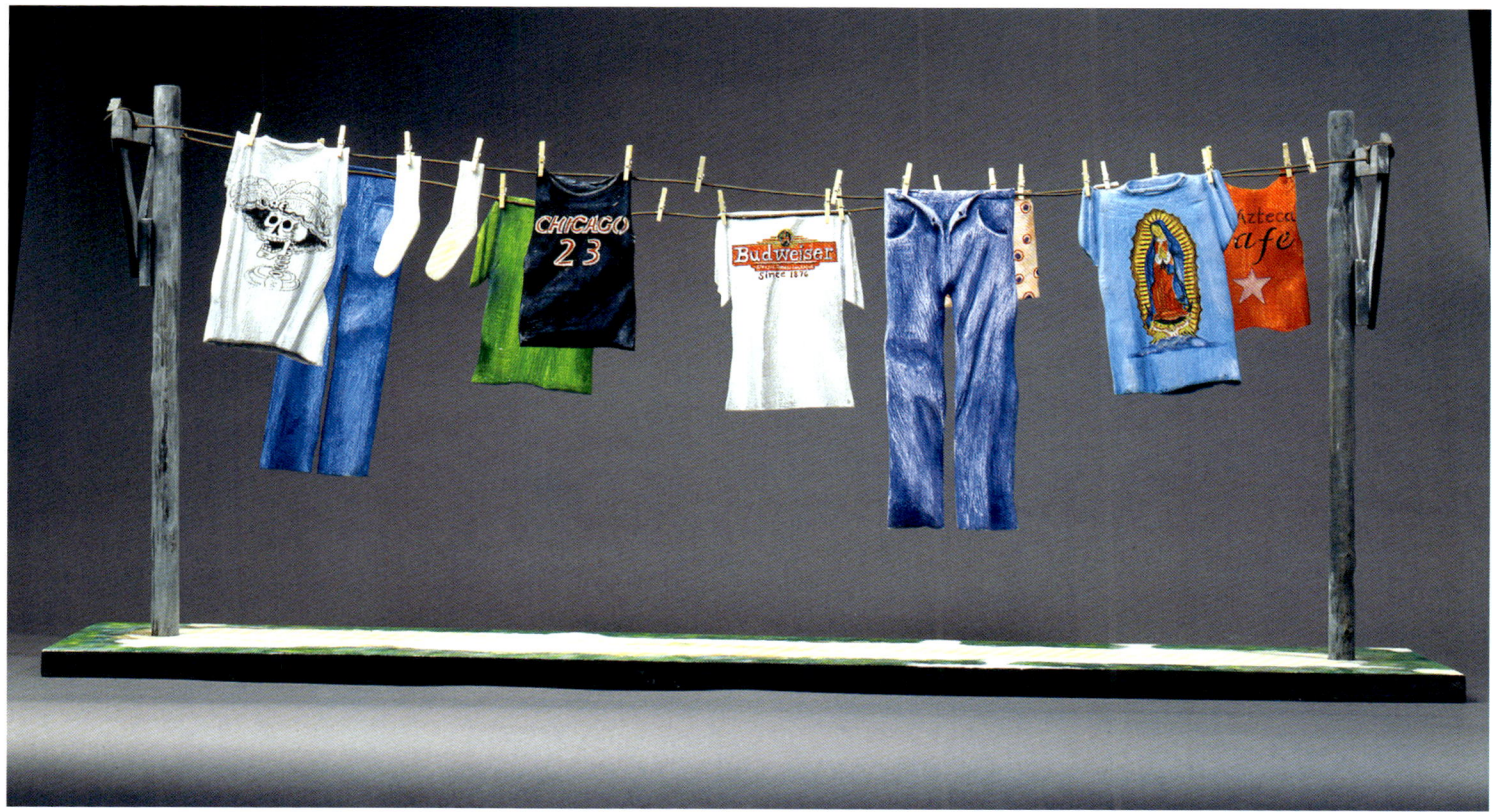

Figure 34. *El Santero*, 1995. Carved and painted wood, 21½ x 12½ x 18½ in. Private collection.
Photo © Dan Morse, courtesy of The Owings Gallery.

Figure 35. *Northern New Mexico Clothesline* (*Two Weeks of Laundry*), 2002. Carved and painted wood,
16⅜ x 38 x 7½ in. Private collection. Photo © Dan Morse, courtesy of The Owings Gallery.

Other examples of Tapia's humor mimic or represent morality plays and cautionary tales embedded in New Mexican folklore. *Good Friday Dance* (1999; Figure 36) is inspired by a common folk tale passed down for generations in northern New Mexico and told to Tapia by his mother. It relays the story of a dance in a village hall on Good Friday, a day that calls for "good Catholics" to stay home in prayer. As the band plays in the background and a singer takes the stage, a young couple dances in proper fashion, at arm's length. Peeking from the hem of the woman's green dress, however, is a long red tail. Her feet are hooves. The price of having a good time on Good Friday is clear. In *Guess Who's Coming to Dinner* (2002; Plate 18), two couples sit around a table on hand-carved New Mexican chairs. Their red chile enchiladas look delicious, but each diner wears a Mexican dance mask—a pig, a black horned goat, a jaguar, and a dog. The piece alludes simultaneously to local folk tales and to the mask traditions of Mexico, of which Tapia is an avid devotee. It also literally interprets the old adage that people are not always what they seem. In *Doña Sebastiana Relaxes after a Hard Day at the Office* (2003; Figure 37), Tapia puts a subtly humorous twist on the female skeletal figure normally depicted riding in a death cart. Here Tapia's rendition of Death as a lady depicts La Doña in a black dress seated comfortably with a drink after a long day's work. She has two halves: on one side she has gray hair and holds a Budweiser, while on the other she has black hair and a glass of wine. Thunderbolts shoot down below her toward a base filled with carved and painted bodies— the souls she has the power to call to the other side. The intricately intertwined figures wait in a tangle of flesh and fear to see if they will meet her after her break. Finally, *Seven Deadly Sins* (2008; Plate 41) brings Tapia's interpretation of life as an ongoing morality play home, encasing our ever-persistent vices in glass. The reliquary-like work is dramatic and powerful, with classic Tapia satire. Seven youthful figures make up the composition. A red-haired Vanity stands on a pedestal and looks anxiously into a gilded hand mirror. Lust, wearing a white "wife beater" T-shirt with a Hooters emblem, is obviously physically aroused as he eyes her from above. The tattooed male Wrath grips a baseball bat, ready to cause immediate destruction. The image on his right arm depicts a gun pointed at the viewer. Gluttony, a female with a muffin-top tummy, appears ready to inhale a fried chicken drumstick and a hamburger with detailed carved and painted lettuce bits spilling out of the bun. Her clothes, and even her shoes, have mustard and ketchup stains. As Sloth leans back on Vanity's pedestal and drinks a beer, a wistful Envy turns slightly green. Pride and Greed, who grasps an armful of money, round out the cardinal sins.

Over time, Tapia's social and cultural commentary has evolved to more effectively weave the authenticity of the Hispano and Chicano communities in New Mexico with local popular culture. In *Holy Toaster* (2008; Plate 42), a devotional image of an elevated toaster radiates symbolic rays around a piece of toasted bread emblazoned with an image of La Virgen de Guadalupe on one side and the head of Christ on the other. Although it's a lighthearted work, the idea of holy images on food products is not so unrealistic. Images of the Virgin Mary, and of Jesus, have been reported worldwide on toast, tortillas, pancakes, grilled cheese sandwiches, and more. In New Mexico, some of these images have

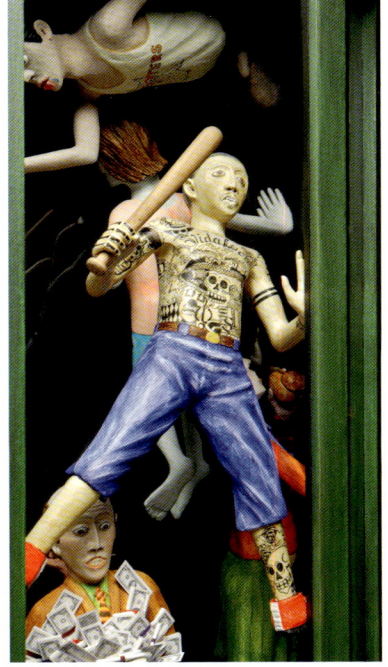

Seven Deadly Sins (detail), 2008; see page 150.

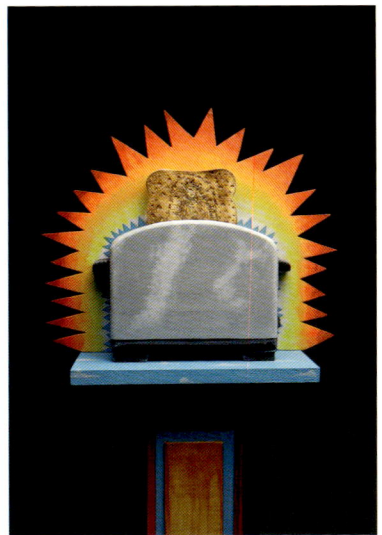

Holy Toaster (detail), 2008; see page 152.

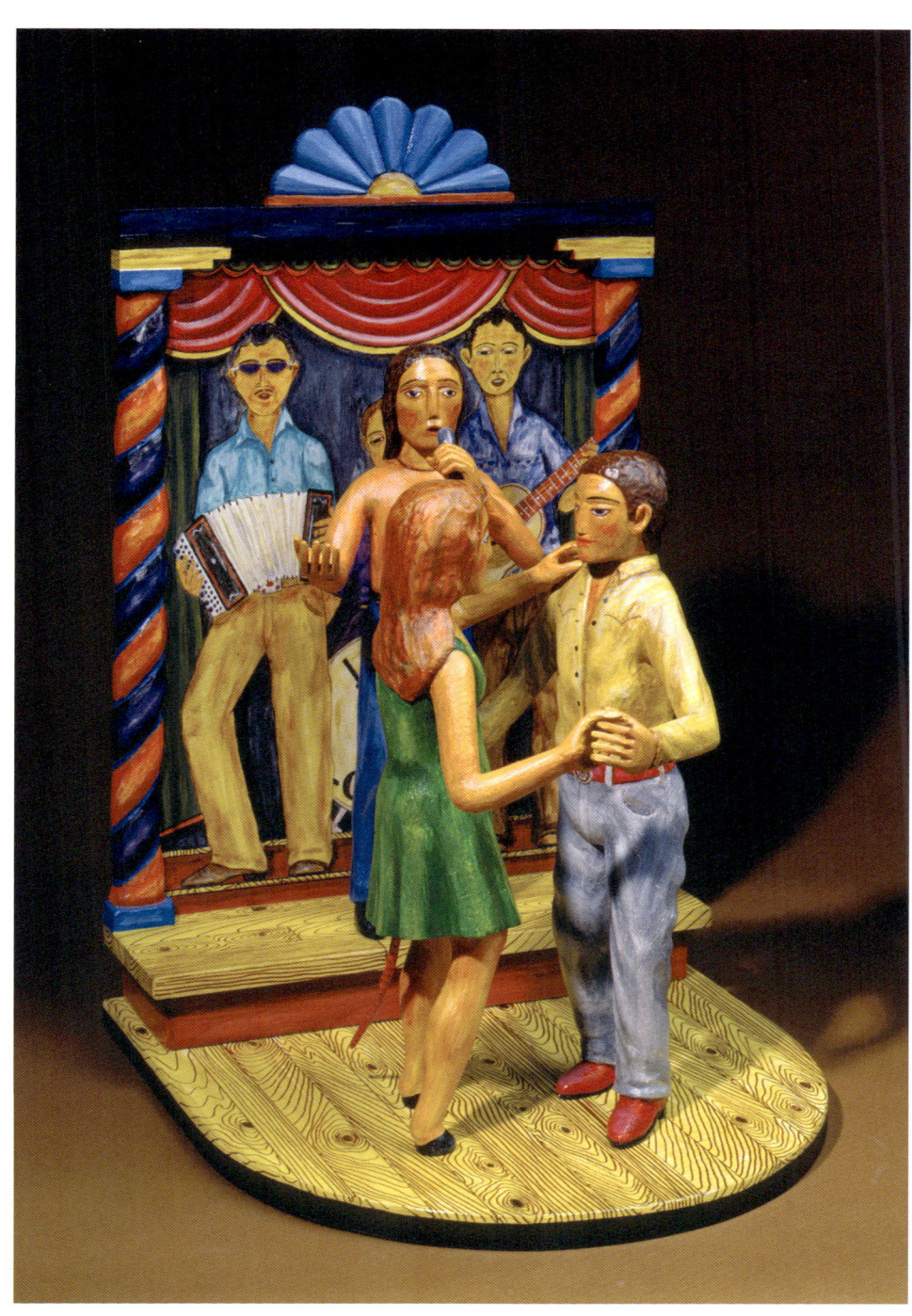

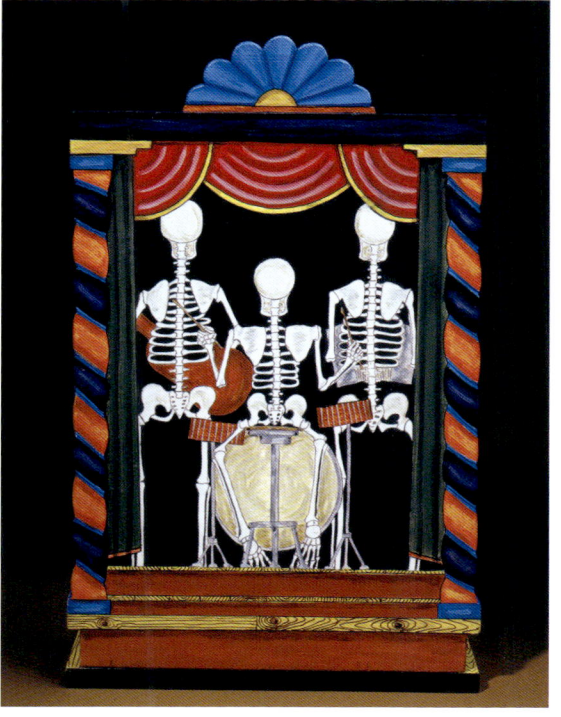

Figure 36. *Good Friday Dance*, 1999. Carved and painted wood. 22 ¾ x 13 ¾ x 15 in. Private collection. Photo © Dan Morse, courtesy of The Owings Gallery.

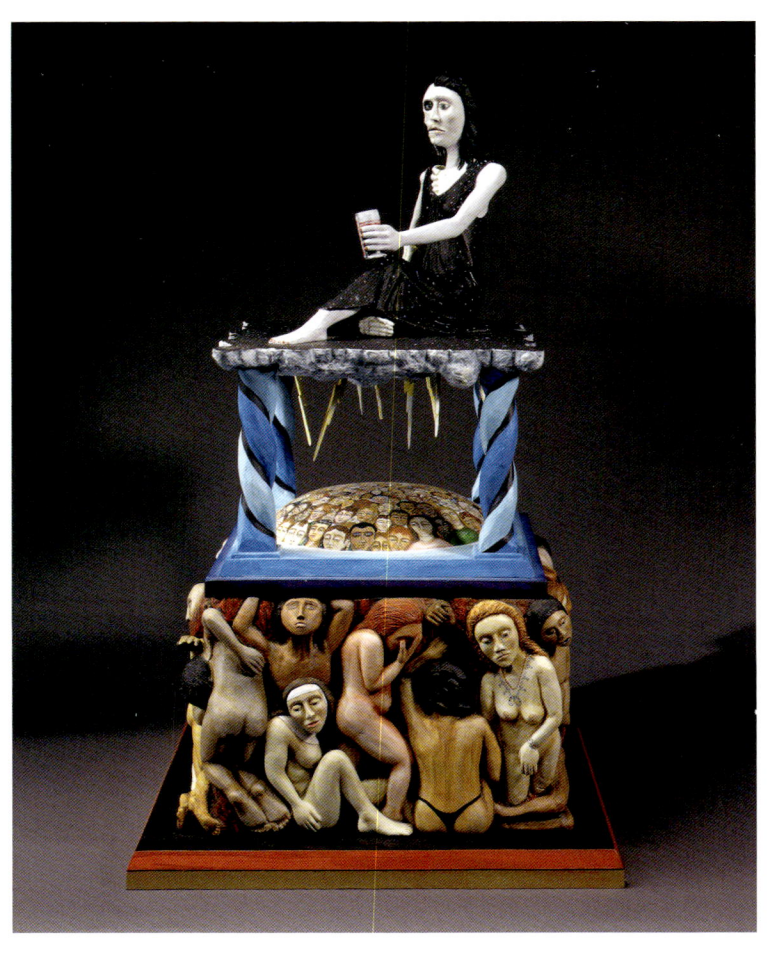 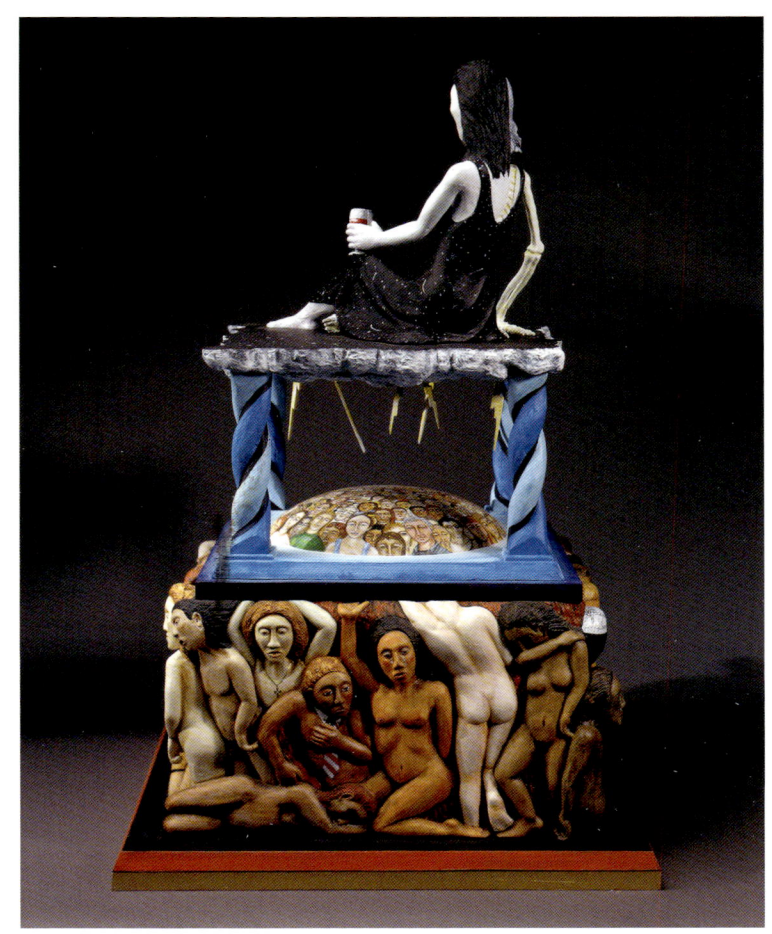

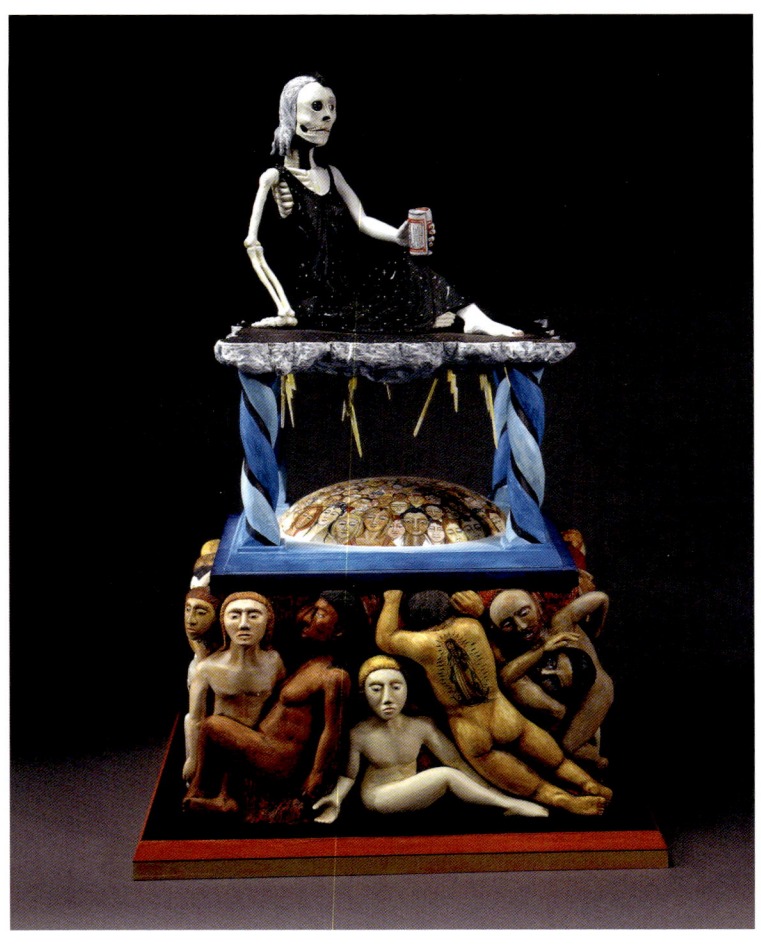 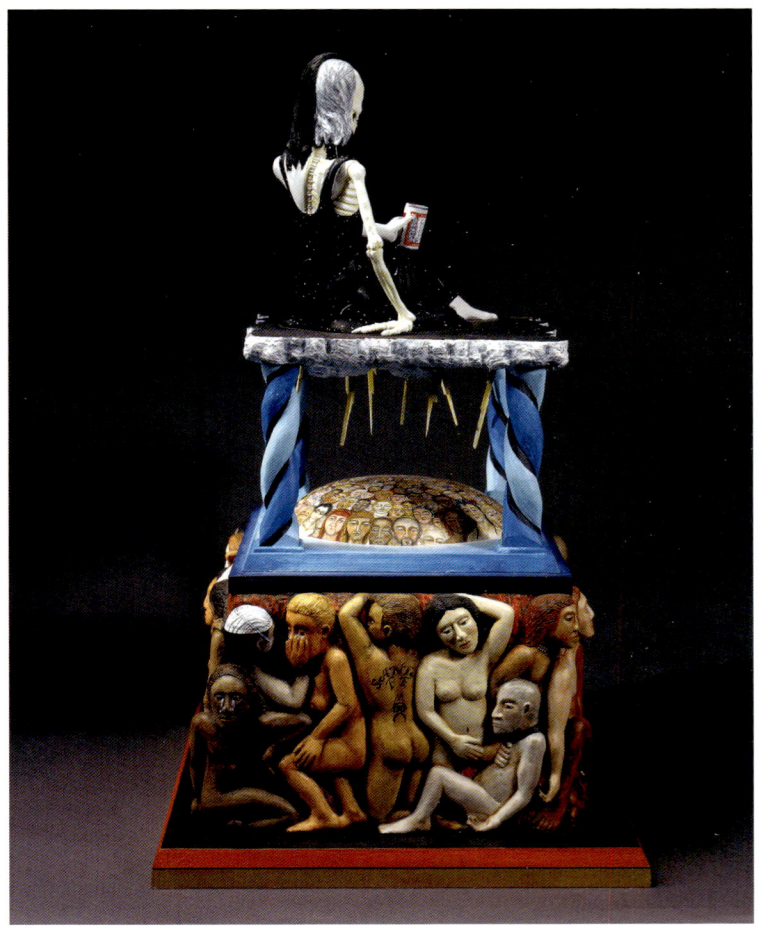

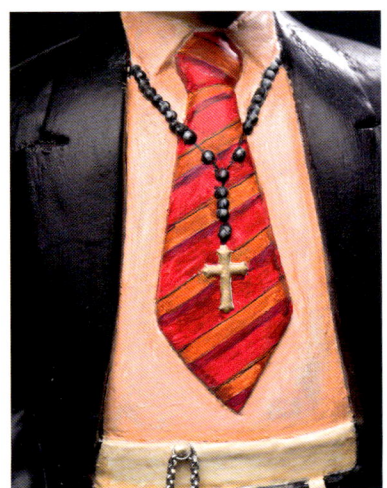

Pachuco Way (detail), 2106, see page 172.

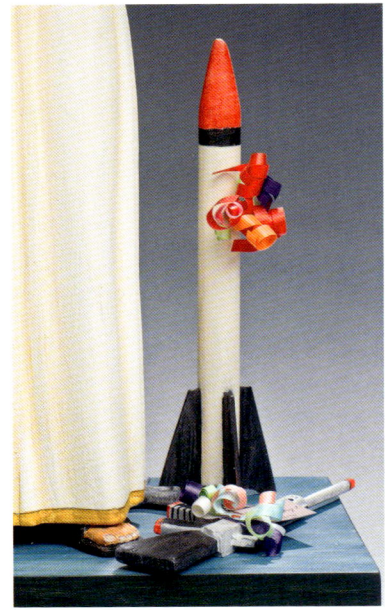

Happy Birthday, Jesus (detail), 2016; see page 168.

OPPOSITE
Figure 37. *Doña Sebastiana Relaxes after a Hard Day at the Office*, 2003. Carved and painted wood, 35 x 22 x 20 in. Collection of the Spanish Colonial Arts Society, Museum of Spanish Colonial Art, Santa Fe. Photo © Dan Morse, courtesy of The Owings Gallery.

been enshrined for visitation. Tapia's more recent *Holy Cow* (2016; Figure 38) is a riff on this same apparitional idea, a virtual companion piece to *Holy Toaster* that, knowing Tapia, may be joined by other works in this highly amusing series. In this sculpture, a brown-and-white cow is poised on all fours on a pedestal. Its white spots of various shapes and sizes reference outlines of cuts of beef and holy images, including the Star of Bethlehem on the cow's forehead and the shape of La Virgen de Guadalupe on its back. Corn motifs are painted along the base, bringing the sacred bovine back down to earth.

Tapia revels in the aesthetics of place making. The full vocabulary of hand-painted images that he has developed through the decades—of Santa Fe and New Mexico landscapes, as well as symbols of Hispano identity, traditions, social issues, life and death, good and evil—is incorporated into his most recent body of work.

"Art is always here," he says, tapping the middle of his forehead. "When people see me working on a figure, they often ask: What is it going to be? And I answer: I don't know yet. In my work now, the figures become individuals with their own stories. I take pride in that. They really start to become a person themselves. I talk to them and have conversations. As I am creating them, I wonder: Who are you? What is your story? Who will you become? Were you born in Agua Fría or were you born in Los Angeles?"

In *Pachuco Way* (2016; Plate 52), Tapia honors a shared Chicano cultural icon of both California and New Mexico: the zoot suiter. The figure, complete with chain and a wide, 1940s-style necktie, also wears a rosary. Here again, Tapia's nod to religiosity in Latino culture connects the religious and the everyday. The single figure stands on a platform, paying homage to both the *pachuco* movement and the devotional appeal of the iconic *santo*. The figure's classic lean and stride are so well done that it seems he could step off his painted platform and walk away. The figure has blue eyes, a tribute to a *pachuco* neighbor nicknamed Blue Eyes from Tapia's Santa Fe youth.

Tapia's *Happy Birthday, Jesus* (2016; Plate 50) features a figure of Santo Niño, the holy child. On first impression, the standing Christ Child appears very traditional, dressed in a long white gown with golden rays around his head. In many Latin American countries, as well as in New Mexico, gifts are given to Santo Niño as *milagros*, miracles, for prayers granted and blessings secured. These include toys, small offerings, and even shoes. (In New Mexico, worshippers believe the Christ Child wears shoes out while traveling and performing miracles.) In Tapia's interpretation, appearances can be deceiving. Instead of innocent childhood toys, Santo Niño is surrounded by guns, a missile, a tiny armored tank, a male GI Joe–like army figure, a plane, and of course an iPhone. Each is carefully wrapped with hand-curled ribbon. The Christ Child's expression is one of confusion and wonderment. Tapia's message is unsettlingly obvious: these symbols of war and contemporary consumer culture are the extreme opposite of what the Prince of Peace would wish for his birthday.

Tapia returns to the theme of women in three recent works. *Venus of Willendorf* (2012; Plate 45) is a takeoff on the famous *Woman of Willendorf* (circa 28,000–25,000 BCE) discovered in Austria in 1908. Tapia's elegantly voluptuous version is rather spare and

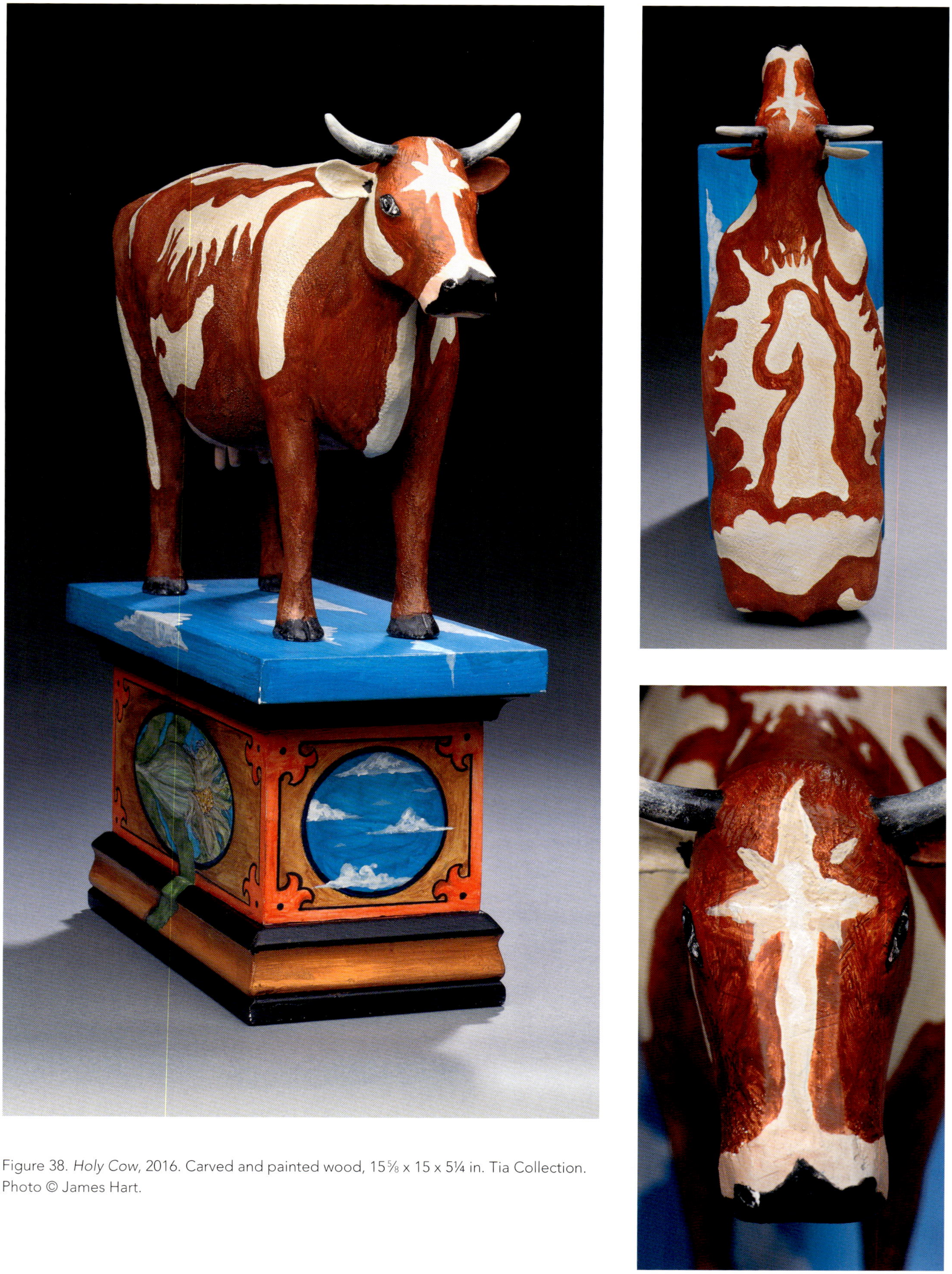

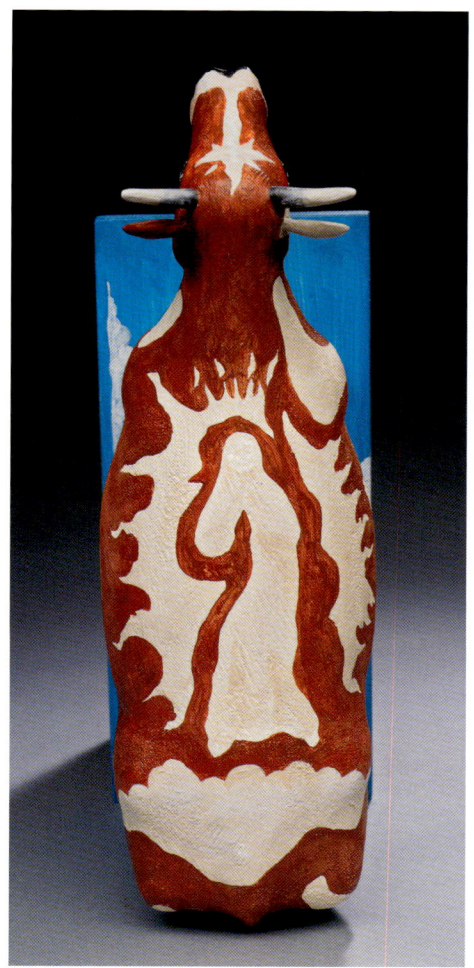

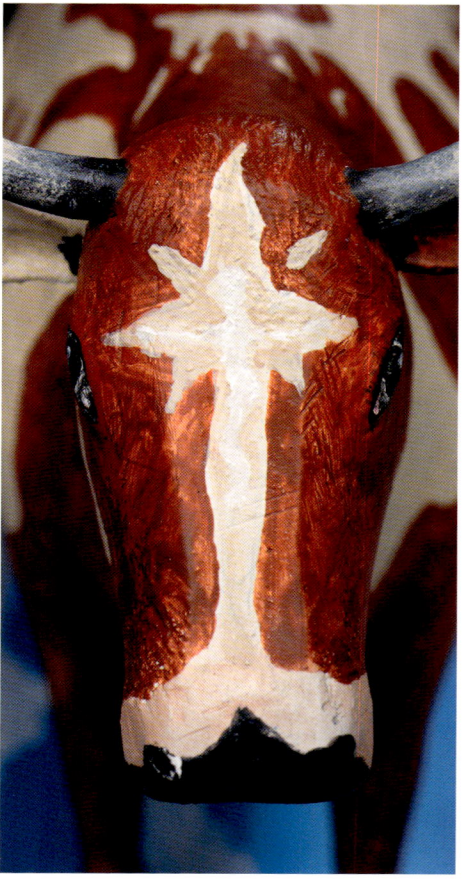

Figure 38. *Holy Cow*, 2016. Carved and painted wood, 15⅝ x 15 x 5¼ in. Tia Collection. Photo © James Hart.

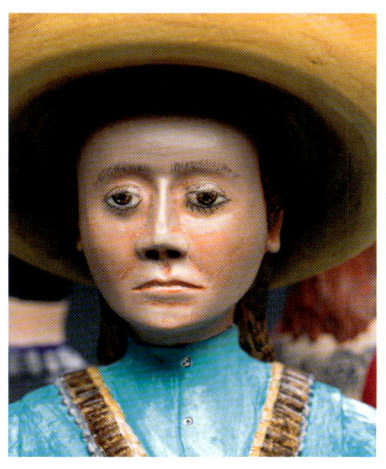

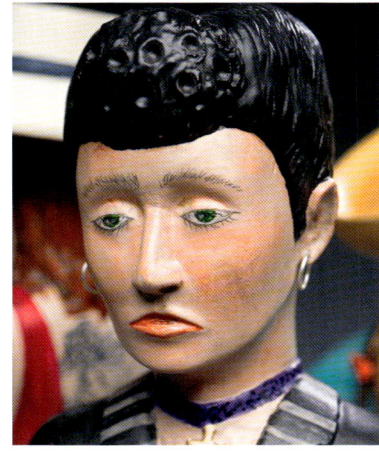

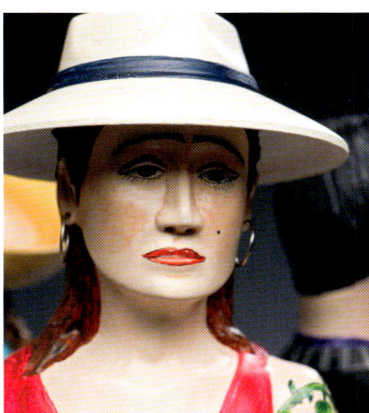

The Three Graces (details), 2016;
see page 174.

straightforward. She is set deeply inside a glass-paned window frame, with a lush New Mexico landscape painted on either side. Her figure is an image of power, enhanced by the "I Am Woman" tattoo on her back and a red apple that she appears to be close to crushing under her left foot. *Sirena del Río Grande* (2014; Plate 46) is another nude, this one with well-defined shape, body ink, and attitude. Tattoos of a half moon and a star frame her heart-shaped belly button. Her imperfect breasts and lower torso boast bikini tan lines. The latter detail is Tapia's tongue-in-cheek reference to *la sirena,* the mermaid, a figure that appears on Mexican *lotería* cards and other popular artworks. The woman leans inside a doorway, a red apple on the ground beside her. One side of the door frame features the northern view of the Río Grande Gorge; the other shows the river's southern course. Tapia takes on contemporary female stereotypes and their effects on modern women with *Barrio Barbie* (2016; Plate 51), at once a reference to the secular Barbie Doll icon and a portrait of an everyday woman. This version, situated on a round pedestal, features a realistic female figure in a form-fitting LBD (little black dress). Her accessories include red platform shoes and a halo-like, gold-rimmed black sombrero. The plunging back of her dress reveals Tapia's signature Guadalupe tattoo. Her face tilts to the right, revealing a beauty mark and a faraway look of strength or sadness.

The Three Graces (2016; Plate 53) is a deeply meaningful and personal statement that connects much of Tapia's work and community in a portrait of cultural power and determination. The sculpture portrays three strong and powerful Mexican women through time—the revolutionary Adelita, La Pachuca, and a twenty-first-century *chula chola chica.* Their different periods of dress and backstories reference significant events for Mexicanas and Chicanas on both sides of the border. As an icon of feminism and strength from the Mexican Revolution, Adelita is meaningful for today's Chicanas and Latinas. La Pachuca is another symbol of resistance; she was an important part of a post–World War II social movement in which Latinos and Chicanos proudly claimed their cultural identity and became more visible in society. Today her image is being reclaimed by both Chicanas and Chicanos of varied ages. Tapia's contemporary Chicana draws inspiration from her two companions. Her tattoos symbolize their collective past and present: on her right arm is an image of the plumed serpent Quetzalcoatl; on her back a detailed portrait of La Virgen de Guadalupe. A tattooed vine of roses and thorns winds down her left arm and leg, as if threading together their lives and legends, struggles and triumphs.

Tapia's recent works also address contemporary issues surrounding the U.S.–Mexican border, so timely in 2017. These bold border commentaries go beyond northern New Mexico subject matter and stereotypes and acknowledge the state's direct connections to Mexico on its southern border, illustrating how national, and in fact global, Tapia's themes are. Despite the pervasiveness of identity politics in New Mexico, Tapia nuances the subject so profoundly that the viewer is often caught unaware of his blatantly political messages.

In *Camino de sueños* (2015) and *Virgen del camino de sueños* (2016), he holds nothing back in addressing the human realities of the immigration debate. *Camino de sueños* (Plate 47) is anchored by a thorny nopal, or prickly pear cactus. Caught in the chaos between the thorns are the possessions left or lost by those crossing the border: backpacks, shoes, underwear, identification cards, family photos, empty cans, and toys. A signpost points to the wealthy "U$A." Above it, a vulture points out the costs of the journey, guarding a list of names of those who have lost their lives. Painted footprints punctuate the base, wandering about the desert sand in aimless circles.

Virgen del camino de sueños (Plate 54) is another powerful statement in the round. The front view depicts a Marian-type figure reminiscent of La Virgen de Guadalupe, her red gown and green manta outlined by golden rays. But a closer look reveals that the images on her manta are not traditional iconographical stars but rather skulls representing those who have lost their lives attempting to cross the border. Draped in front of La Reina are the human remains—a skull, an arm, and a foot—of Juan Diego, the Mexican peasant to whom La Virgen de Guadalupe originally appeared. Red roses, another iconographic element of Marian representations, are strewn around the figures. These too are dead. On the reverse of the manta are detailed portraits of those who have died or disappeared on the dangerous journey north from Mexico through the centuries. Their faces are haunting and powerful, as familiar as one's family member or neighbor, as ancient as the Aztec warrior Tapia places among them. Tapia extends their meaning by depicting people of all races and colors who comprise the Mexican—and American—diaspora. Peeking through the nopal pads, they represent the horrors faced by immigrants of all nationalities. The small white crosses that stick out from the painted earth mark the global graveyard of migration.

Tapia exposes what is real, what communities live every day. He is at his best when he demystifies the legends surrounding identity and the oversimplification of "the pure" in Latino communities. Not all his works are religious, but he makes a personal religion of his sculptural topics and themes. In his hands, the sacred becomes the secular, the everyday. Nowhere is this more evident than in Latino culture.

"I take a lot of credit and pride that I have introduced a lot of people to Hispano art," he says. "But it is important to me to merge this art. I hope this will be a bridge between our Chicano cultures so we can unite and value each other."

Tapia's global view and profound visual record speak for themselves. To limit descriptions of his production to sweet and simple examples of centuries-old traditional New Mexican folk art denies Tapia, and by extension those who follow his path, the critical means by which to expose a larger art world to integral and timely cultural commentary. There is nothing sweet or simple about Tapia's visual production (and I mean that sweetly). Even when creating more straightforward images—of a Saint Francis or a sacred heart, for example—Tapia never fails to be progressive or to hold a message. "I work hard for my imagery," he says, "to strive to make everything fresh, new, one of a kind."

What Tapia has achieved by defying Anglo definitions of New Mexican traditions is profound. He has broken through barriers indicative of a mythos that continues to pervade the art scene not only in New Mexico but also in California, the greater Southwest, and

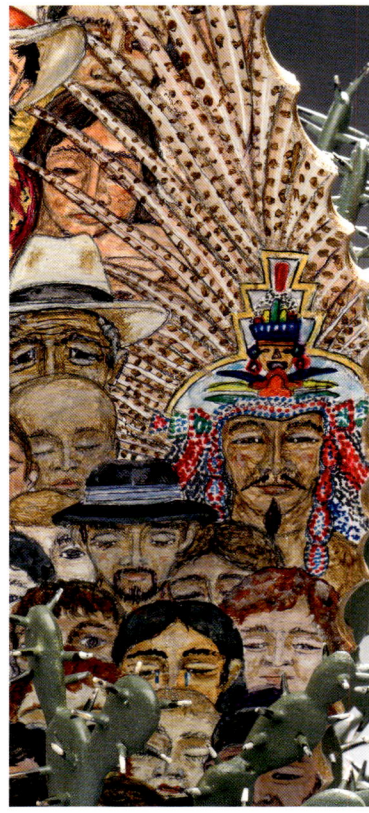

Virgen del camino de sueños (detail), 2016; see page 176.

nationwide. Still, one rarely reads about Hispano, Latino, Chicano, or Mexican contributions to New Mexican and American art history. Instead, it is Georgia O'Keeffe (good grief) and the Santa Fe and Taos artists who continue to be cast as the true masters.

During the past forty-five years, Tapia has demanded—and crafted—a different narrative. What if the narrative were turned on its head? Maybe, at long last, it would read like this:

> Luis Tapia, a contemporary Chicano sculptor represented by major galleries nationally and internationally, has completed his recent body of work addressing issues of identity, economy, inequity, power, war, drugs, gender, religion, good versus evil, injustice, immigration, cultural politics, and their global impact. *¡Órale!*

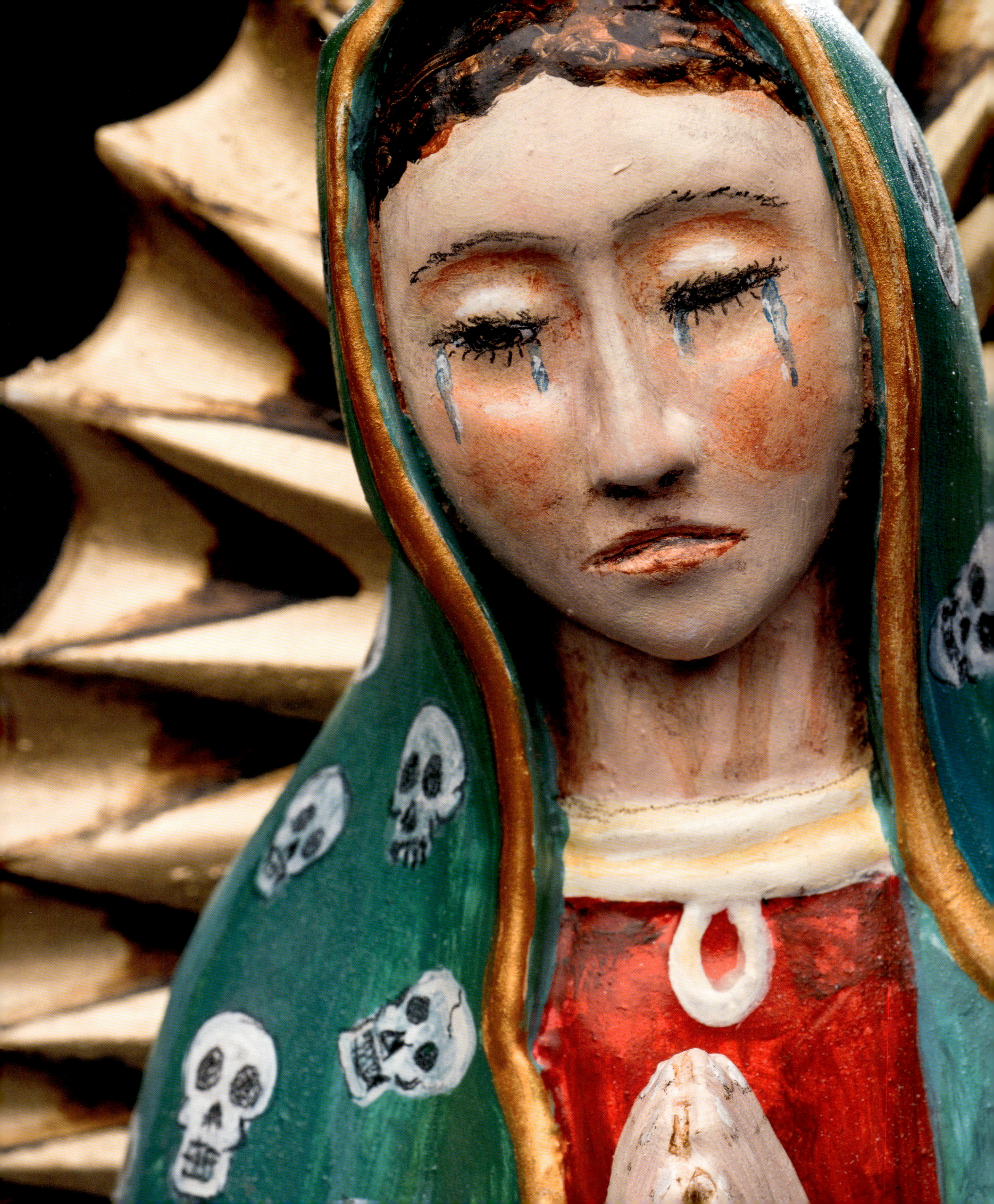

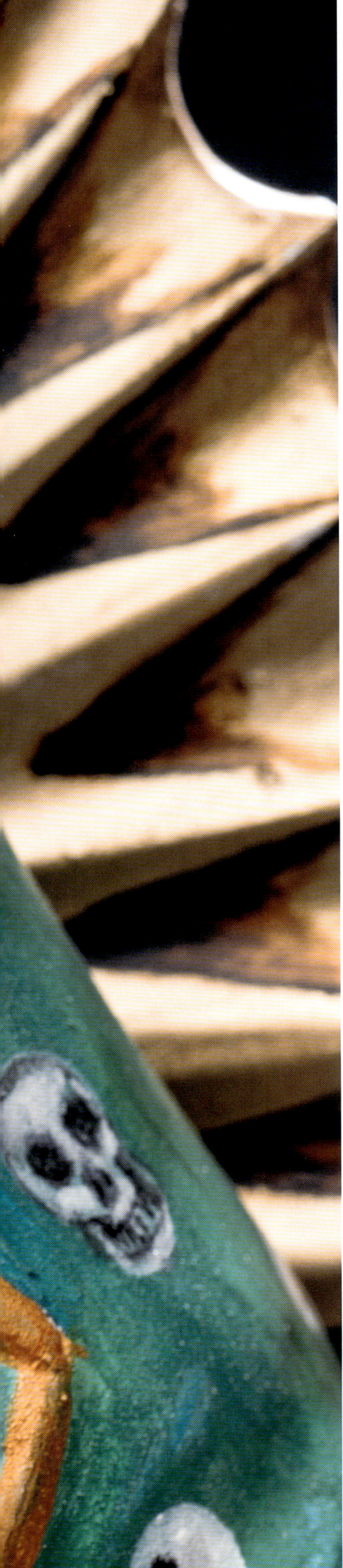

Luis Tapia: Firme*

DENISE CHÁVEZ

THE BRAVE NEW WORLD PORTRAYED in George Orwell's classic novel by the same name depicts an outland colony—a place removed from mainstream society. Set in a New Mexico described by Orwell as a "savage reserve"—a place removed from place—this society on the fringes of the cultured and known world is designated the Other Place, the Other World. By this calling out of the remote and bucolic still untouched, New Mexico became in the minds of many a historic, epic, and still virgin place to be loved, revered, and, sadly, used.

To those born and raised in that New Mexico of myth and magic, imposed and real, the ancestral ground of our Hispano and Native ancestors, the appellation Land of Enchantment often masks the irony of a state depleted, denied, denigrated, and disallowed. Los Alamos. Trinity Site. Dulce. Roswell. Kirtland Air Force Base. White Sands Missile Range. Holloman Air Force Base. WIPP. Jemez Springs. The Servants of the Paraclete. All are familiar names in the local lexicon of New Mexico. But what more do we need to know about a land dreamed about, revered, and lovingly and wondrously called enchanted?

Whose enchantment? Whose land? Whose dream?

The true reality of this homeland is what sculptor Luis Tapia knows and explores.

"¿Quién te parió?" our grandmothers asked when someone came into the house. Who are you? Who are your people? Where do you come from? And most importantly, who gave you birth?

It was important to know the lineage of the person standing before you, who your family was, your parents, their parents, and where they lived. A ranchito in Agua Fría, a small village on the southern outskirts of Santa Fe, was the wellspring of lineage and life for Luis Tapia.

The New Mexico of Luis's youth was dynamic and mercurial. He grew up in Agua Fría, the son of Ben and Pauline Leyba Tapia. His father, a firefighter at the then-nascent Los Alamos National Laboratory, died mysteriously when Luis was thirteen months old. Only fifty years later did the family learn he had likely died of beryllium poisoning. Exposure to, and death from, this highly toxic metal has all too frequently been linked to work at the Lab. Luis's mother

*Chicano slang for Firm. Resolute. Steady. Solid. Stable. Grounded. And Cool.

Virgen del camino de sueños (detail), 2016; see page 176.

never remarried. Instead she went to work, first cleaning houses and eventually working as a counselor at the New Mexico School for the Deaf. Raised close to his grandmother Doloritas, Luis learned Spanish as his first language.

To be a native Spanish speaker in oft-segregated New Mexico was a harsh lesson of assimilation, as such children were classified, punished, and often put into classes with slow learners or those who were called retarded. Many primarily Spanish speakers faced humiliation, denigration, and goading from both peers and teachers. It was an insensitive and long-remembered punishment for someone who was different.

Luis had to learn English within an unsympathetic system. He was embarrassed by others' unconscious lack of understanding when he explained that he had no indoor plumbing. He was often called huérfano, orphan, as if losing one's father meant he belonged to no one.

Guided and nurtured by his grandmother and mother, he learned valuable life lessons. On his family's ranchito and those surrounding, Luis's kin were the goats, sheep, pigs, horses, apple trees, and acequias. The rich Mother Ditch—the Acequia Madre—gave life and sustenance with water from the Santa Fe River. It also sustained the trees that supplied his village and nearby Santa Fe with wood.

It was here in Agua Fría—Cold Water—that Luis learned to work. At the age of five, he was digging wells. His mother and grandmother instilled in Luis a sense of pride in his labor, and from them he understood the power of a strong work ethic. "Before women's lib, there was my mom," he says.

This foundation, this anchoring and rootedness in his family, his community, and terreno, his beloved earth, fed Luis's sangre, his soul, his spirit. From a young age, he had the grace to know where he stood and to whom and to what he belonged. Agua Fría, built on two abandoned Indian pueblos, was a place special and powerful. It parió, informó, y elevó—birthed, informed, and elevated—Luis's understanding of his place in the world. The solidity of his beloved New Mexico later found expression in his artistic work.

Despite the odds, including undiagnosed dyslexia, Luis completed high school with honors. He never learned to love English class, but to express himself in elementary school, he taught himself to draw. He had no formal art education, but growing up, the spirit of creativity was all around him. His resourceful gente, his relatives and neighbors, carved, wove, or otherwise crafted the material culture of daily life. Art was his essence. In time he would follow his own instincts to carve.

As a young man, Luis moved to Las Cruces to study engineering at New Mexico State University. When academia proved less interesting than the sights, sounds, and experiences of the city's pulsing and vibrant border reality, he left school and returned to Santa Fe. Much later, he moved for a time to Los Angeles. There he shared a studio with his close friend and kindred spirit Gilbert "Magu" Luján, a pioneer in the Chicano art movement of the sixties and seventies. Magu was a founding member of Los Four, a collective of political and intellectual activists that rocked the art world with fresh and daring style. Their groundbreaking 1974 exhibition *Los Four: Almaraz, de la Rocha, Luján, Romero* at the Los Angeles County Museum of Art legitimized Chicano art in the Anglo American art world.

But like many who were born in and are bound to New Mexico, Luis always returned to his heartland, his centering place. The *Tao Te Ching* describes this deeply embedded sense of place as a point of power—the power of those who return, those who stay, to mine the rich depth of their own communities without feeling the restless call of the world:

> People enjoy their food, take pleasure in being with their families, spend weekends working in their gardens, delight in the doings of the neighborhood. And even though the next country is so close that people can hear its roosters crowing and its dogs barking, they are content to die of old age without ever having gone to see it.

Luis came of artistic age in the tumultuous 1960s and 1970s, a time more idyllic in New Mexico than in other parts of the United States. By then, Santa Fe was already Arts Central. Los de Afuera—the Outsiders—had long moved in to claim their stake of the New American Art Scene. The history of Los de Afuera is rife with the stories and deeds of those who saw New Mexico's magic, its allure, and its need. They came to a state that had always been poor economically but rich in so many other ways. Some attempted to conquer a people and their art and culture, others to use and transform that art and culture for their own purposes in the guise of altruism and goodwill. Some, like Mabel Dodge Luhan and D. H. Lawrence, were internationally known by the time they arrived. Others, like Georgia O'Keeffe and Willa Cather, made an international name for themselves primarily in relation to New Mexico. Some interpreted New Mexico in all its complexity, sincerely and with great love. Others did not. All found the spell of New Mexico tangible and life changing. It was a haven of incredible natural beauty alongside ancient and rich cultures—a place from which to draw light to their hungry souls.

For those born into this New Mexico of veiled enchantment, it has often been hard to justify the takeover and appropriation of the sacred aspects of our cultures, whether Hispano or Native American or one of the many other cultures that have flourished here. Yet always, underneath the hoopla of the newly discovered, the bedrock of those who craft their art in their own fashion, and in keeping with their traditions, has remained.

Being a traditional artist, however, is not always as romantic or as easy as it seems. For many, the traditional must remain undifferentiating, bound in time and by techniques. Some believe that traditional artists can never be traditional or authentic enough, and any deviation is seen as a betrayal. As a result, traditional artists often repeat the same formulaic interpretation of their respective art forms because their audience and the marketplace demand it.

But things have changed, as well they should. The contemporary artist must retain what is best and most powerful of the past. One must also stand at the precipice of the new and examine what needs to be transformed. The world of tradition does not have to collide with the ever-expanding creative tension to comprehend the new. This understanding is what propelled Luis to bridge this fractured, appropriated, up-for-the-highest-bidder cultural spirit grab and forge his own way.

In 1978 Luis, along with Frederico Vigil, Wilberto Miera, Star Tapia, and María Luisa Delgado Roybal, founded a collective, La Cofradía de Artes y Artesanos Hispánicos (the Confraternity of Hispanic Art and Artisans). La Cofradía was a brotherhood and sisterhood of Hispano artists who embraced the conocimiento, the understanding of the ancestors, but who, according to Mary Caroline Montaño's book *Tradiciones Nuevomexicanas: Hispano Arts and Culture of New Mexico,* "did not allow or accept Anglo criteria of what constituted traditional art." The group looked at traditional art with a new vision and clarity that was fresh, startling, and so appropriate, claiming its own métier of what was authentic. By breaking new ground and establishing an alternative to a largely Anglo-derived definition of what was "Spanish," La Cofradía members discovered a newfound autonomy and power.

La Cofradía was a familia de artistas who knew the reality of market sales and the pressure to Make It Bigger and More Western or Quainter and More Rustic. For his part, Luis had already begun to establish himself as a talented sculptor of santos, and his works were best sellers at Santa Fe's annual Spanish Market. But Luis was not driven by a desire to duplicate or bend his work to the mythologies of the marketplace. He self-identified as a Chicano. With the verve and energy of the Movimiento Artístico Chicano that rippled across the United States, Luis and his fellow Cofradía members committed to manejarlo mejor—work it better.

La Cofradía comprised a stellar group of artists, writers, and other visionaries who strove to discover, explore, educate, and empower not only themselves but others across New Mexico. Driven by a mandate to create a space for Chicano artists that did not exist, the collective supported a range of artists like Luis and myself, then an up-and-coming playwright and writer from Las Cruces. Living at that time in Santa Fe, I participated in various Cofradía community exhibitions and presentations. I remember a young, dynamic Luis, front and center, manifesting an unbounded and heartfelt energy. Across the vast expanse of our New Mexico, we recognized each other as kin.

Simultaneously and in spirit connection with La Cofradía came La Academia de La Nueva Raza, the Academy of the New Race, an organization spearheaded by native New Mexican scholars, poets, teachers, artists, and lovers of the land. Academia members included Vicente Martínez from Taos, a direct descendant of Padre Antonio Martínez, as well as Facundo Valdez, Tomás Atencio, Consuelo Pacheco, Eduardo Lavadie, Juanita Jaramillo Lavadie, Alejandro López, E. A. "Tony" Mares, Cecilio García-Camarillo, Enrique Lamadrid, Ellen Arellano, and others. Also among them was the great scholar and writer Juan Estevan Arellano, who chronicled "Manito" culture and whose translation of Spaniard Gabriel Alonso de Herrera's classic 1513 book, *Obra de la Agricultura,* detailed the old but still unfailing methods of agriculture employed both in Arellano's village of Embudo and in Luis's querencia of Agua Fría. These homegrown artists and scholars collected traditional stories and folk wisdom and learned and perfected traditional art. Academia founder Tomás Atencio created the concept of La Resolana, which promoted dialogue and discourse in a place comfortable, sunny, and inherently New Mexican.

Coming of age in the creative ferment and excitement of this time was life changing. We all envisioned a new and empowered world that was De Lo Nuestro—ours and of our own—something wholly original and of its time that had not existed before. Personally, my southern reality had a choque, a jolt, as I was baptized, politically and artistically, during my time in northern New Mexico. These were especially powerful years of growth and expansion for Luis as well.

Luis understood the legacy of the great New Mexican wood carvers and saint makers who had come before—José Rafael Aragón, José Dolores López, Celso Gallegos, Patrocino Barela, and others. He understood their creative challenge to either adhere to, or move away from, certain forms prescribed by Catholic tradition. It was difficult knowing that to become a contemporary artist in one's own right in New Mexico, it was necessary to sell to mainstream galleries patronized mainly by those from outside the culture. It was equally difficult to keep true to one's vision of art and credo of belief.

Luis, however, transcended the expected. He evolved as a self-taught Chicano sculptor with roots grounded in his spiritual homelands of both Spain and Mexico, and in the mythical Chicano homeland of Aztlán. He also took significant inspiration from the original forms and colors of Henry Moore and Alexander Calder and the unbounded vision of Pablo Picasso. He learned his craft by learning his craft. As he moved into his own expression, his work deepened and its roots took stronger hold.

It was no easy task for Luis, moving those sometimes interminable miles through the invisible membrane that existed between Agua Fría, Santa Fe, and beyond. His was a giant leap of hope, perseverance, sheer will. And work.

Racism has been a subtle and destructive issue in New Mexico. Even among native New Mexicans, it can be divisive. You can date this person but not that person, travel here but not there. You are a northerner or a southerner. In the north or the south, someone might call you a greaser or a spic or a mojado, and you, not the aggressor, might land in jail.

Sometimes you are made to feel like an immigrant, an outsider, and when you walk into a room, you might be the only Chicano, Hispano, or Latino there. And then there is the push and pull of language—the division between those who speak Spanish and are proud to be able to do so; those who can speak Spanish but don't want to; and those who understand but can't speak Spanish, resent those who can, or are embarrassed by it.

Every day, one crosses liminal spaces of culture and language.

There were—and still are—so many borders to navigate in this New Mexican world within a world in which Luis became a visionary contemporary Chicano artist. Beyond the borders of his home state, in the art world at large, the Slumpy Mexican phase of art, with its cultural denigration and tacky stereotypes, has featured countless poor and overheated Mexicanos, their faces hidden under the wide brims of enormous sombreros, taking a siesta next to a large saguaro. Tired? Yes. Lazy? Of course. Poor? Naturally. From one overused stereotype to another—if not the Slumpy Mexican then the battered, overextended Frida Kahlo and the weary Guadalupe, the Mother of a Thousand Forms. These images have often been lumped into miscast motifs of Mexican/New Mexican/indigenous art. They are often simplistically applied to the cultural complexities of the New Mexican mestizaje, and though rife with historical inaccuracies and continued stereotypical attachment, they are embedded nonetheless.

But Luis's work jolts us awake with its bold and truthful interpretations of the same old same old. He sidesteps categorizing and pigeonholing, creating his work knowingly, with irony, thoughtfulness, and a seriousness that is both challenging and life affirming. He takes a tongue-in-cheek stance with great humor and zest. He has moved, unapologetically and with great understanding, from being a traditional New Mexican santero to being a Sculptor Sin Fronteras, a borderless world artist whose work offers social and personal commentary to all cultures, all people.

Luis challenges viewers to look at his art and make a decision. A decision about who they are; who, in this precious world of illusion and truth, they wish to be. He asks viewers to decide how they want to live.

Viewing such powerful and sobering pieces as *Man without a Heart* (2007; Figure 3), which deals with pedophilia in the Catholic Church, we in New Mexico are deeply touched. We are reminded of the disturbing and tragic legacy of the Servants of the Paraclete, the rehabilitation center for priests in Jemez Springs that returned seriously troubled clergy to other congregations with only minimal healing and acknowledgment of their transgressions, only to have them continue their abuse. The story of Jemez and its priests is part and parcel of the dysfunctional local and global history of the Catholic Church, with its oversight, neglect, and dismissal of evil.

In another brave and powerful sculpture on the subject, *See No Evil, Hear No Evil, Say No Evil* (2011; Figure 4), Luis again confronts the abuse perpetrated by those in authority. The evil bishop sees no evil, the evil cardinal speaks no evil, and the evil priest hears no evil. This piece is reminiscent of the sad saga of New Mexican archbishop Robert Sánchez, who left the Archdiocese of Santa Fe in disgrace after being accused of having sex with young women. The clergy has too long shielded the darkness in its midst, and yet Luis's work makes us want to believe things are changing. Surely, the three roosters atop the marble mansion of religion that shelters these men will call out the truth in the light of early morning and heal the countless men, women, and children who have endured oppression at their hands.

In *Man Trapped in His Religion* (2004; Plate 34) we see a man boxed in, and bent over, by dogma. The dogma not only of Catholicism but of any religion. When will he be freed? It is a haunting rendition of spiritual pain and helplessness. What Luis has accomplished in this single piece is groundbreaking and important, particularly as he comes from an artistic and cultural tradition that in many ways has been repetitive, dependent on the past, silent and constrained in the stranglehold of religious beliefs. This jarring and unforgettable sculpture is a masterpiece.

The spirit behind all art calls out to the artist to interpret the seemingly uninterpretable, to link the divine to the human. With searing humanity, in the work *Camino de sueños* (2015; Plate 47), Luis chose to follow the devastation of man's cruelty to other

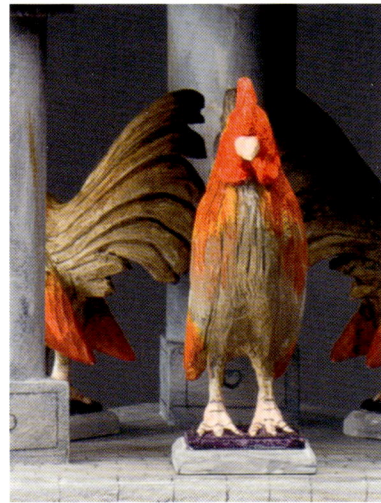

See No Evil, Hear No Evil, Say No Evil (detail), 2011; see page 26.

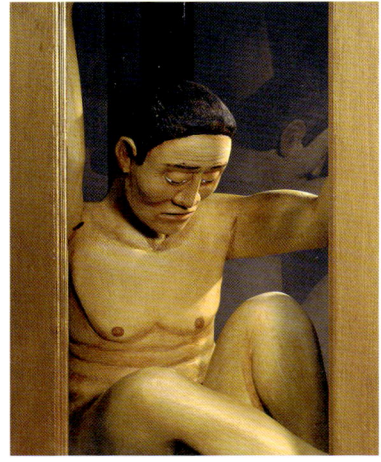

Man Trapped in His Religion (detail), 2004; see page 138.

men, women, and children. Luis shows the woman's abandoned handbag, the child's teddy bear, the man's battered huarache made from woven leather. He reflects, as the buitre does with his dark vulture's eye, on the names of Los Desaparecidos, those disappeared and lost and dead in the desert. A bottle of water and a dried holy card can't help but escape the bony hand of La Muerte, who waits on the Cross of Cactus. Ironically, Luis calls this crushing piece the Road of Dreams.

Meanwhile, *Virgen del camino de sueños* (2016; Plate 54) shoulders her countless lost children: the vato loco, the pachuco y pachuca, the cholo and the cholitas, the indigenous, the Spanish, the Mexican, the young and the old. Each face is a precious incarnation of humanity. It was Our Lady of Guadalupe who said to Juan Diego: "Am I not here who am your Mother?" In Luis's interpretation, the Divine Mother's back is strong enough to carry the world's children. She sees the skeletal Juan Diego, now a saint, through his death as well, desiccated roses gracing his remains.

In a less somber sculpture, *Juan Diego* (2015; Plate 48), the careworn, fragile, and humble nativo is wonderfully transformed into a modern-day vato de esos, a dude from the vecindad. You know him: he's young and old, todo tatuado with his cerveza in hand, wearing his black Guadalupe T-shirt looking a lo todo—you know, tranquilo. La Guadalupe always has m'ijo's back, and he knows that is a great blessing. For she is the mother of her mestizo son, and she will always be there, en la buenas y en las malas, in the good and in the bad times.

In *Pachuco Way* (2016; Plate 52), Luis takes the dude from the vecindad back to the earlier era of the pachuco. Pachuco culture had its origins in Ciudad Juárez, Chihuahua, Mexico, in the 1940s. It was made popular by iconic comedian, singer, and actor Tin Tán and later immortalized by the mainstream film *Zoot Suit,* from a play by Chicano playwright Luis Valdez. In this sculpture, Luis captures the bravado, endurance, and boundless chispa, the spark of life energy, of the Chicano/Mexicano, who once again flaunts who he is. ¡Órale! OK. All right. Así es. That's how it is. You got a problem?

Luis's pachuco has it all: the stride, the walk, the attitude, and the traje, a costume like no other. He is Firme. Solid. Steady. Stable. Resolute.

Firme. Like the artist himself.

"We are historians," Luis says in a phone interview so private and personal that I felt I was in confession. "My work stands for itself." I think I talked more than he did, and for this I am sorry. But Luis inspires anyone to drag out the stories and share them.

The Chicano slang term "con safos"—C/S for short—literally means "with respect." It is used as a seal, an imprimatur, on one's work, like saying "amen." Luis's art makes an equally definitive statement in which we learn about our past, see the present, and dream of a better future. He is a sculptor who presents us with options and ways of seeing political and societal issues, even as we consider with humor or pain the rucas and rucos in our own familias. They are our boyfriends, our girlfriends, our loves, but ay, sometimes it's hard to love them! ¡Por Dios! Our neighborhood is on display in all its beauty and ugliness! ¡Caray! Luis offers us a thoughtful, intense, and reflective look at what is. So wake up, cabrones!

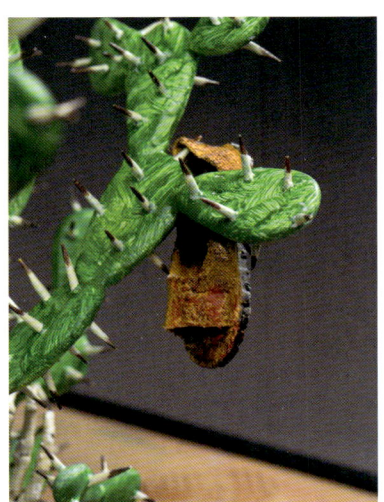

Camino de sueños (detail), 2015; see page 162.

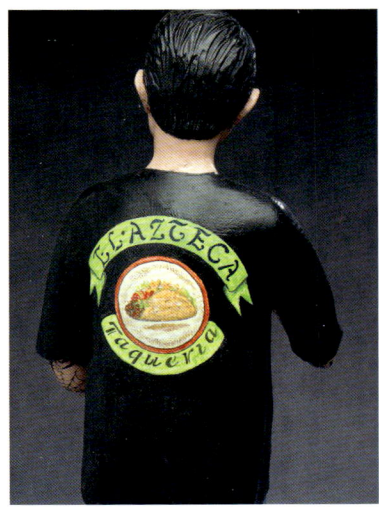

Juan Diego (detail), 2015; see page 164.

Luis's work encourages us to look long and hard and lovingly at our neighbors, friends, and familia. We might see a little bit of ourselves locked in the wooden altar of our beliefs. Our hearts throb and burn with understanding and rock and roll with laughter at his surprising wit and wisdom. While the work is deeply subjective and personal, the horizon of social commentary is always there; it allows us to grow taller and see farther as we stand in the landscape of our understanding.

Luis's credo is life. It is the blessing we have all been given to hold. "Life is a gift and we are challenged to give back. I have a beautiful life," he says with a sanctity and gratitude that I understand.

When asked about the future of his work, Luis reflects on his long and hard-fought creative journey. When he exhibited at Spanish Market forty years ago, there were maybe thirty artists. Now there are hundreds. While Luis no longer exhibits there, he understands the creative impetus that Spanish Market gave him and how it uplifts and supports upcoming and seasoned artists alike.

"New Mexico will never lose its artistic soul. I see the traditional work, and it is good that artists are educating themselves and other people," he says. "For many, Spanish Market is an opportunity for artists to support themselves financially and to make their work known."

Luis forged his way in a sometimes provincial, very traditional, and often restrictive New Mexico. Thankfully for all of us, he rose up and found his true calling. He created a unique vision that has greatly impacted many—not only those from New Mexico and the Southwest but those who seek expression of the unformed, untold story of the world: the student, the educator, the art lover, those who have stayed, those who have gone away, those still to return, those yet to be born.

There is no greater legacy for a man than the power of his creation. Luis gives ánimo to those who doubt their ability to testify to their truth. He gives energy, encouragement, hope, and above all courage, the ultimate blessings of a great artist.

Luis is of his times, of all times. No better compliment can be given to an artist who knows who he is, where he comes from, and, yes, where he is going. Firme. A todo dar. Así es.

An acknowledgment because it is necessary: I want to thank Luis Tapia for sharing his art, spirit, and a few tequilitas in this fortunate confessional. It was my great honor to revisit our times, here and there, with this true brother, hermano de veras. Long live El Noa Noa!

—Denise Chávez. C/S.

OPPOSITE
Pachuco Way (detail), 2016; see page 172.

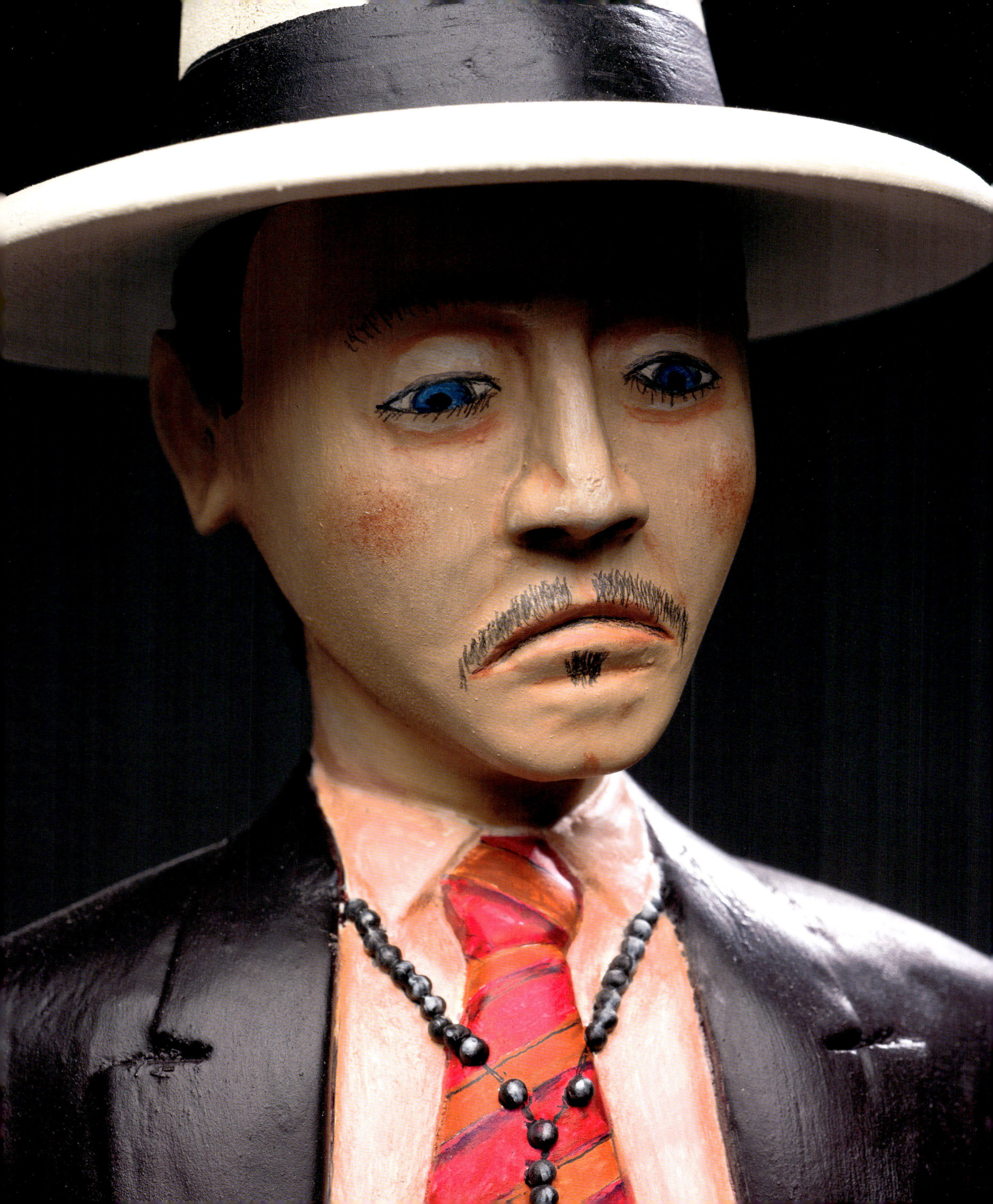

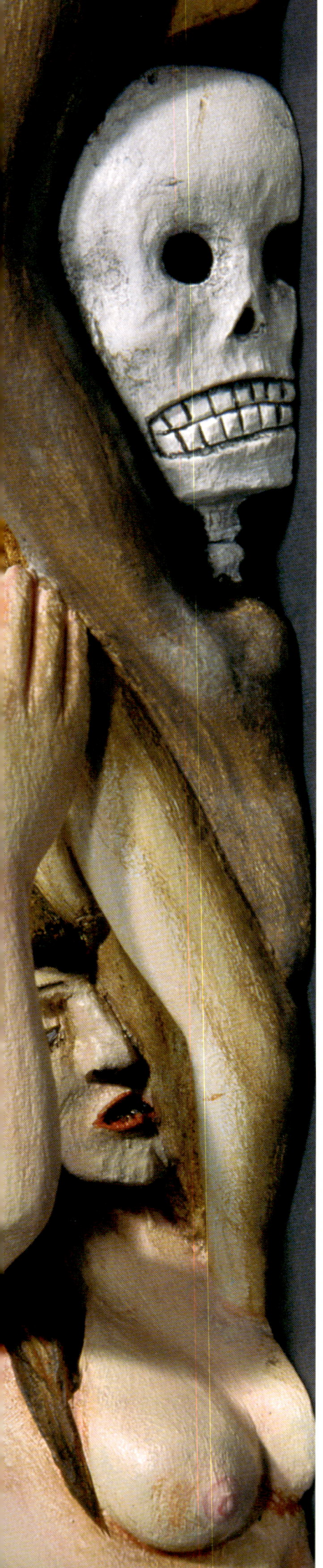

Luis observes. Luis ponders.

Life triumphs. Tradition lives.

—James Moore, Former Director, Albuquerque Museum

Borderless
The Art of Luis Tapia

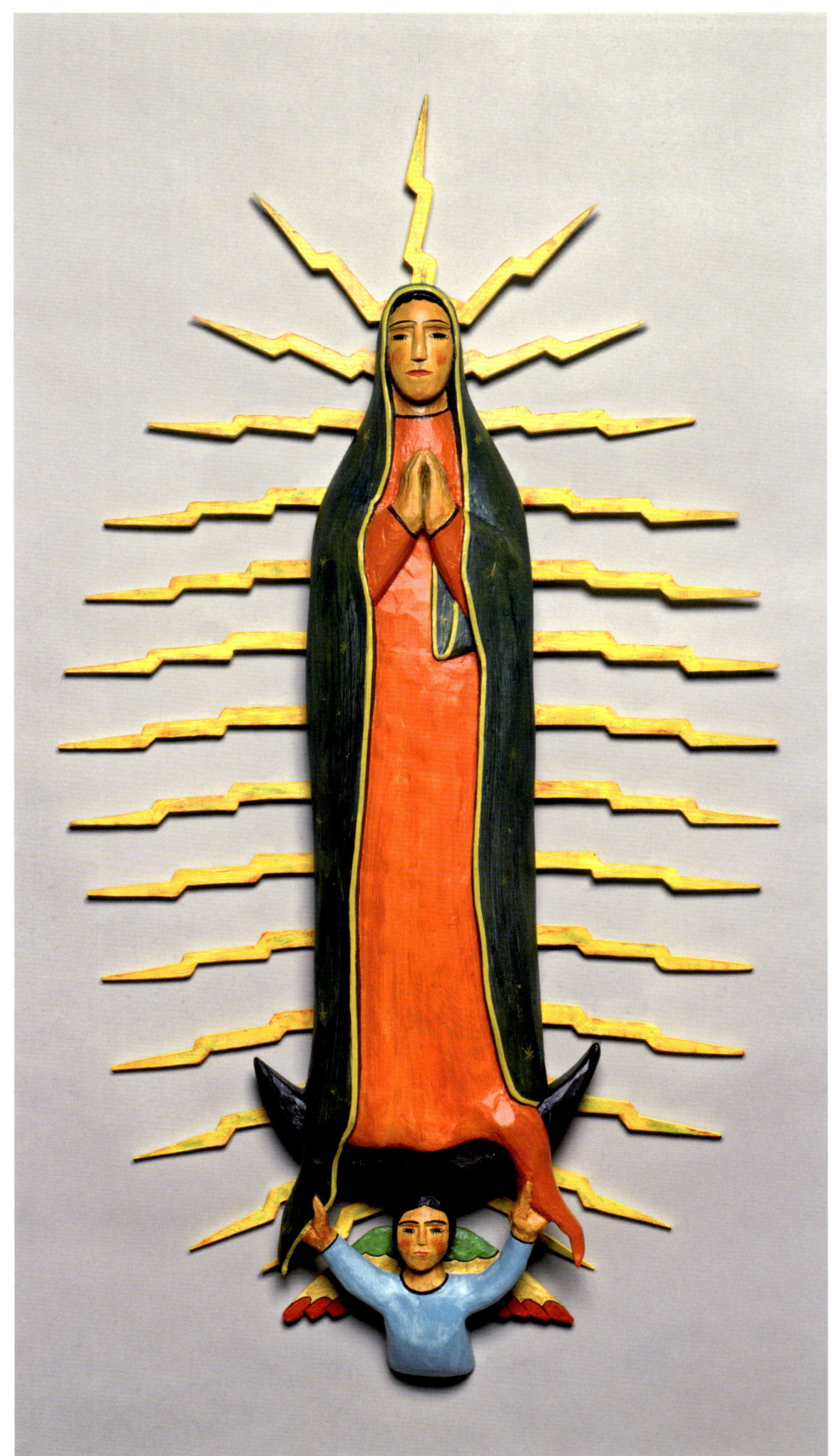

Plate 1. *Nuestra Señora de Guadalupe*, 1991. Carved and painted wood, 35 x 20 x 3¾ in. Collection of Mr. and Mrs. H. Earl Hoover II. Photo © James Hart, courtesy of The Owings Gallery.

OPPOSITE
Plate 2. *Cristo*, 1991. Carved and painted wood, 38 ½ x 33 ½ x 3¾ in. Collection of Arthur and Bernadette López. Photo © James Hart, courtesy of The Owings Gallery.

PREVIOUS SPREAD
Cruz de las ánimas (detail), 2002; see page 125.

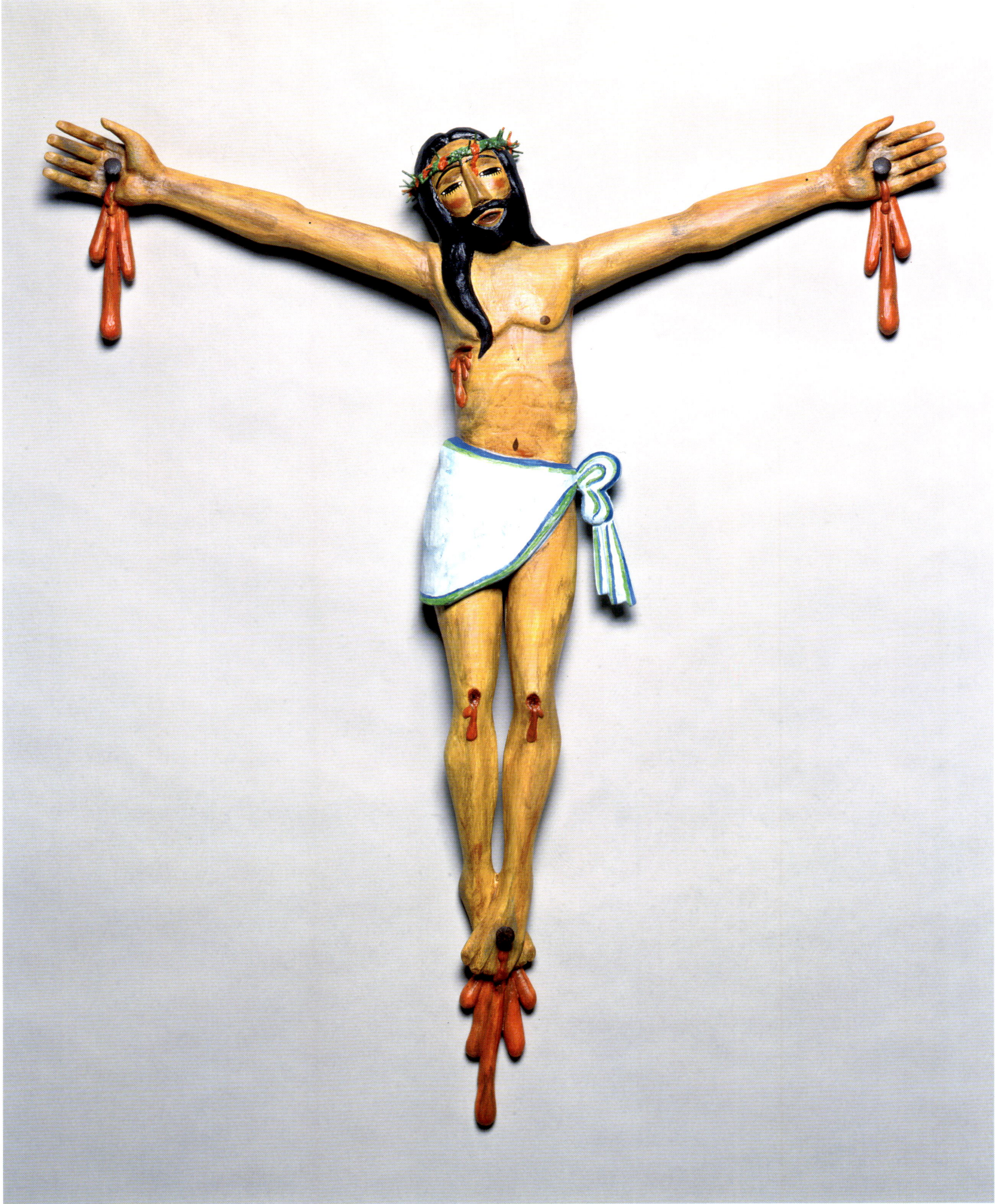

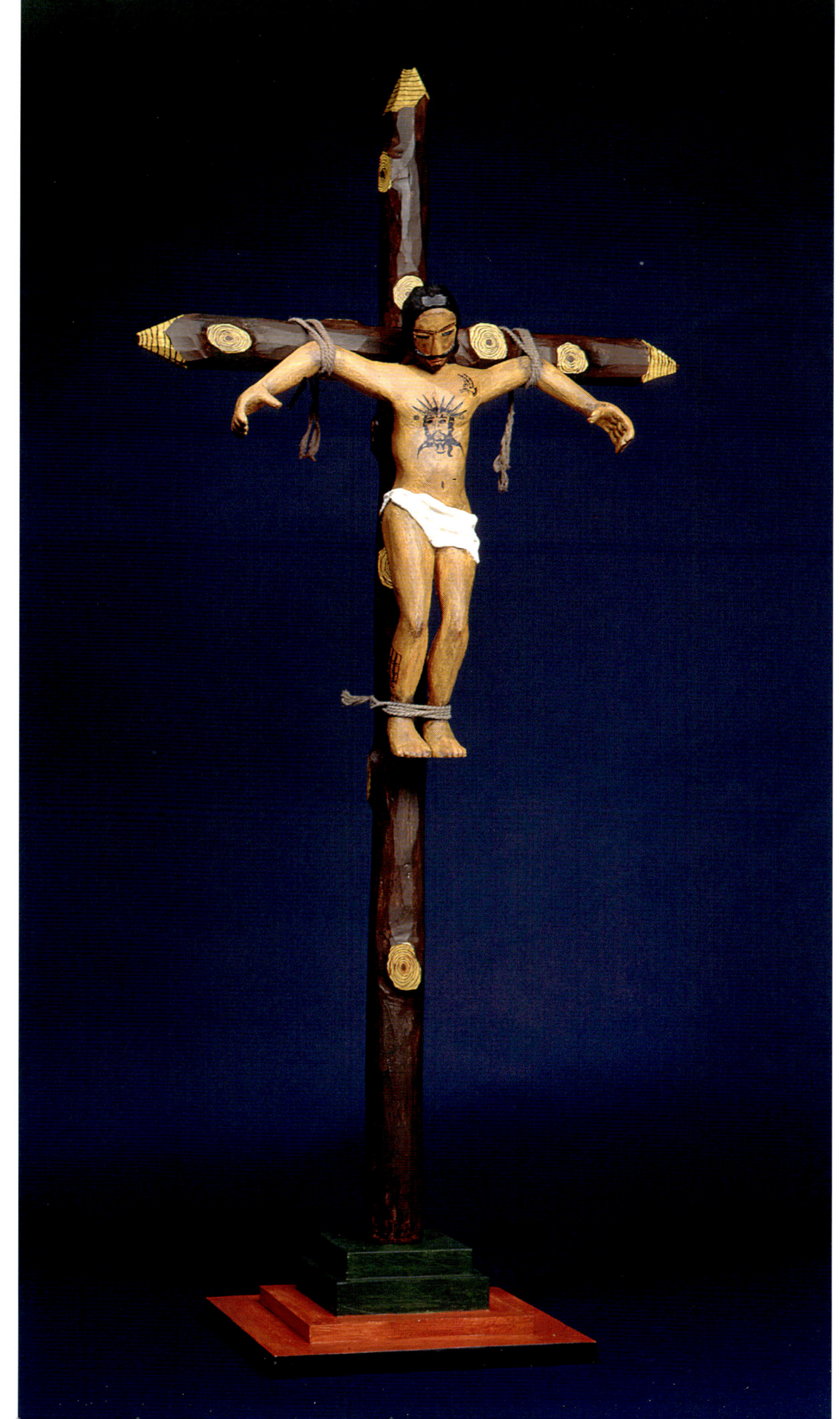

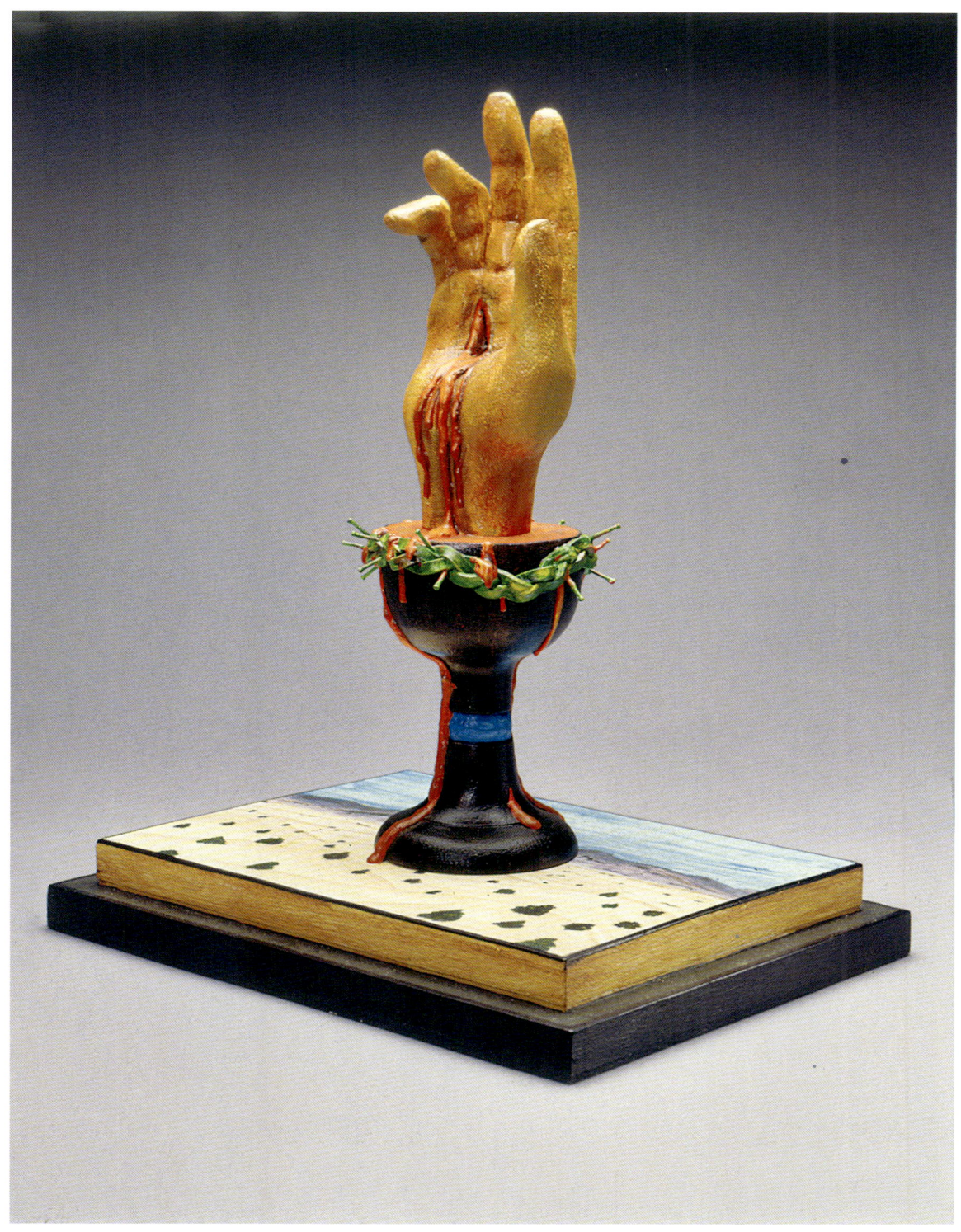

Plate 3. *San Dismas*, 1992. Carved and painted wood, 17¼ x 15⅛ x 8⅛ in.
Collection of the Spanish Colonial Arts Society, Museum of Spanish Colonial Art,
Santa Fe. Photo © Dan Morse, courtesy of The Owings Gallery.

Plate 4. *Sangre de Cristo*, 1992. Carved and painted wood, 16¾ x 15 x 11½ in.
Collection of the Spanish Colonial Arts Society, Museum of Spanish Colonial Art,
Santa Fe. Photo © Dan Morse, courtesy of The Owings Gallery.

Plate 5. *Broken Christ*, 1993. Carved and painted wood, 26 x 15¾ x 11⅜ in.
Collection of the artist. Photo © Dan Morse, courtesy of The Owings Gallery.

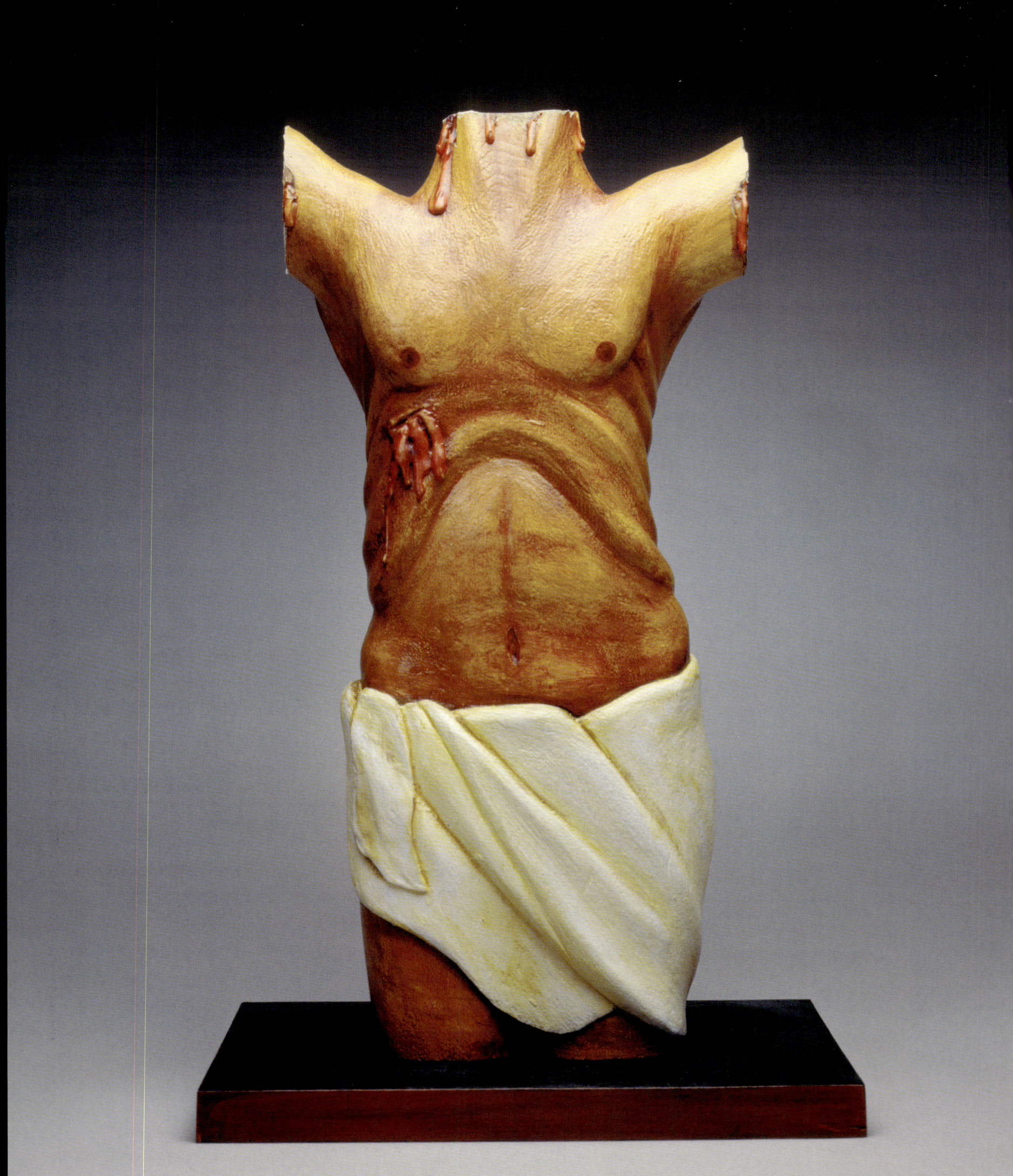

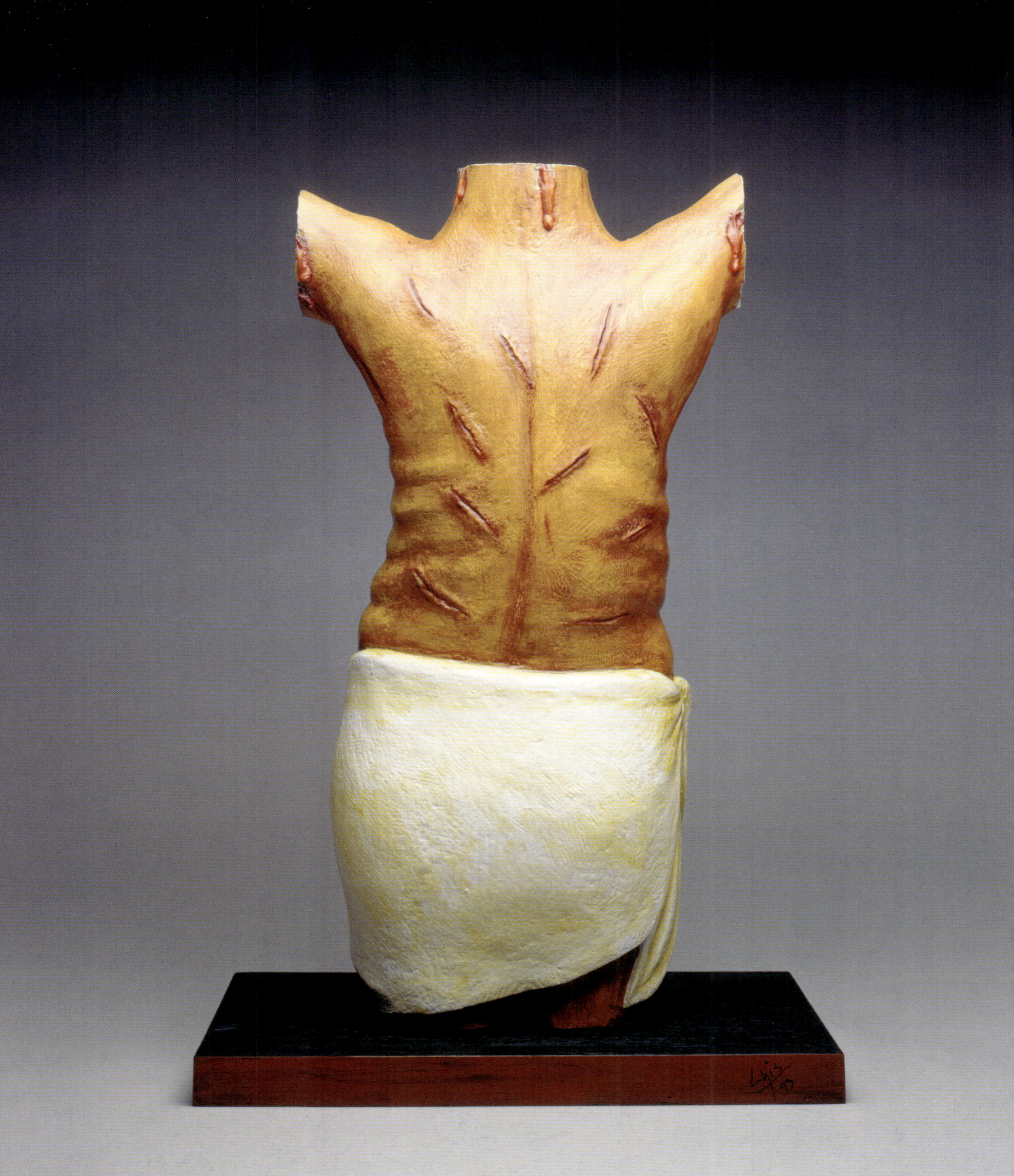

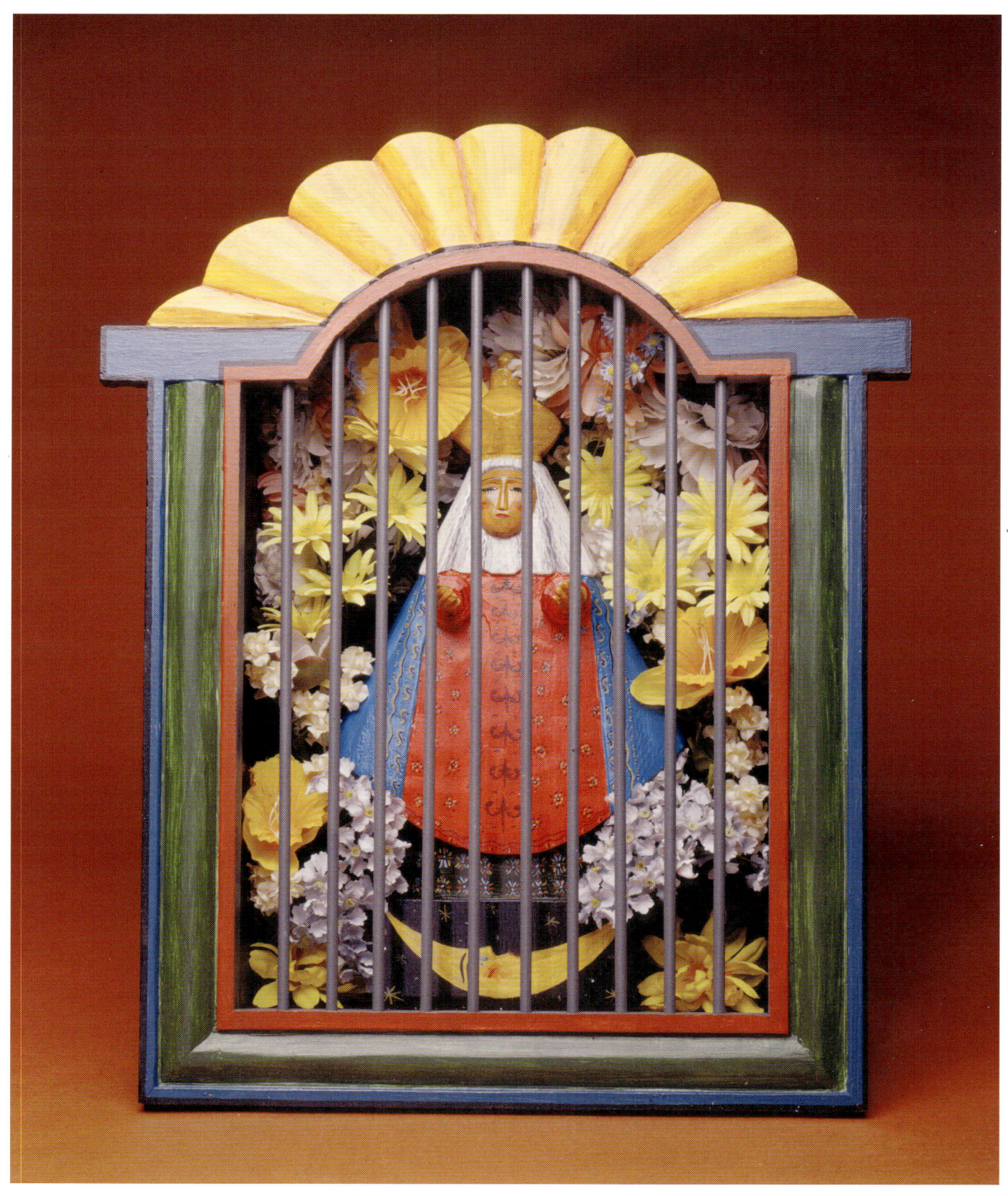

Plate 6. *Virgen de la castidad*, 1993. Carved and painted wood, cloth flowers, 21 x 15 x 6 in.
Collection of the Spanish Colonial Arts Society, Museum of Spanish Colonial Art, Santa Fe.
Photo © Dan Morse, courtesy of The Owings Gallery.

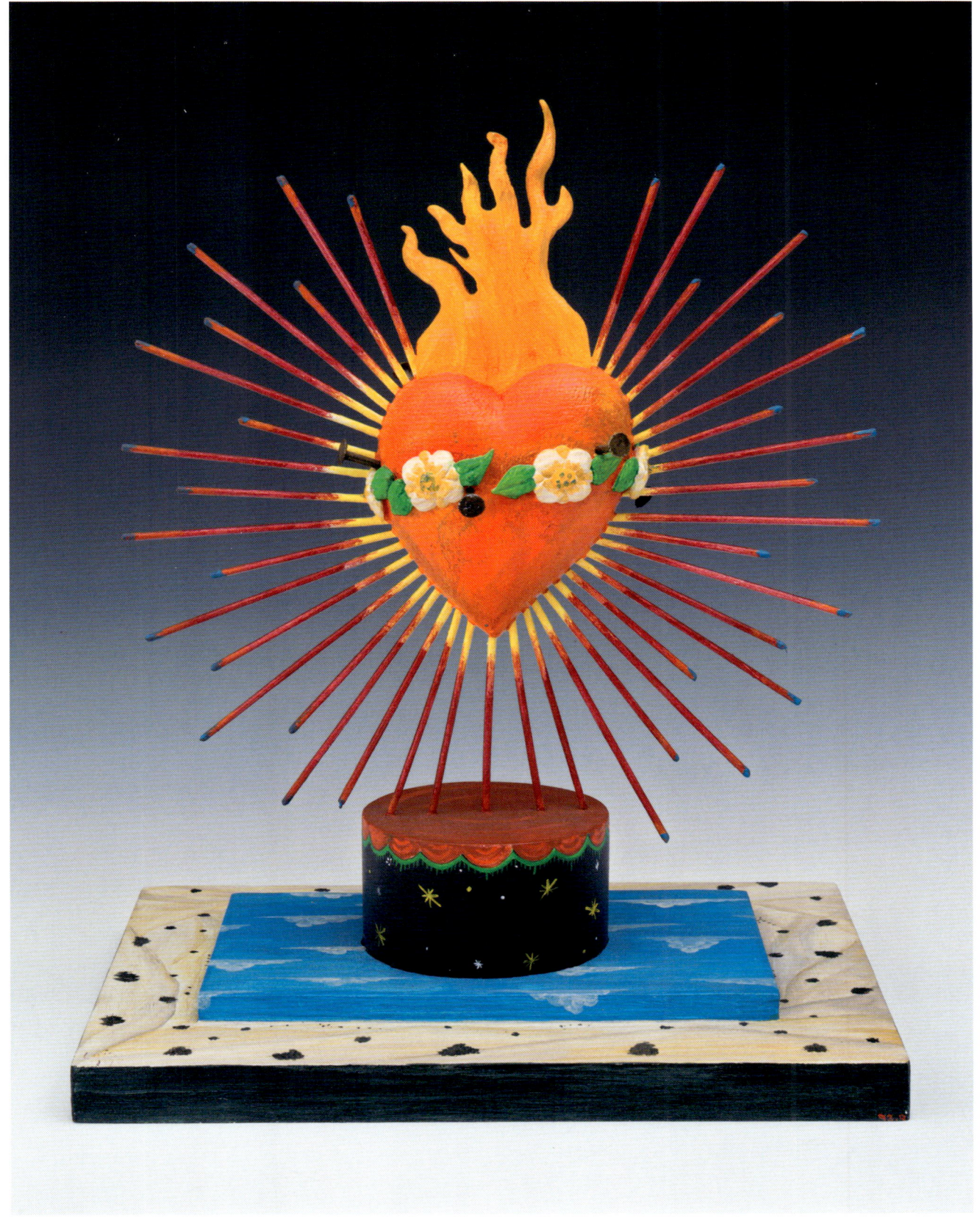

Plate 7. *Our Lady of Sorrows*, 1992. Carved and painted wood, nails, 17 3/8 x 13 7/8 x 10 in. Collection of the University of New Mexico Art Museum, Albuquerque; museum purchase with funds from the Friends of Art (93.9). Photo courtesy of Geistlight Photography, Albuquerque.

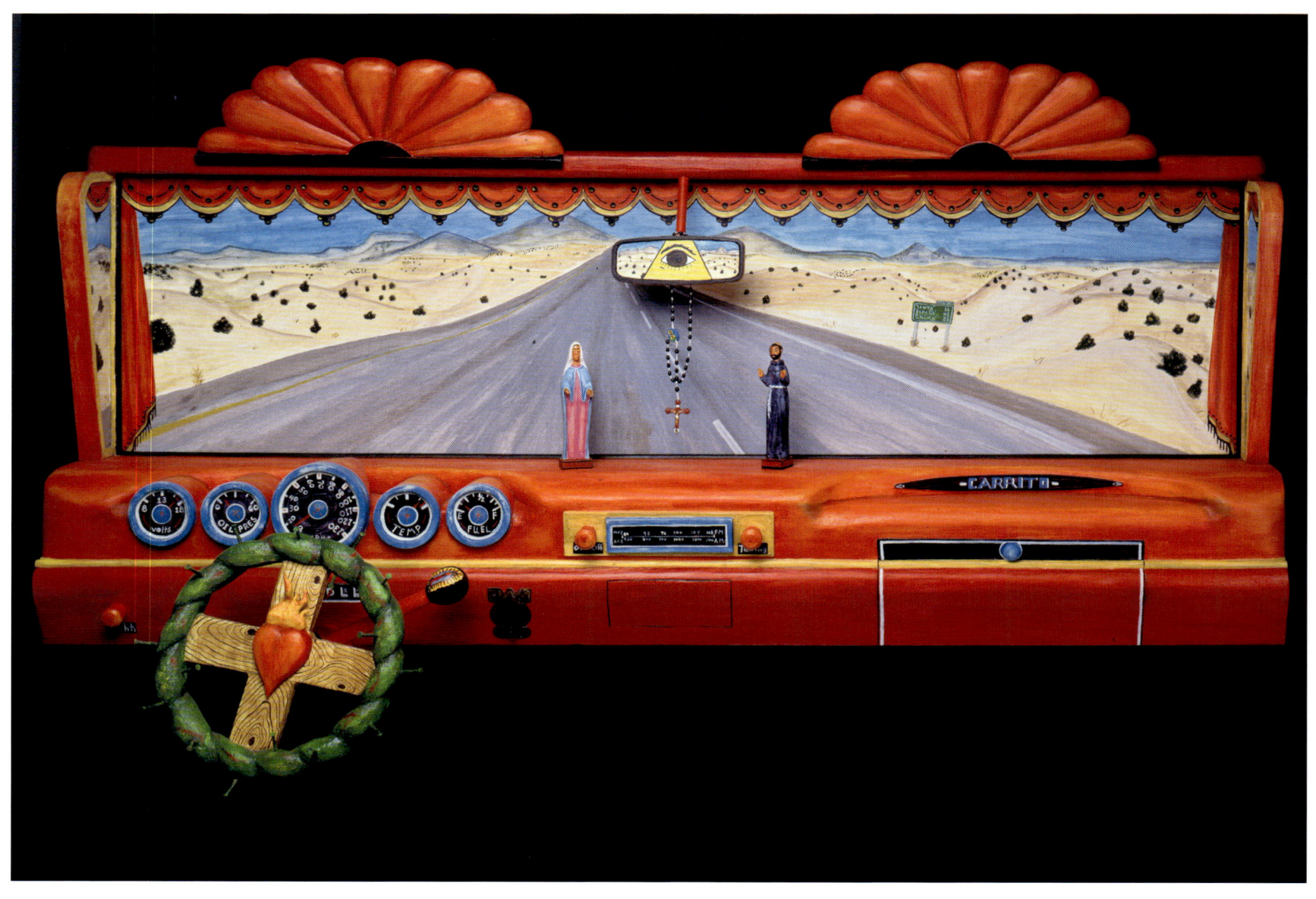

Plate 8. *Chima Altar III*, 1992. Carved and painted wood, metal, glass beads, nails, 35 x 60 x 17 in. Collection of the Albuquerque Museum; museum purchase, 1991, general obligation bonds and private donation (1992.79.1). Photo © Dan Morse, courtesy of The Owings Gallery.

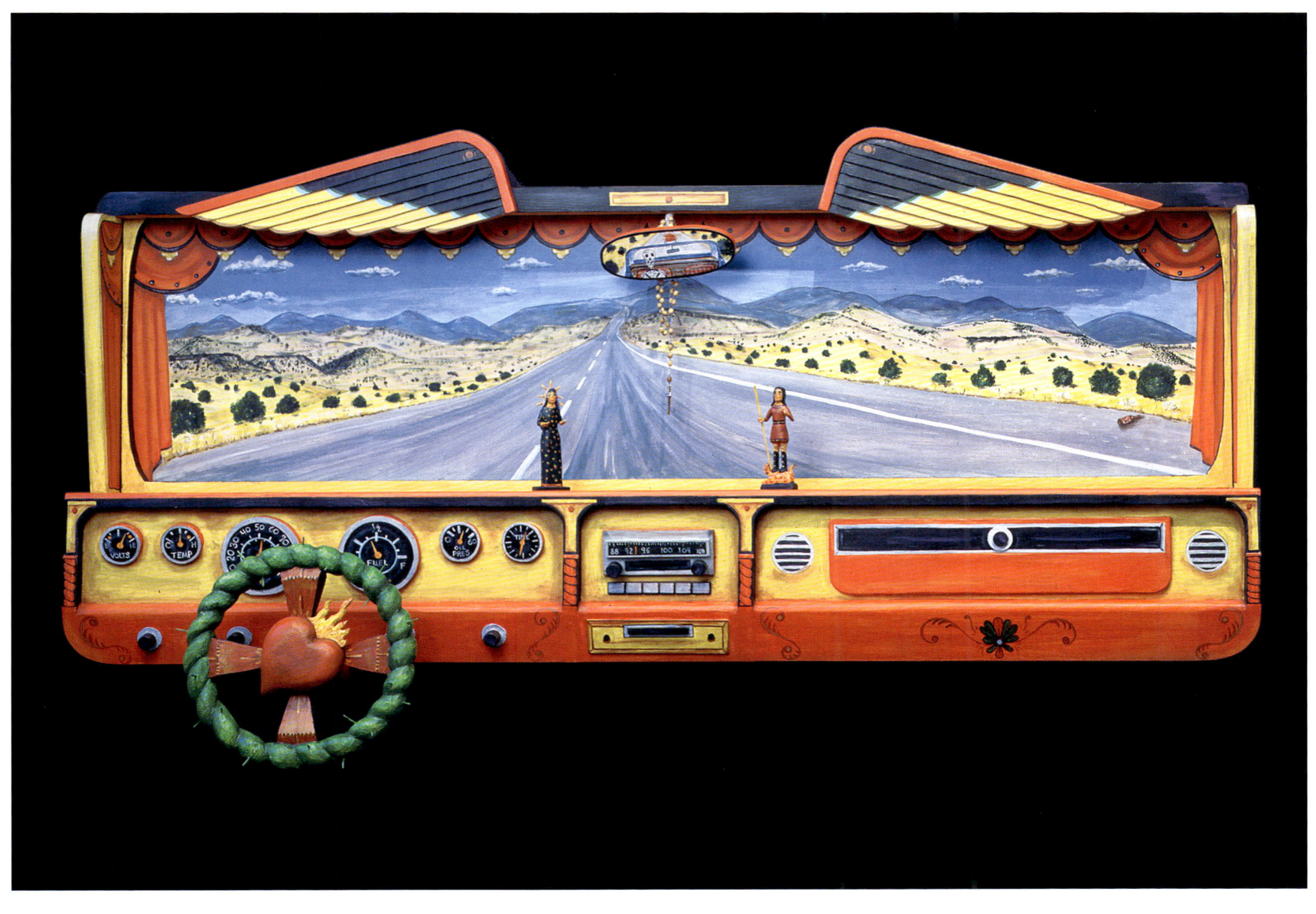

Plate 9. *Chima Altar IV*, 1994. Carved and painted wood, 24 x 60 x 12 in. Private collection.
Photo © Dan Morse, courtesy of The Owings Gallery.

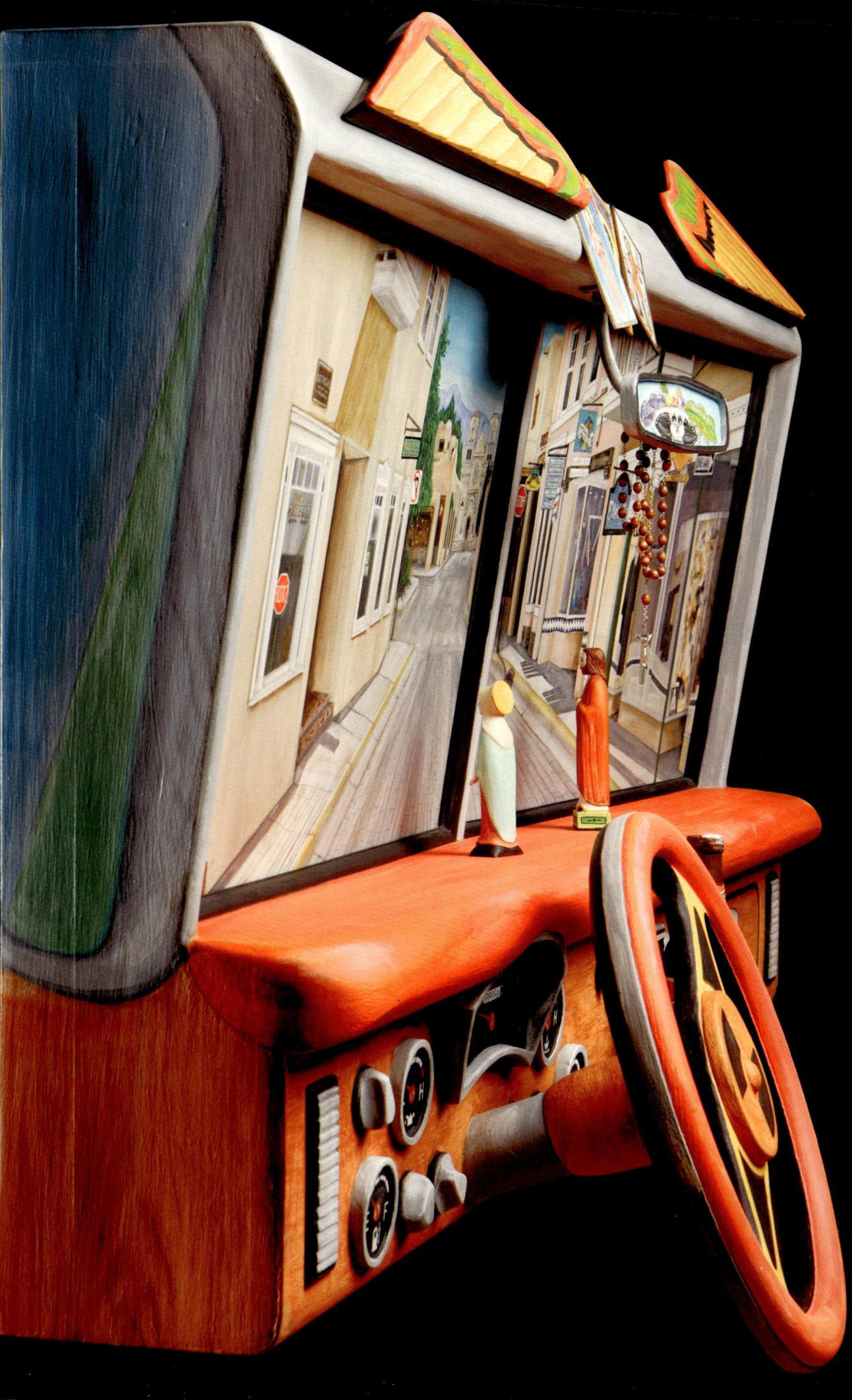

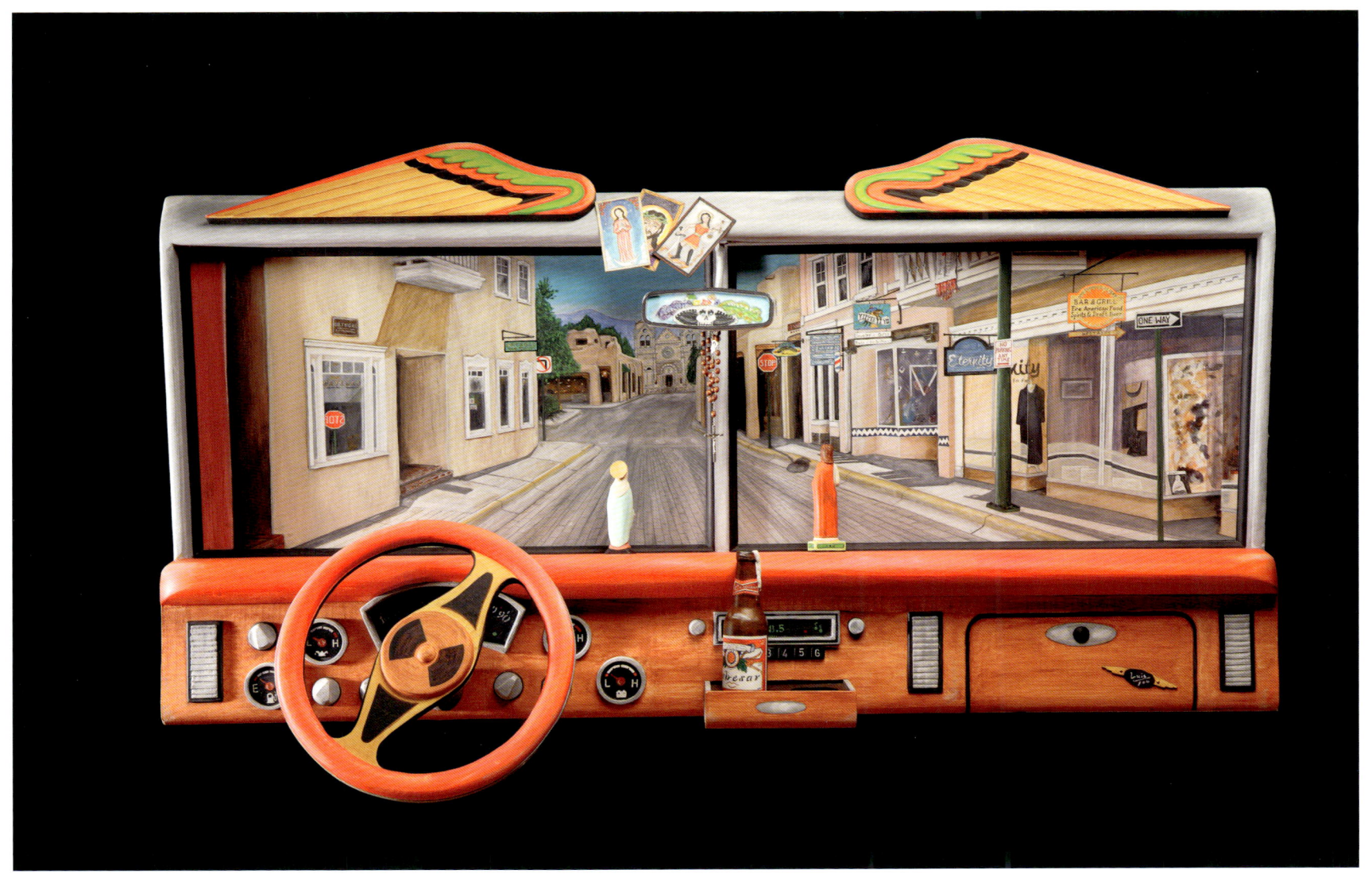

Plate 10. *Santa cruz.* 2006. Carved and painted wood, 30 x 58 x 15 in. Collection of Curt, Christina, and Jonah Nonomaque. Photo © Addison Doty, courtesy of The Owings Gallery.

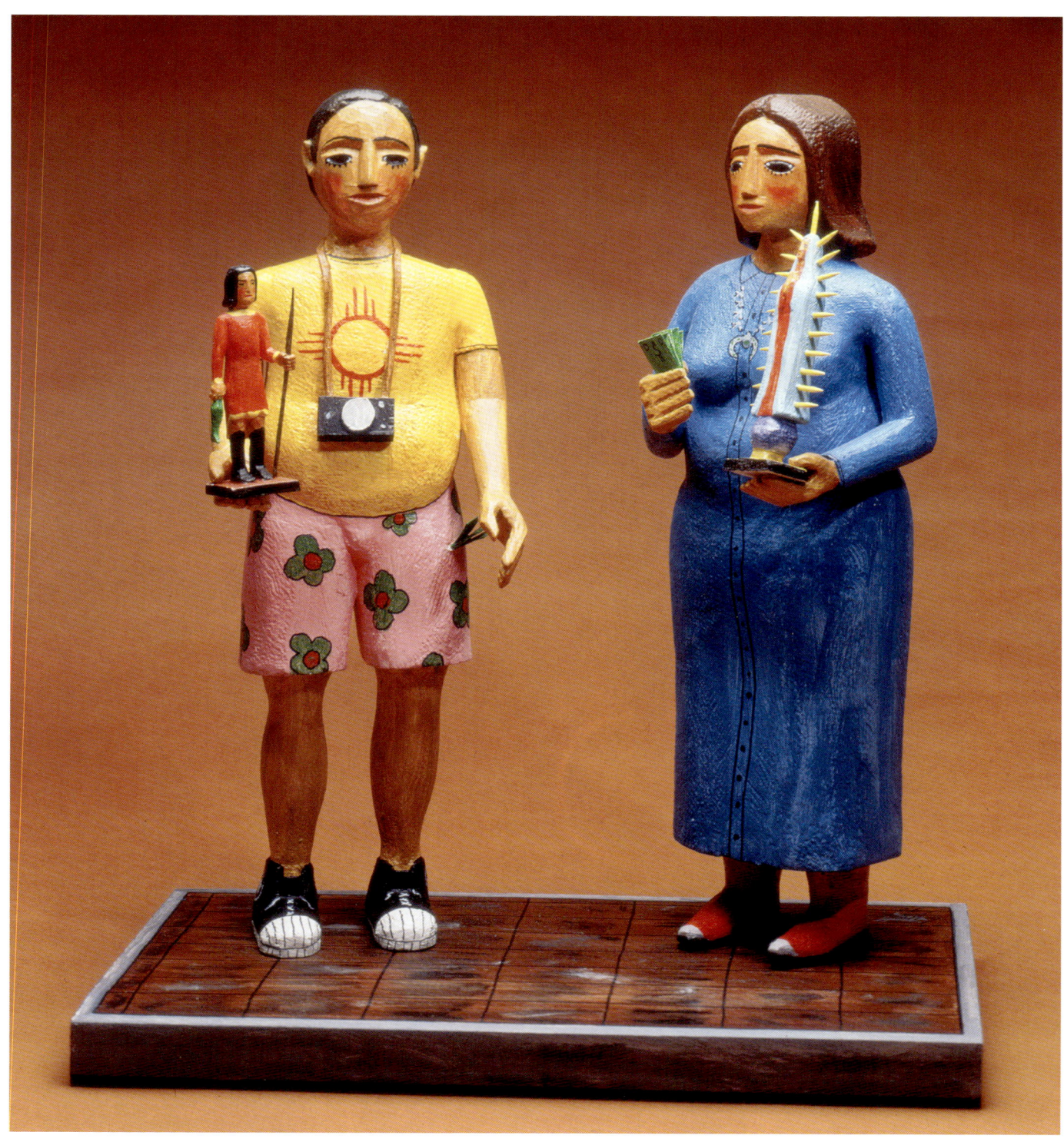

Plate 11. *The Folk Art Collectors*, 1992. Carved and painted wood, 17¼ x 15⅛ x 8⅛ in. Collection of the Spanish Colonial Arts Society, Museum of Spanish Colonial Art, Santa Fe. Photo © Dan Morse, courtesy of The Owings Gallery.

OPPOSITE
Plate 12. *¡Viva La Fiesta!* (*Zozobra*), 1996, carved and painted wood, 36 x 39 x 39 in. Collection of the New Mexico Museum of Art; museum purchase with funds from the Boeckman Acquisition Fund, 1997 (1997.8.1). Photo © Blair Clark, courtesy of The Owings Gallery.

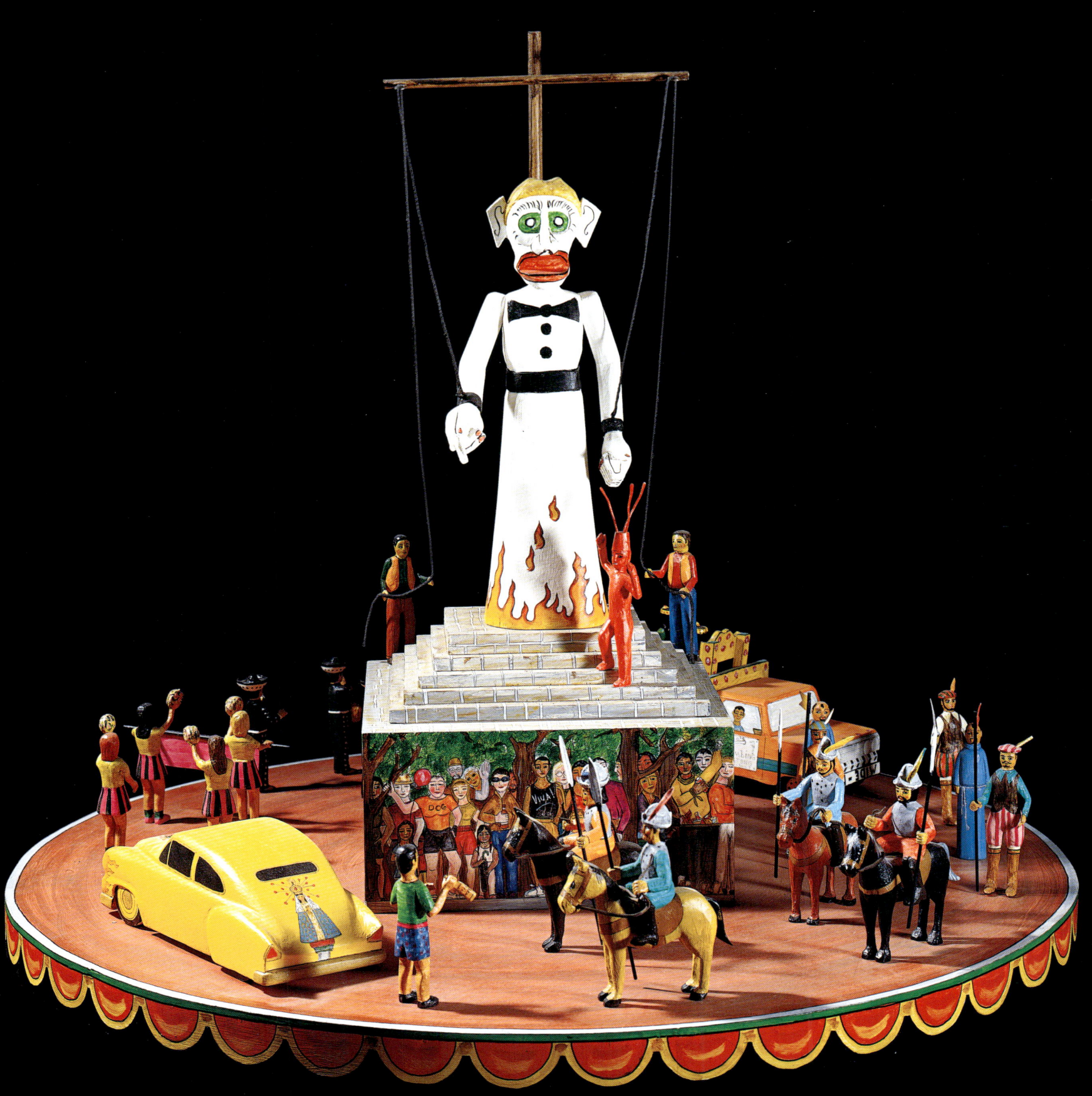

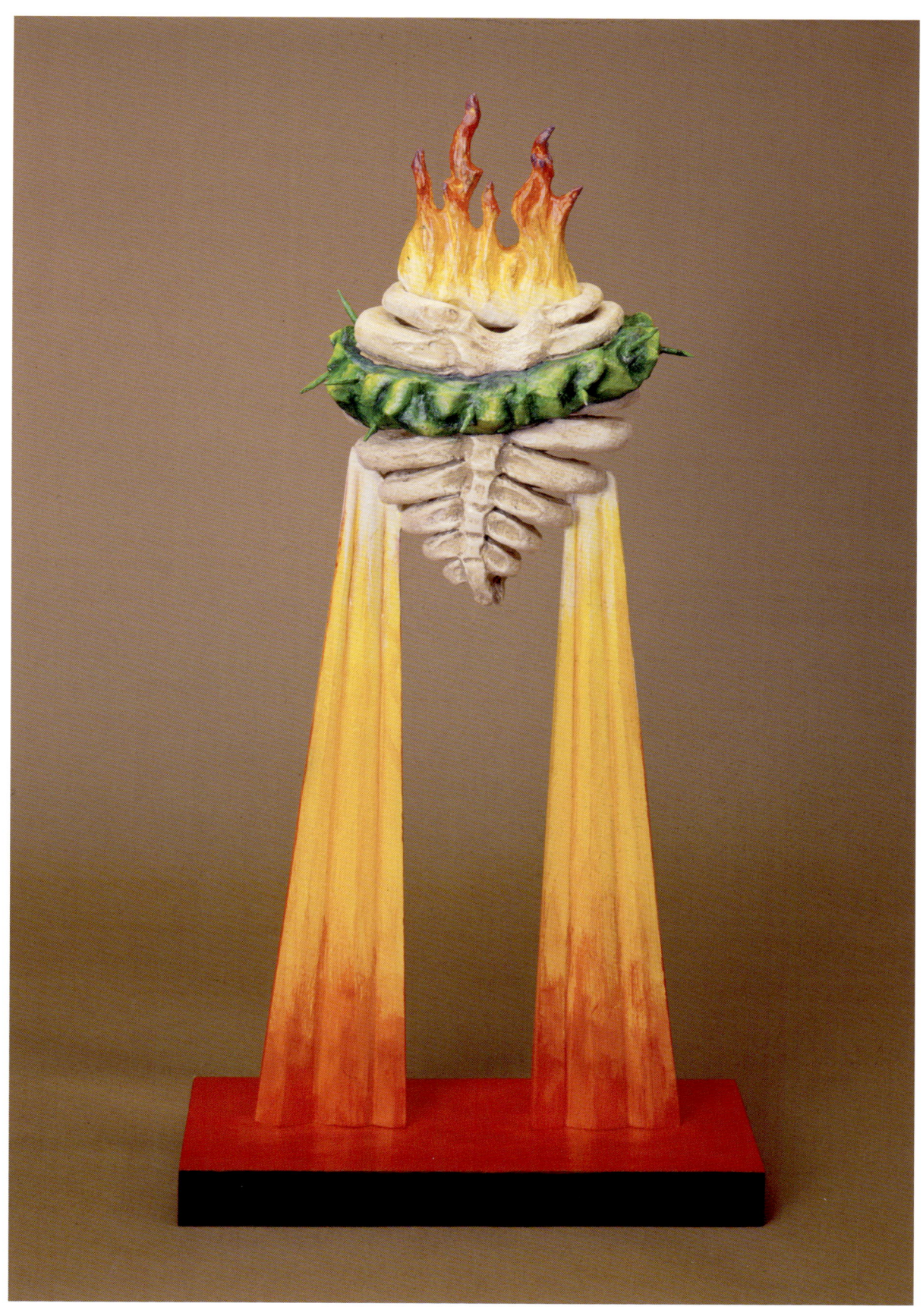

Plate 13. *The Passion of Christ*, 1996. Carved and painted wood, 23¾ x 12 x 6 in.
Private collection. Photo © Dan Morse, courtesy of The Owings Gallery.

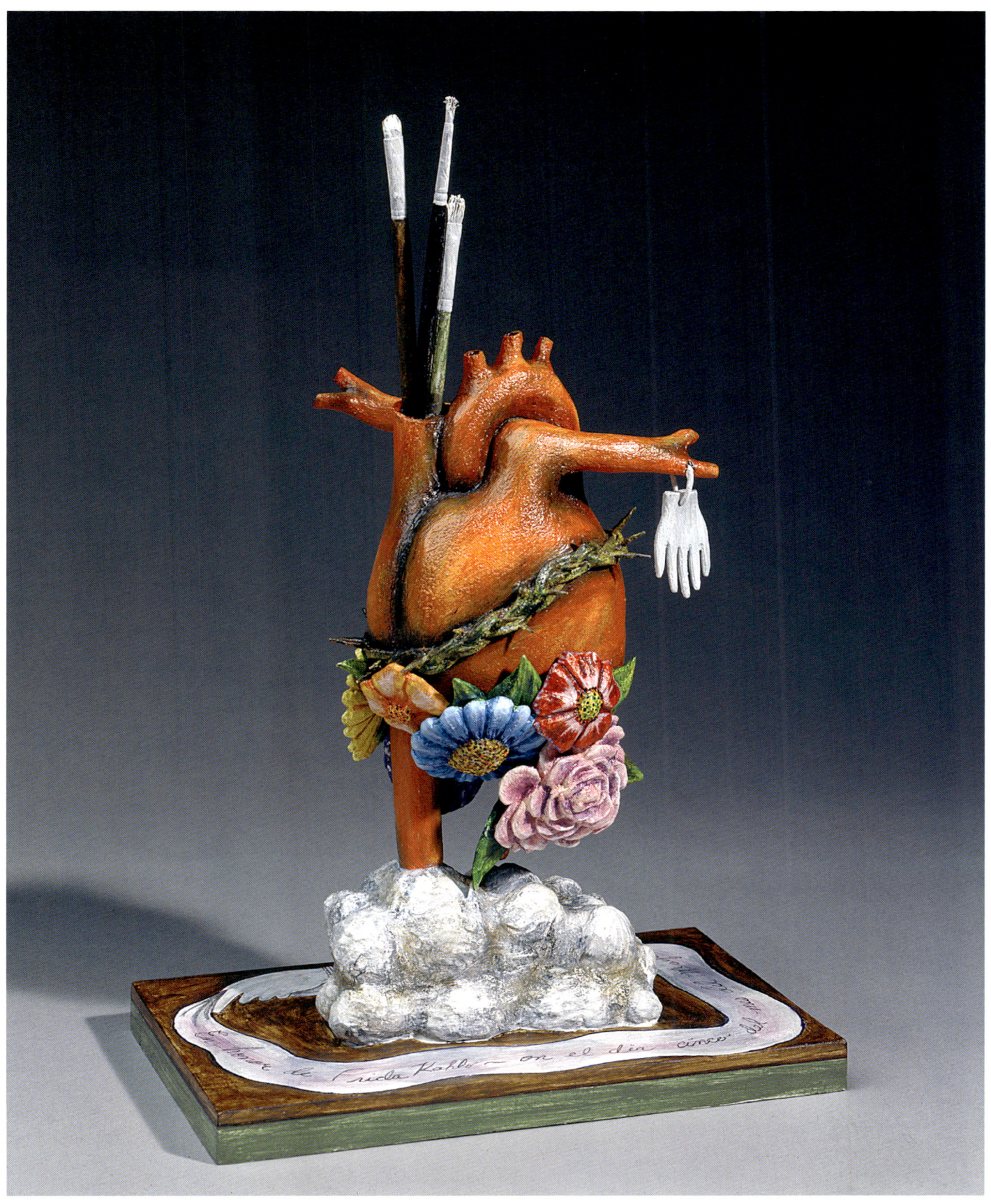

Plate 14. *En Honor de Frida*, 1999. Carved and painted wood, 16 x 10 x 6 in.
Private collection. Photo © Dan Morse, courtesy of The Owings Gallery.

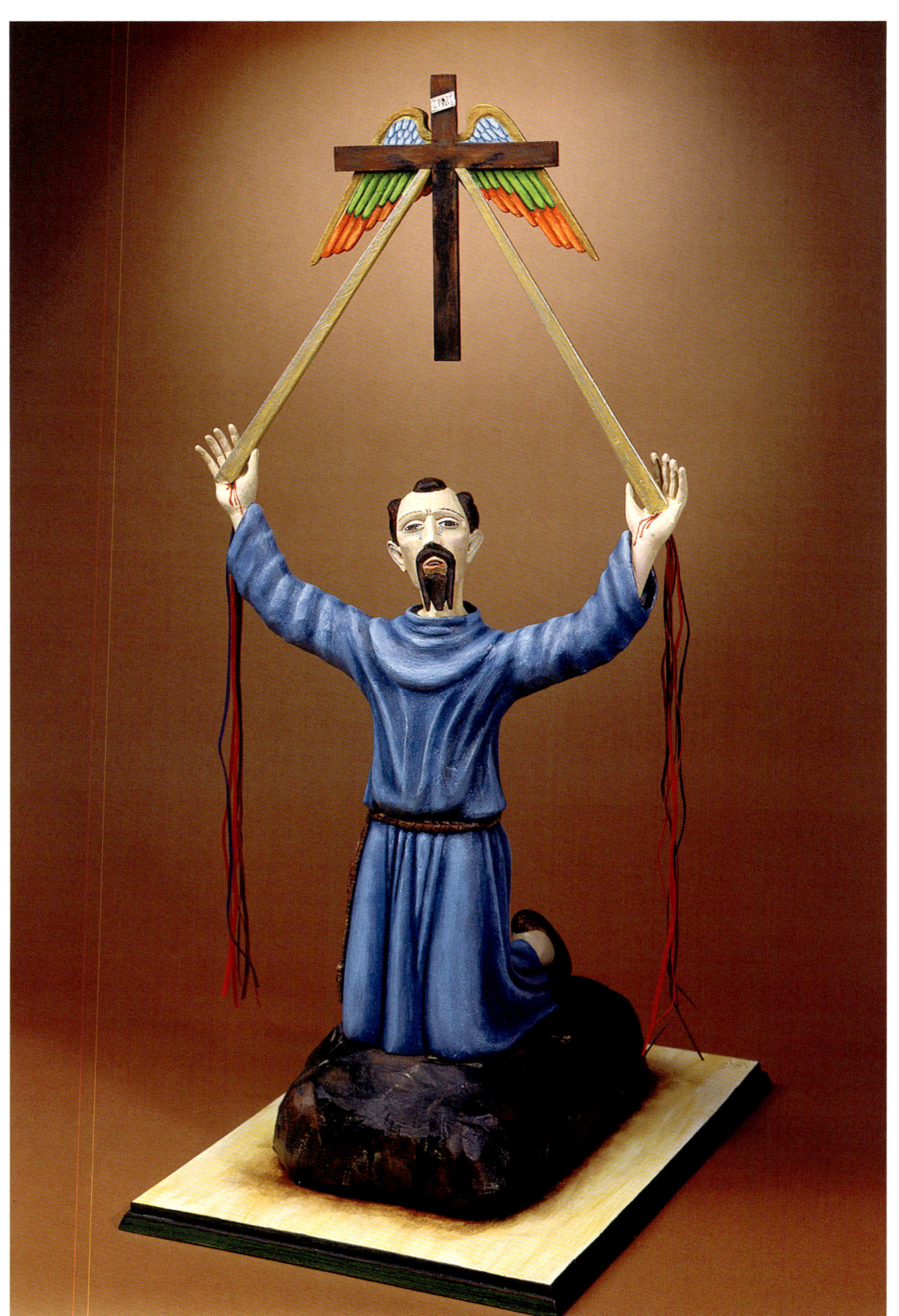

Plate 15. *Saint Francis Receives the Stigmata*, 2002. Carved and painted wood, ribbon, 33½ x 15¾ x 19 in. Denver Art Museum Collection; gift of Hope and Edward Connors (2010.500). Photo © Dan Morse, courtesy of The Owings Gallery.

OPPOSITE
Plate 16. *Earthly Temptations*, 2001. Carved and painted wood, 20½ x 17¾ x 10¾ in. Collection of the Spanish Colonial Arts Society, Museum of Spanish Colonial Art, Santa Fe. Photo © Dan Morse, courtesy of The Owings Gallery.

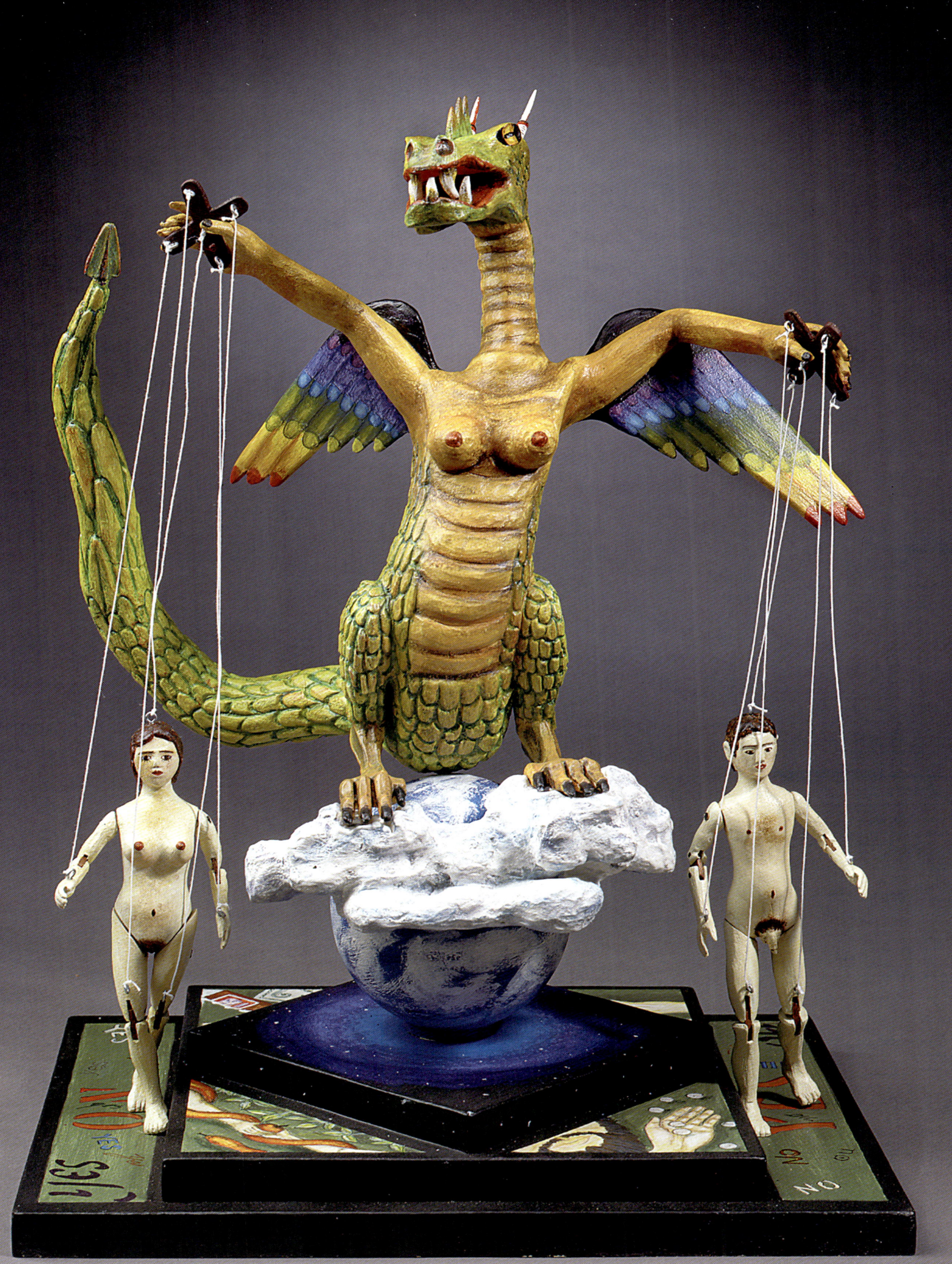

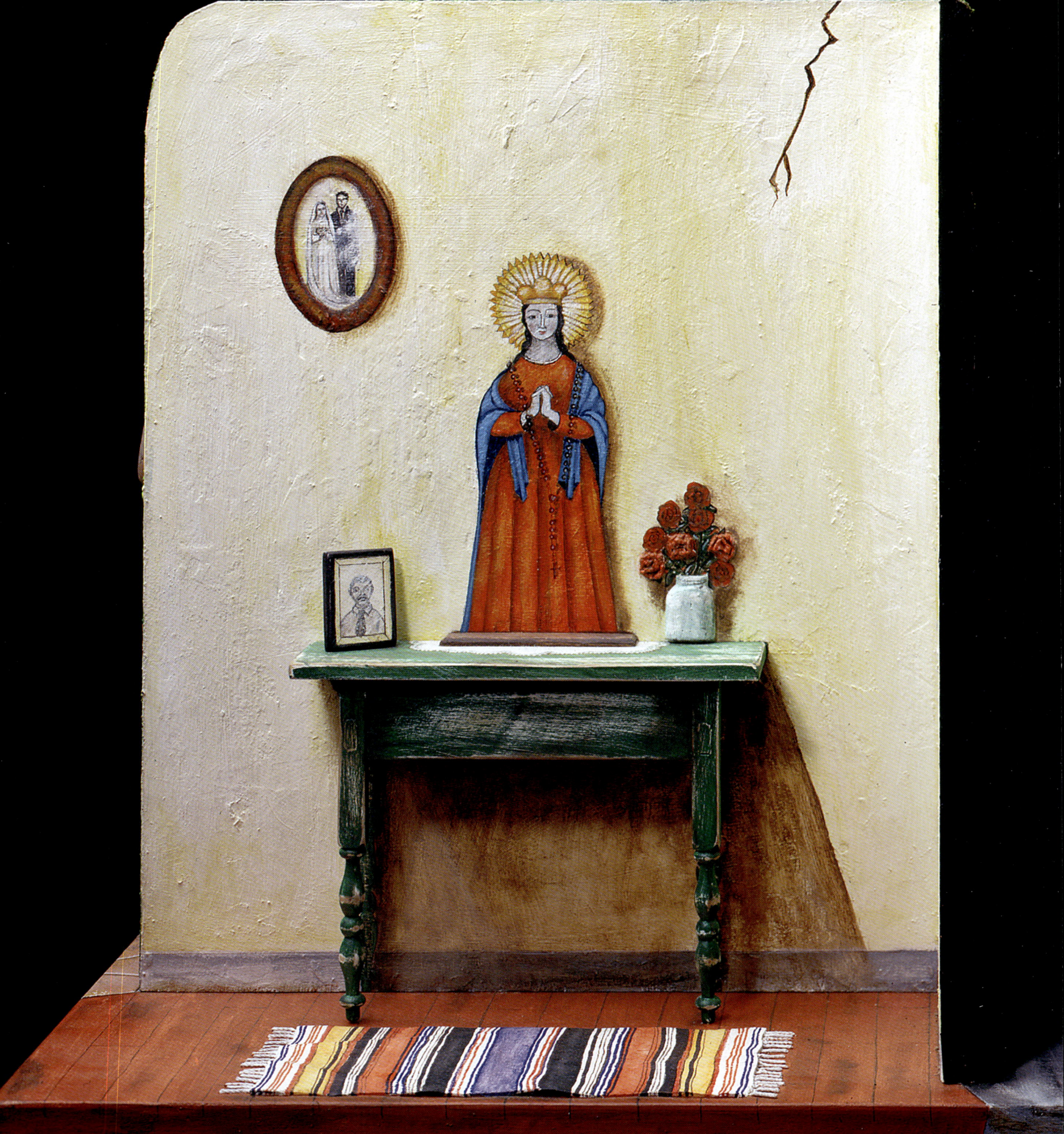

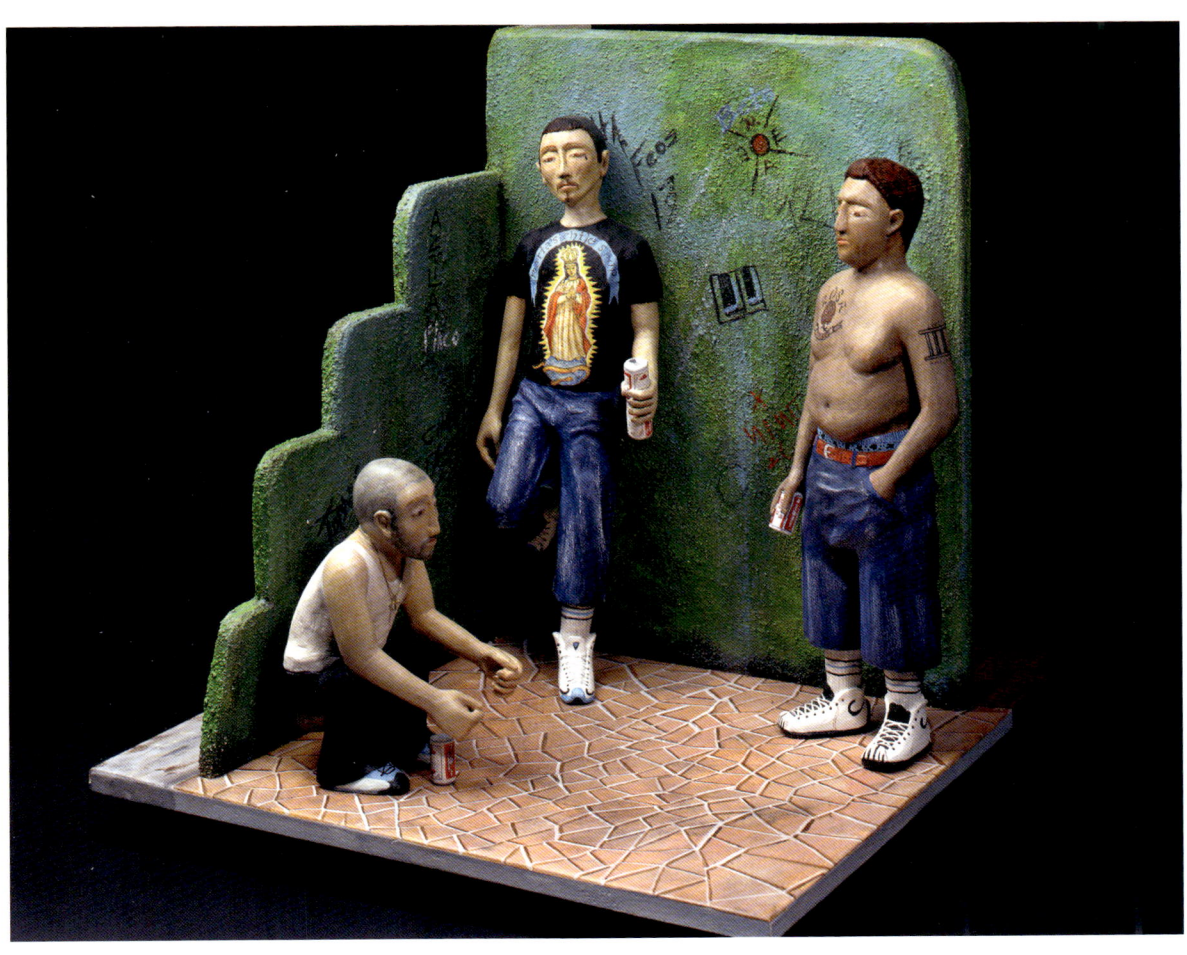

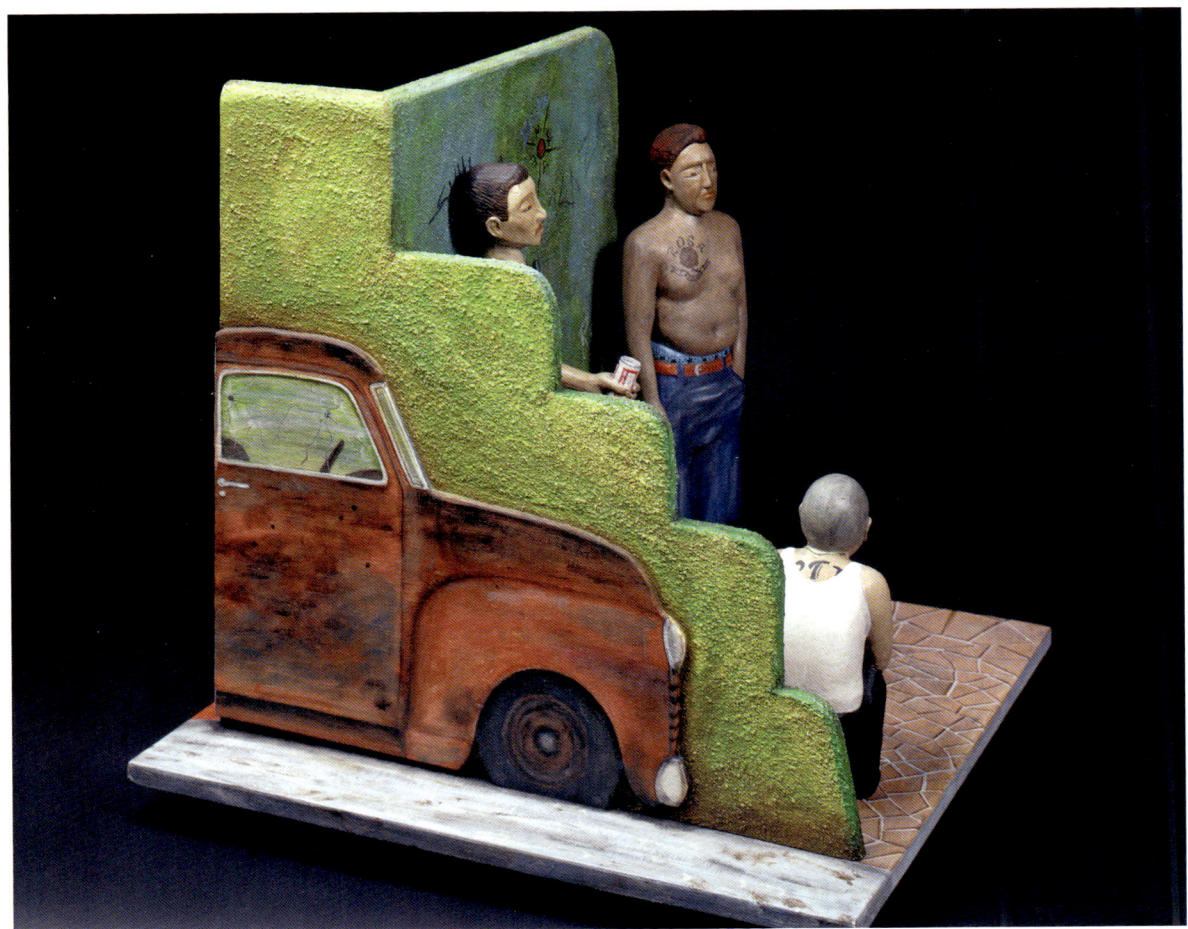

TOP, LEFT, AND OPPOSITE
Plate 17. *Untitled*, 2002.
Carved and painted wood,
21¼ x 19¾ x 21¾ in. Private
collection. Photo © Dan Morse,
courtesy of The Owings Gallery.

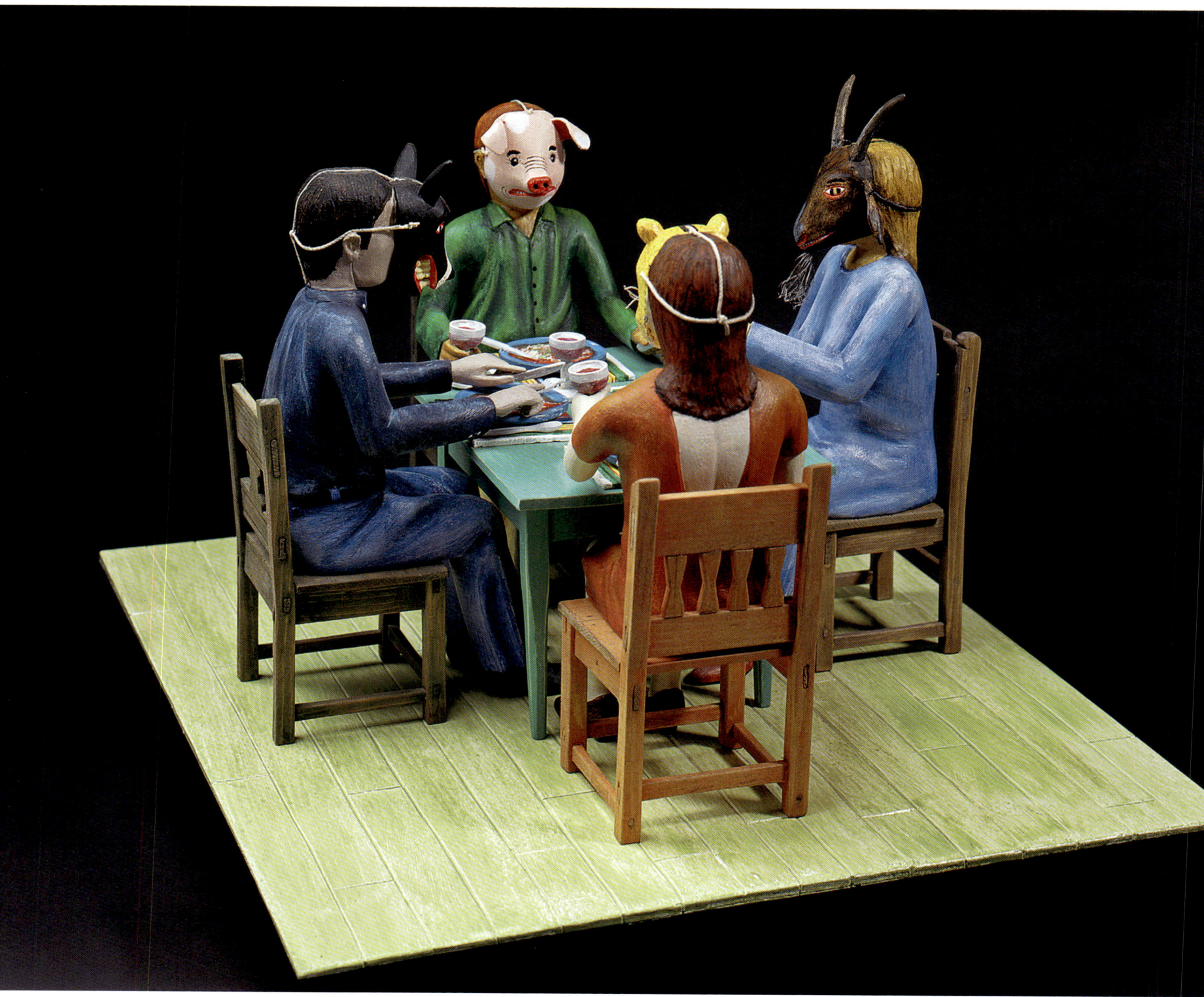

Plate 18. *Guess Who's Coming to Dinner*, 2002. Carved and painted wood,
17 ¾ x 23 x 20 ½ in. Collection of Curt, Christina, and Jonah Nonomaque.
Photo © Dan Morse, courtesy of The Owings Gallery.

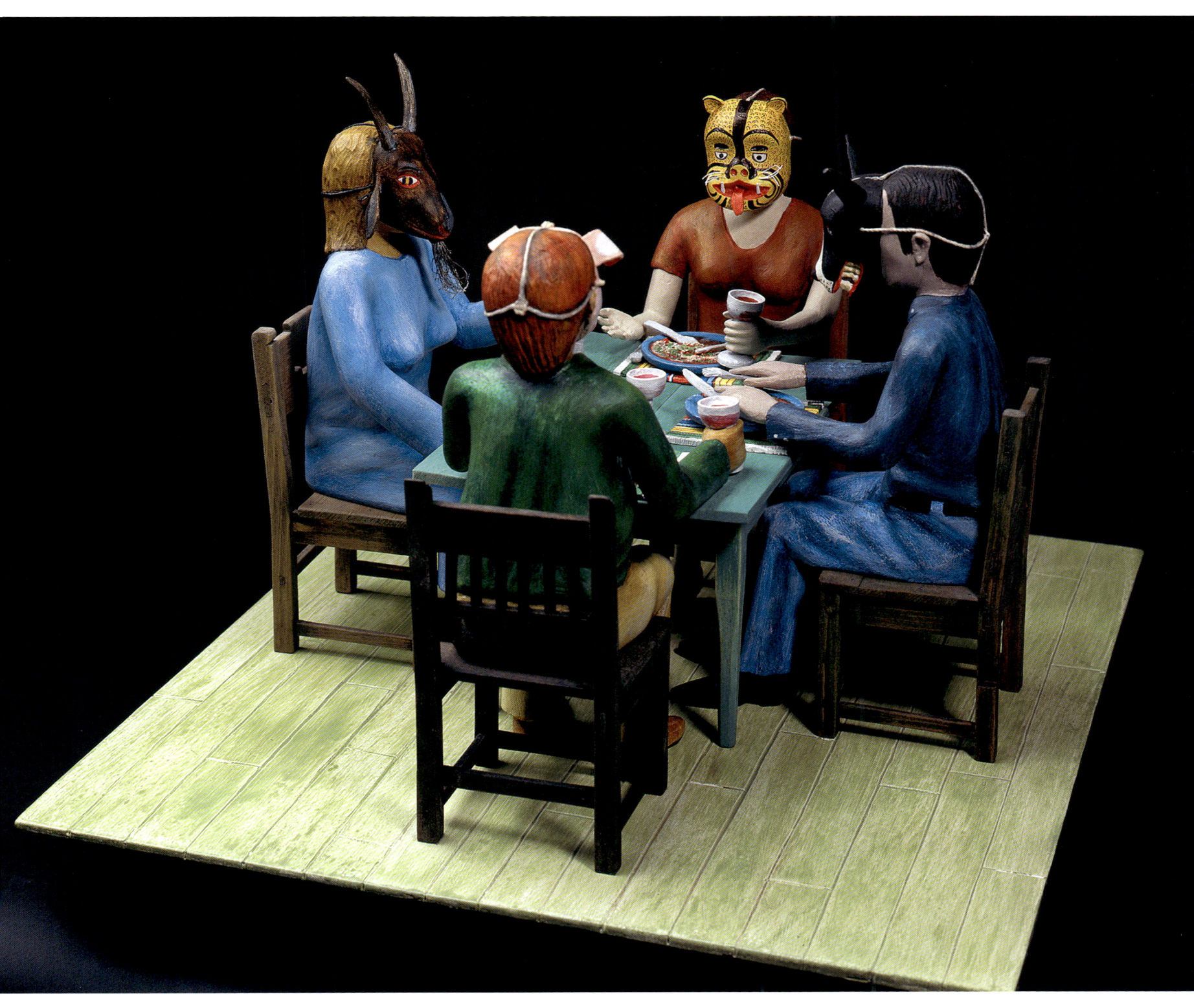

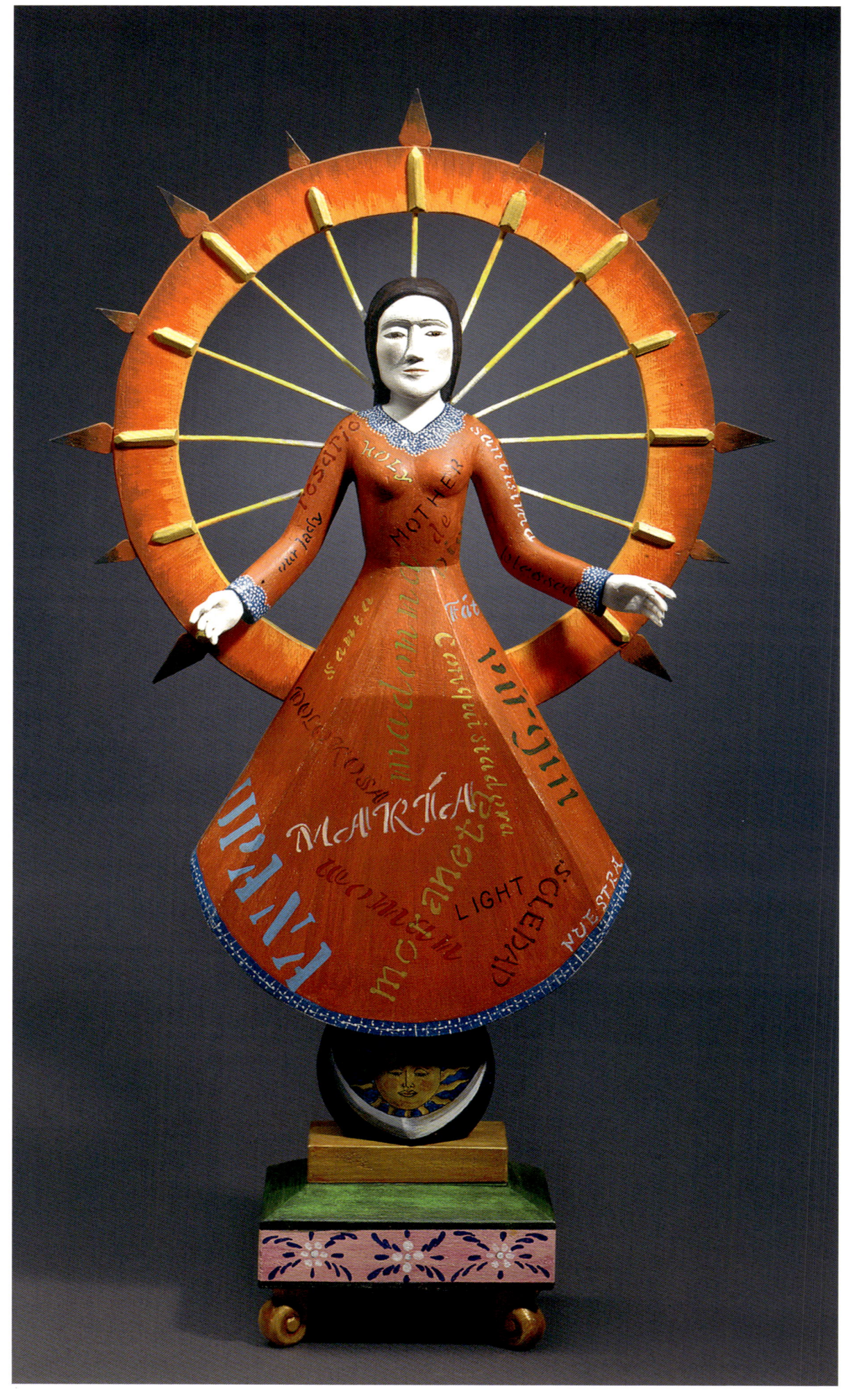

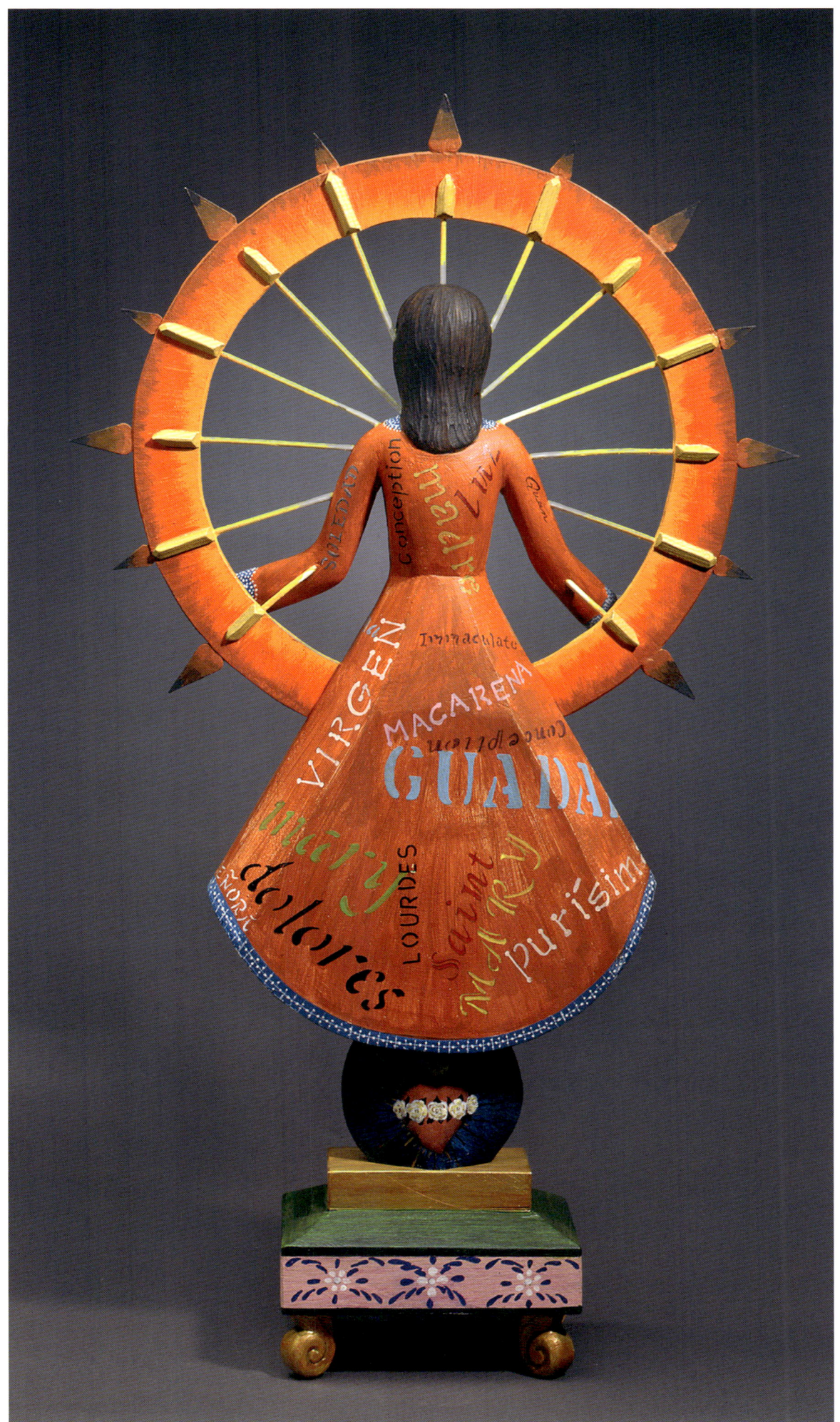

Plate 19. *Ave María*, 2002. Carved and painted wood, 28 7/8 x 16 1/2 x 4 1/2 in. Private collection. Photo © Dan Morse, courtesy of The Owings Gallery.

FOLLOWING SPREAD
Plate 20. *The Passion of Christ*, 2002. Carved and painted wood, 40 3/4 x 26 5/8 x 8 in. Collection of the Spanish Colonial Arts Society, Museum of Spanish Colonial Art, Santa Fe. Photo © Dan Morse, courtesy of The Owings Gallery.

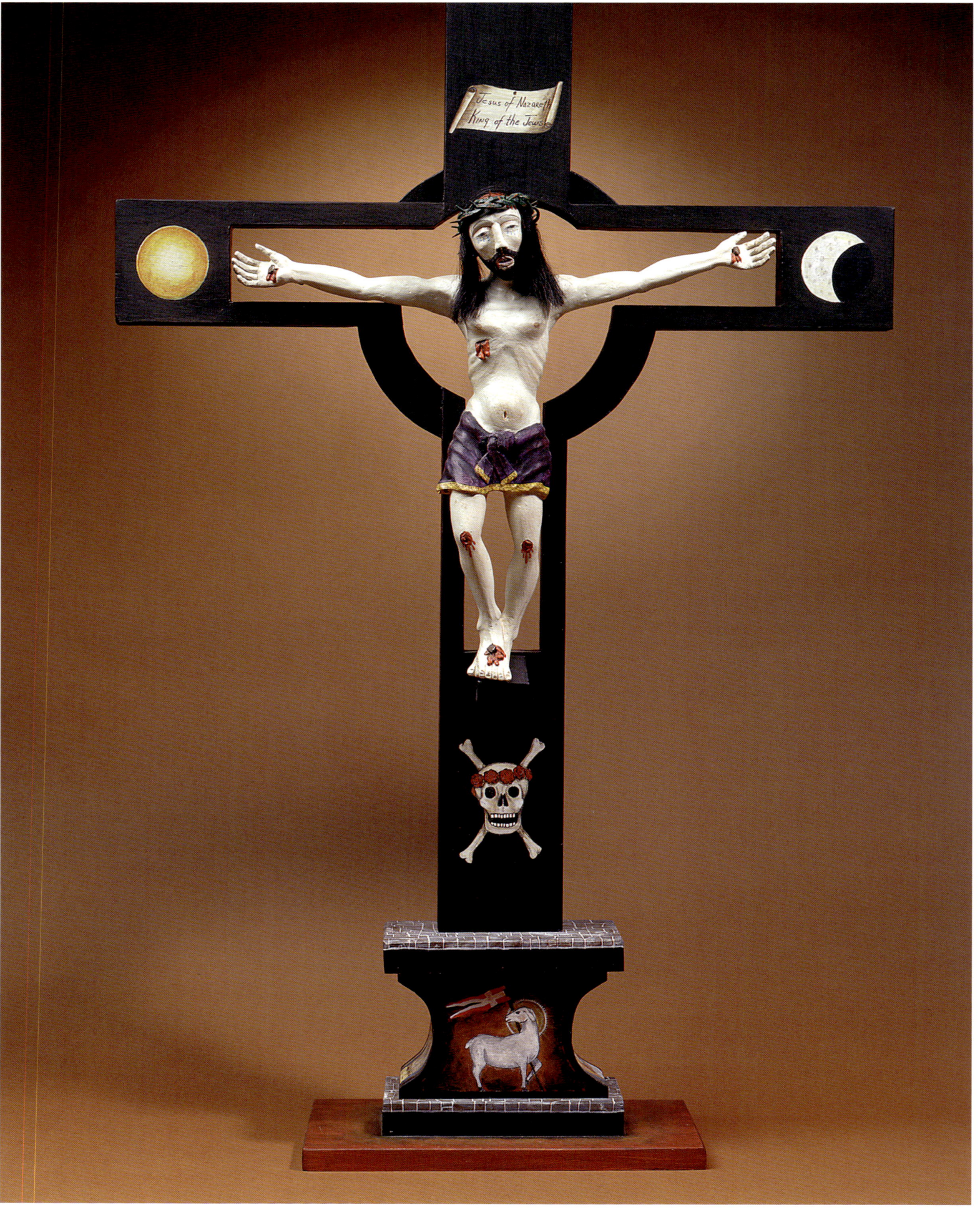

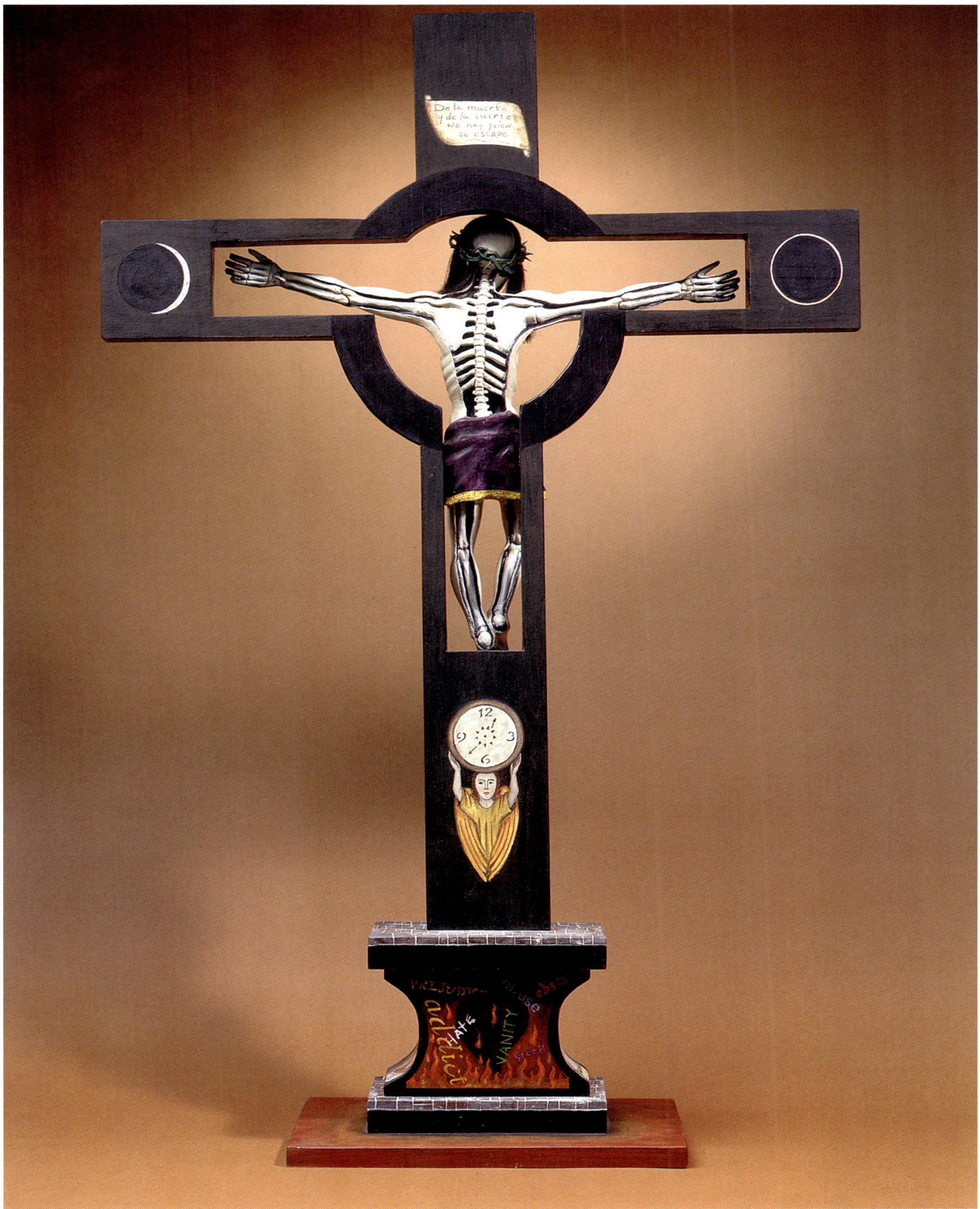

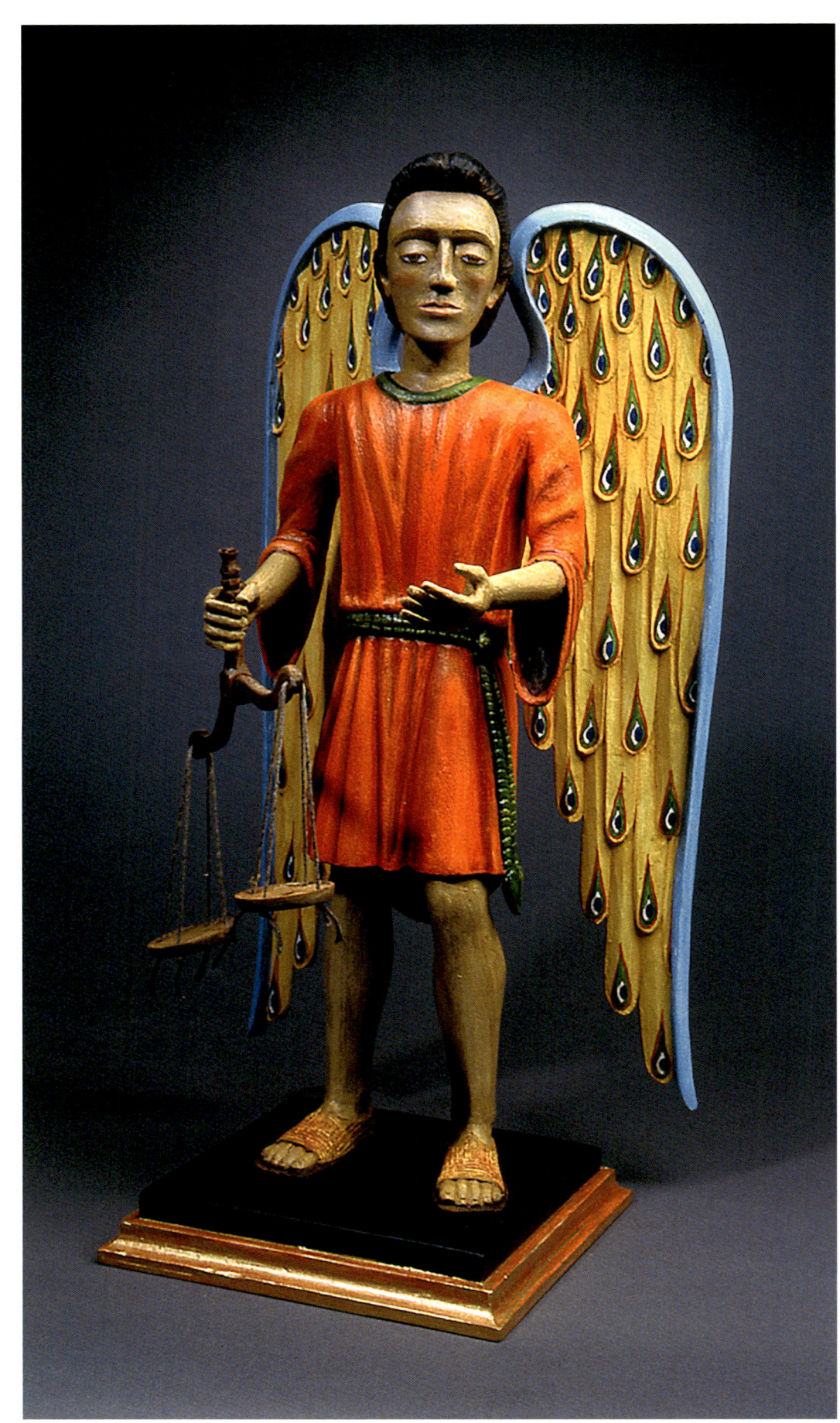

Plate 21. *Angel of Color*
(*San Miguelito*), 2002. Carved
and painted wood, 24 ½ x 12 x 9 ½ in.
Private collection. Photo © Dan Morse,
courtesy of The Owings Gallery.

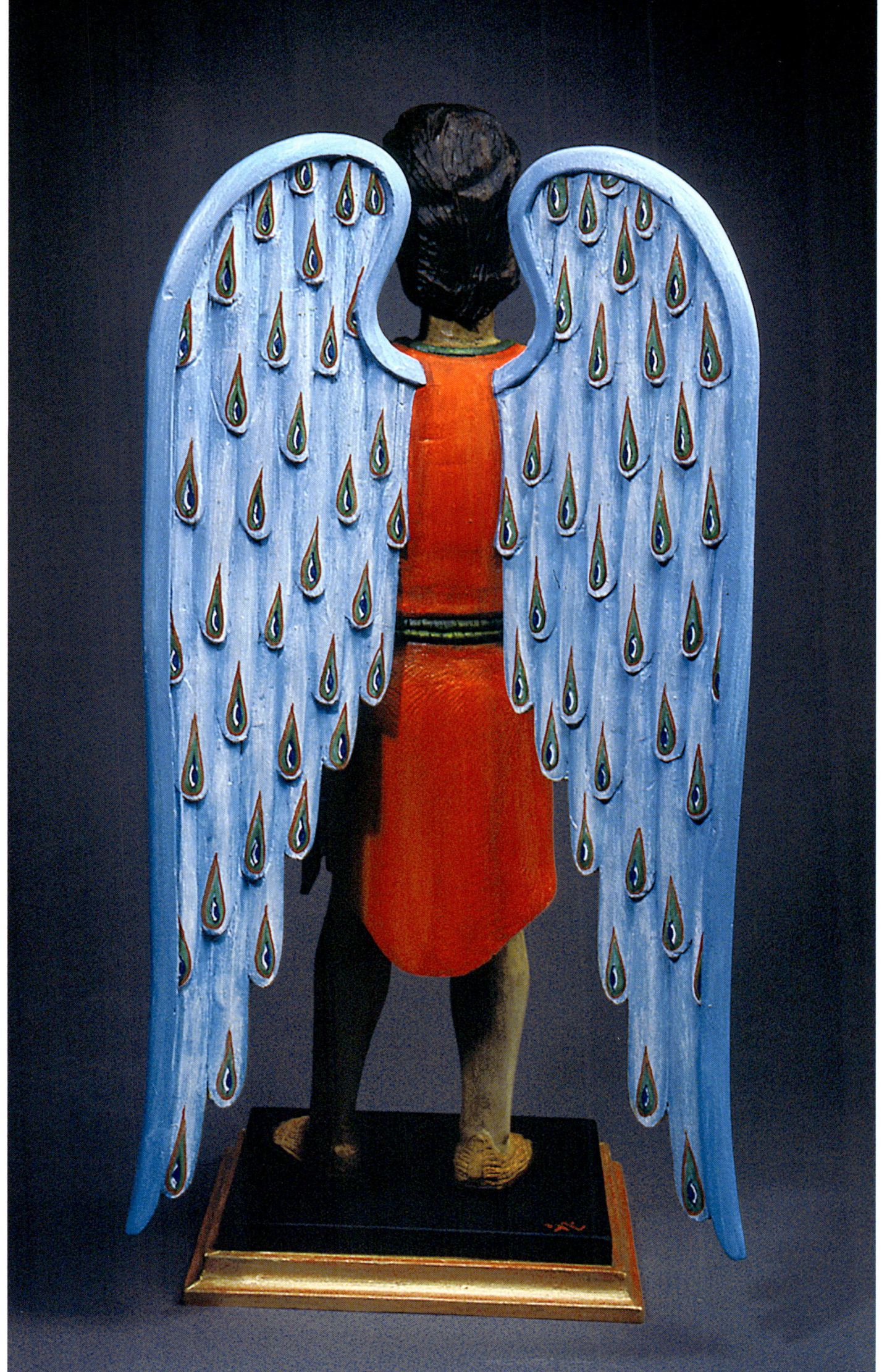

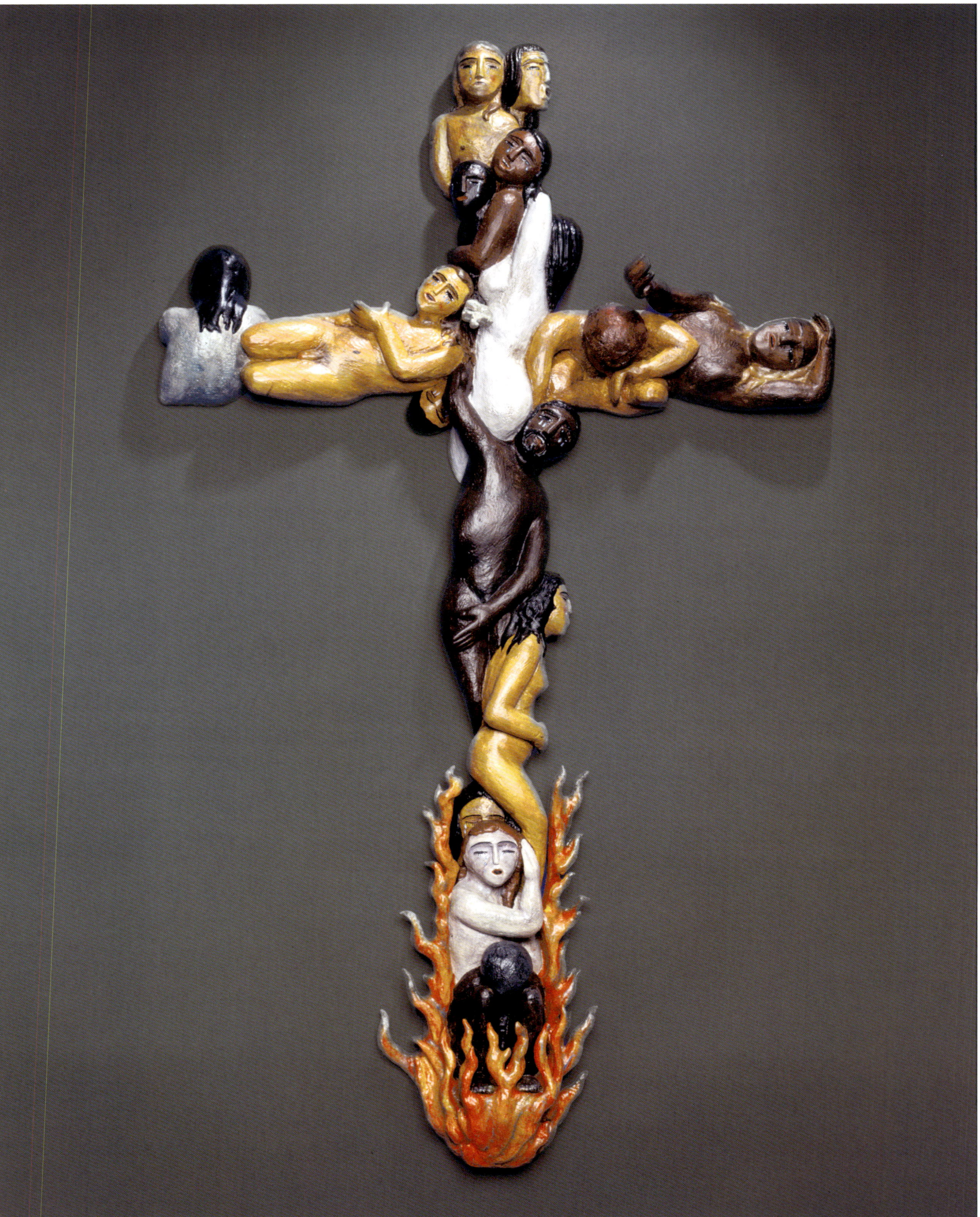

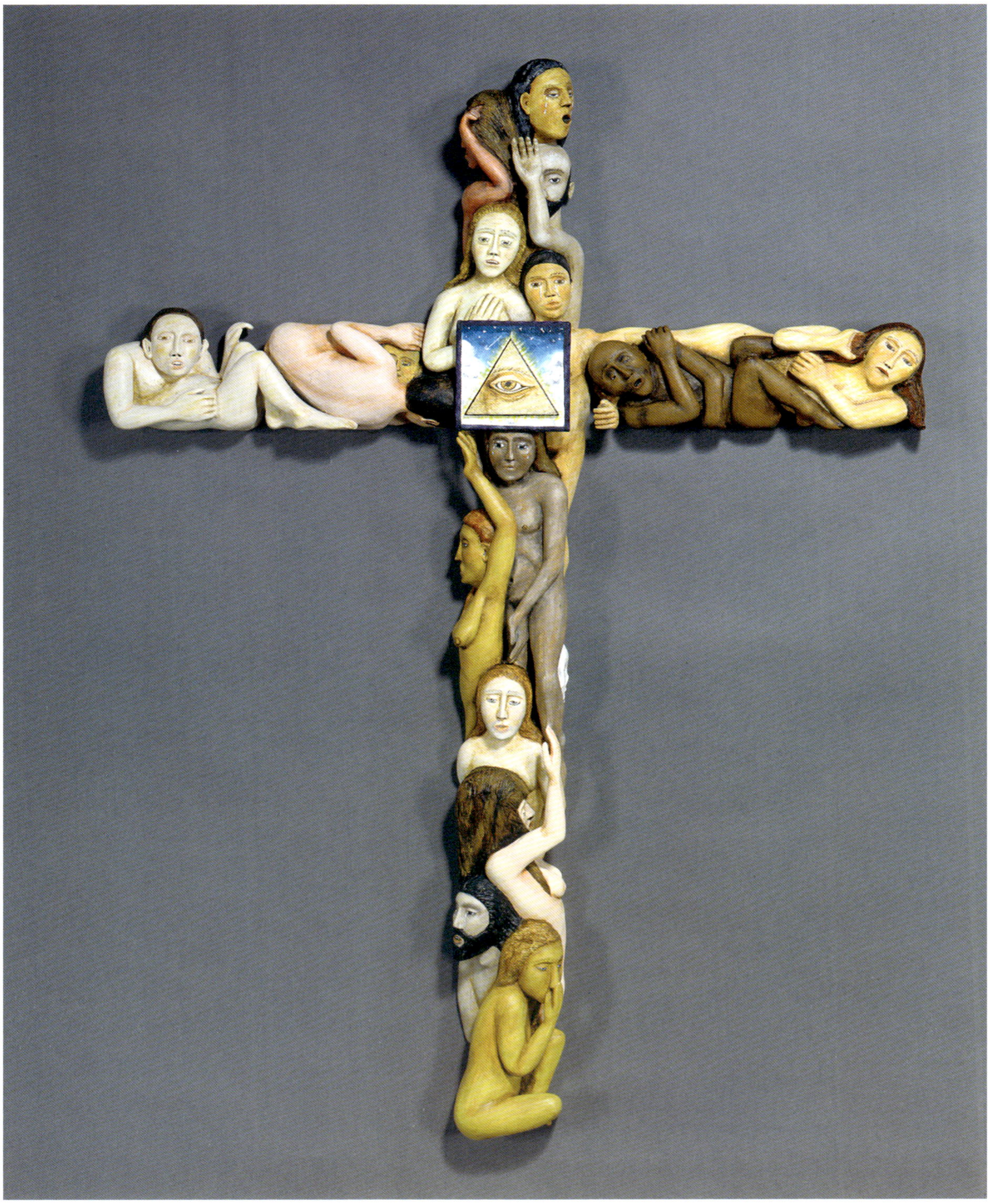

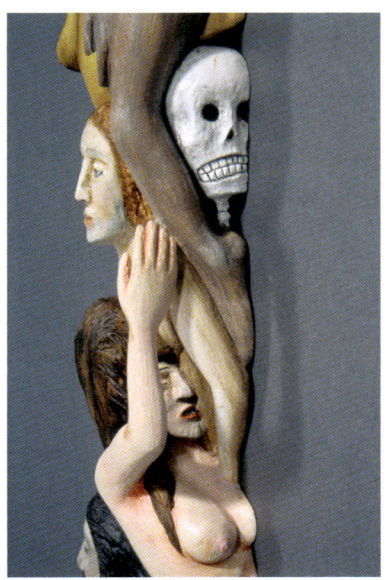

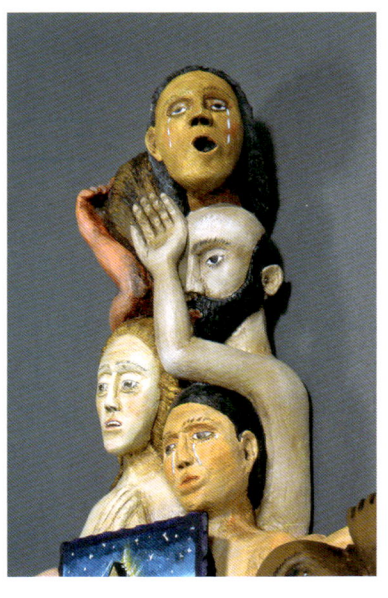

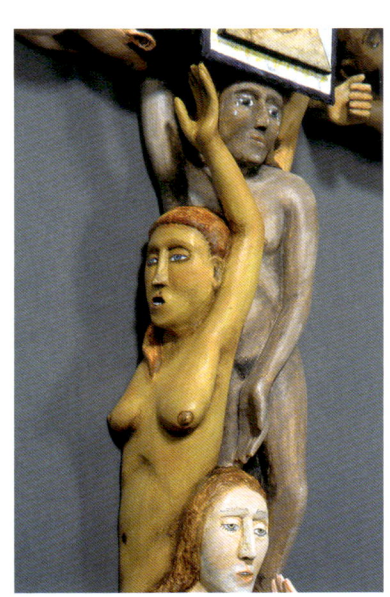

Plate 22. *Cruz de las ánimas,*
1993. Carved and painted wood,
39 x 23 x 5 in. Collection of
Mary and Michael Mahaffey.
Photo © Dan Morse, courtesy of
The Owings Gallery.

Plate 23. *Cruz de las ánimas,* 2002.
Carved and painted wood, 30 x 20 x
2 in. Collection of Curt, Christina, and
Jonah Nonomaque. Photo © Dan
Morse, courtesy of The Owings Gallery.

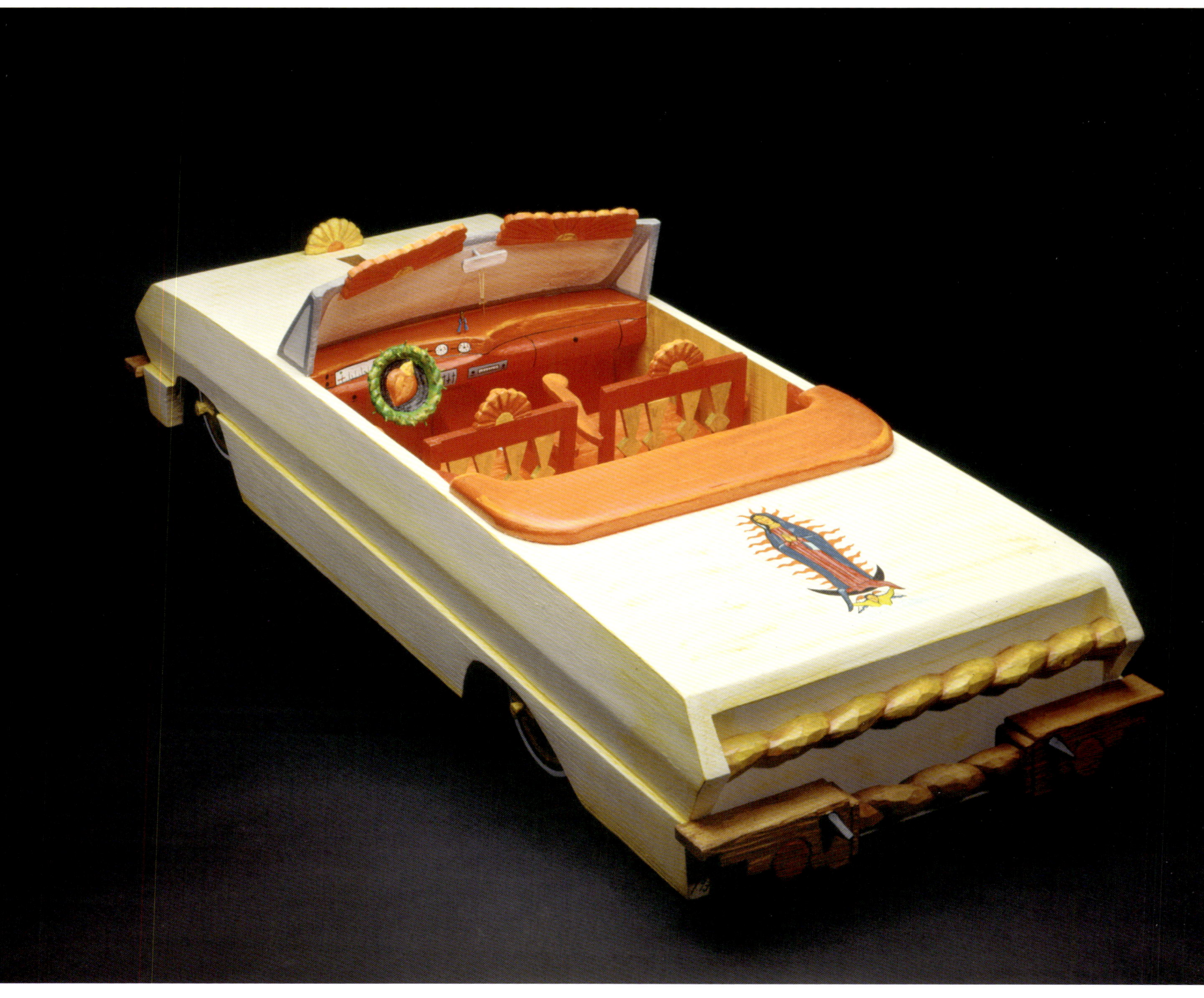

Plate 24. *Spanish Colonial Carreta*, 1993. Carved and painted wood, 10⅝ x 38⅜ x 14 in.
Collection of Terry and Eva Herndon. Photo © Dan Morse, courtesy of The Owings Gallery.

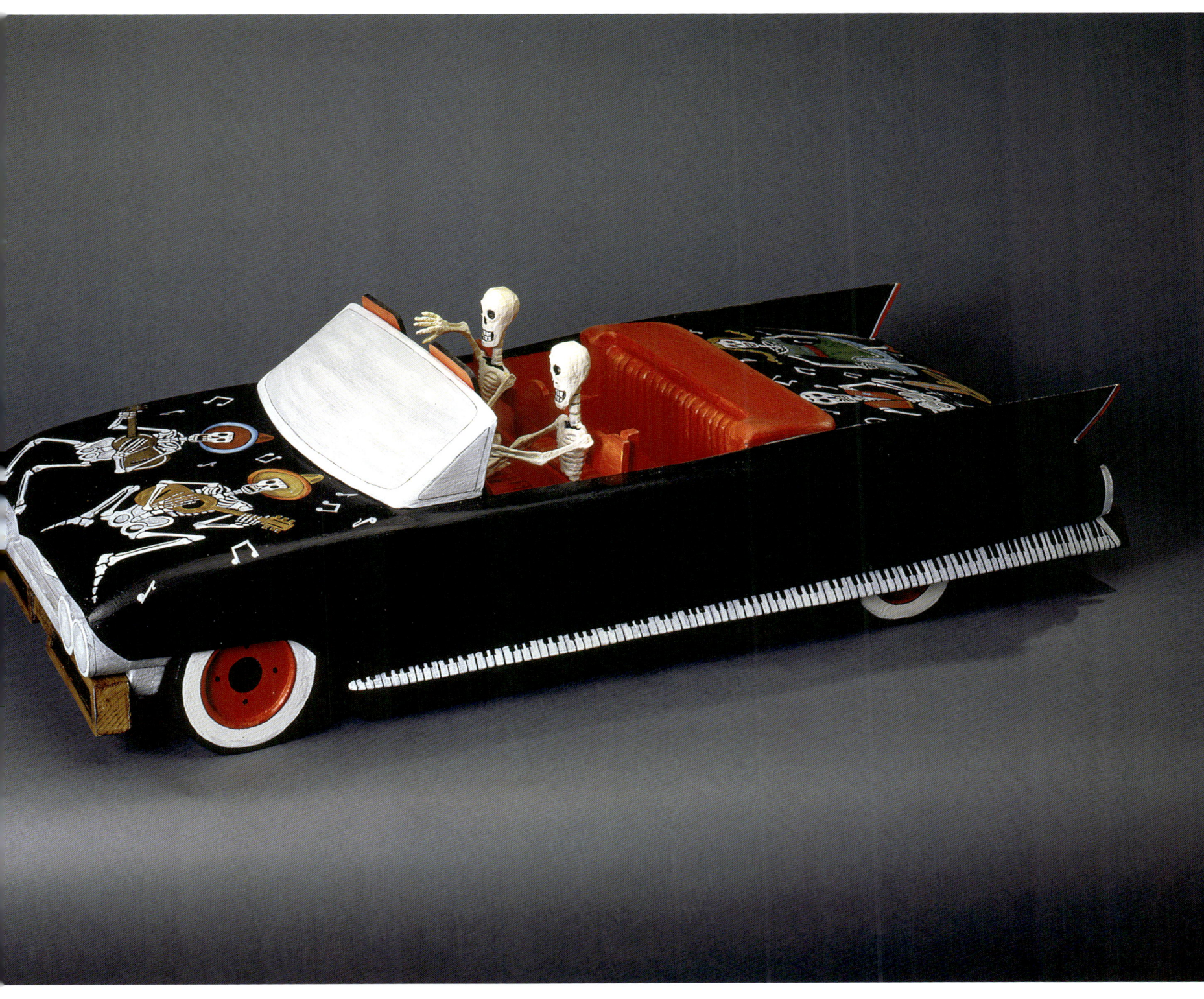

Plate 25. *El gato negro*, 1995. Carved and painted wood, 10 x 38¾ x 15½ in. Private Collection.
Photo © Dan Morse, courtesy of The Owings Gallery.

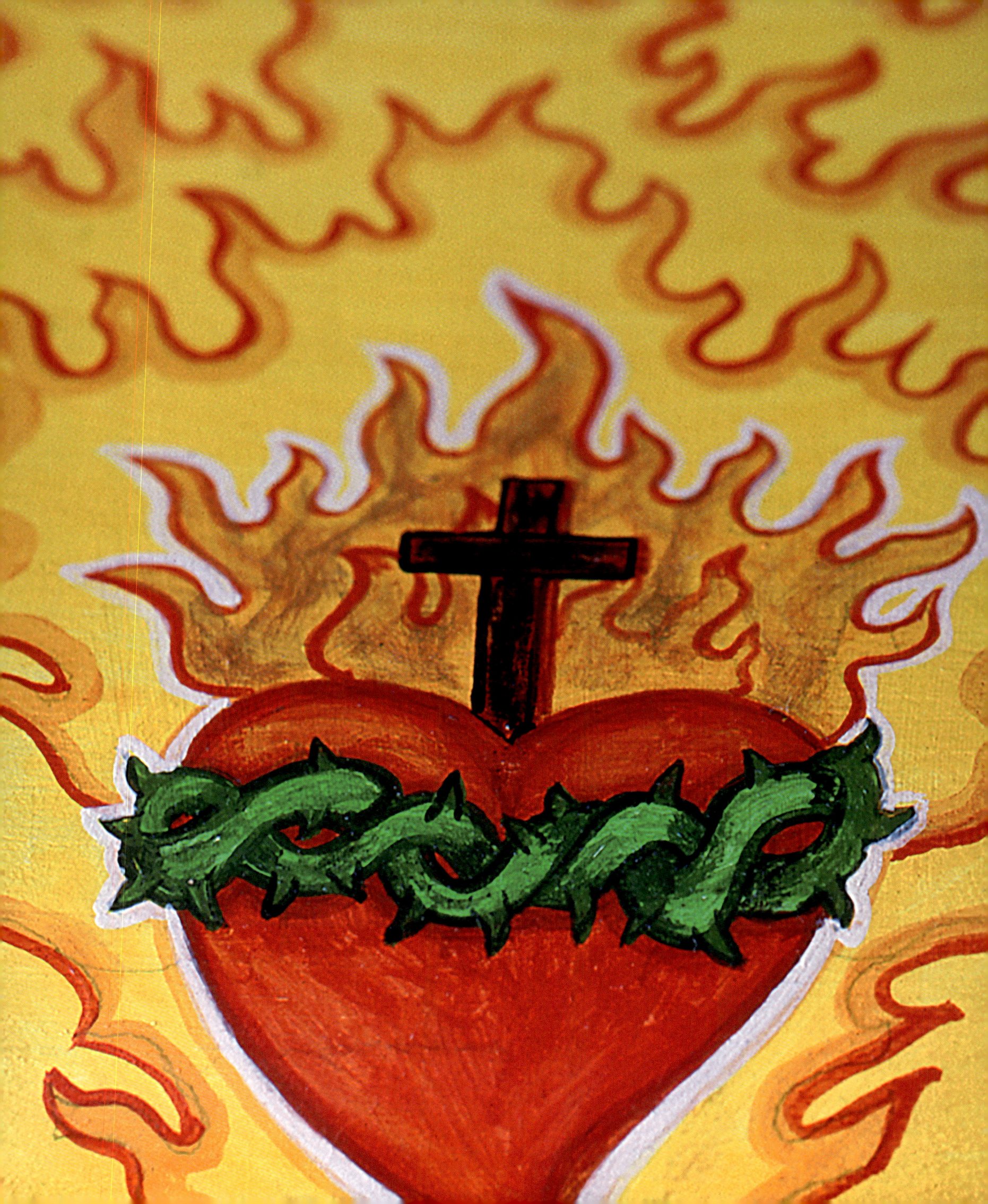

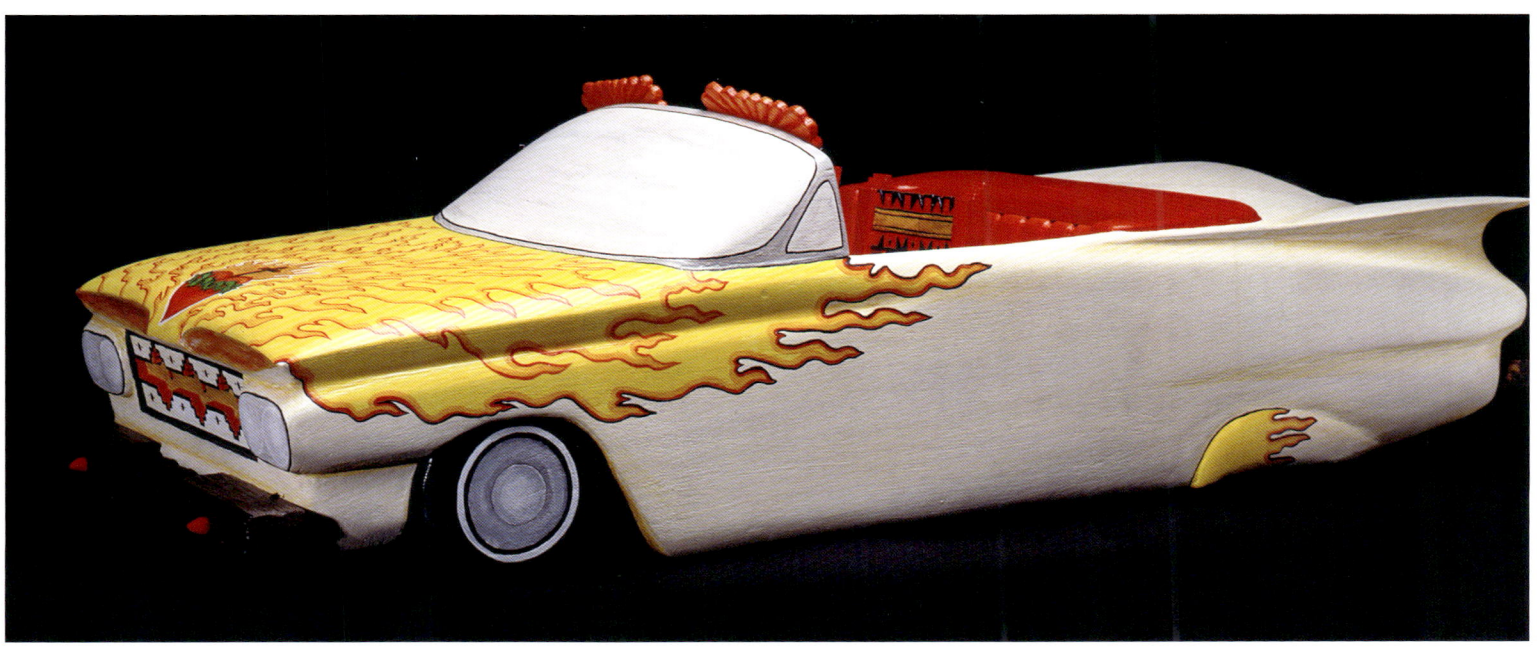

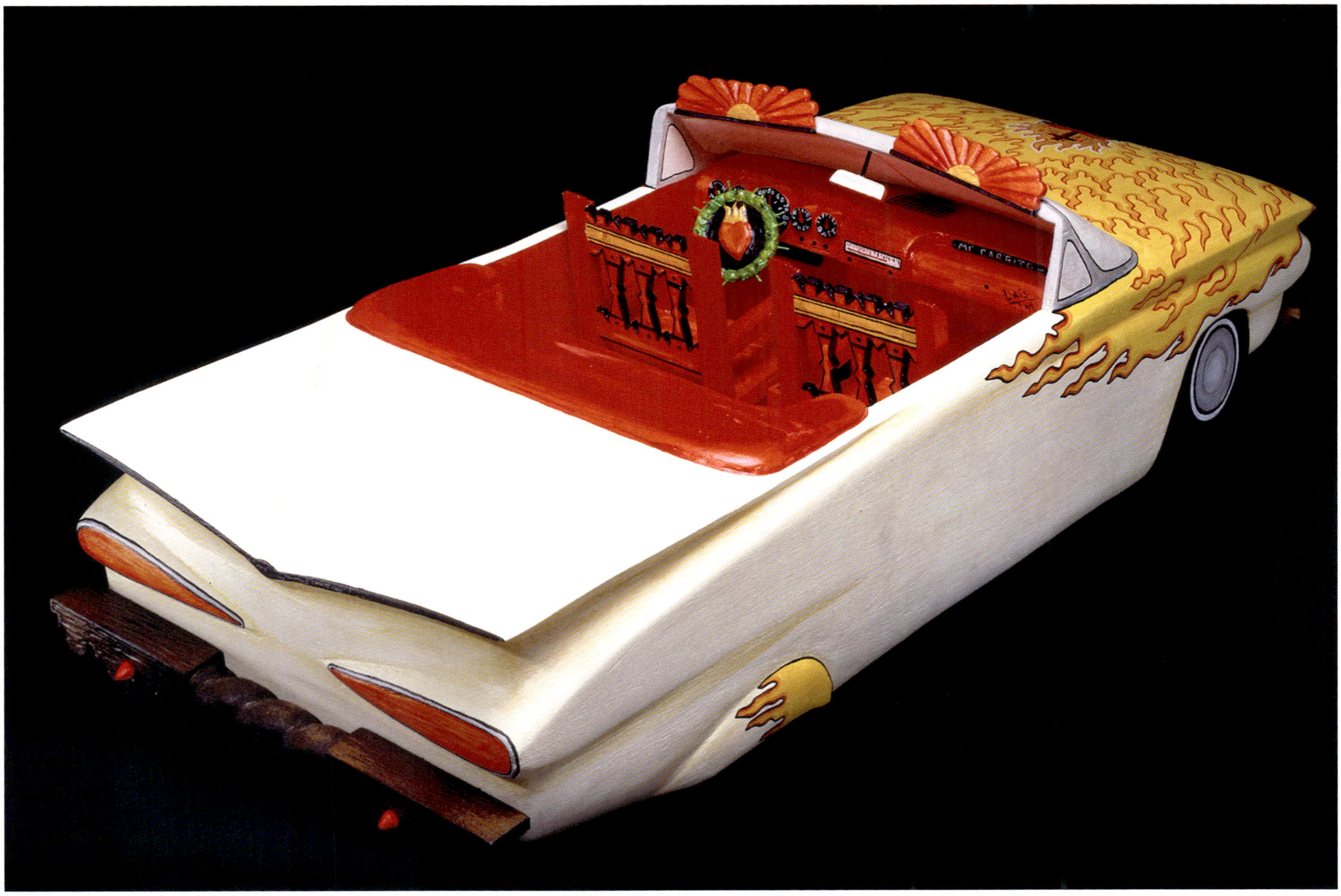

Plate 26. *Mi carrito*, 1994. Carved and painted wood, 11 x 38 x 14 in. Collection of the Autry Museum, Los Angeles (2004.25.1).
Detail photo (left) © and courtesy Jack Parsons. Photos (right) © Dan Morse, courtesy of The Owings Gallery.

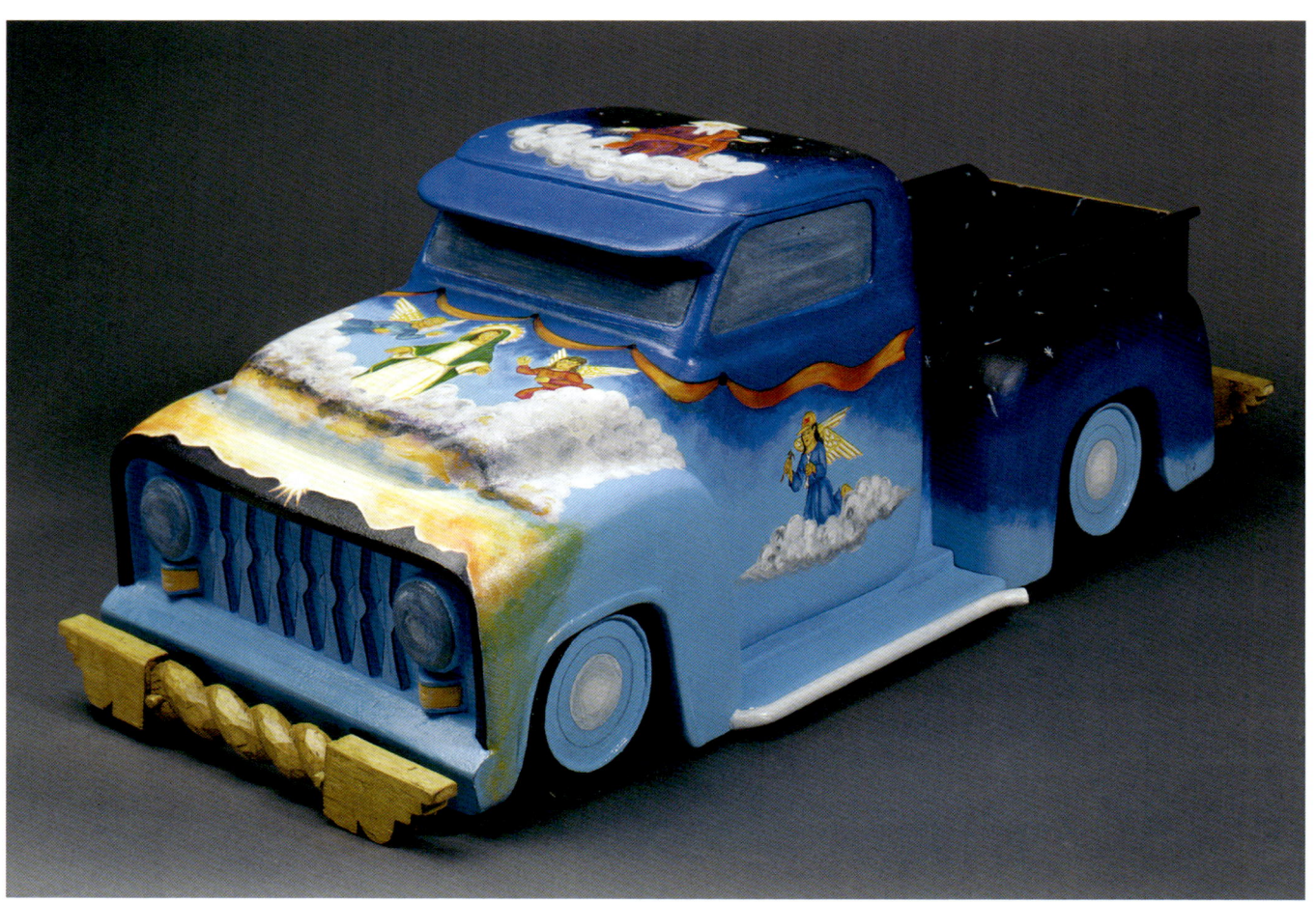

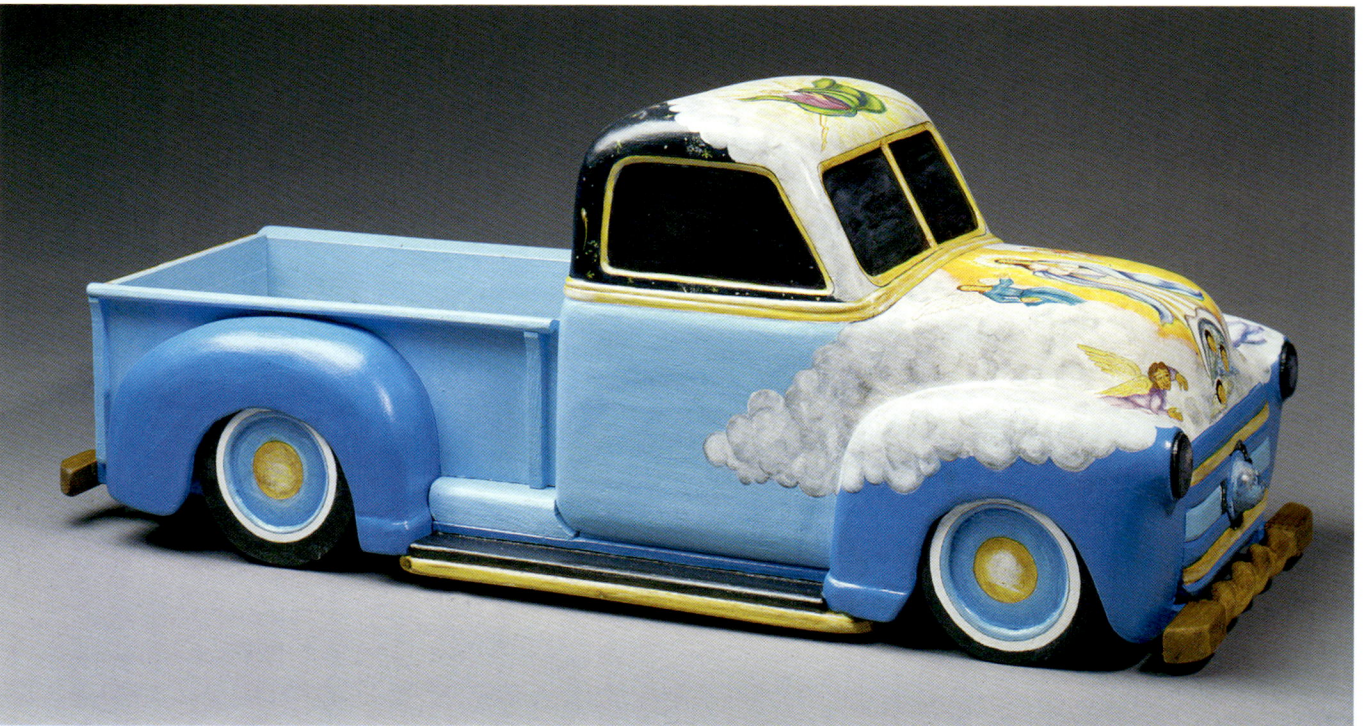

Plate 27. *1954 Ford*, 2001. Carved and painted wood, 12¾ x 32½ x 12½ in. Private collection.
Photo © Dan Morse, courtesy of The Owings Gallery.

ABOVE AND OPPOSITE
Plate 28. *New Mexico Sky Truck*, 2000. Carved and painted wood, 12¾ x 32½ x 12½ in.
Collection of Curt, Christina, and Jonah Nonomaque. Photo © Dan Morse, courtesy of The Owings Gallery.

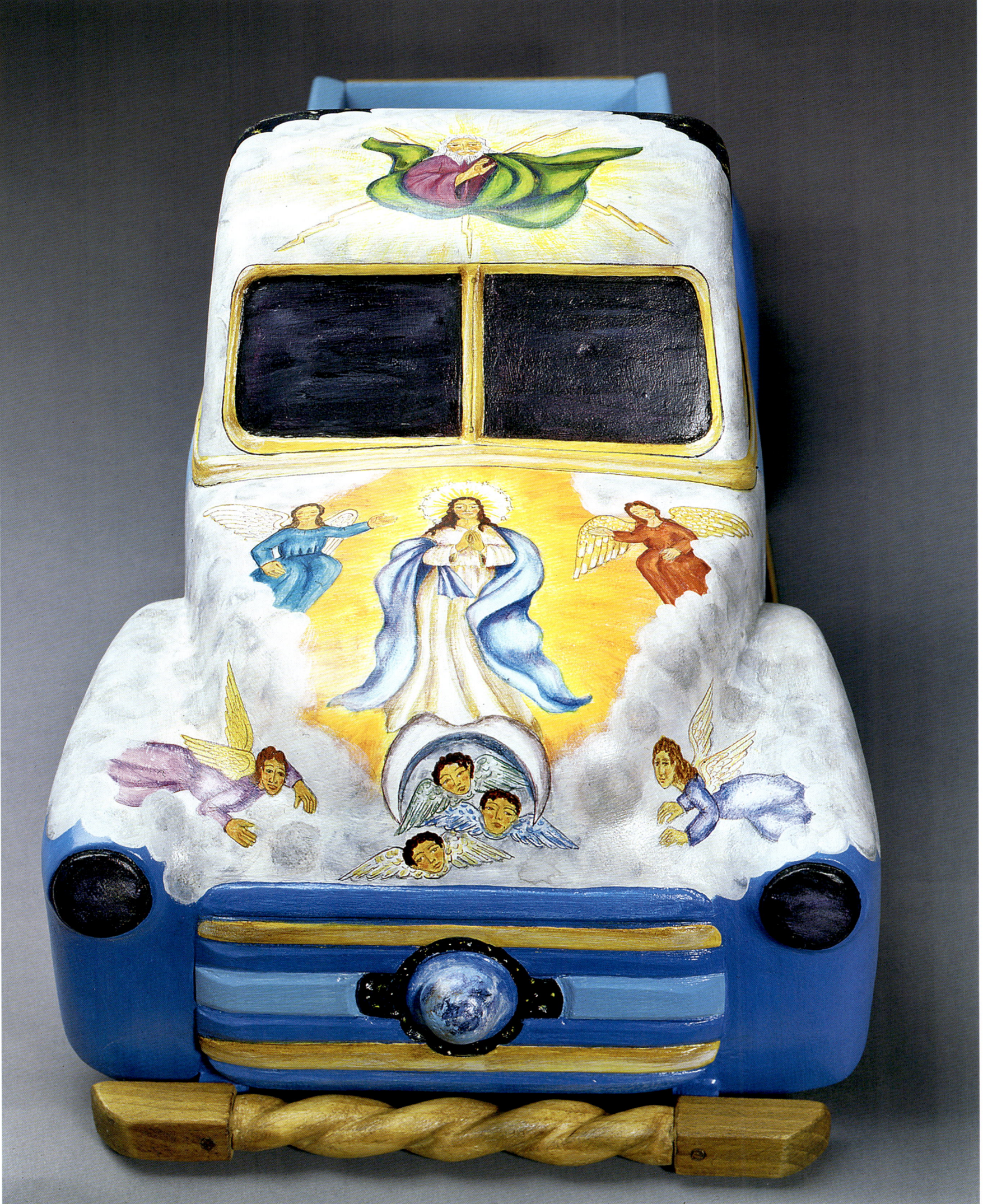

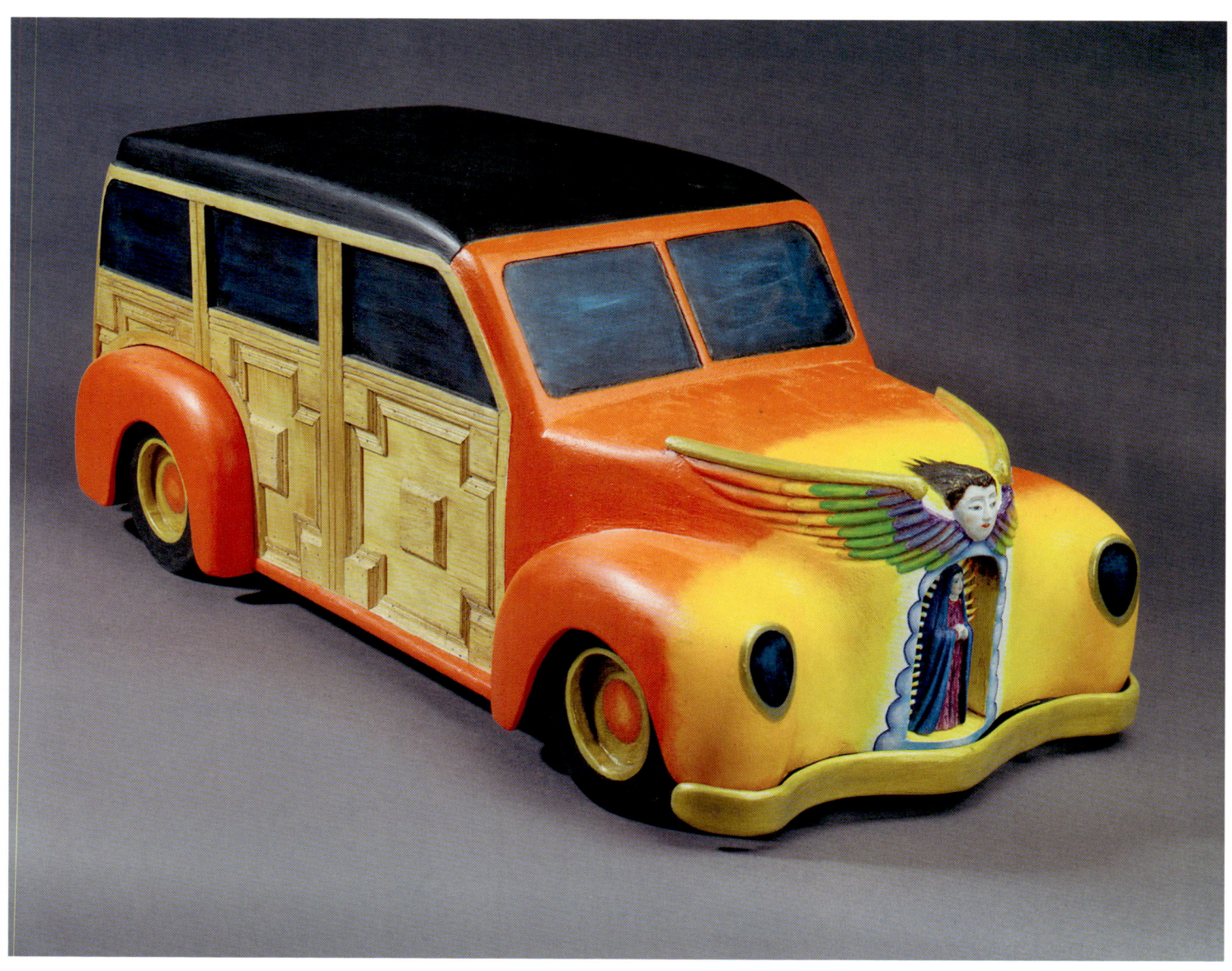

ABOVE
Plate 29. *Northern New Mexico Woody (Peñasco Truck)*, 2002. Carved and painted wood,
11¾ x 30½ x 12¾ in. Collection of Jack and Rebecca Parsons. Photo © Dan Morse,
courtesy of The Owings Gallery.

OPPOSITE TOP
Plate 30. *Carmela's Cruz*, 1996. Carved and painted wood, 10 x 39 x 15½ in. Private collection.
Photo © Dan Morse, courtesy of The Owings Gallery.

OPPOSITE BOTTOM
Plate 31. *Pat and Ray's Cruise*, 1996. Carved and painted wood, 9¼ x 32¾ x 12¾ in.
Collection of Ray and Pat Paige. Photo © Dan Morse, courtesy of The Owings Gallery.

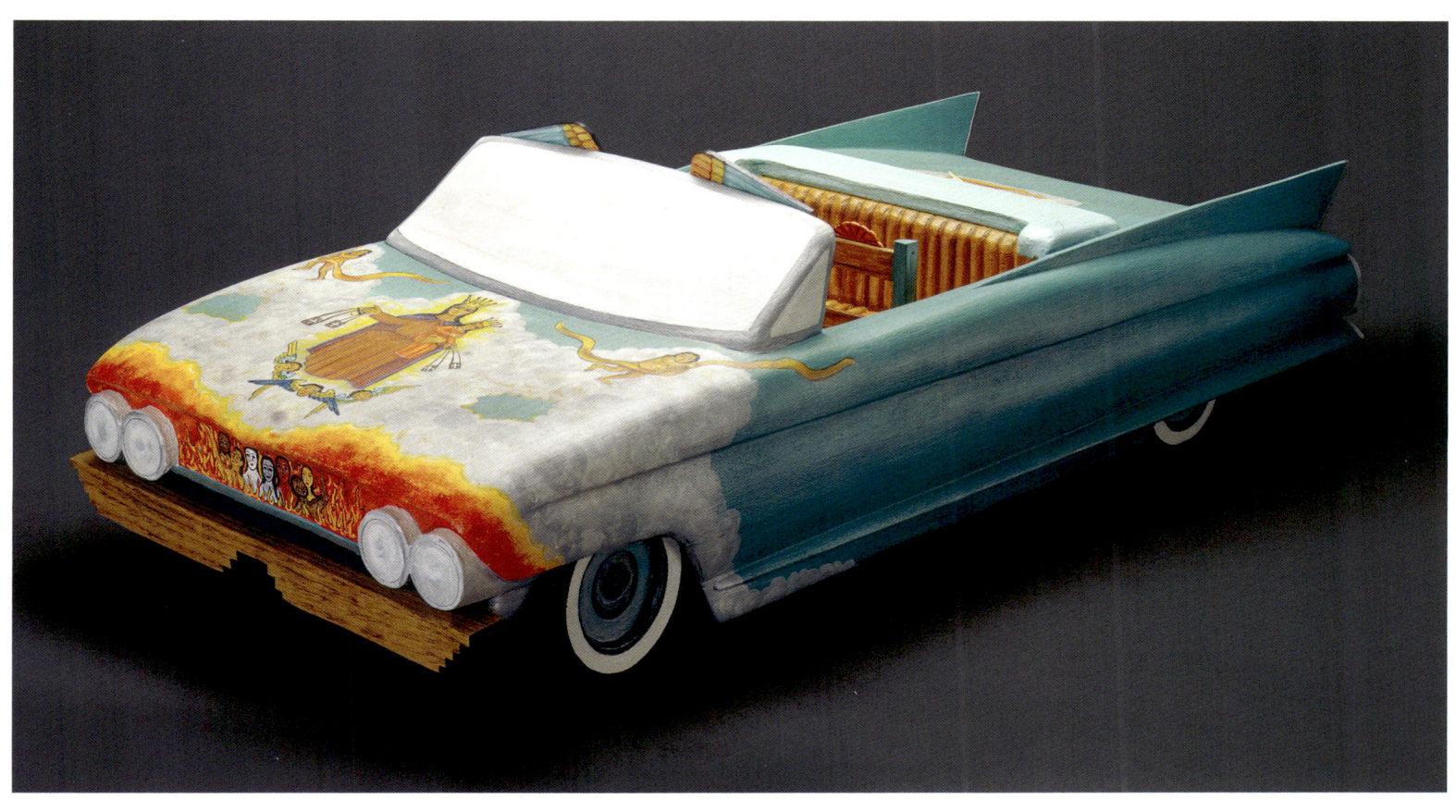

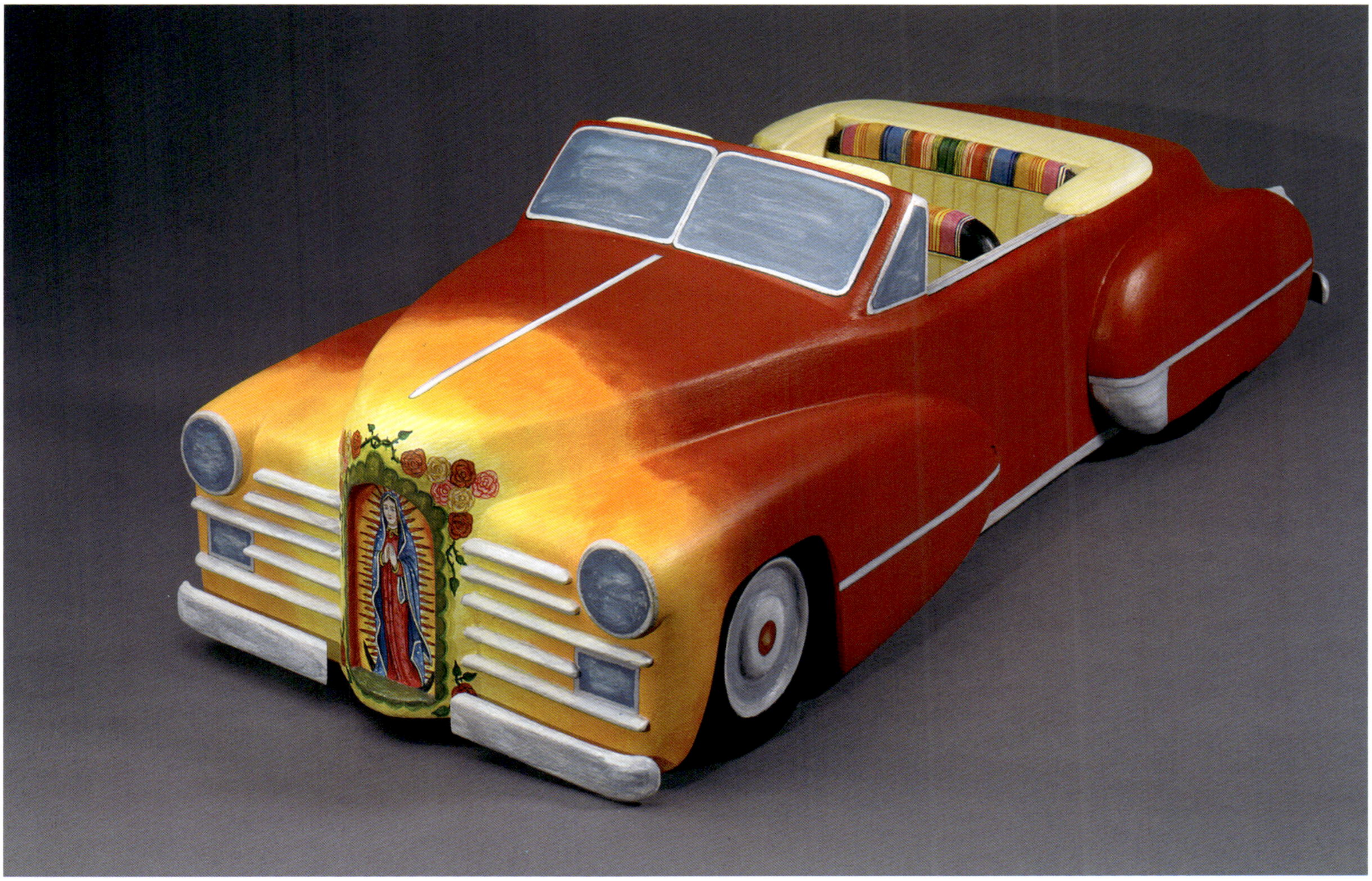

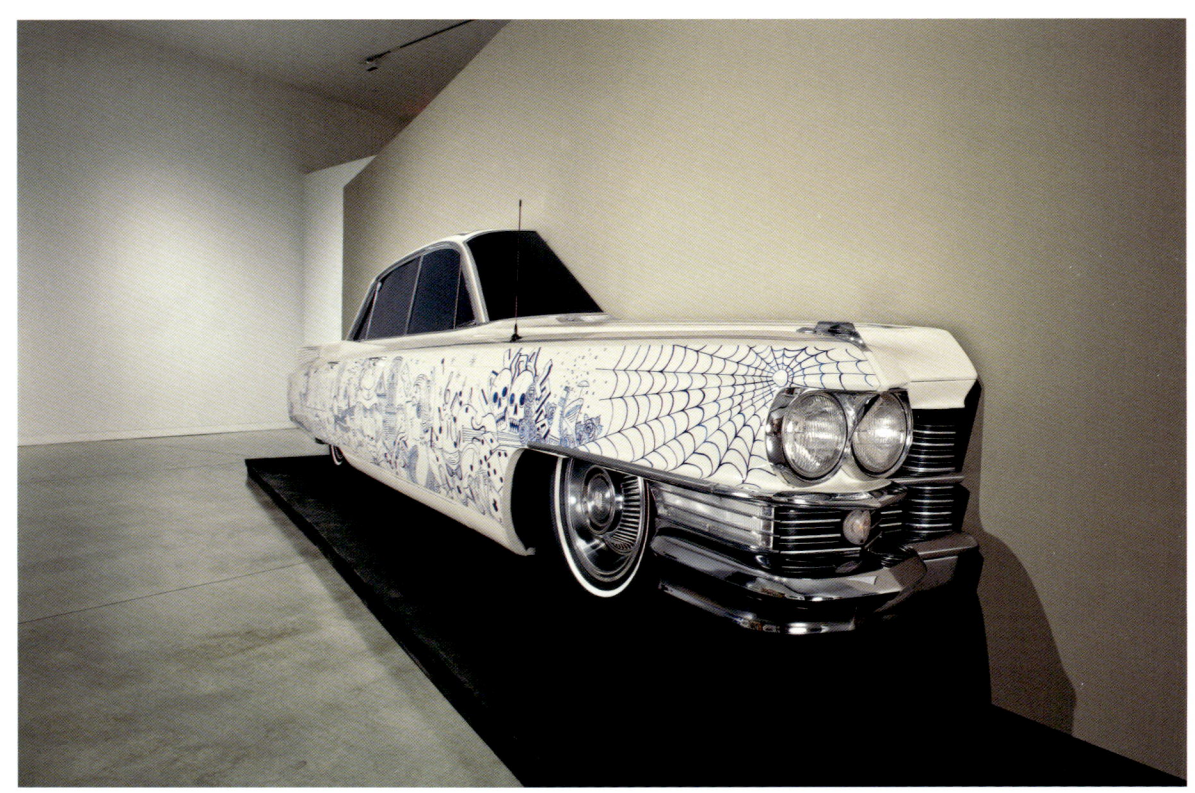

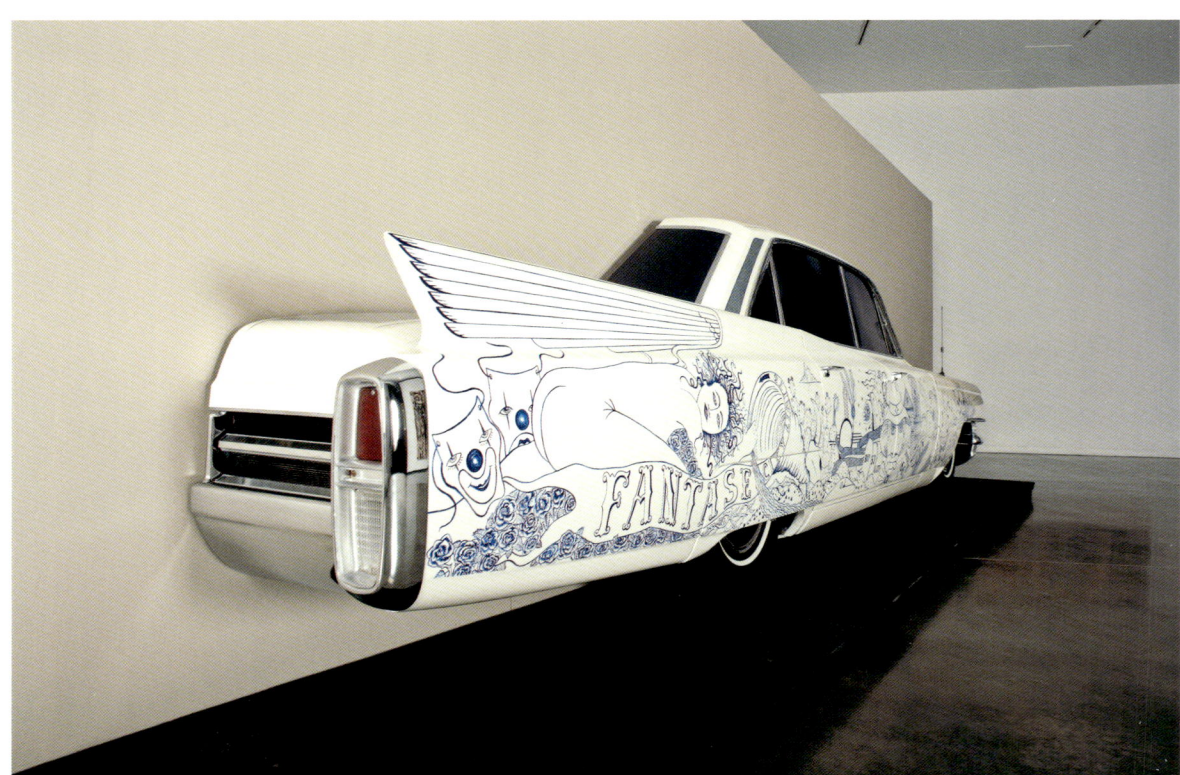

Plate 32. *A Slice of American Pie*, 2008. Painted metal, 56 x 210 x 23 in., 700 lbs. Collection of the National Hispanic Cultural Center, Albuquerque; museum purchase funded through Art in Public Places, New Mexico Arts, New Mexico Department of Cultural Affairs. Photo © Addison Doty.

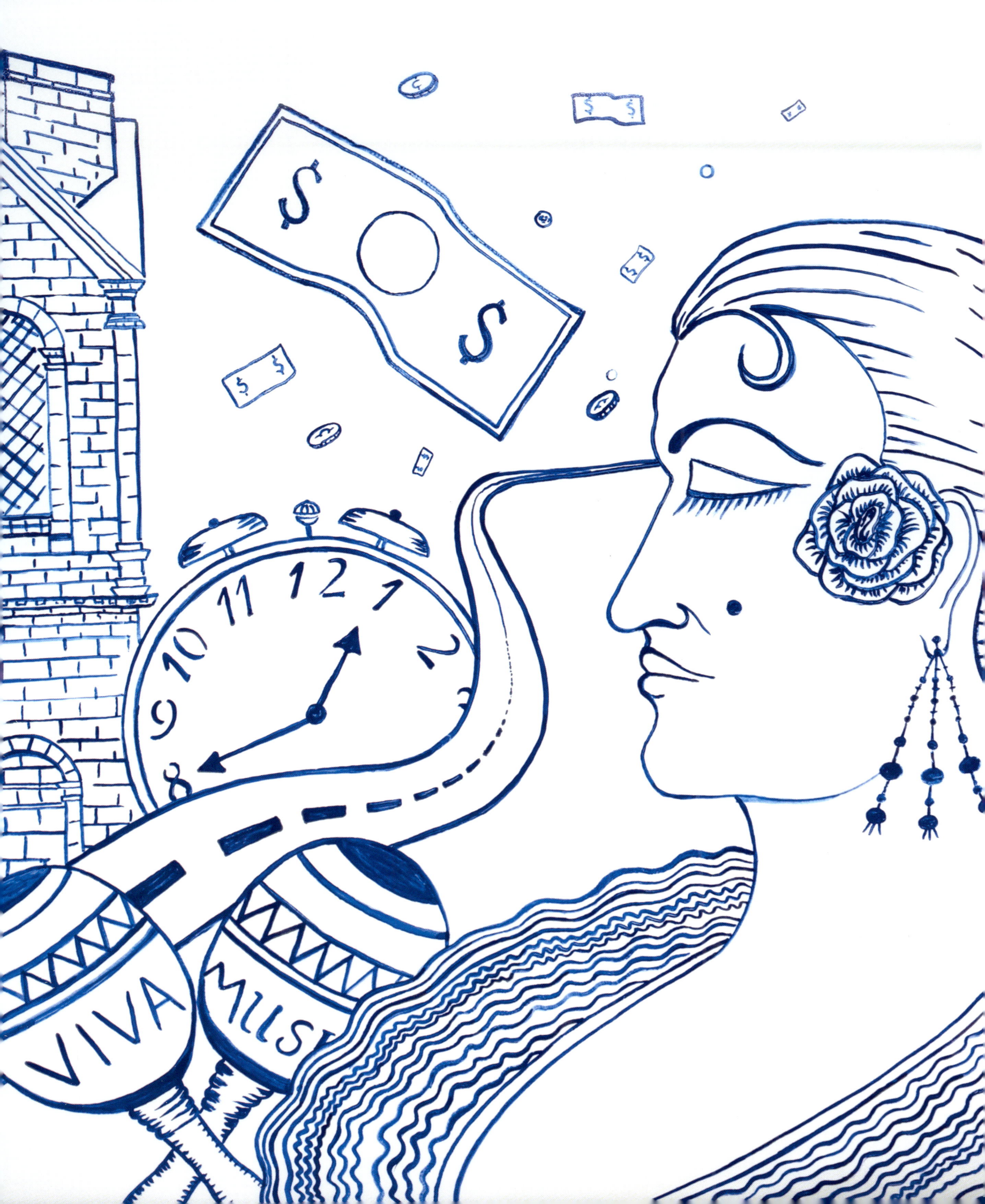

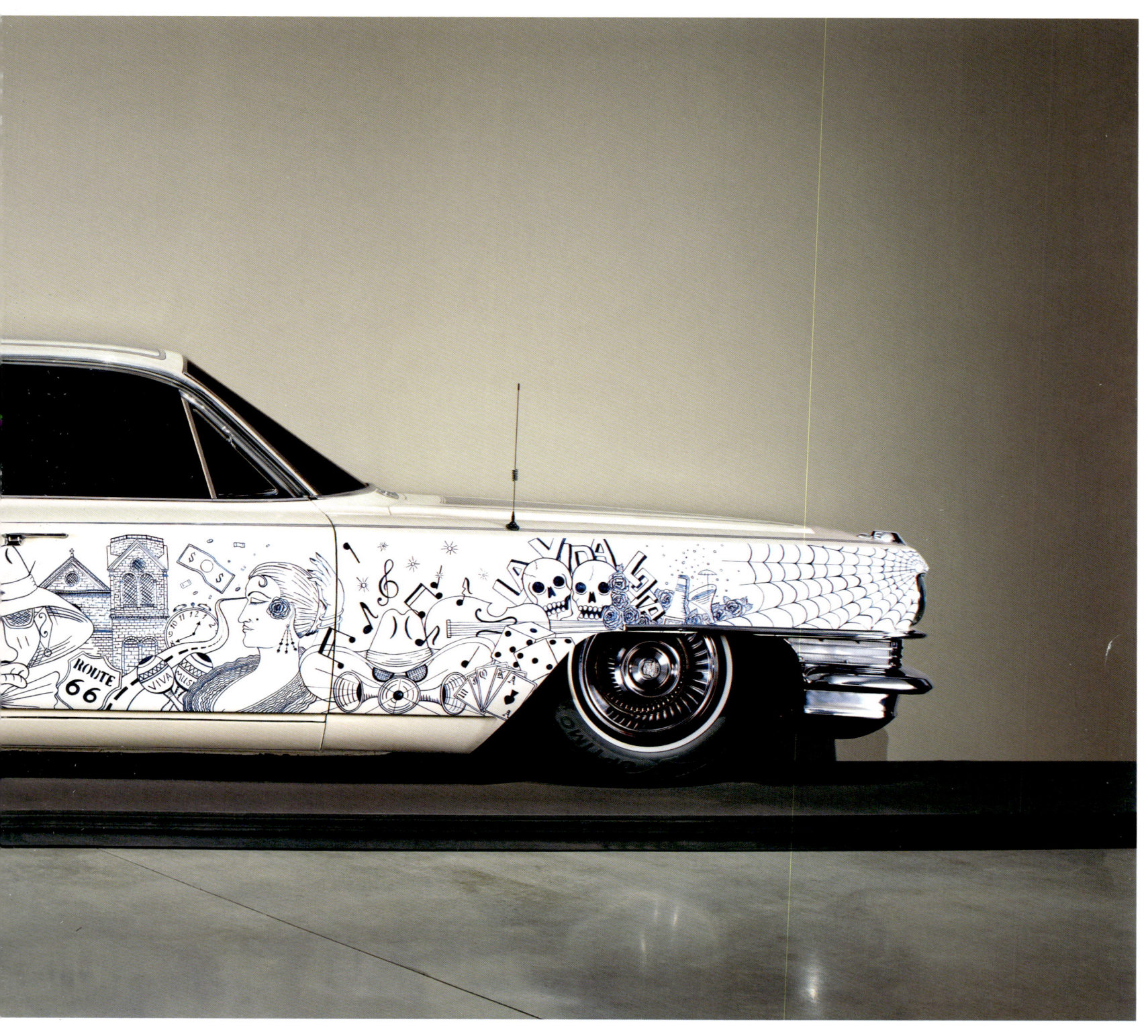

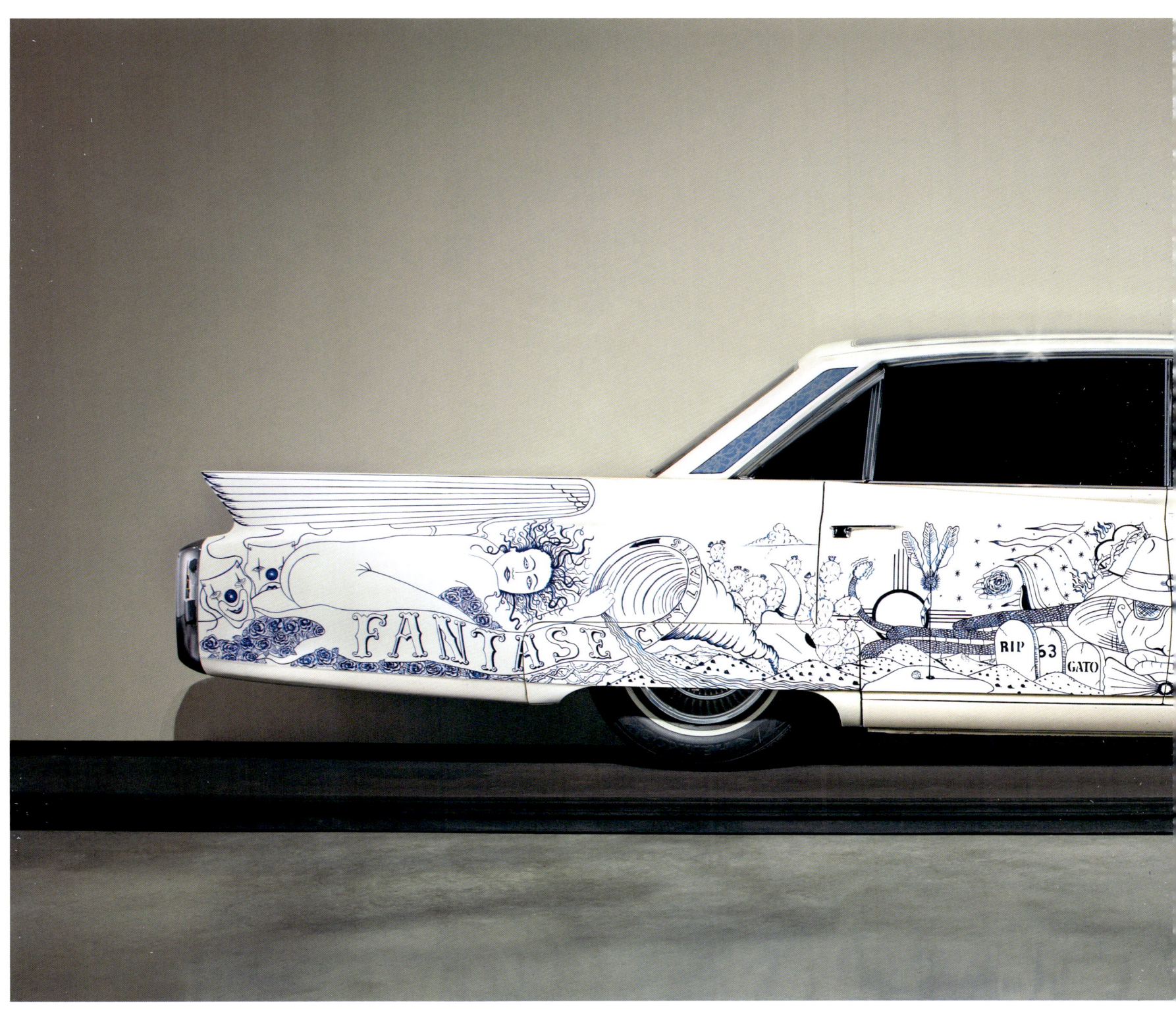

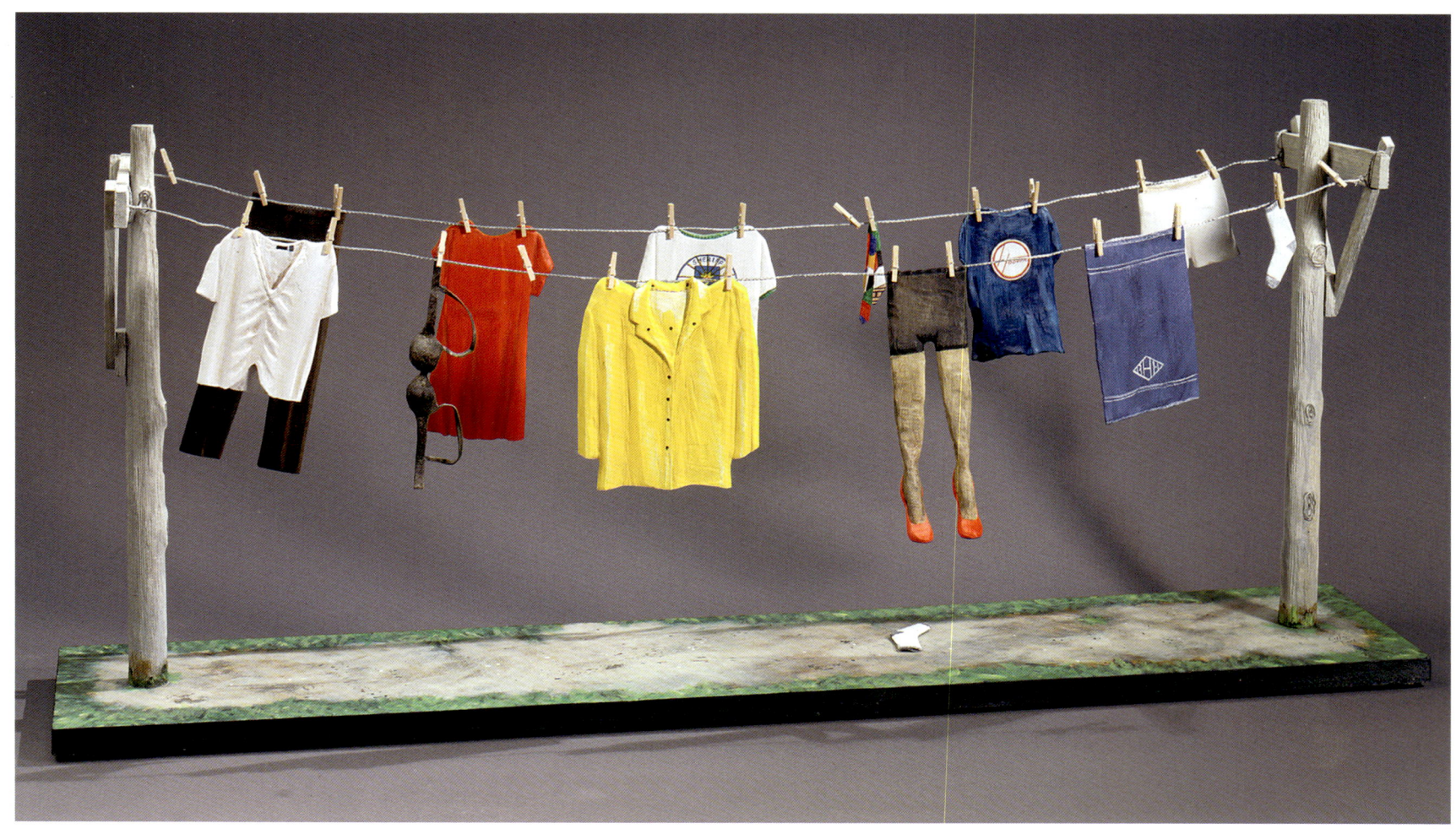

ABOVE AND OPPOSITE

Plate 33. *Bud and Barbara's Clothesline*, 2002. Carved and painted wood, 16⅜ x 38 x 7½ in.
Collection of Mr. and Mrs. H. Earl Hoover II. Photo © Dan Morse, courtesy of The Owings Gallery.

FOLLOWING SPREAD

Plate 34. *Man Trapped in His Religion*, 2004. Carved and painted wood, 33 x 25⅜ x 16⅜.
Collection of Tom and Kimberly Padilla. Photo © Dan Morse, courtesy of The Owings Gallery.

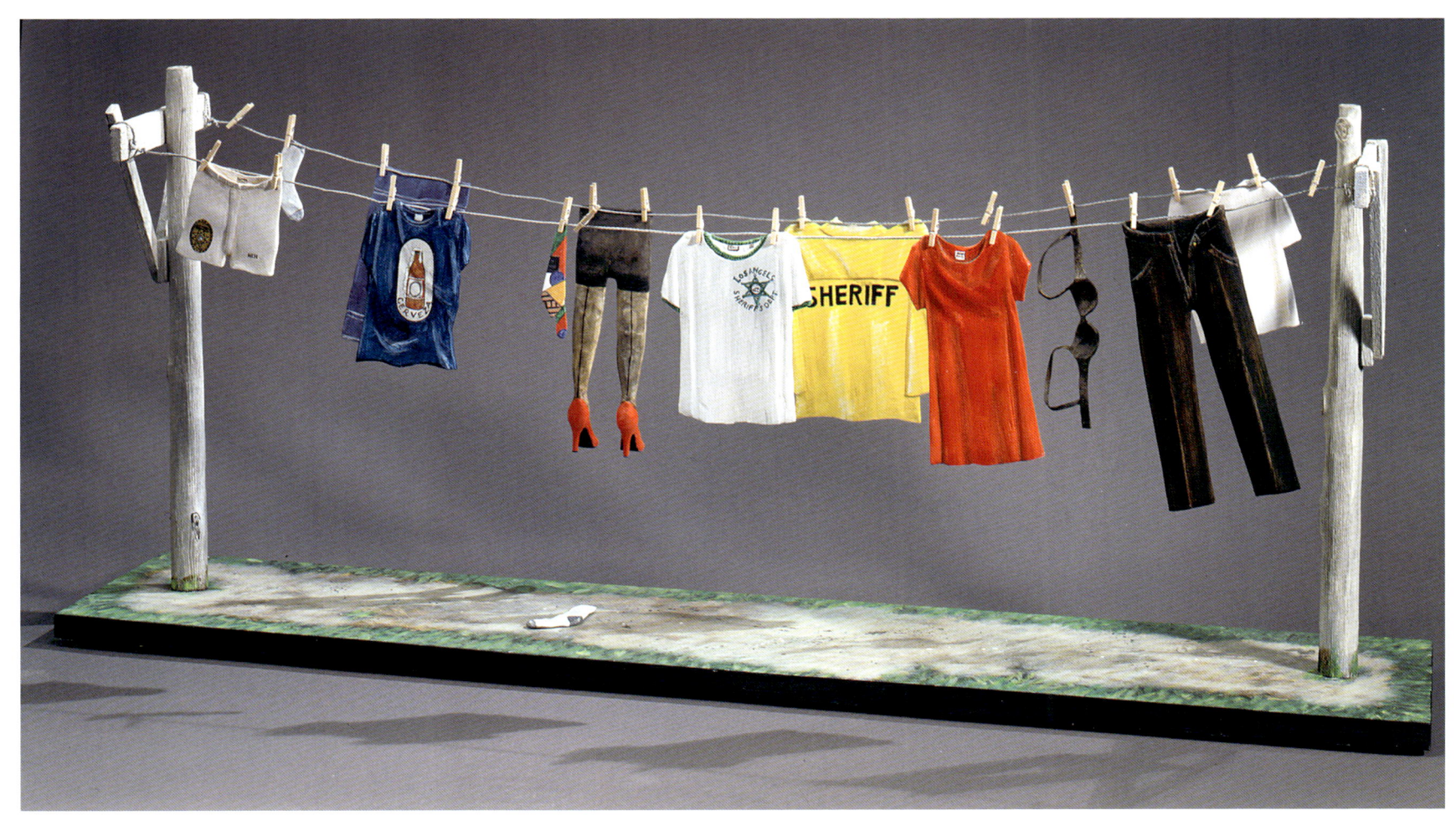

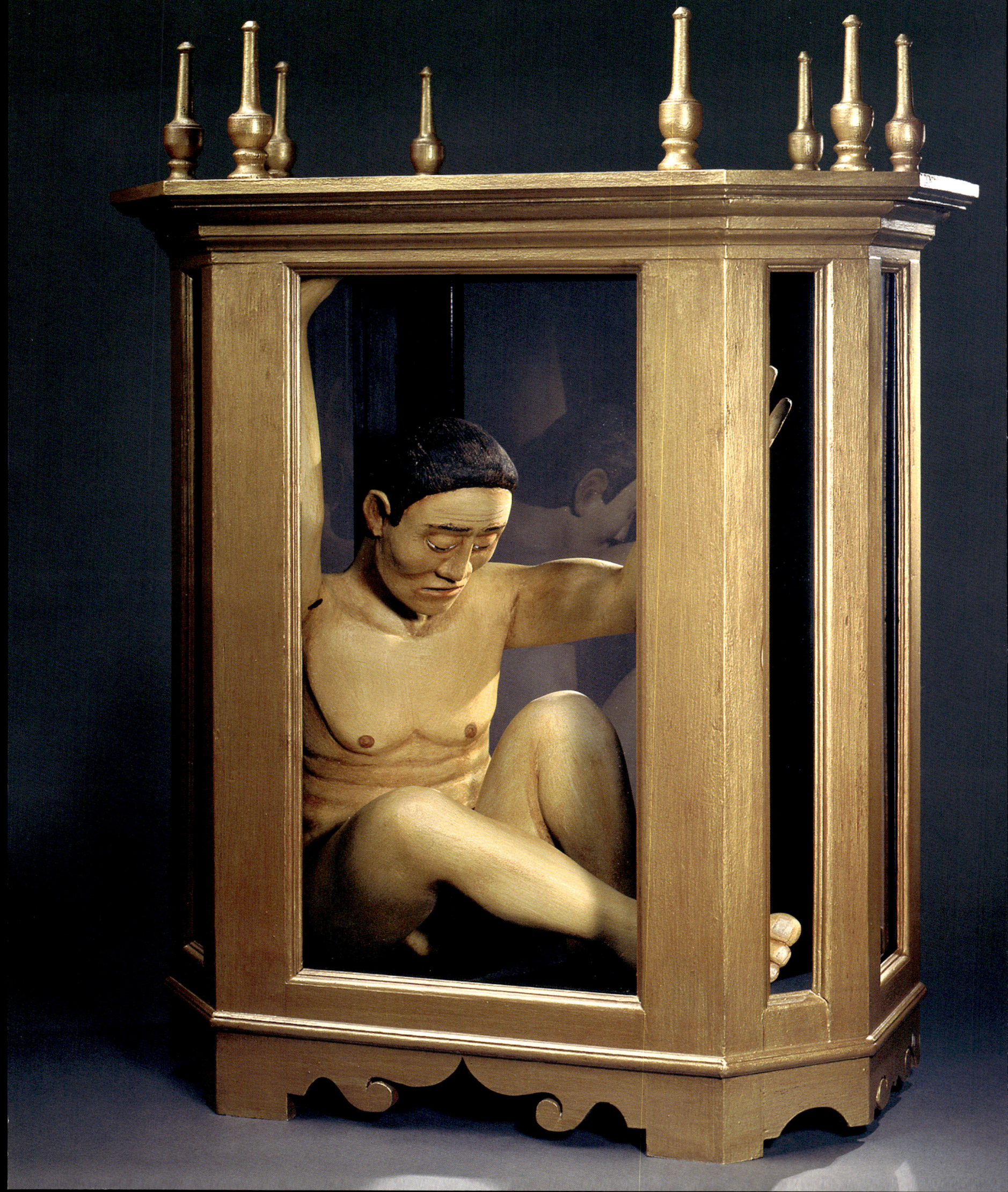

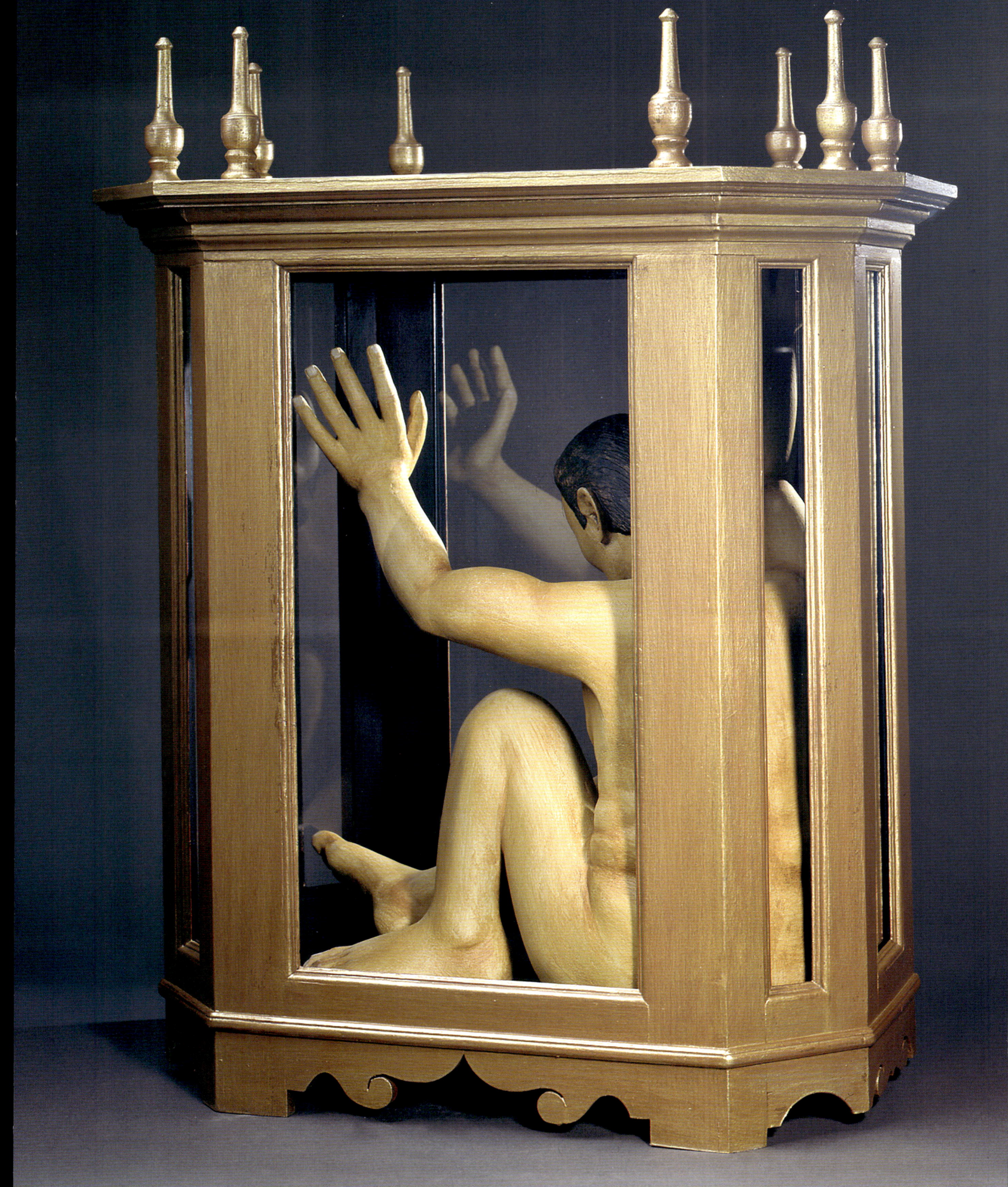

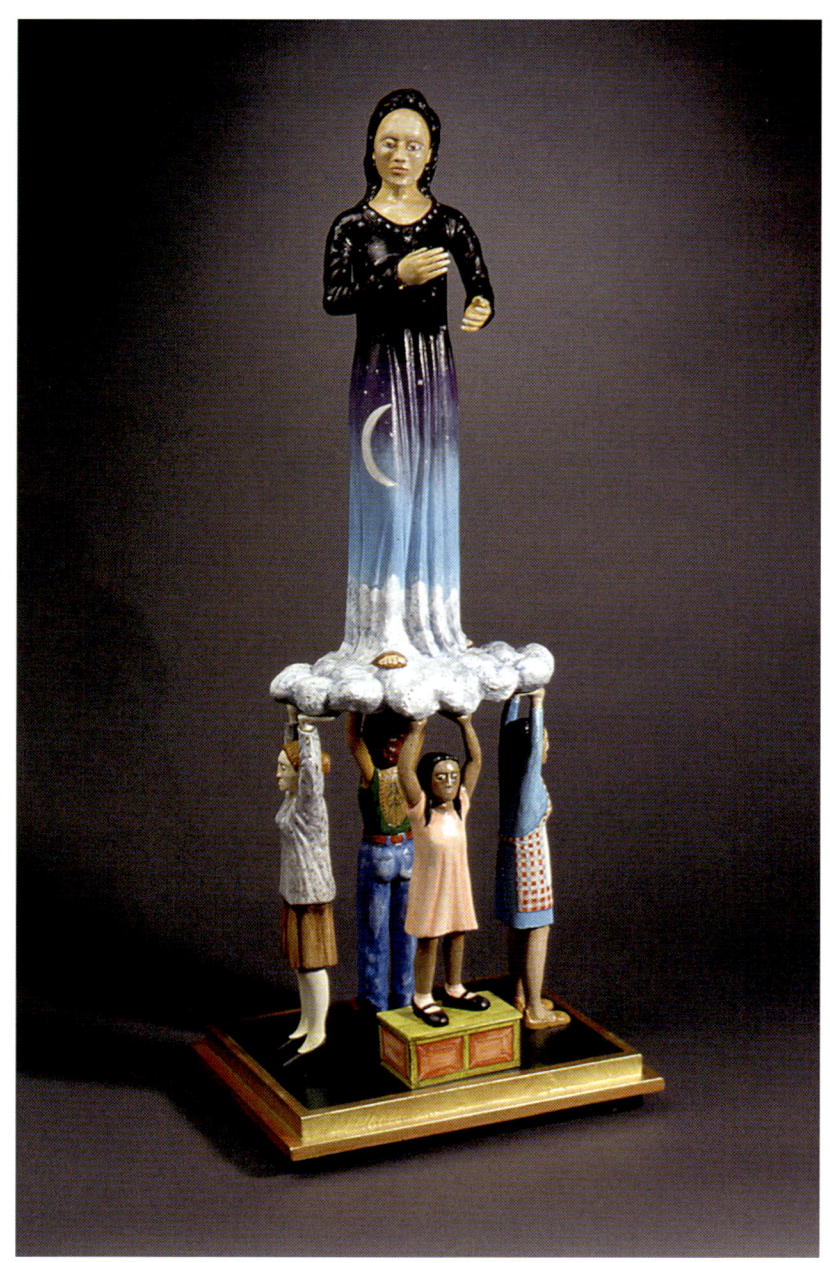
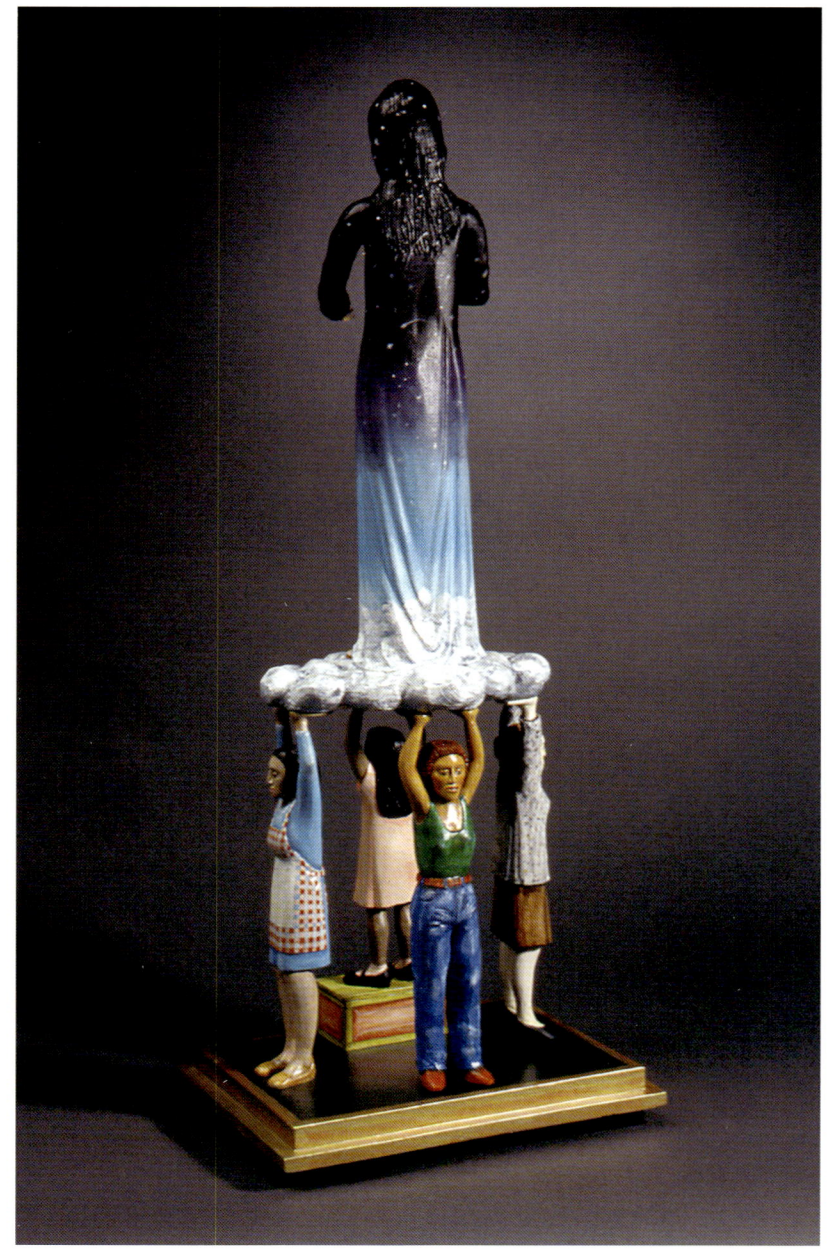

Plate 35. *A Temple Sacred by Birth Built by Hands Divine*, 2004. Carved and painted wood, 36 x 10½ x 14 in.
Collection of the Autry Museum, Los Angeles (2013.46.1). Photo © Dan Morse, courtesy of The Owings Gallery.

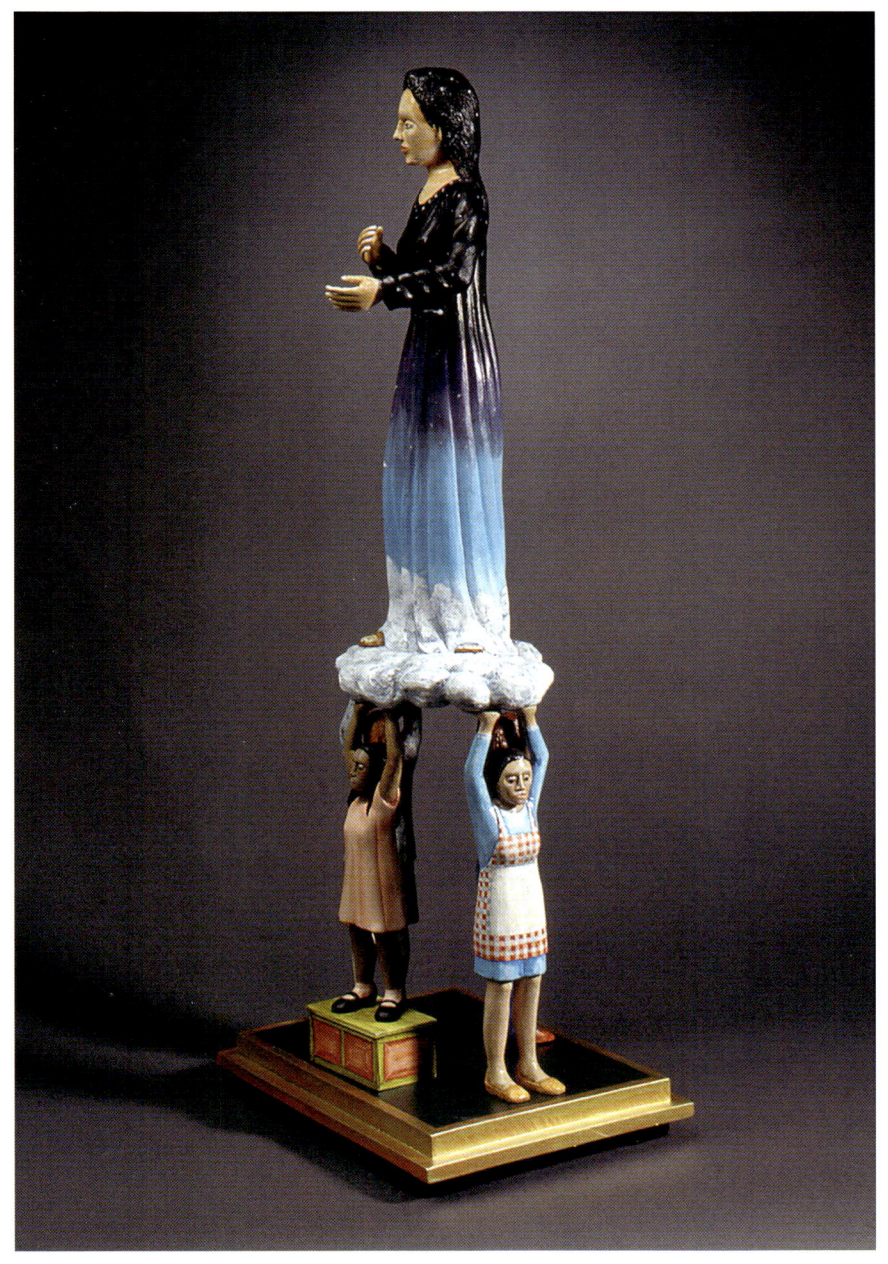
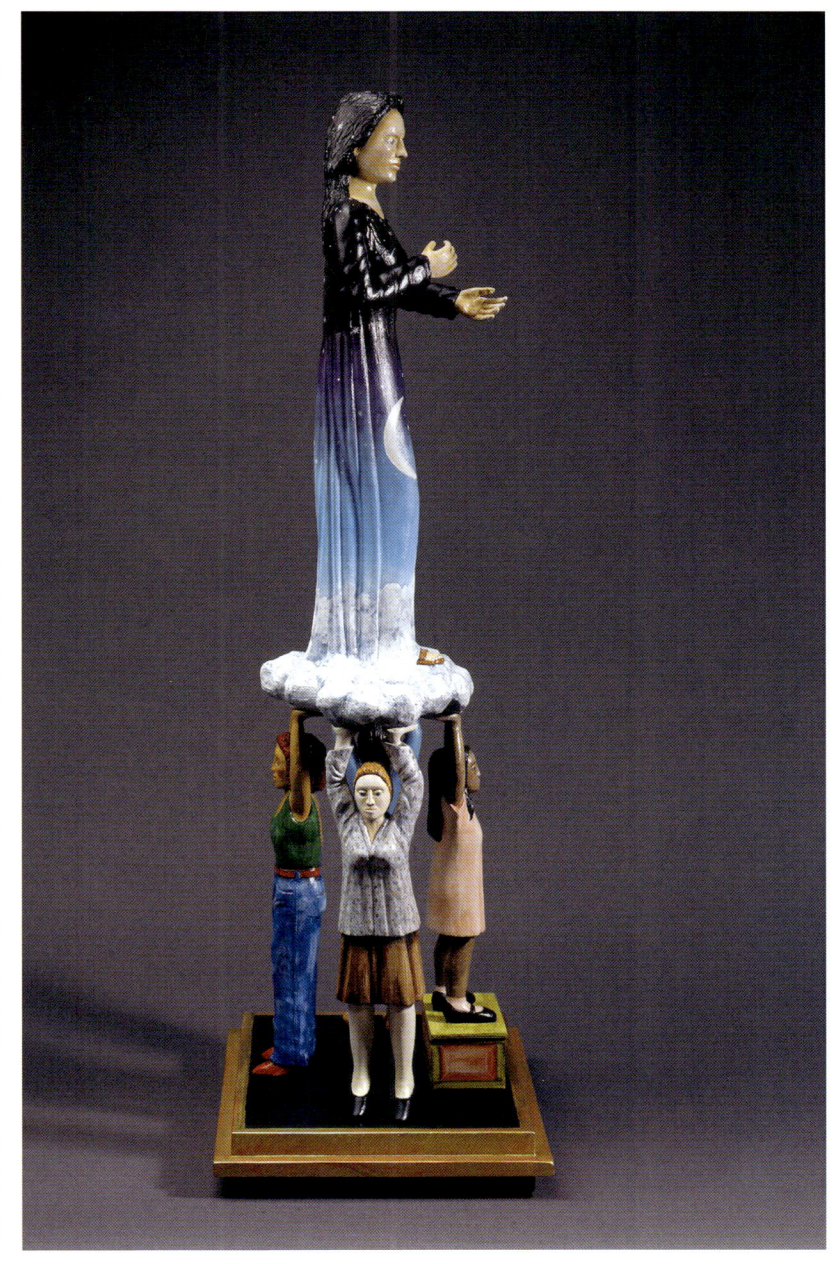

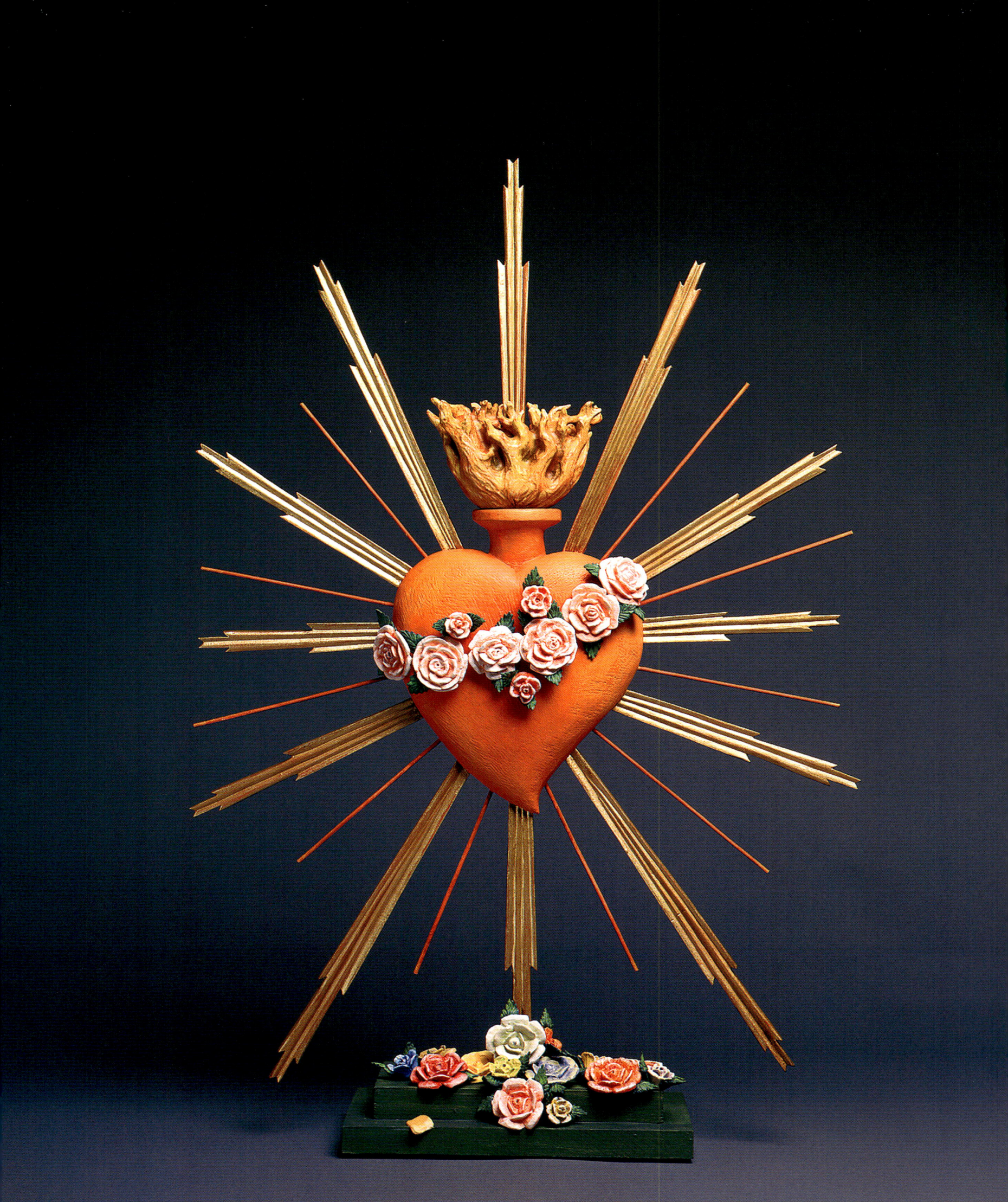

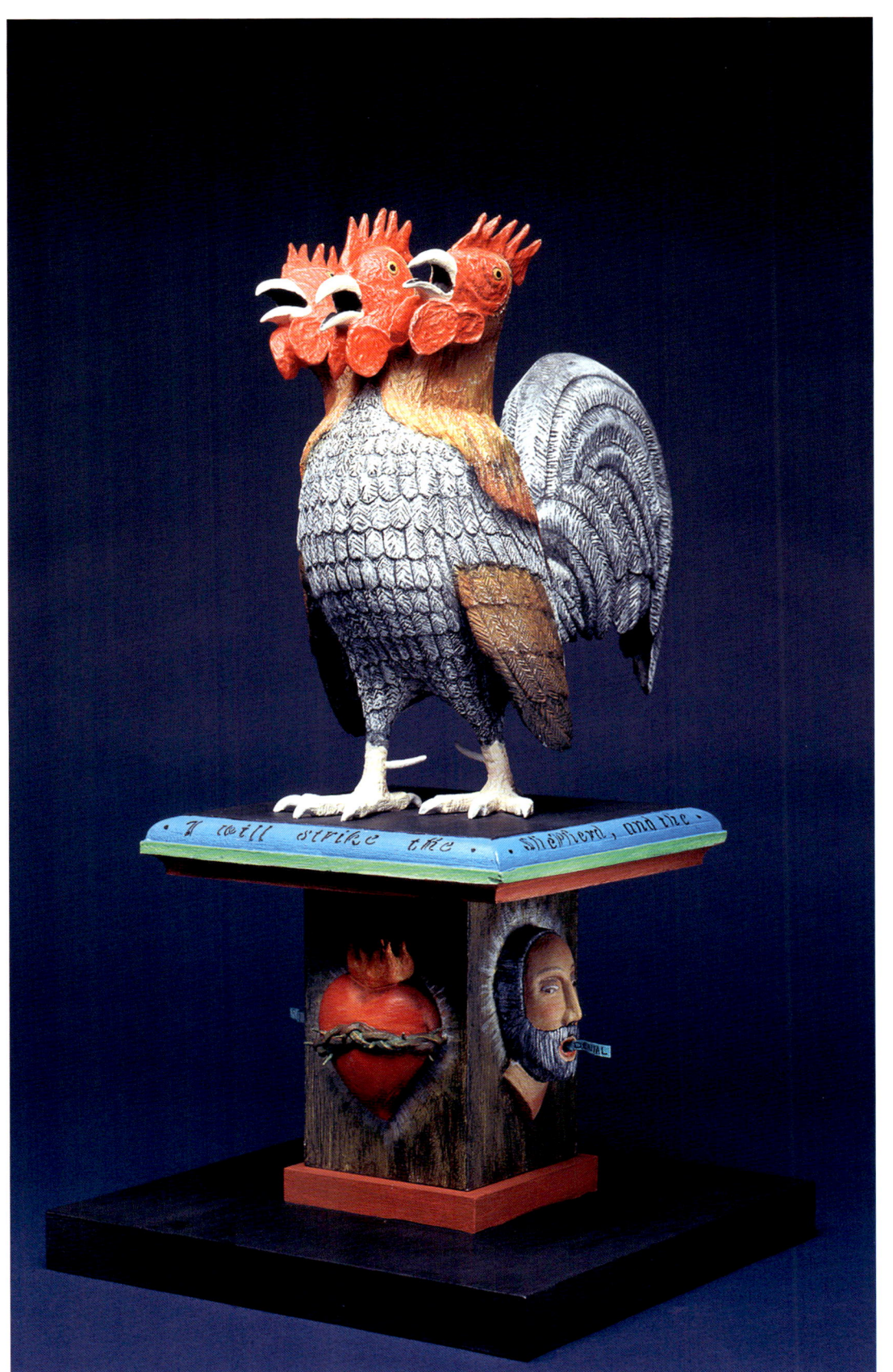

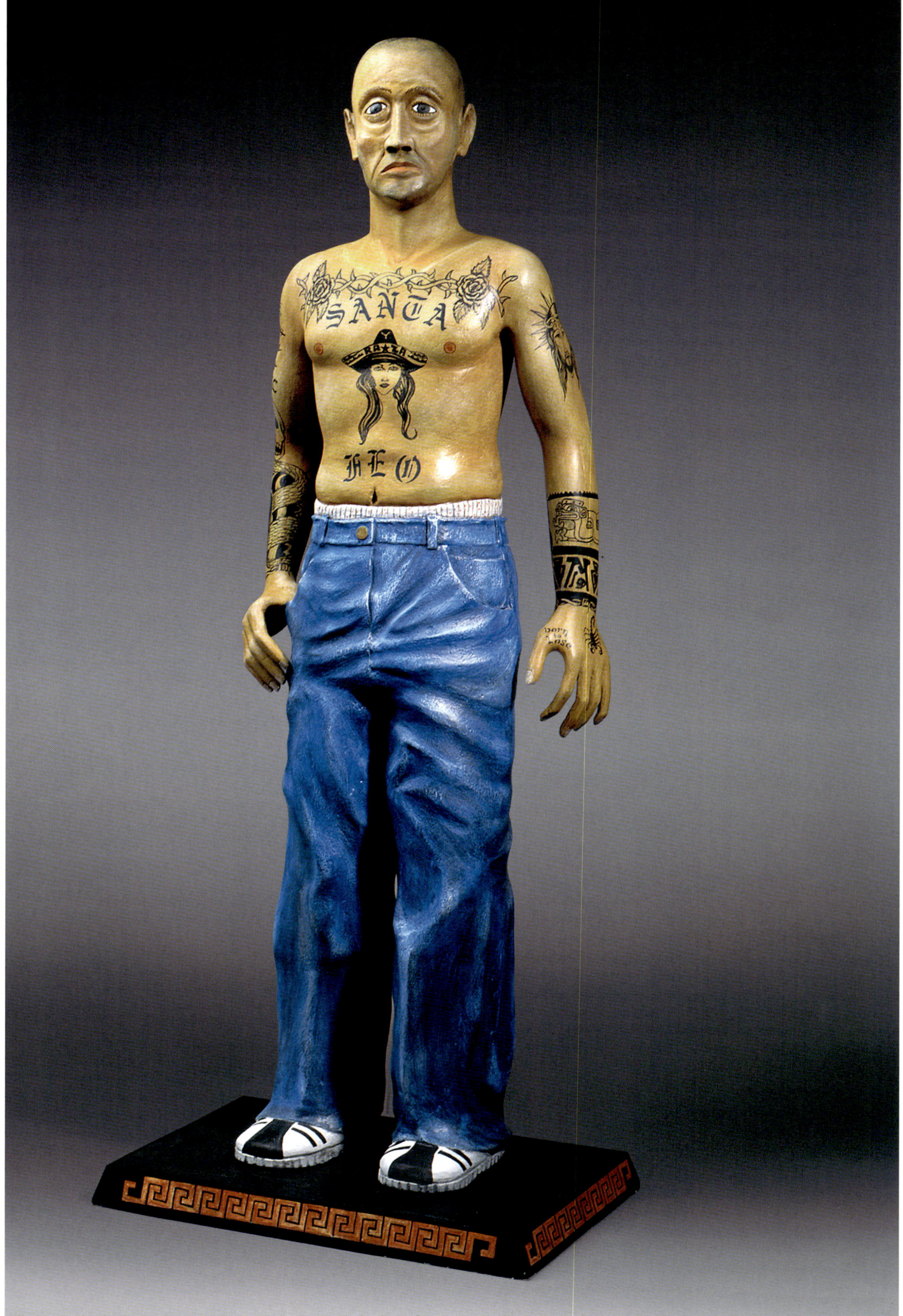

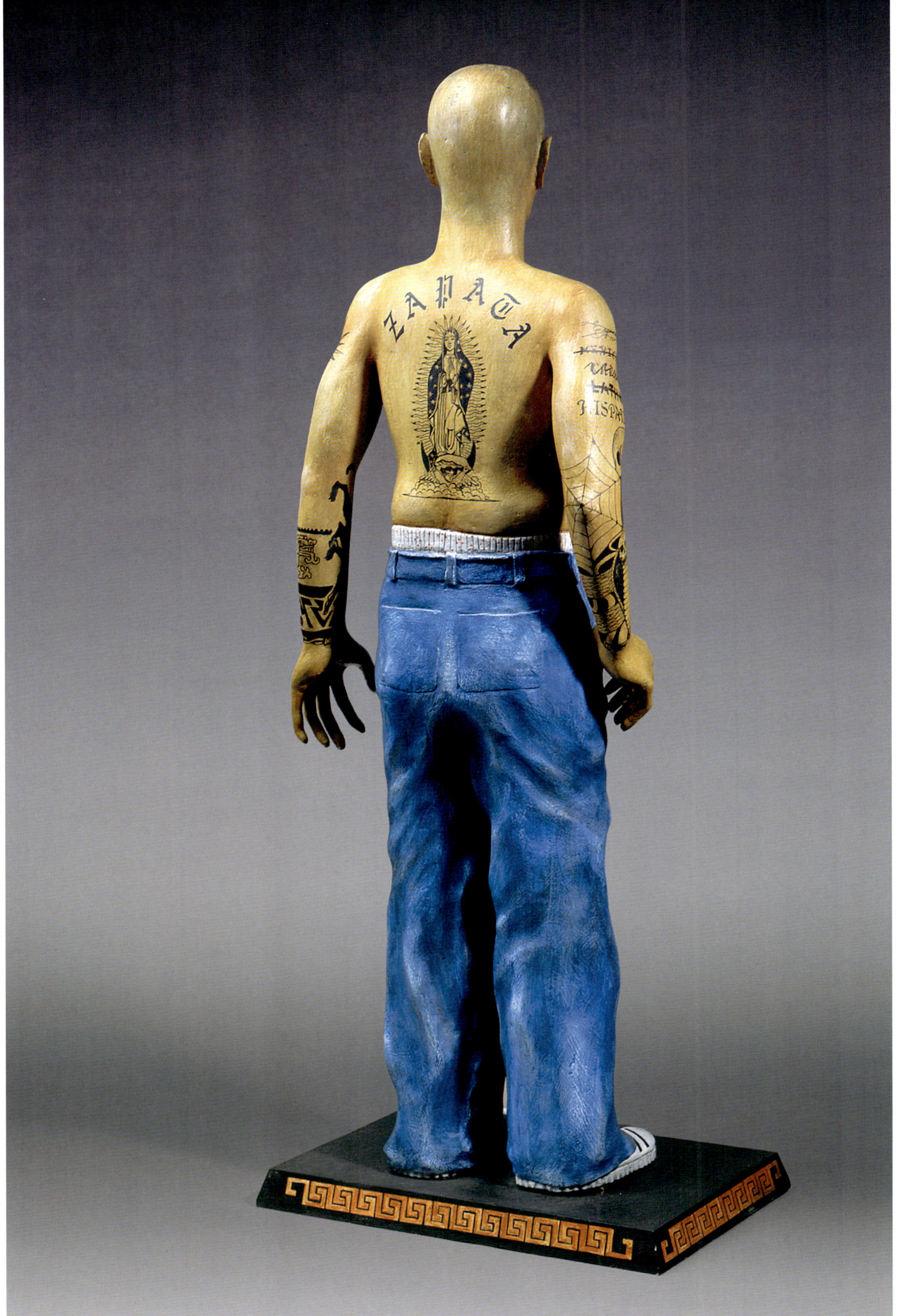

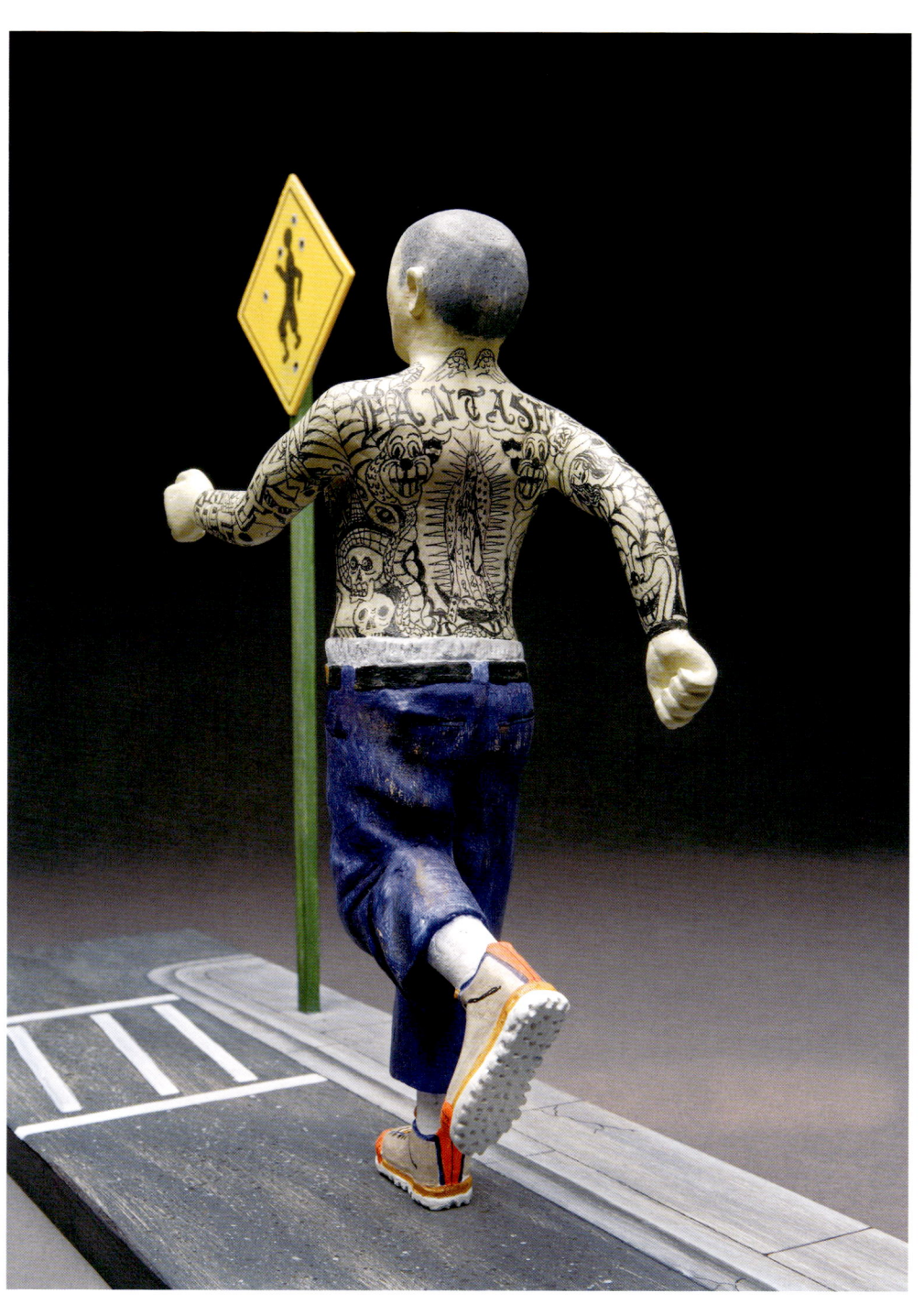

Plate 39. *Gangster Crossing*, 2008. Carved and painted wood, 30 x 20⅜ x 8¾ in.
Collection of John Robertshaw. Photo © Addison Doty, courtesy of The Owings Gallery.

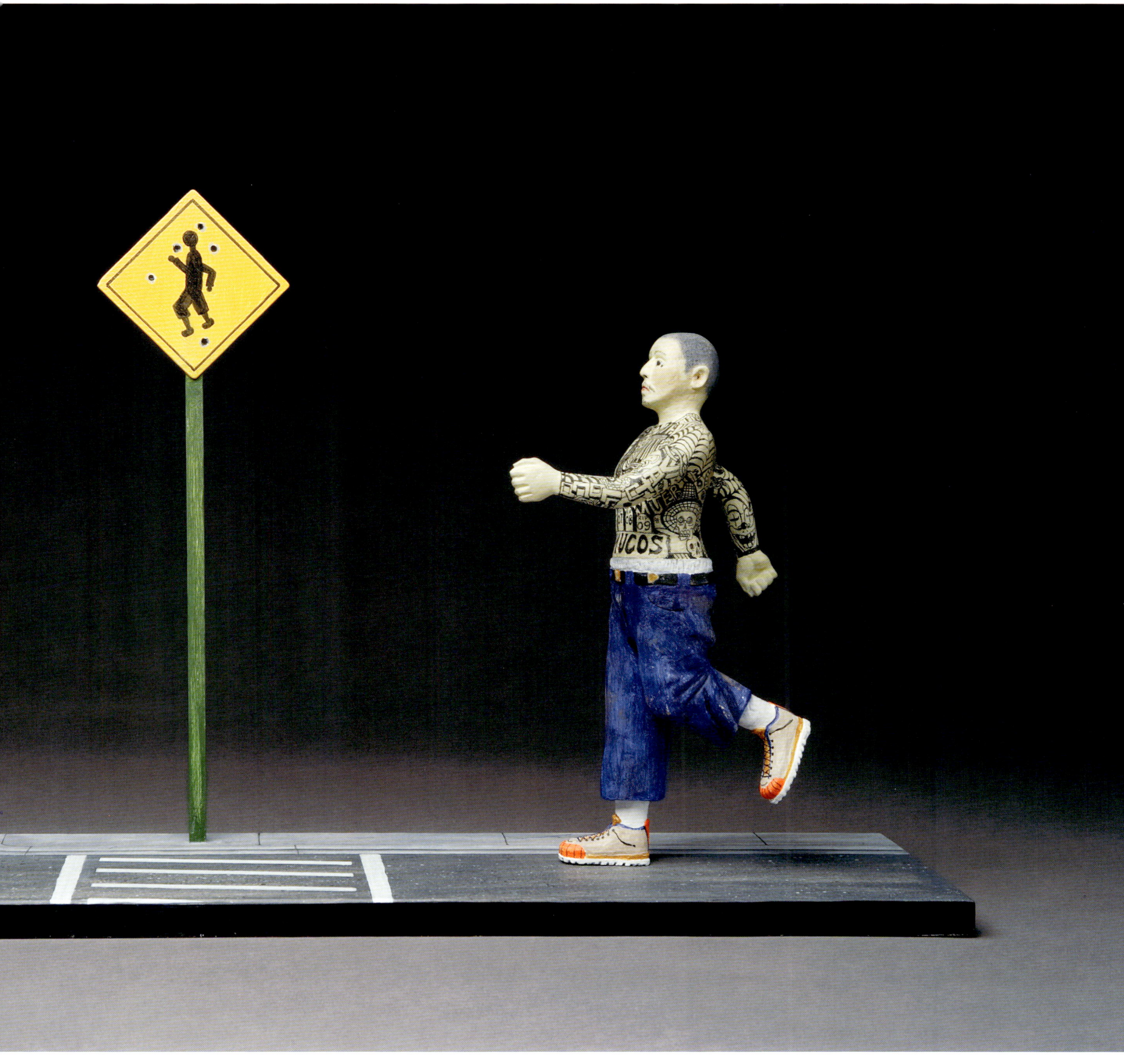

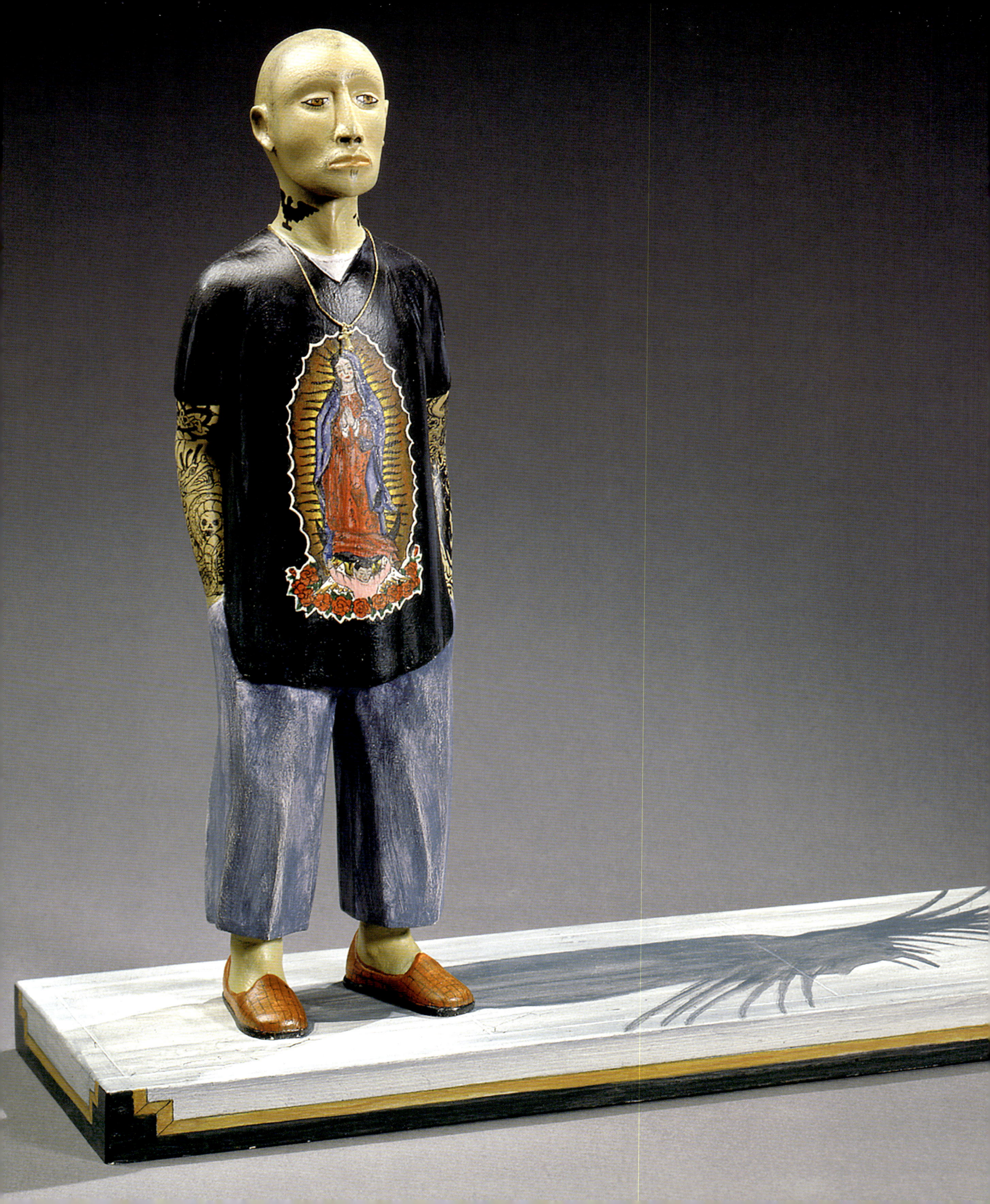

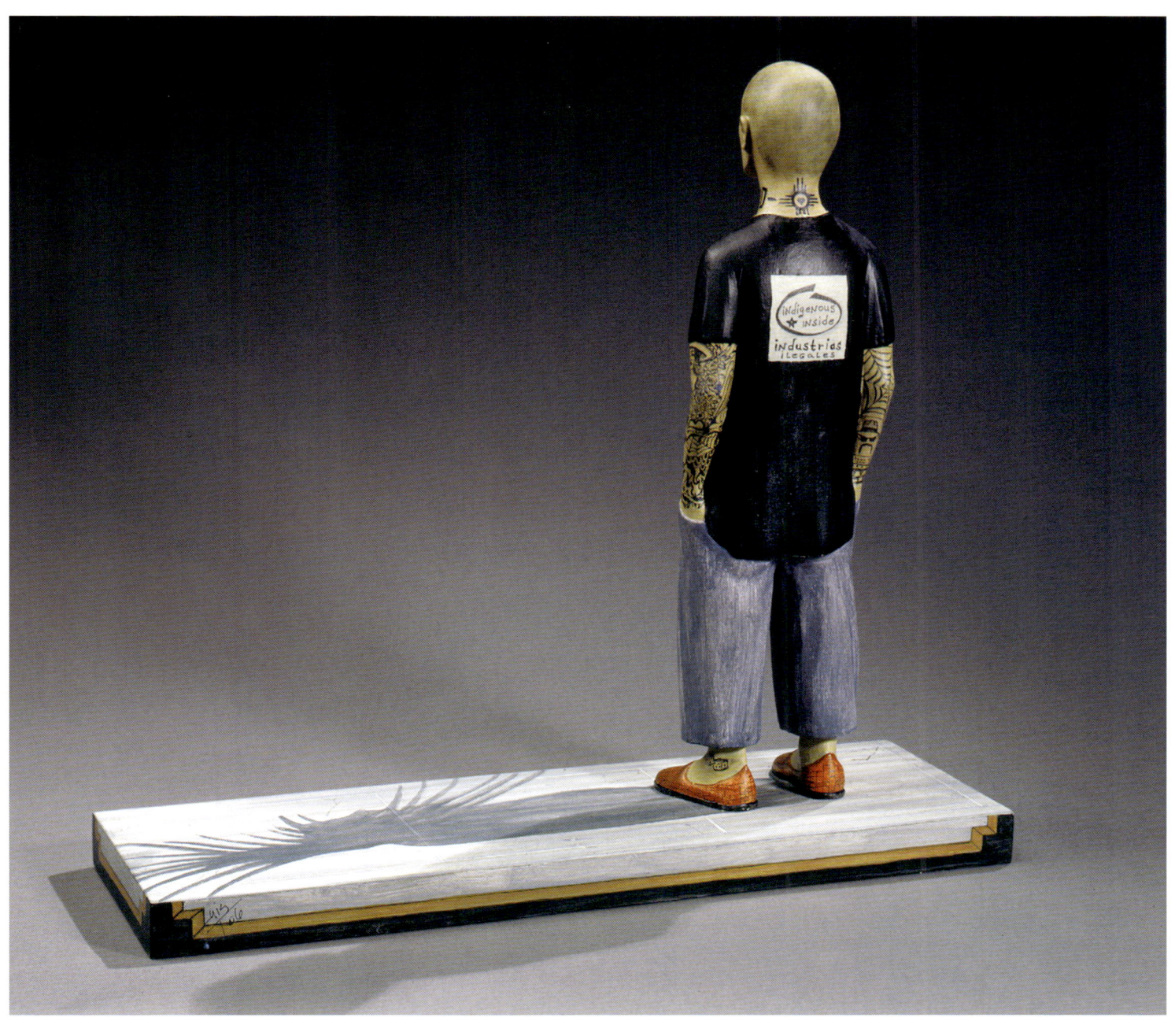

Plate 40. *Juan Diego*, 2011. Carved and painted wood, 27 ¾ x 12 x 6 in. Collection of Ed Blount.
Photo © Dan Morse, courtesy of The Owings Gallery.

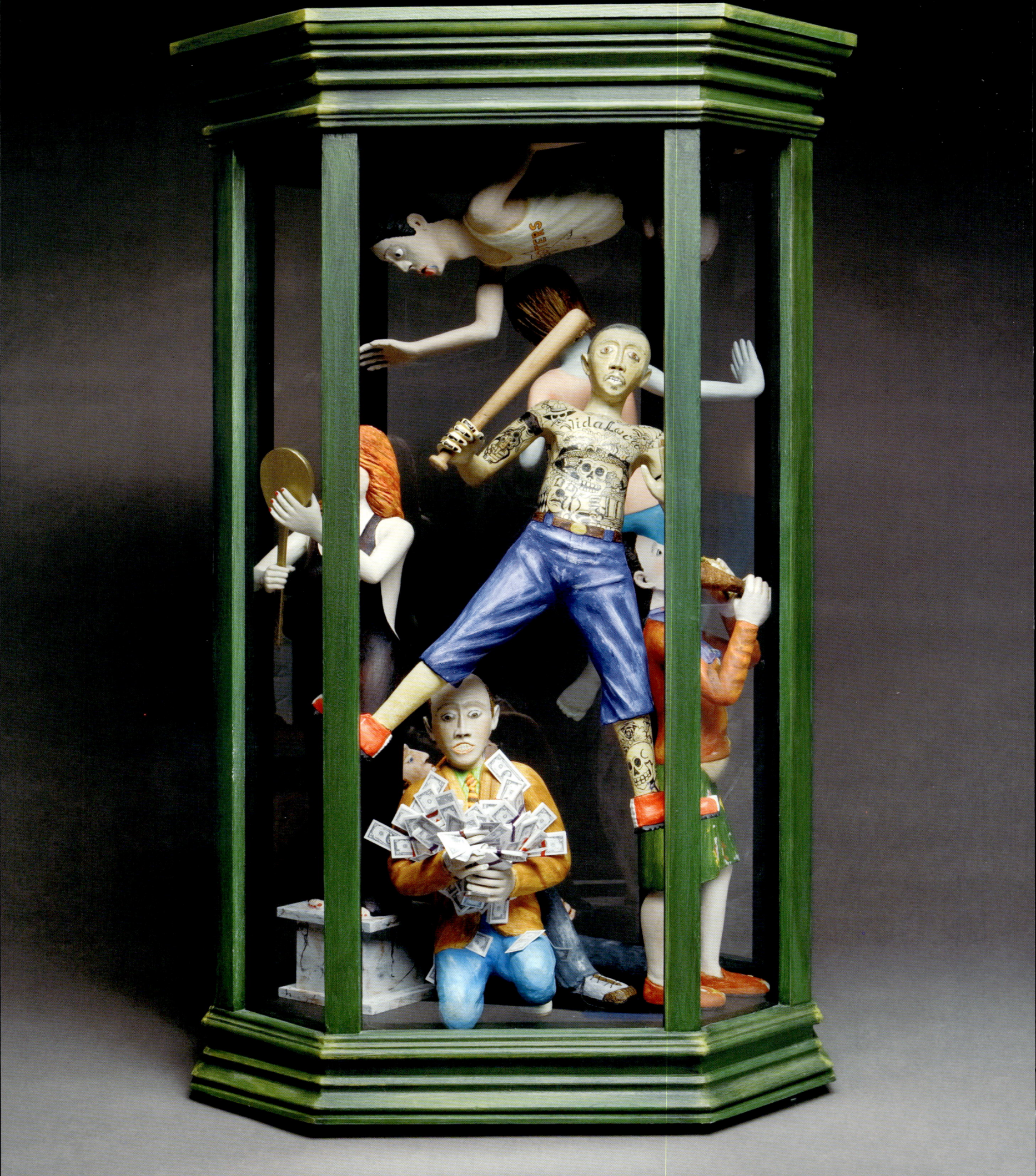

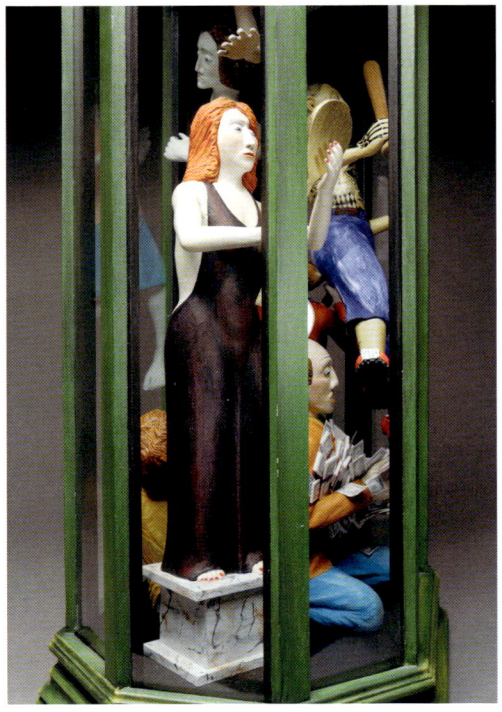
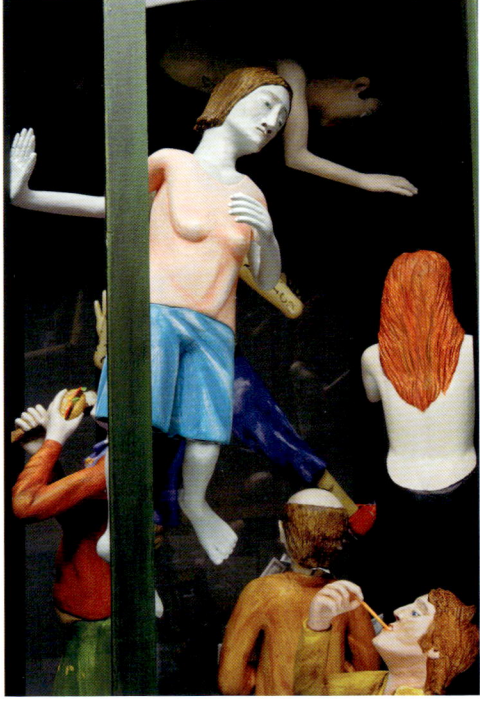
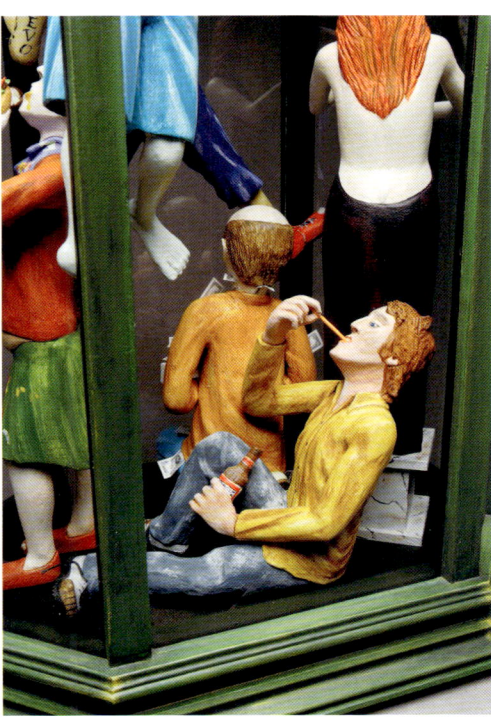
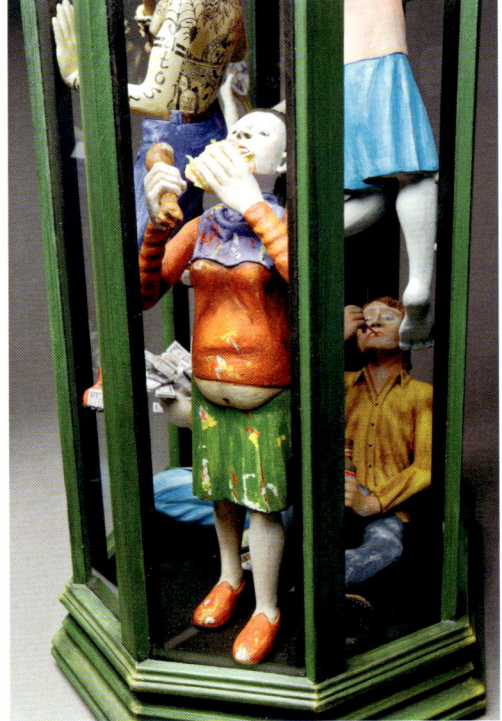
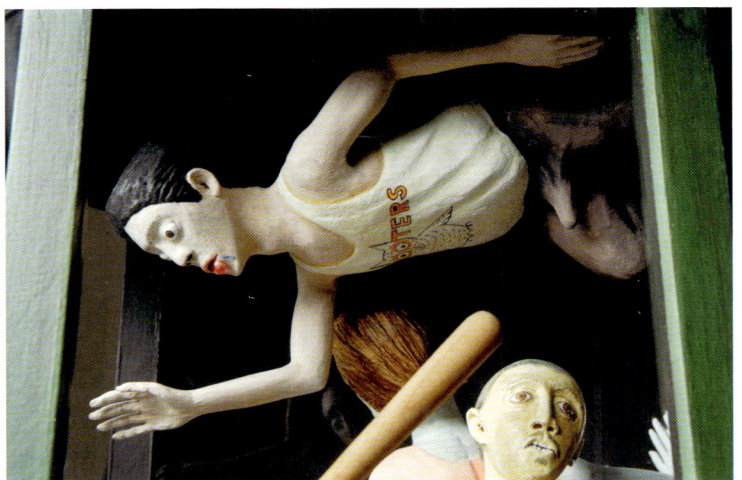

Plate 41. *Seven Deadly Sins*, 2008. Carved and painted wood, 33 x 15¼ x 21¼ in. Collection of Kathryn Minette and Stan Biderman. Photo © Addison Doty, courtesy of The Owings Gallery.

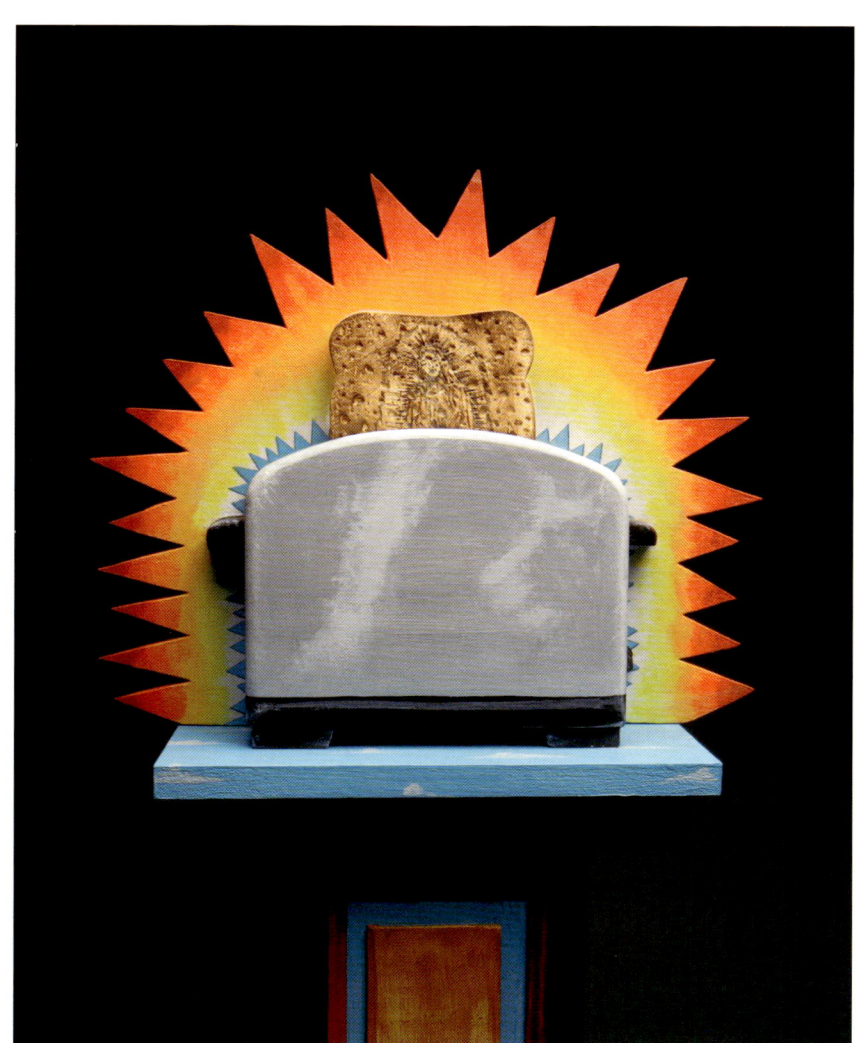
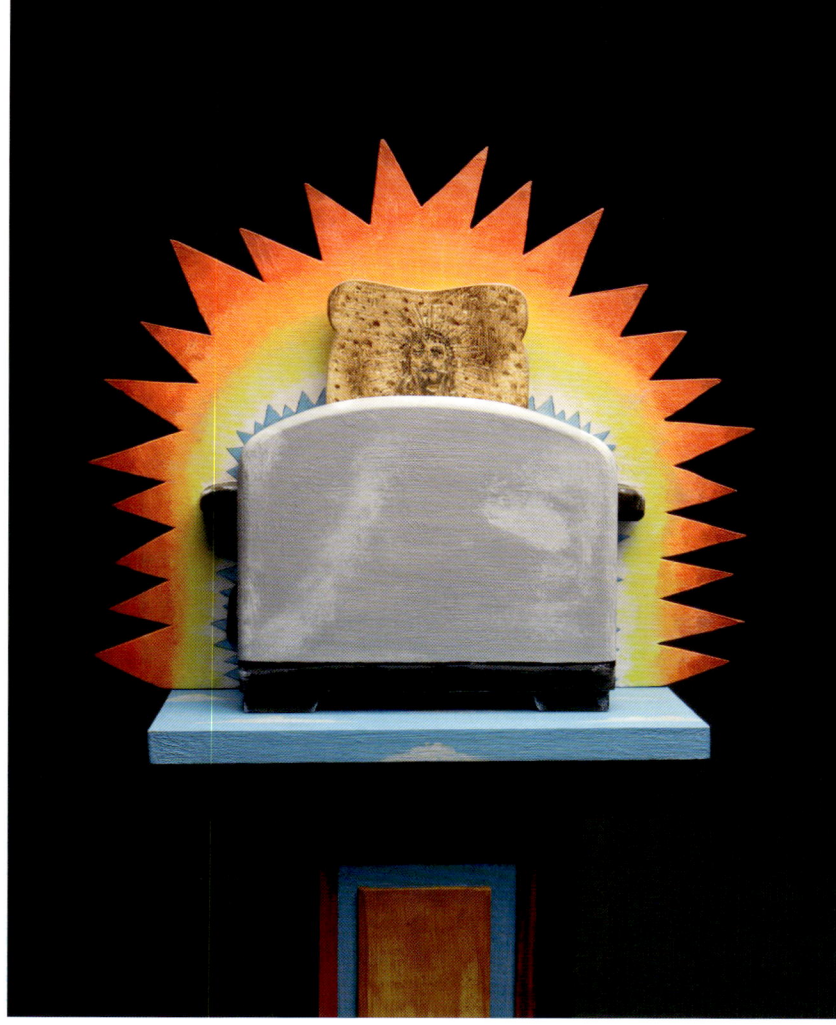

Plate 42. *Holy Toaster*, 2008. Carved and painted wood, 55 x 16 x 10 in.
Denver Art Museum Collection; funds from Nancy L. Benson (2011.272A-D).
Photo © Addison Doty, courtesy of The Owings Gallery.

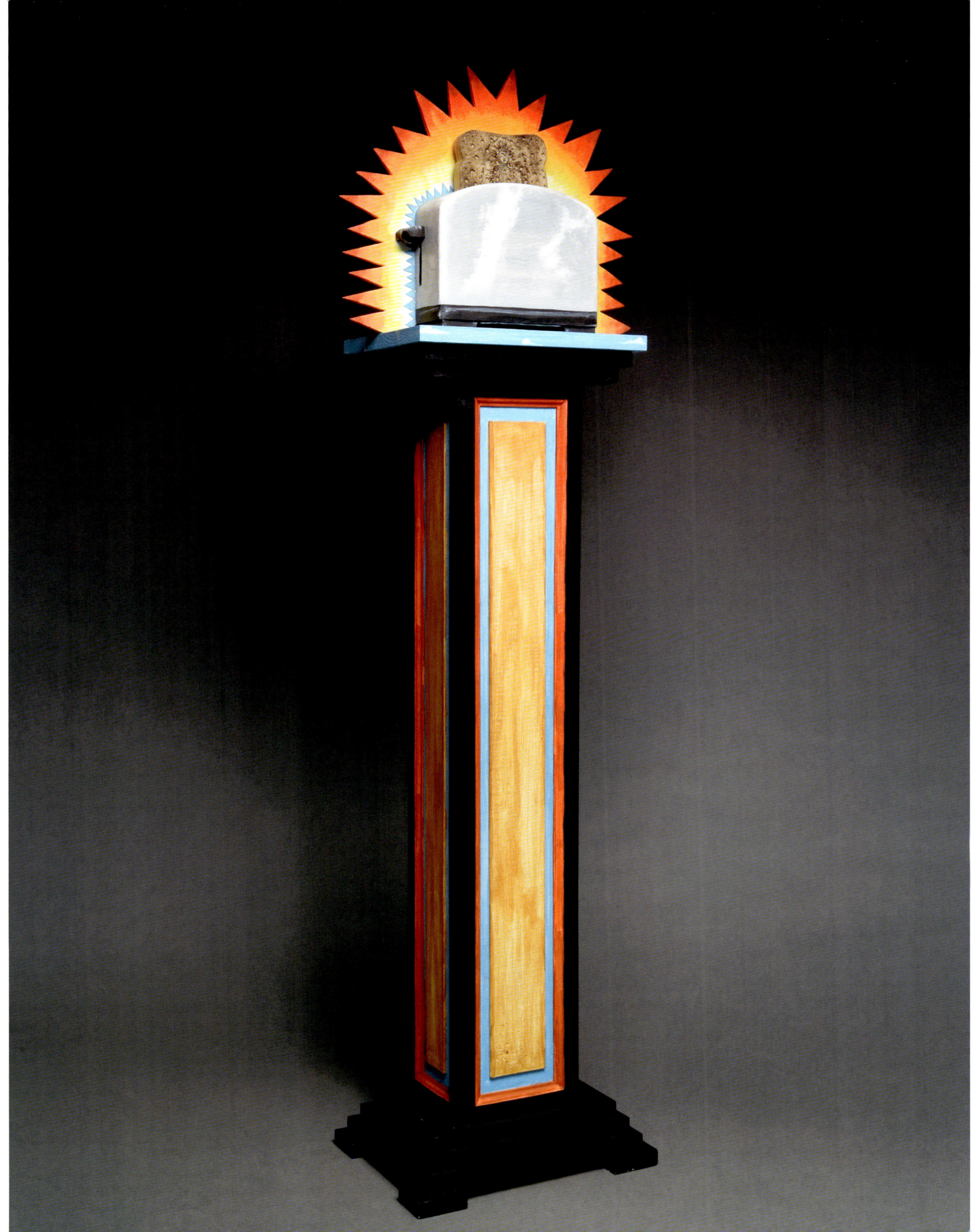

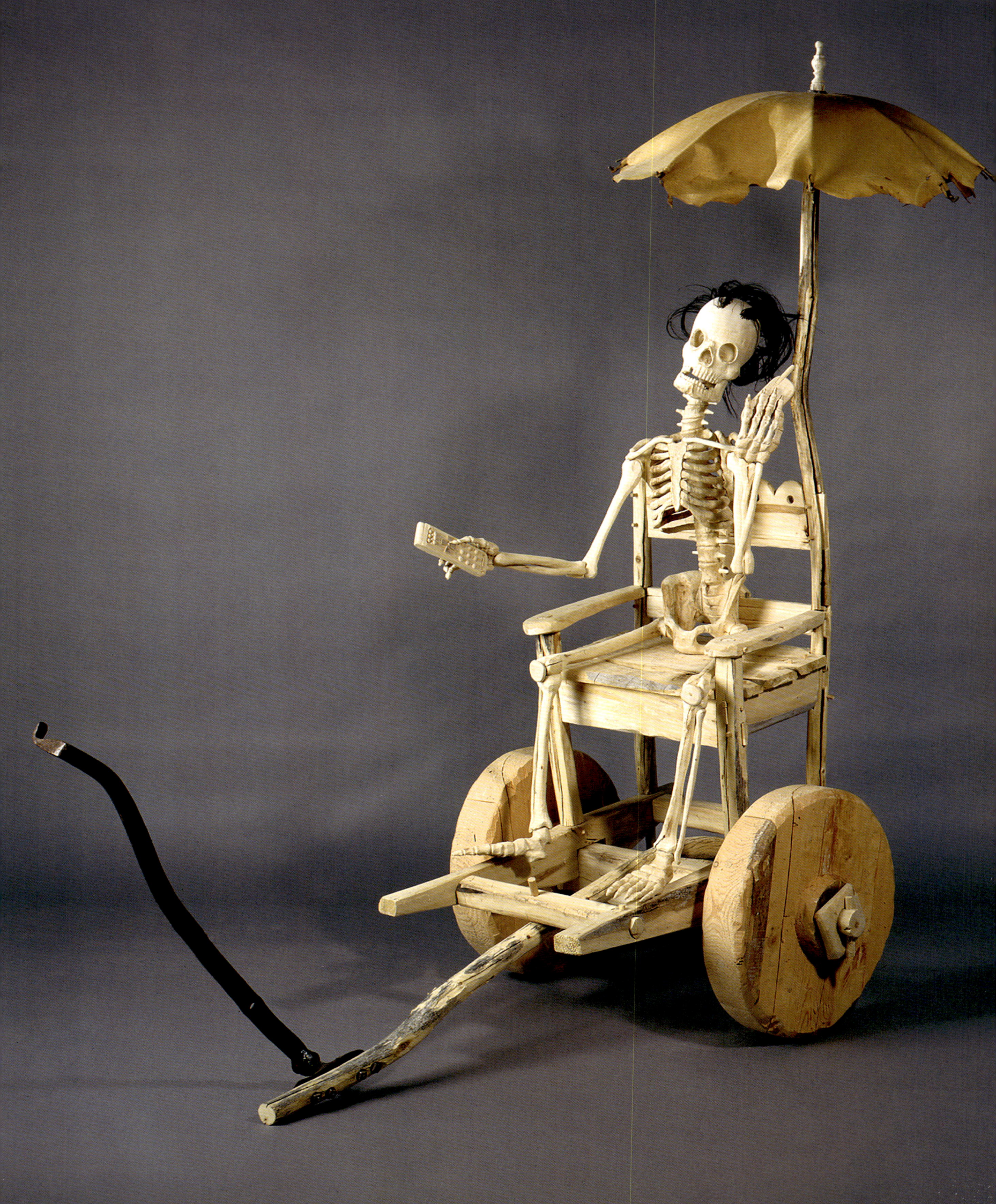

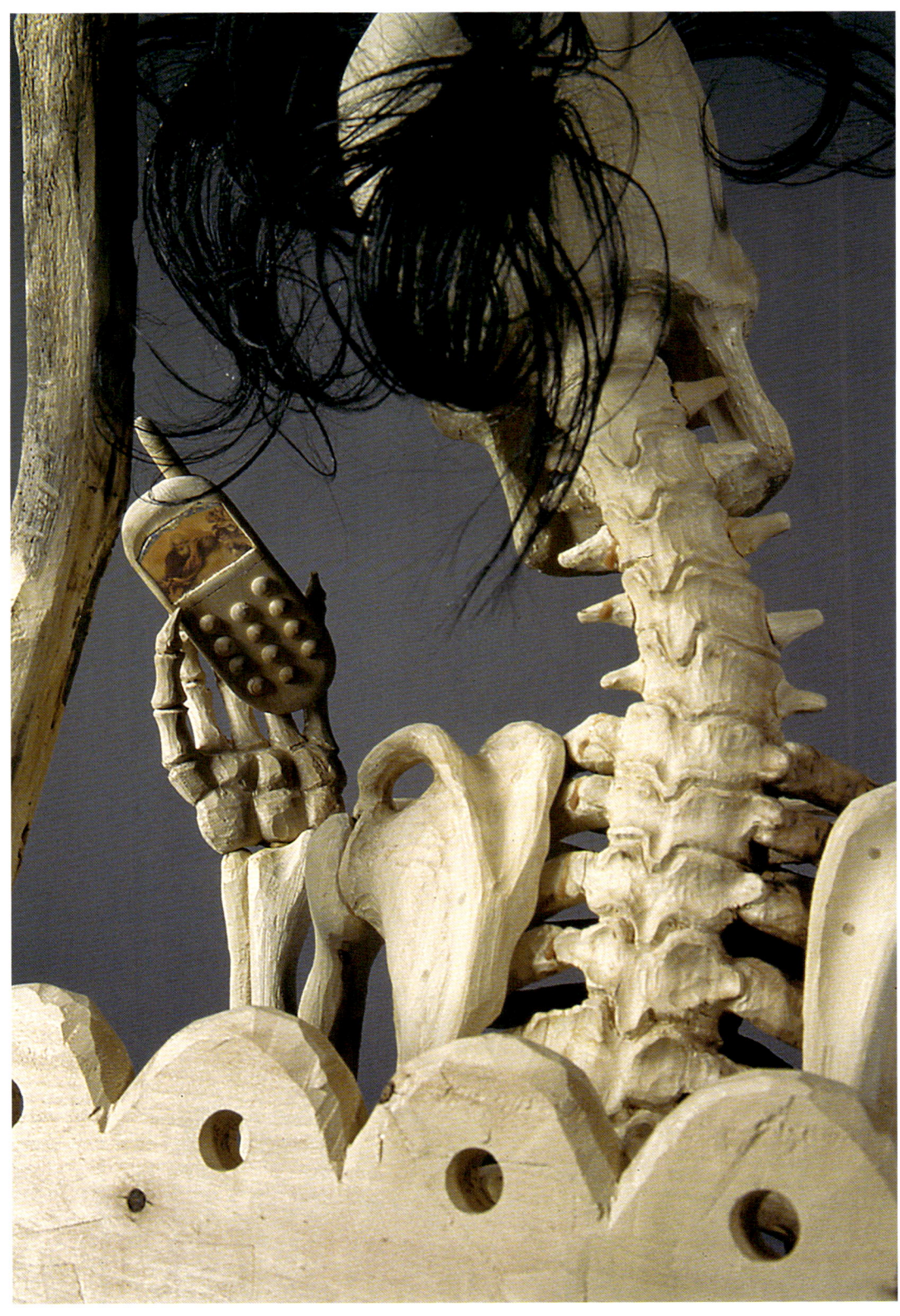

Plate 43. *State of the Art Sebastiana*, 2006. Carved wood, iron, human hair, 69 x 61 x 33 in. Collection of William Paul Wanker and Pamela Kelly. Photo © Addison Doty, courtesy of The Owings Gallery.

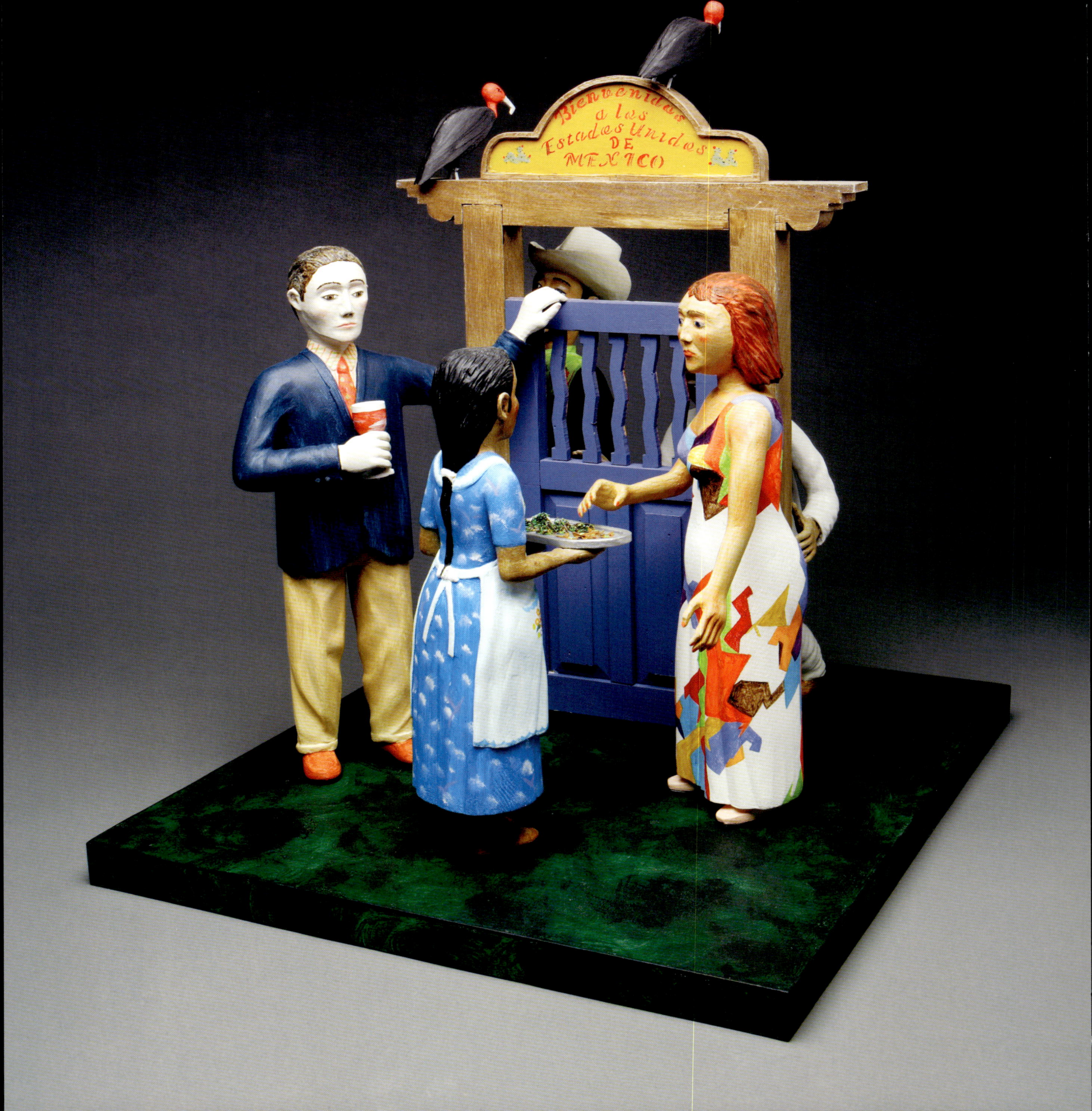

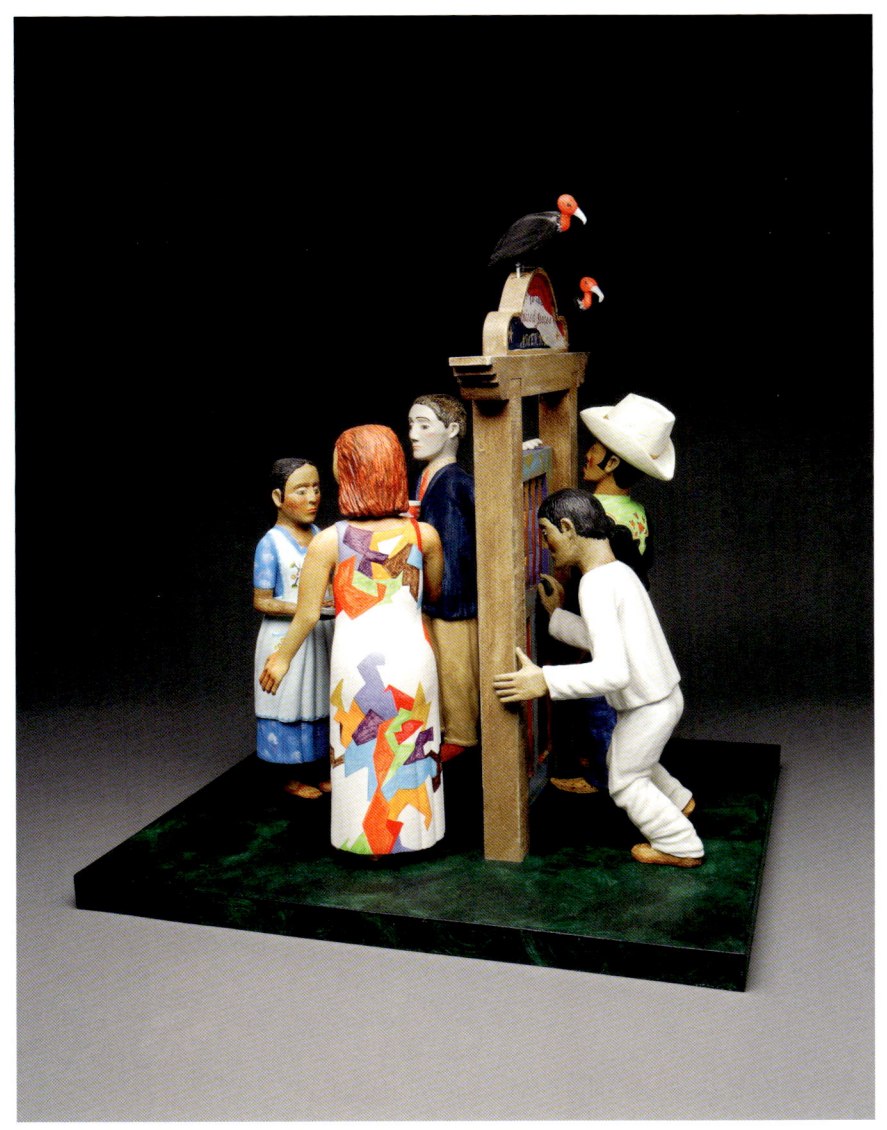
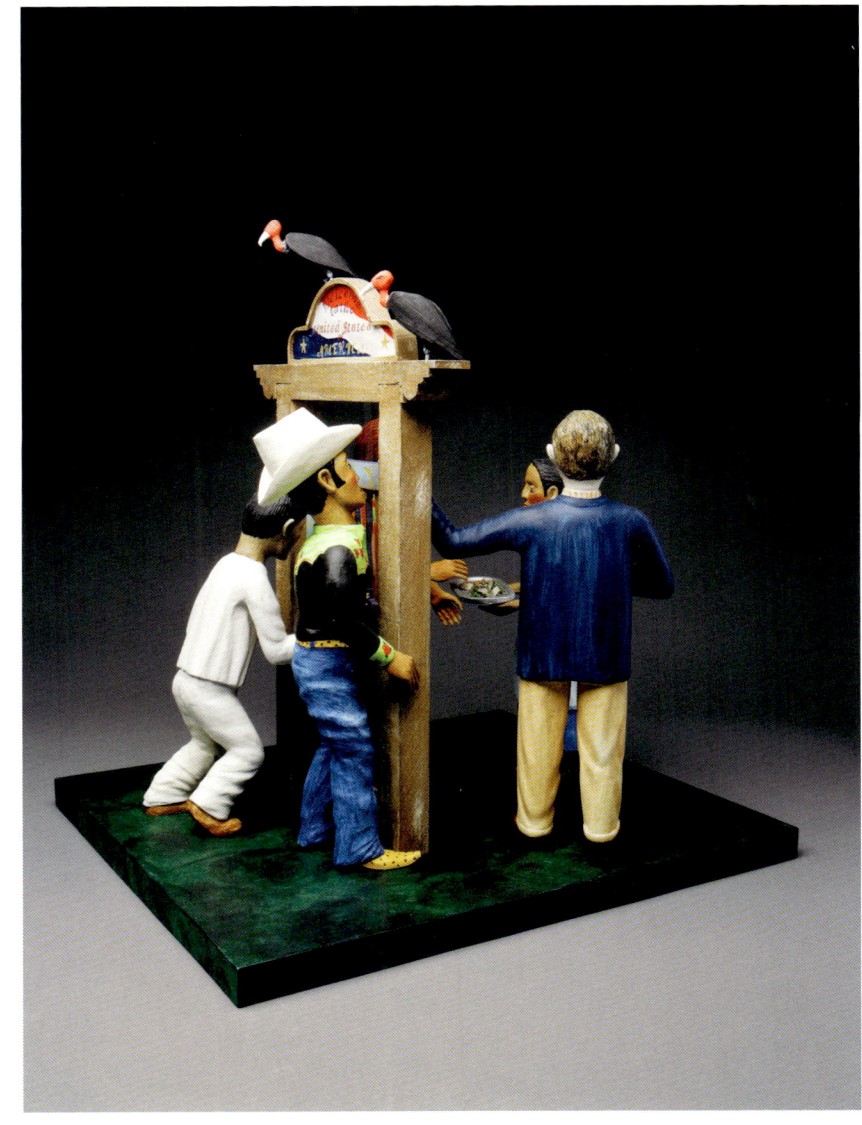

Plate 44. *Fiesta at the Border*, 2007. Carved and painted wood, 22 x 24¹⁄₁₆ x 19½ in. Collection of Museum of International Folk Art; museum purchase (A.2010.22.1), Santa Fe. Photo © Addison Doty, courtesy of The Owings Gallery.

FOLLOWING SPREAD
Plate 45. *Venus of Willendorf*, 2012. Carved and painted wood, 26⁷⁄₈ x 15¼ x 6⁵⁄₈ in. Collection of Robert and Ellyn Feldman. Photo © James Hart.

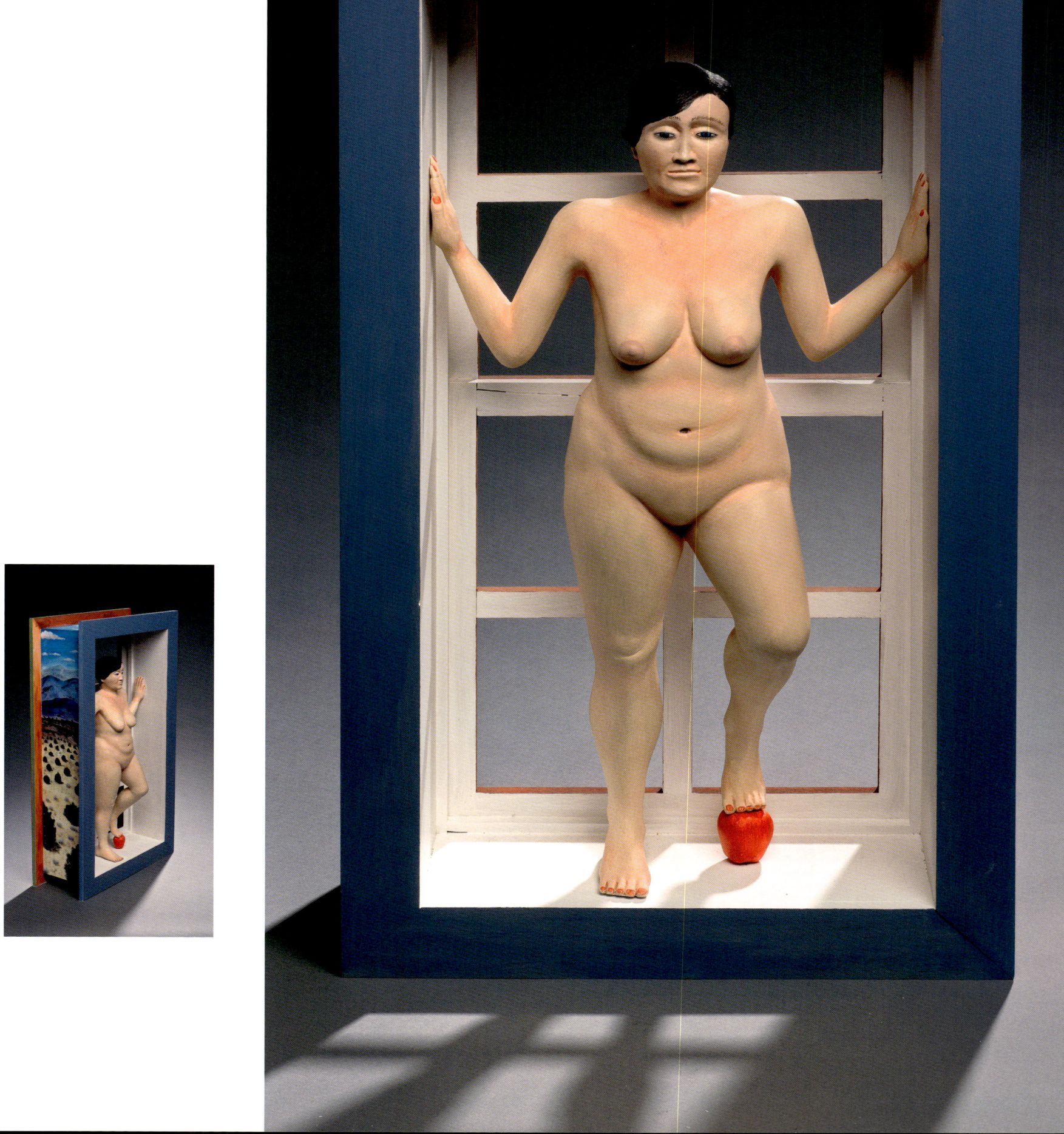

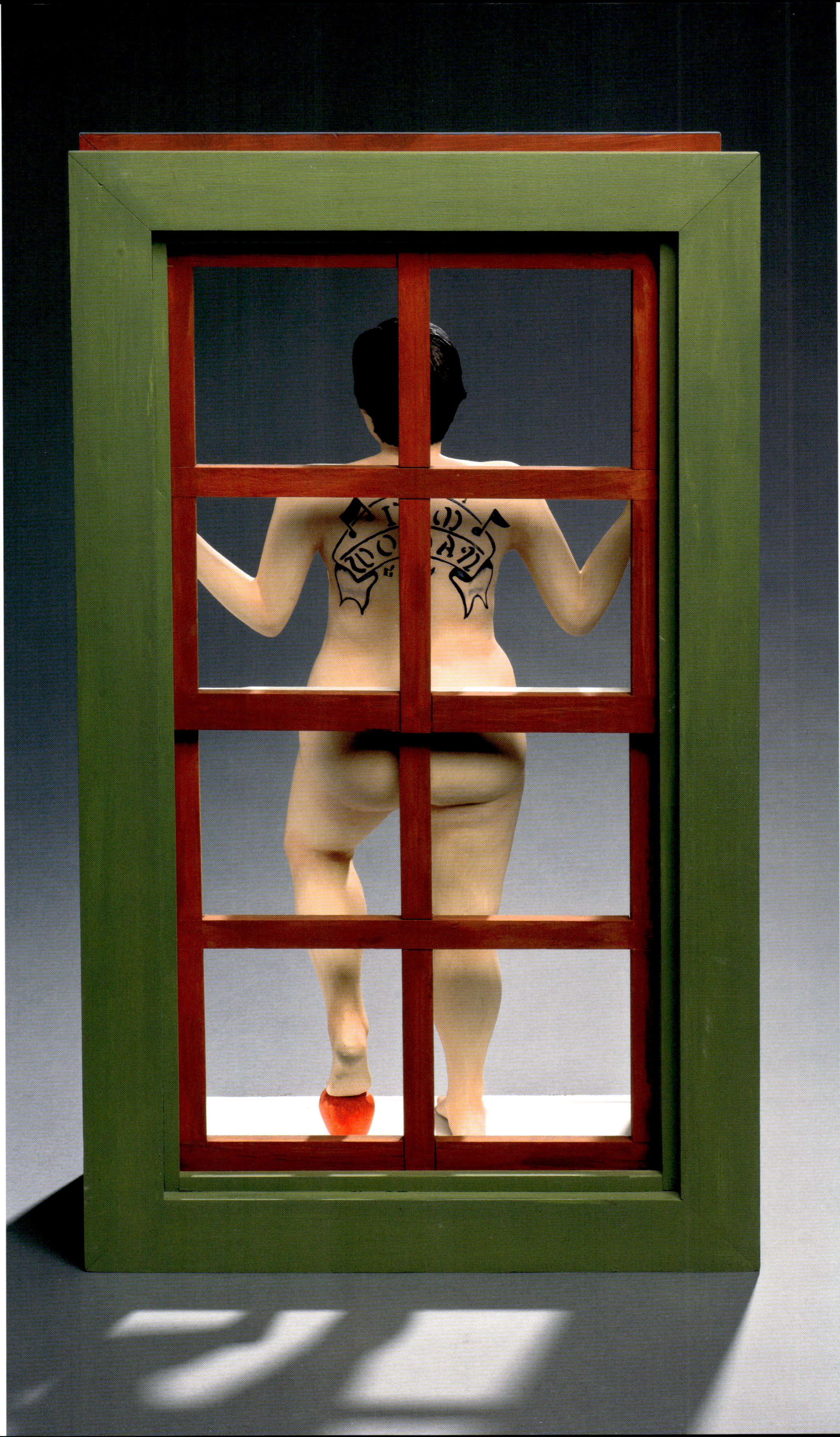

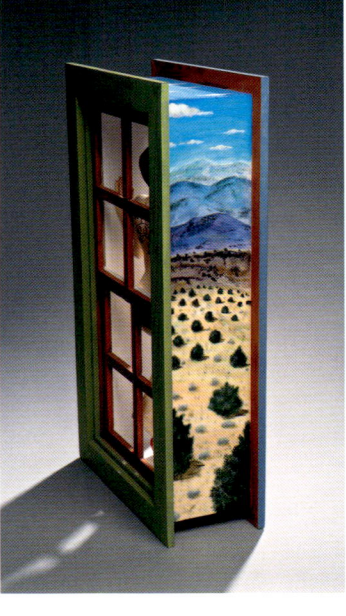

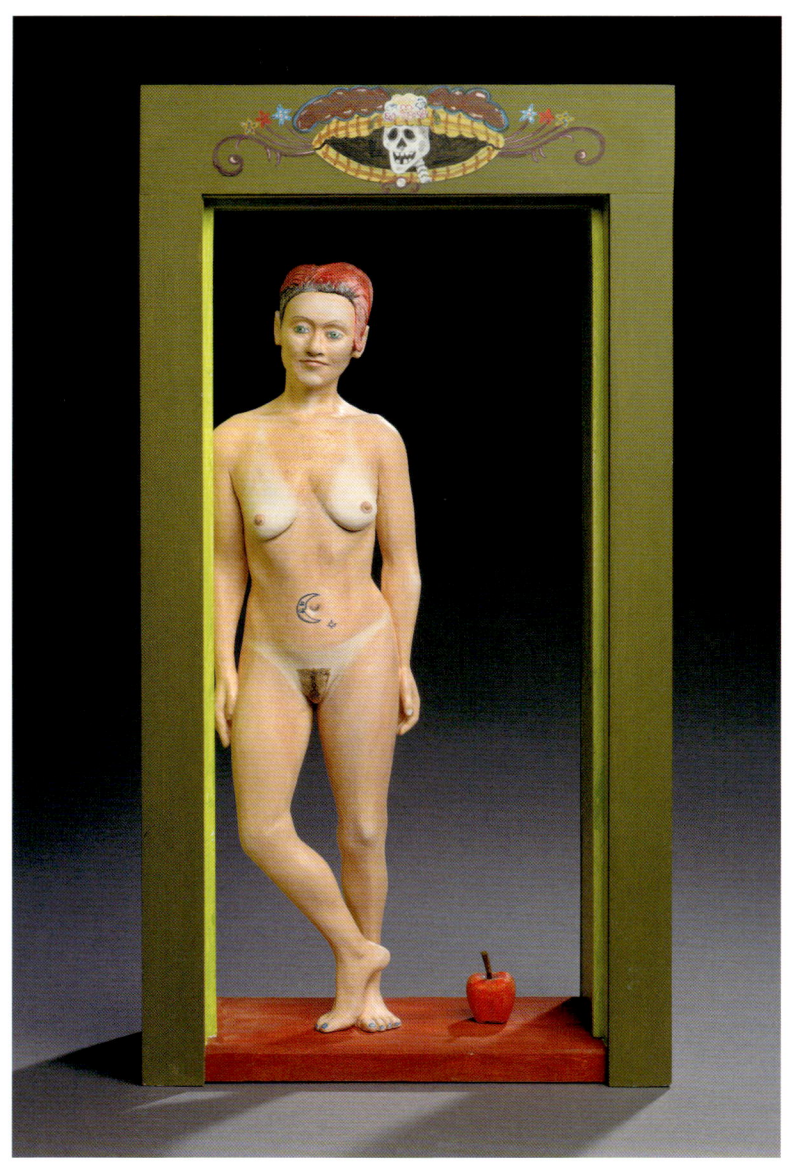
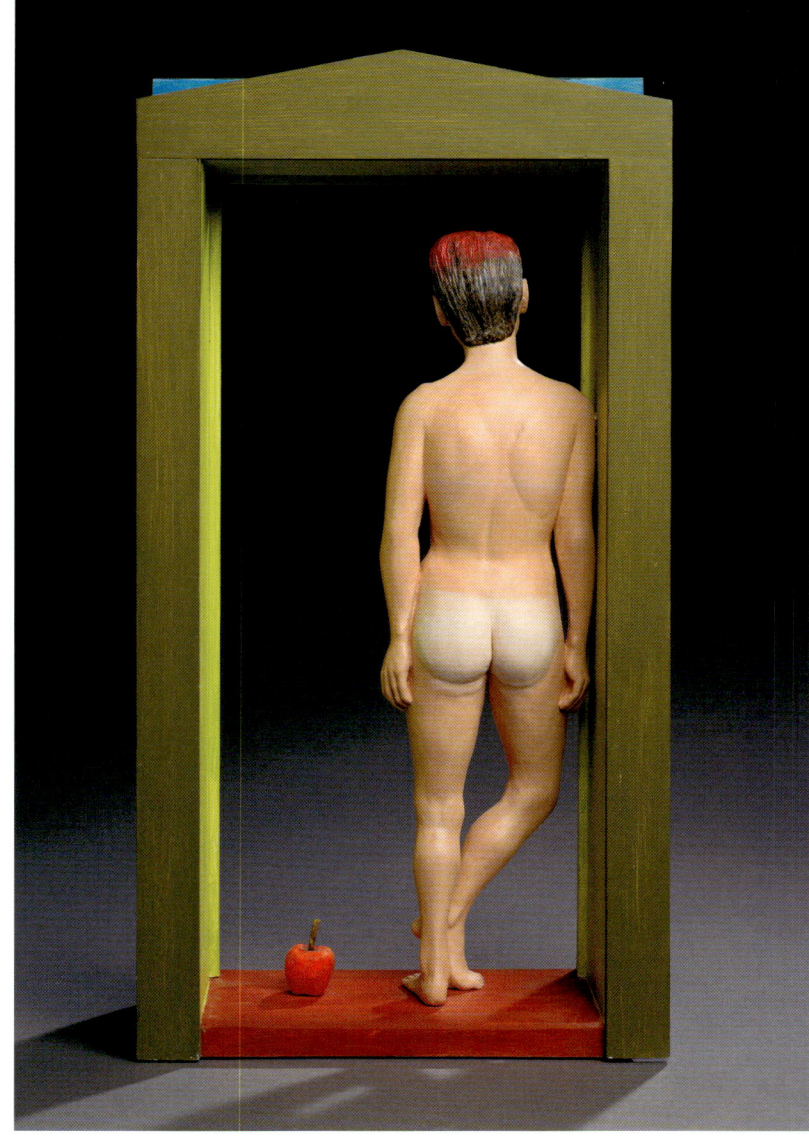
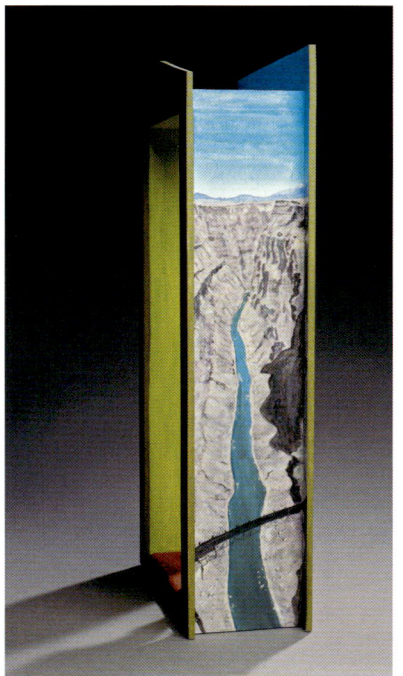
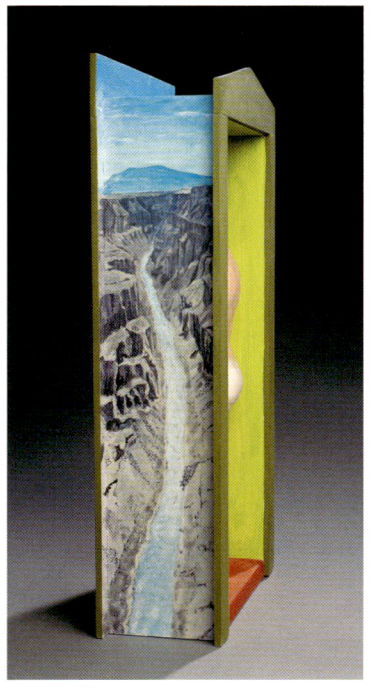

Plate 46. *Sirena del Río Grande*, 2014. Carved and painted wood,
26 x 13¼ x 6 in. Collection of the artist. Photo © James Hart.

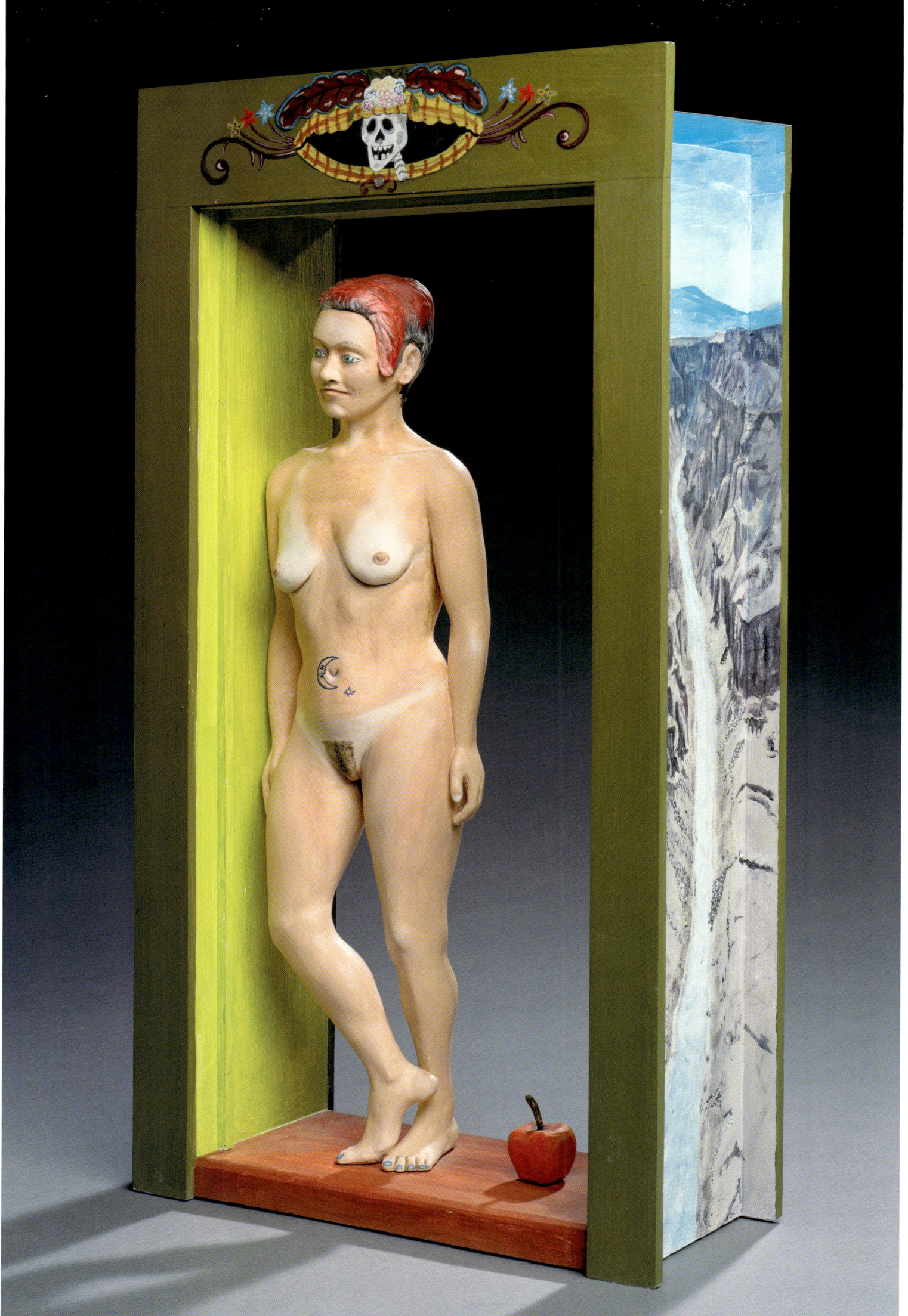

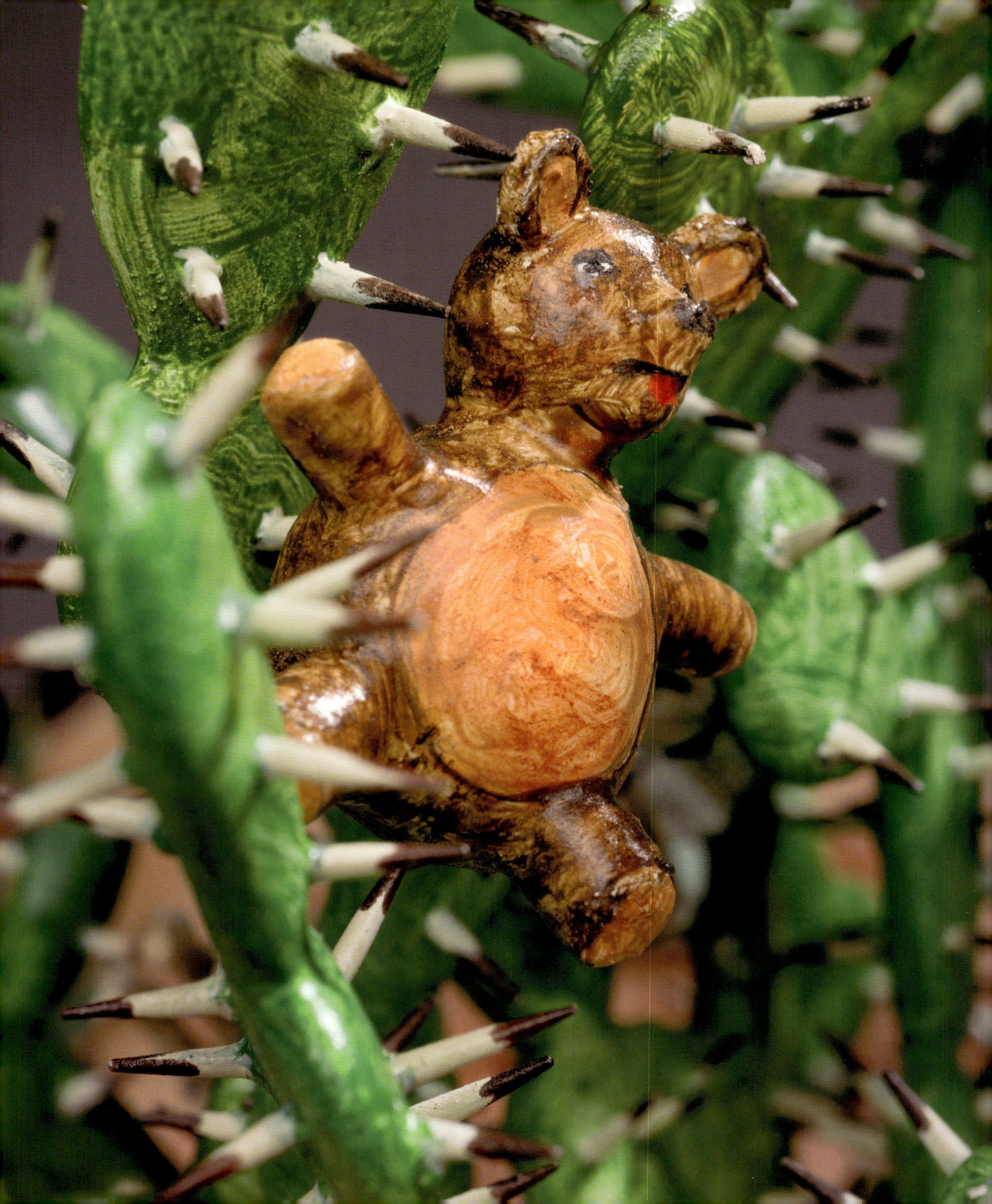

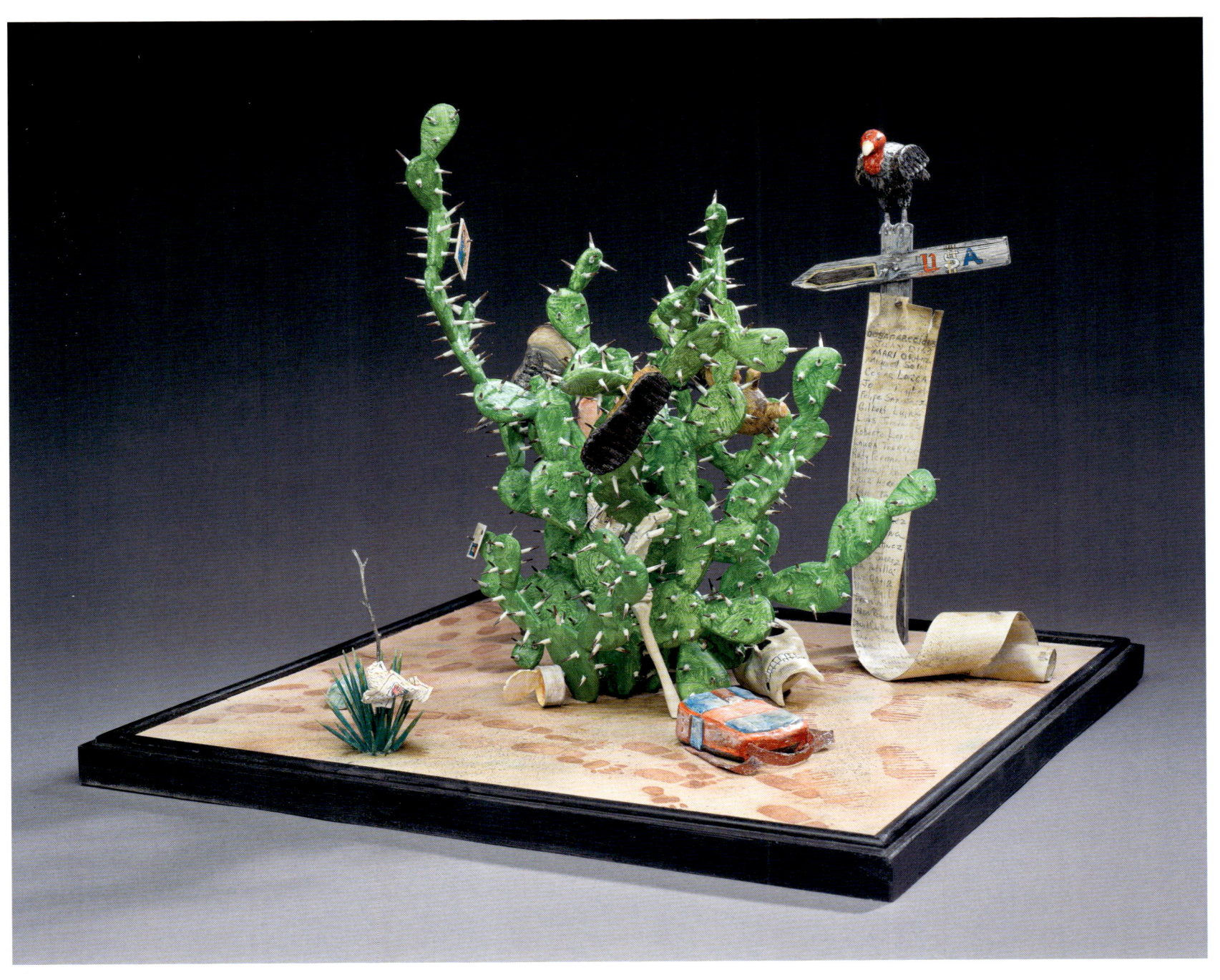

Plate 47. *Camino de sueños*, 2015. Carved and painted wood, 12 ¼ x 15 x 15 in.
Collection of the artist. Photo © James Hart.

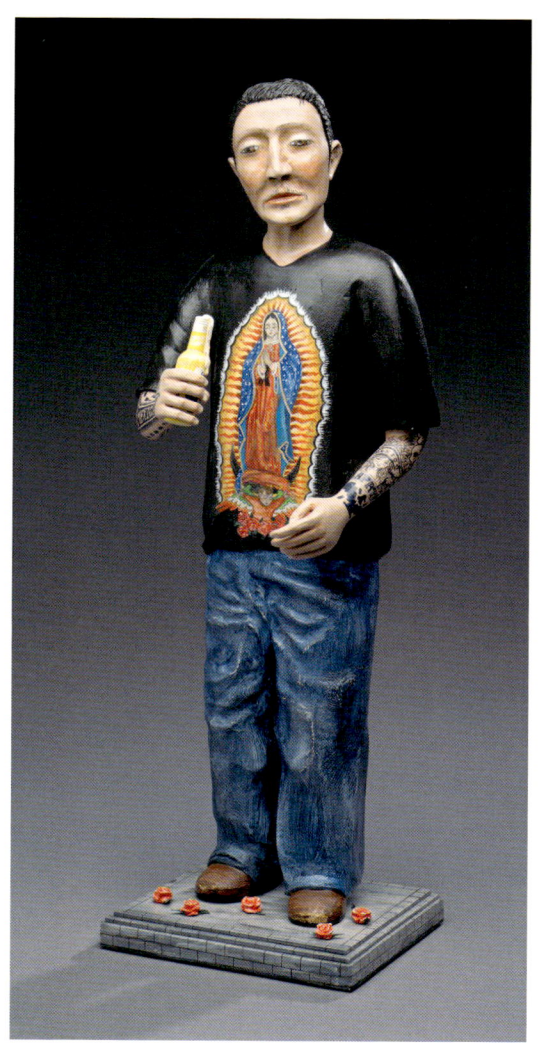
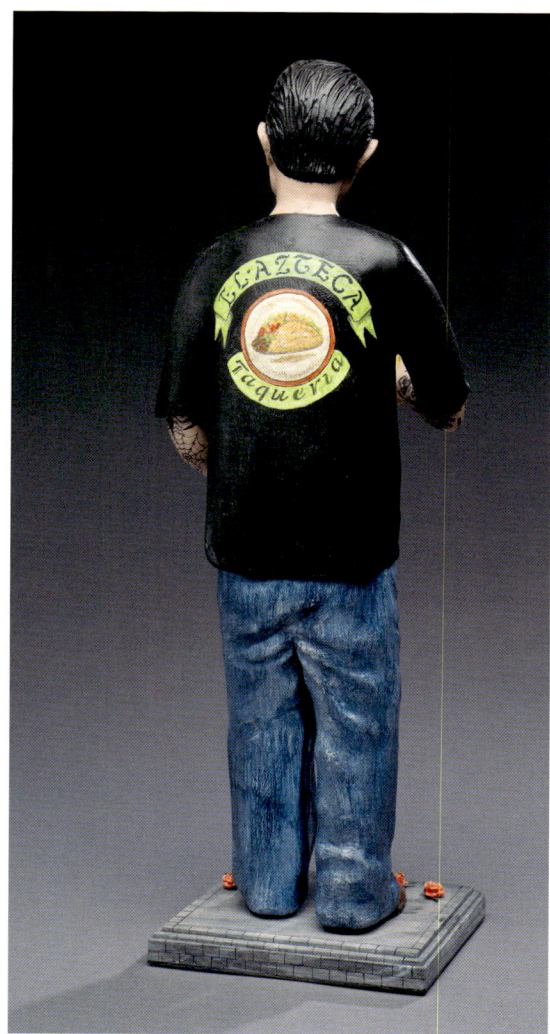
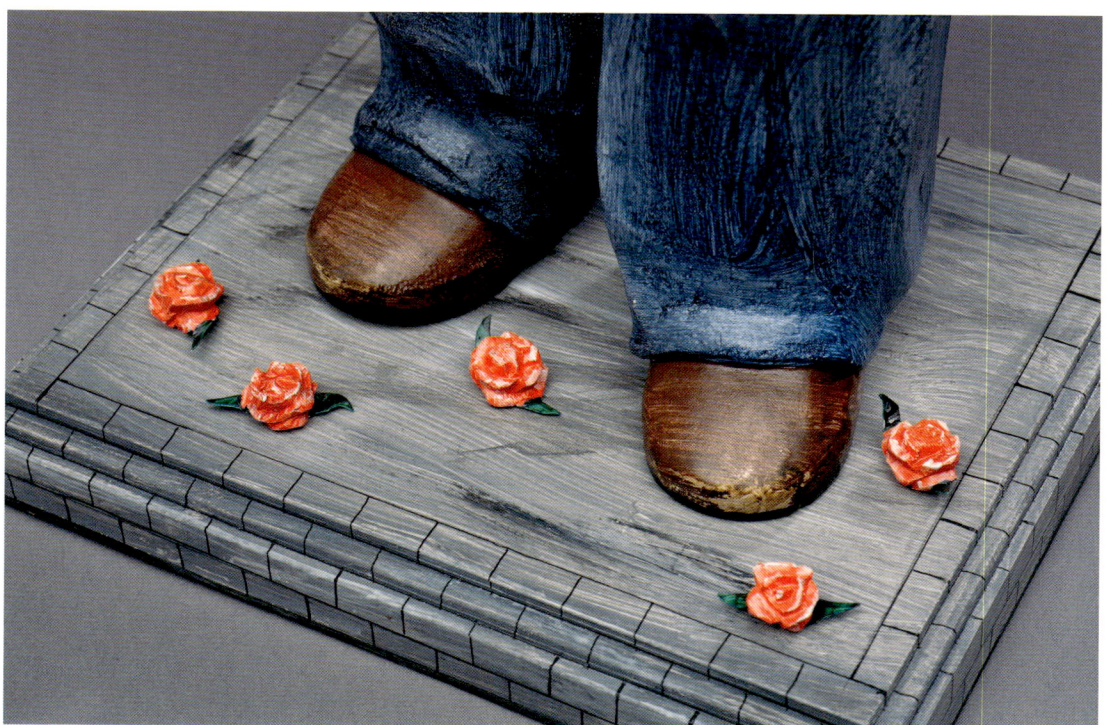

Plate 48. *Juan Diego*, 2015. Carved and painted wood, 24 x 7¼ x 6½ in. Collection of Curt, Christina, and Jonah Nonomaque.
Photo © James Hart.

164

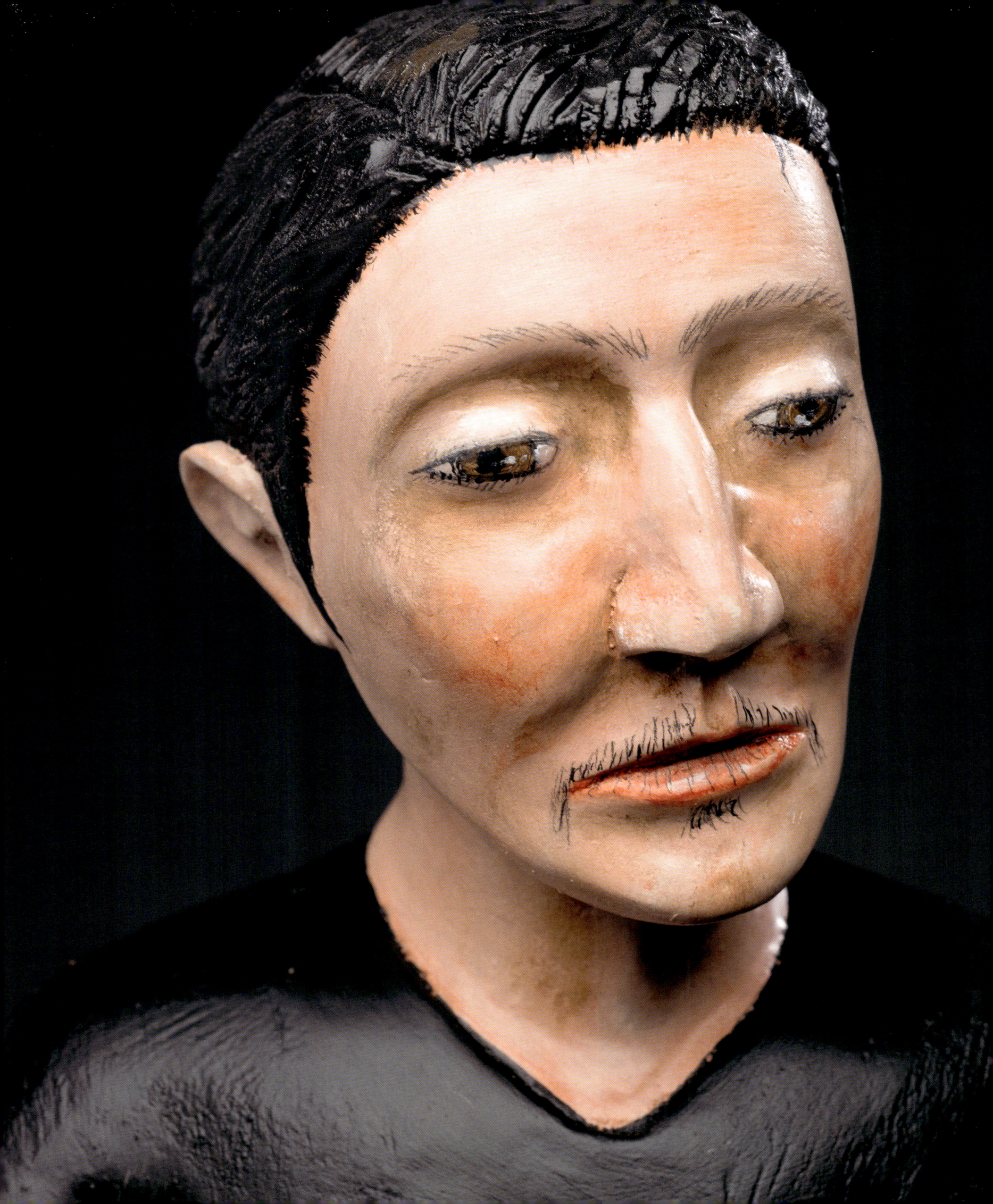

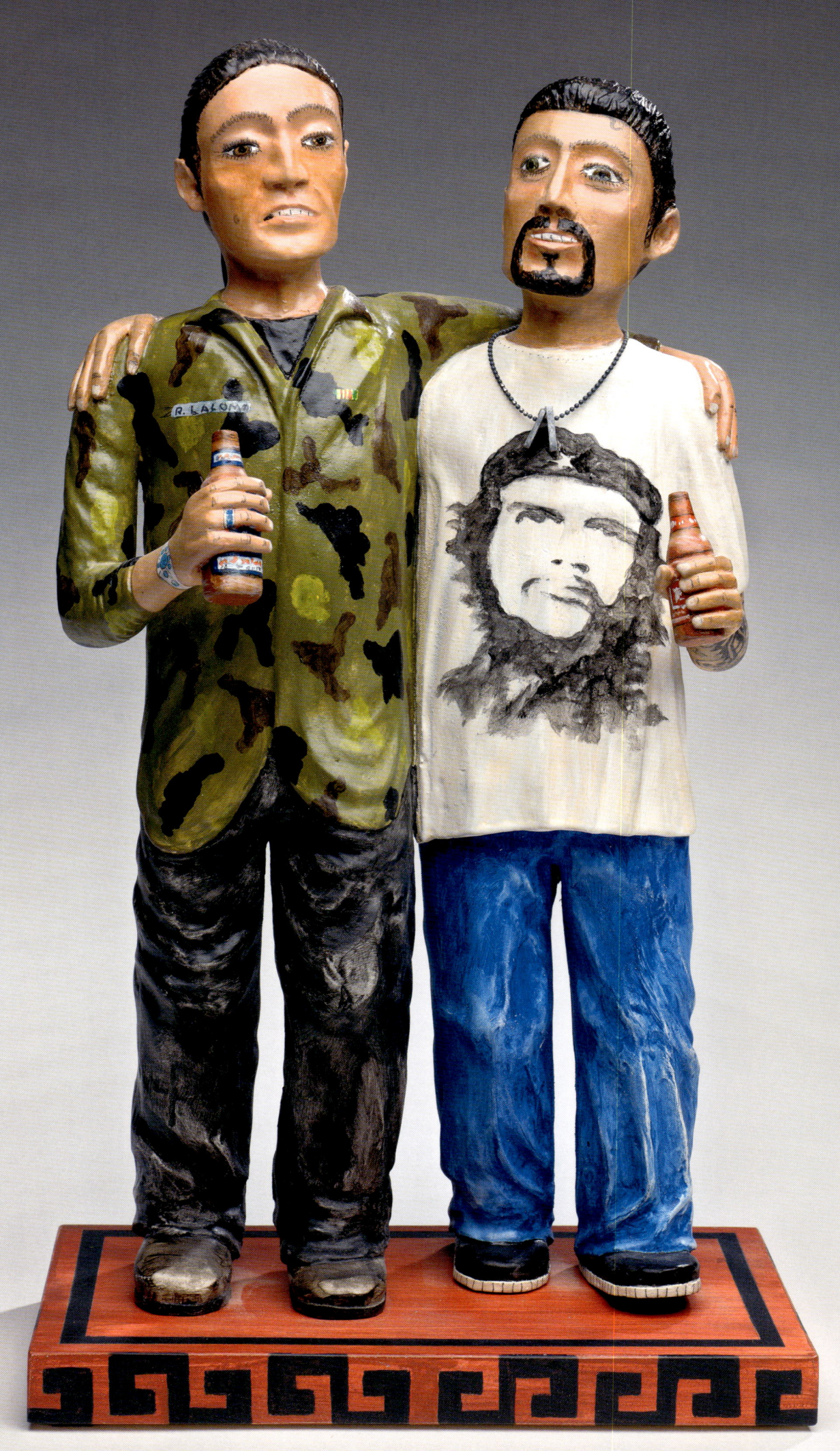

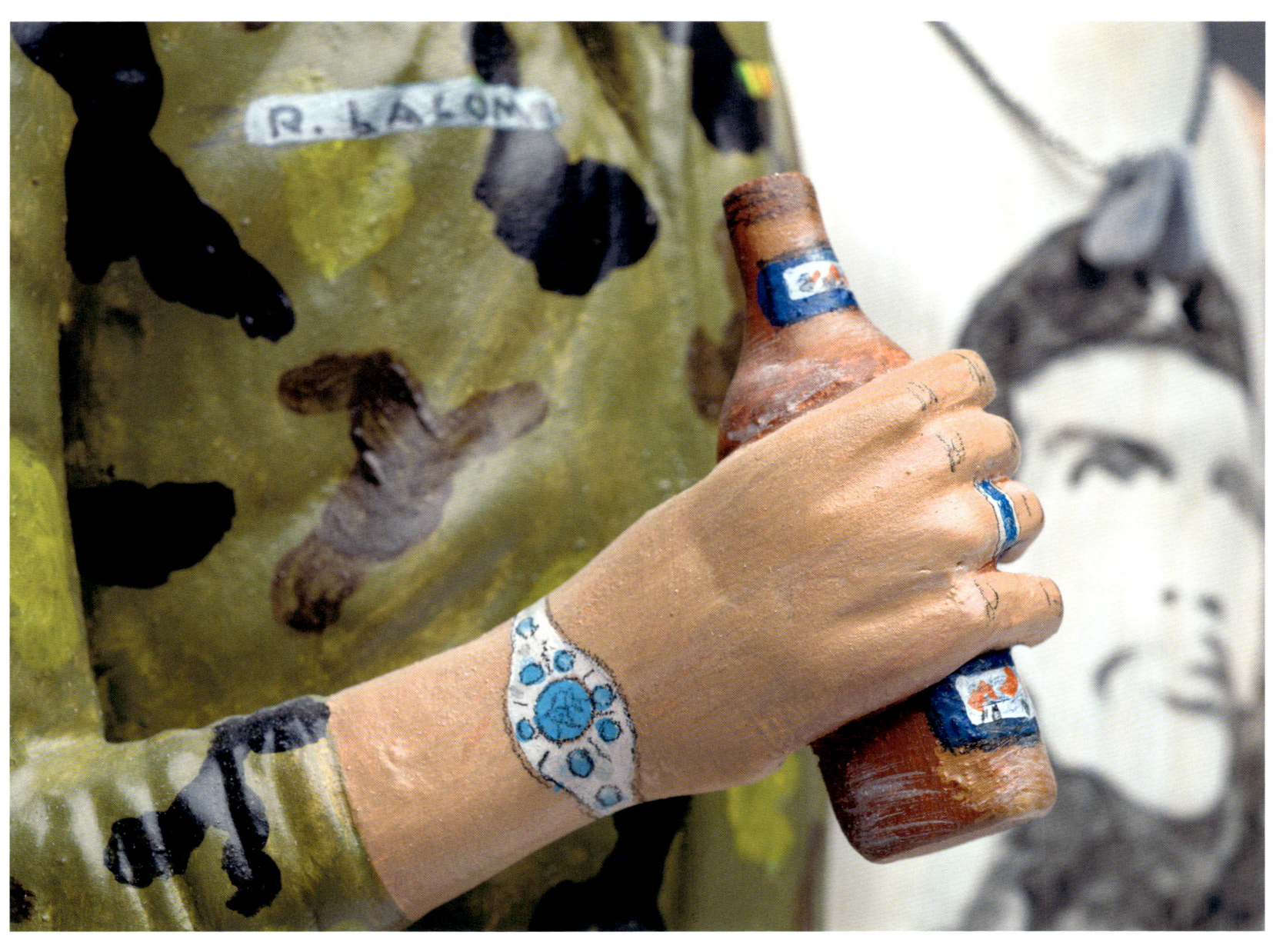

Plate 49. *Dos amigos con sus vicios*, 2015. Carved and painted wood, 18 x 10¼ x 7 in.
Collection of the artist. Photo © James Hart.

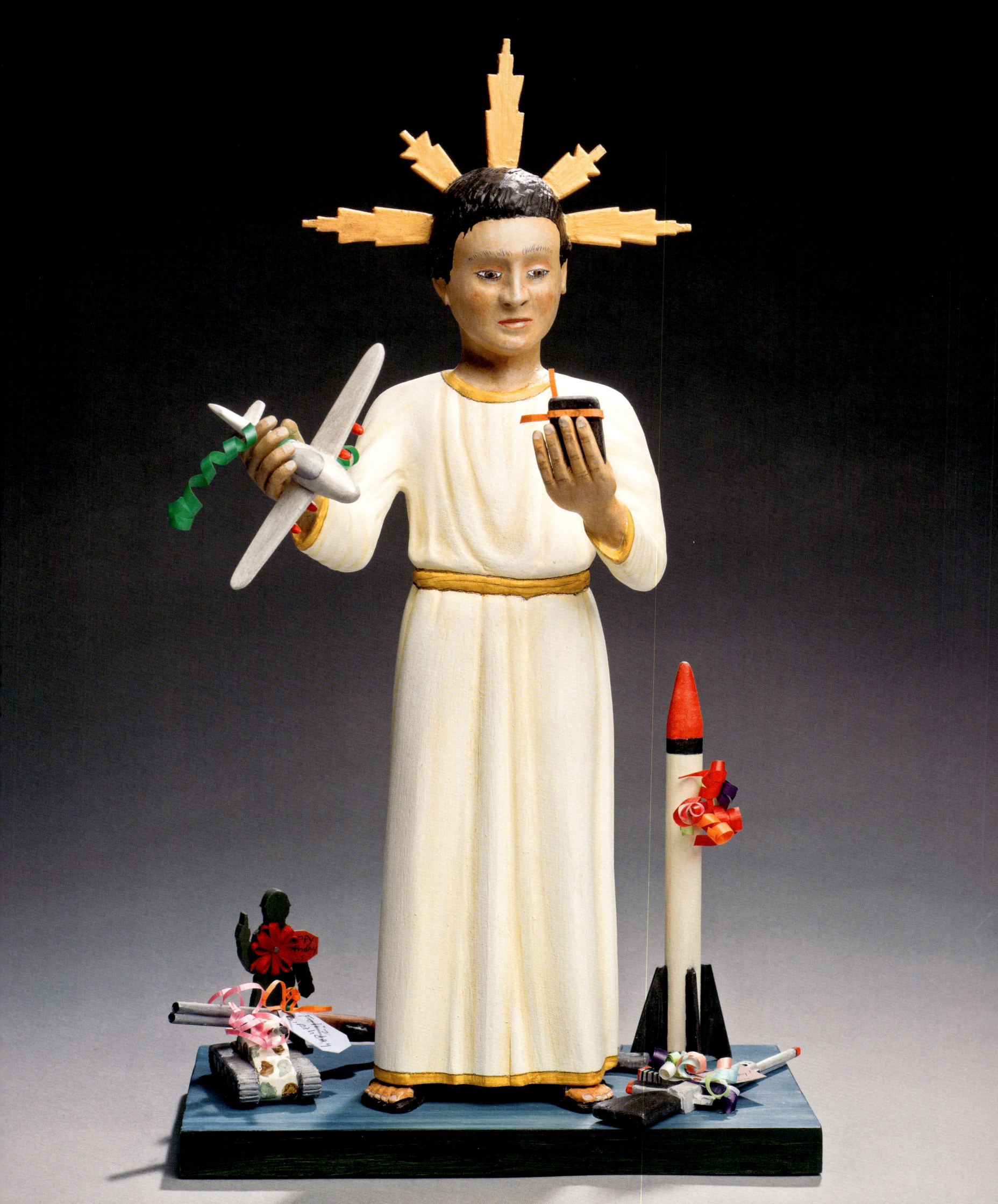

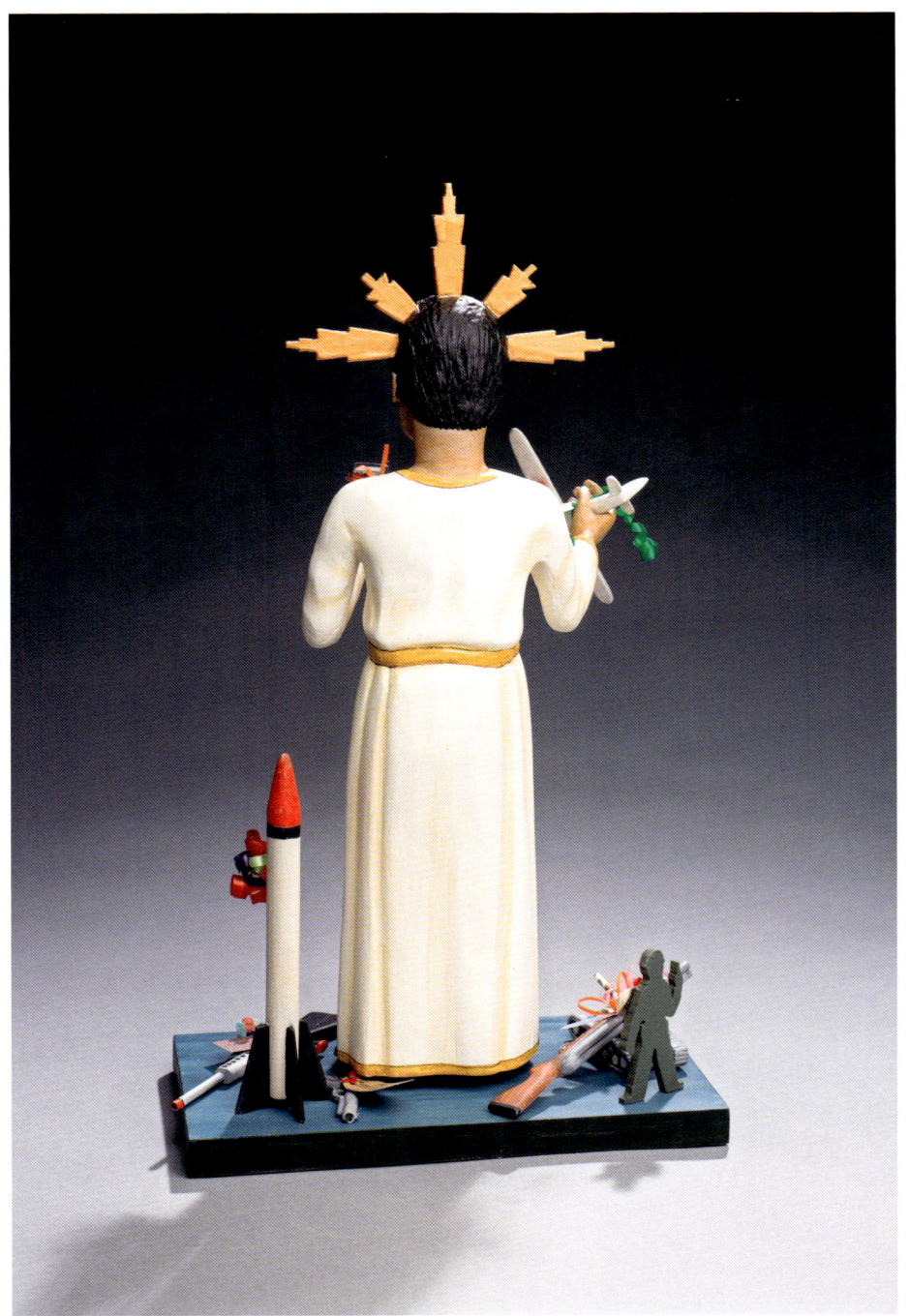

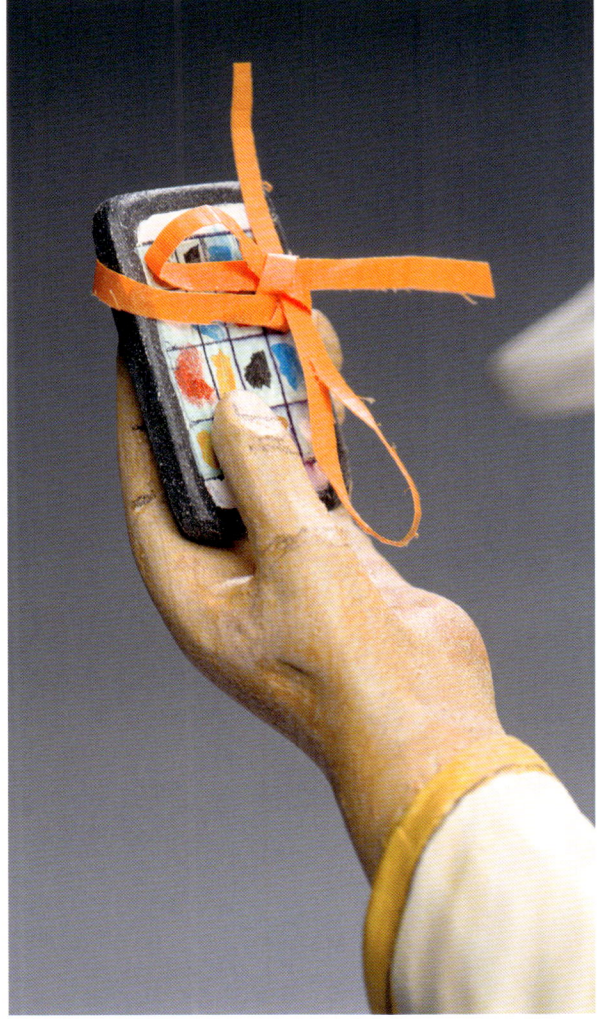

Plate 50. *Happy Birthday, Jesus*, 2016. Carved and painted wood, 19¼ x 10¼ x 7 in.
Collection of the artist. Photo © James Hart.

FOLLOWING SPREAD
Plate 51. *Barrio Barbie*, 2016. Carved and painted wood, 23 x 9 x 9 in.
Collection of Gary, Brenda, and Hayley Ruttenberg. Photo © James Hart.

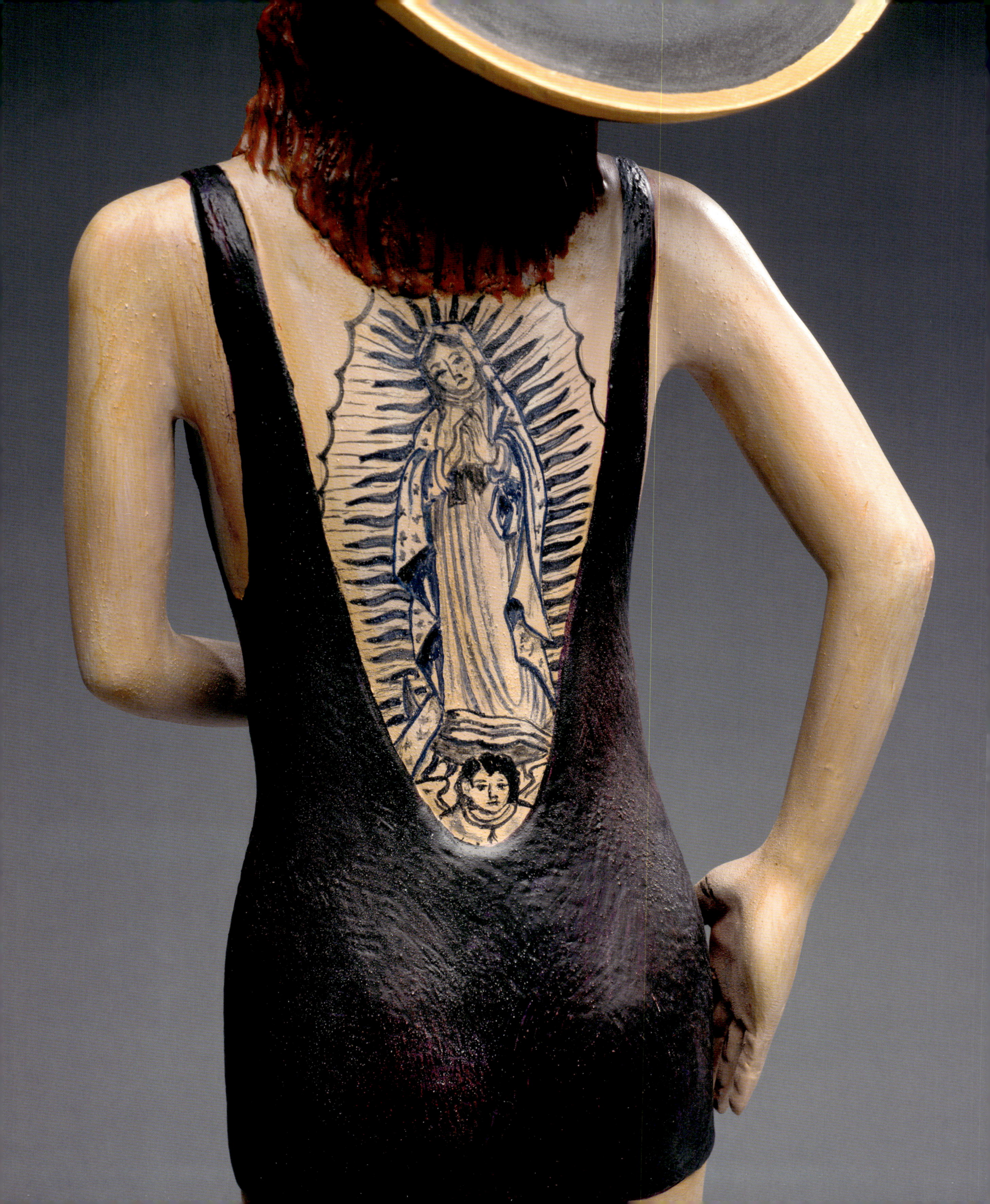

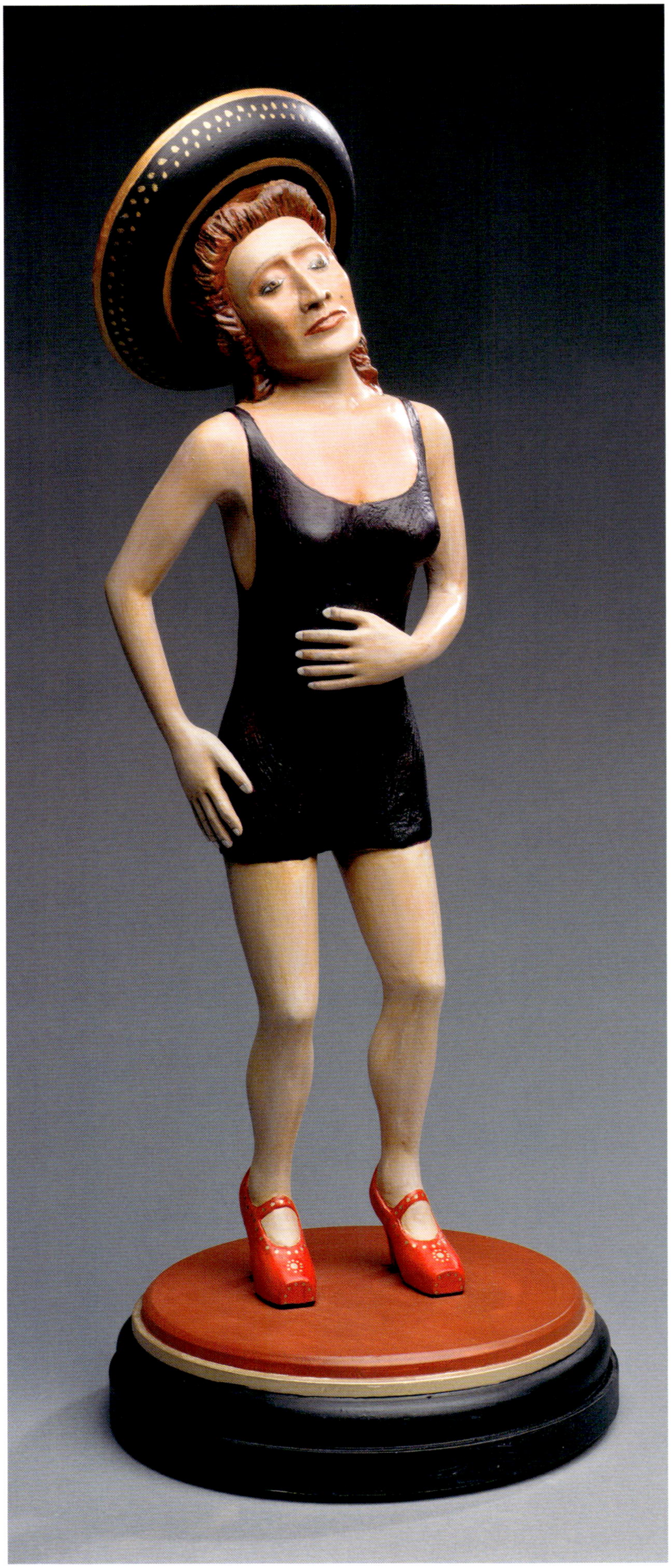

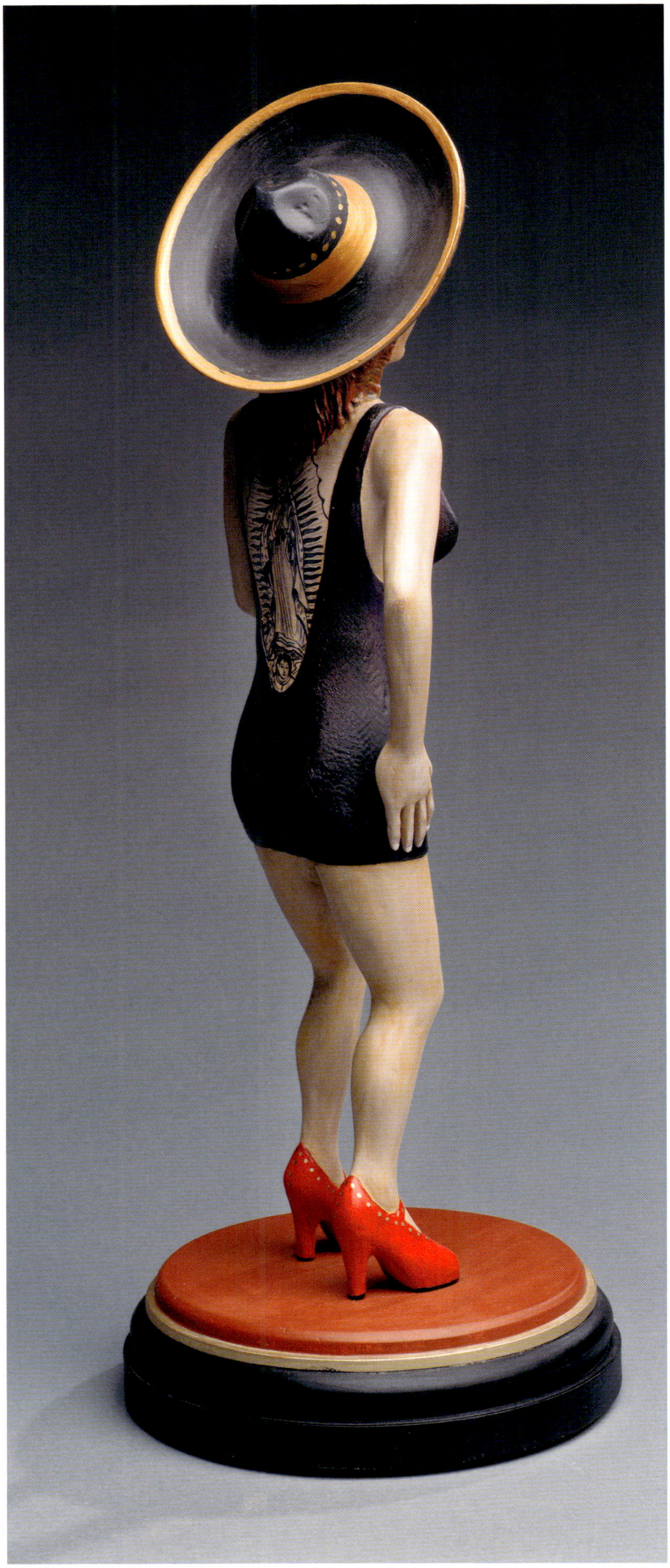

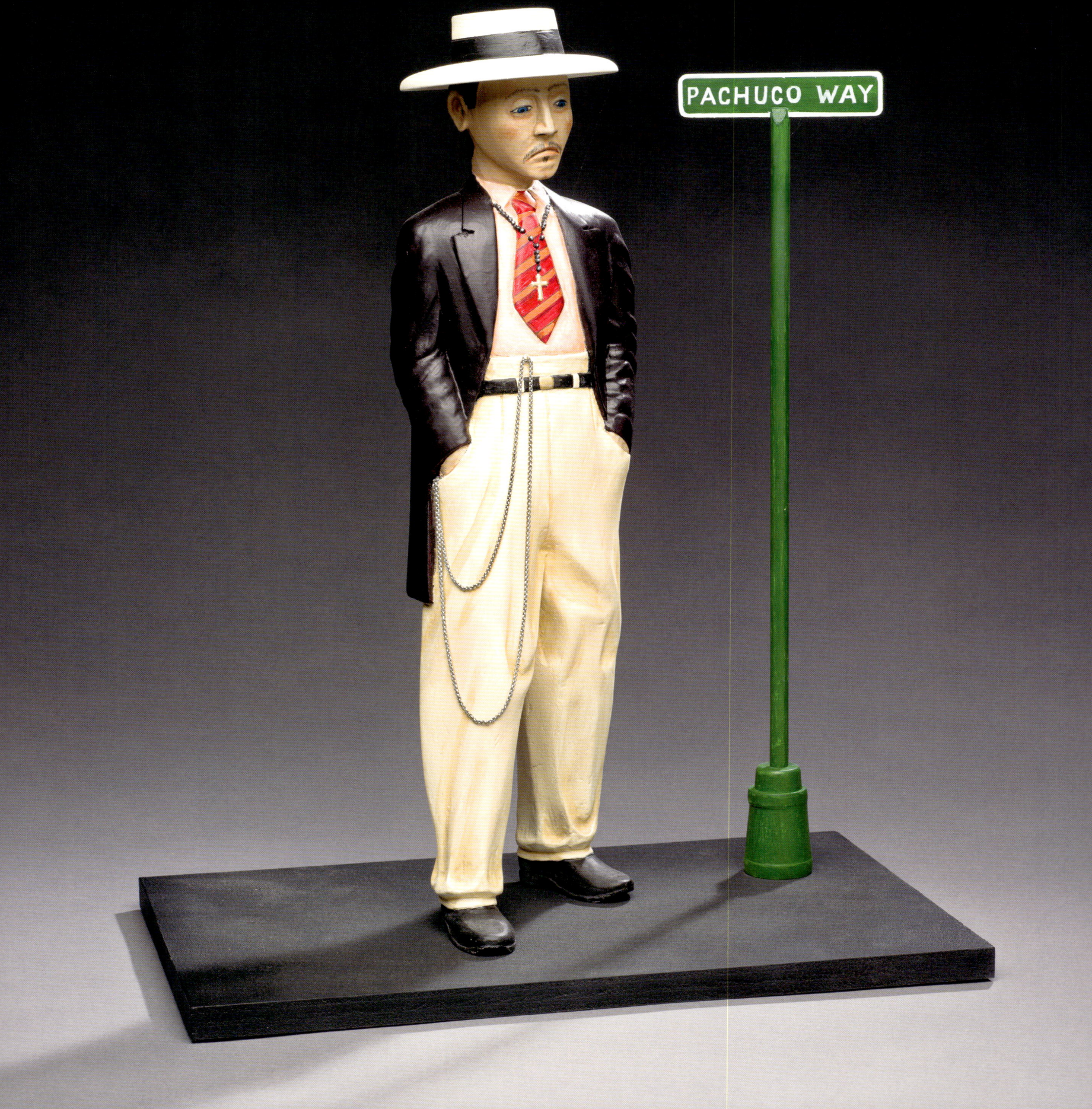

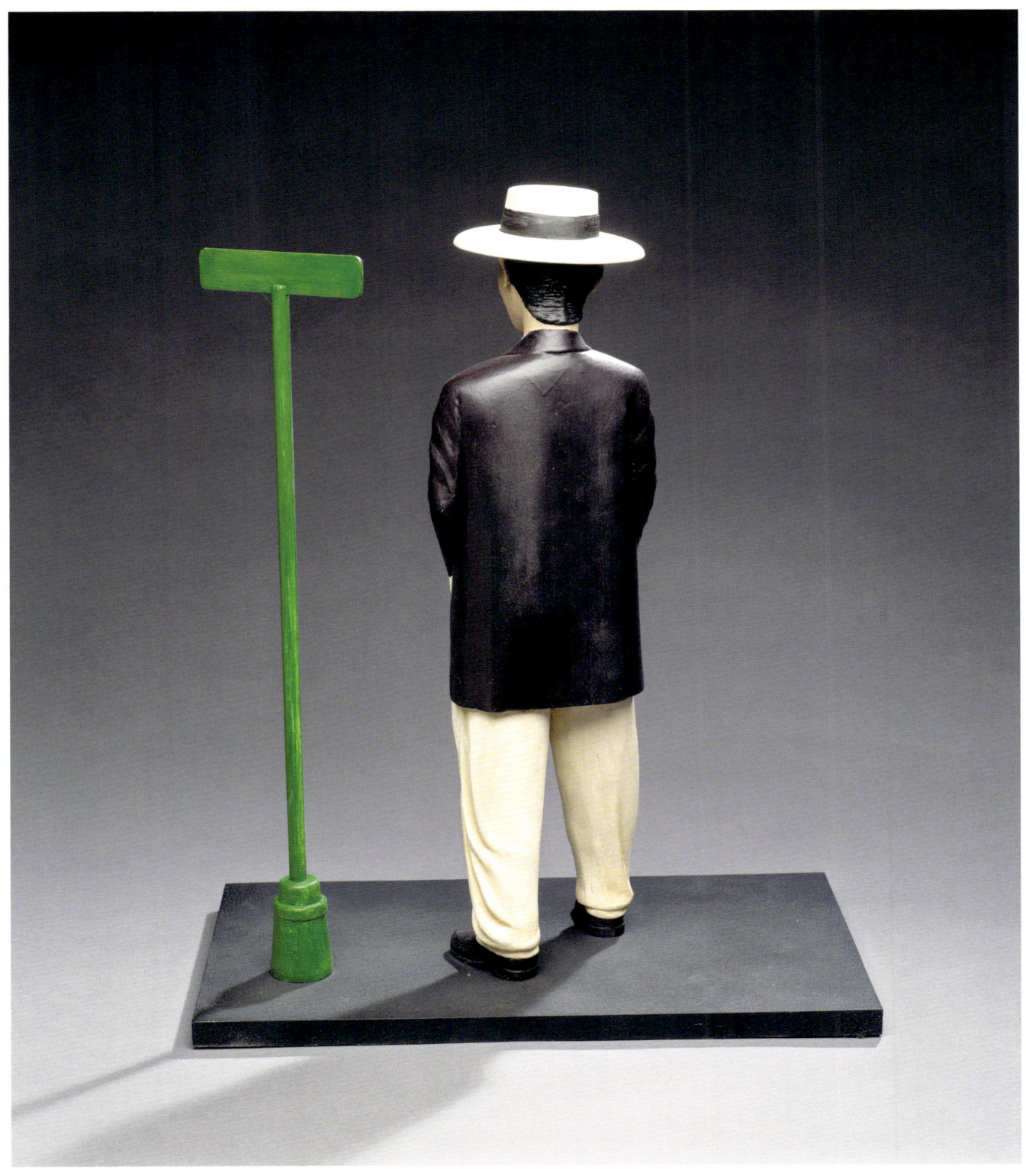

Plate 52. *Pachuco Way*, 2016. Carved and painted wood, 22 x 18 x 11 in. Collection of the artist.
Photo © James Hart.

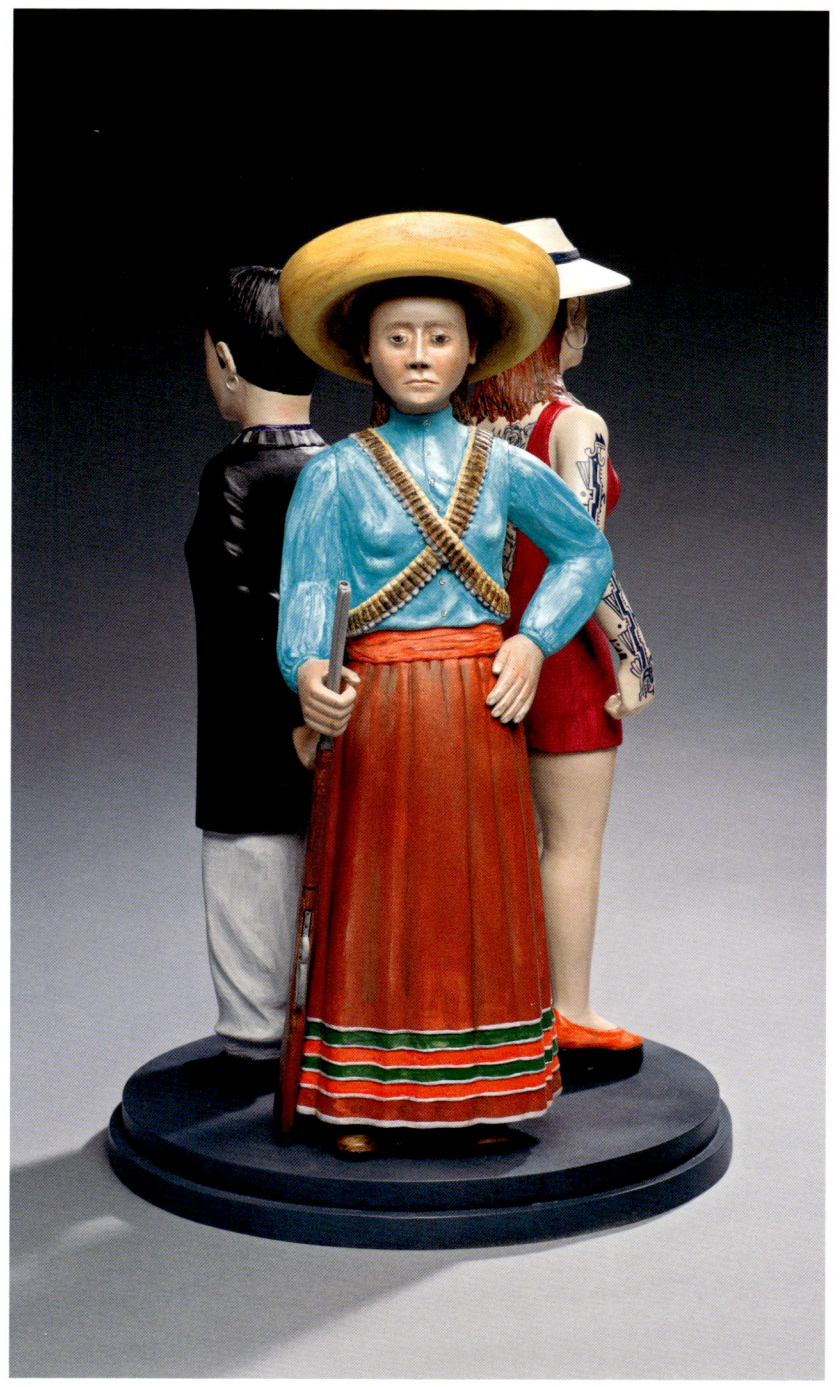
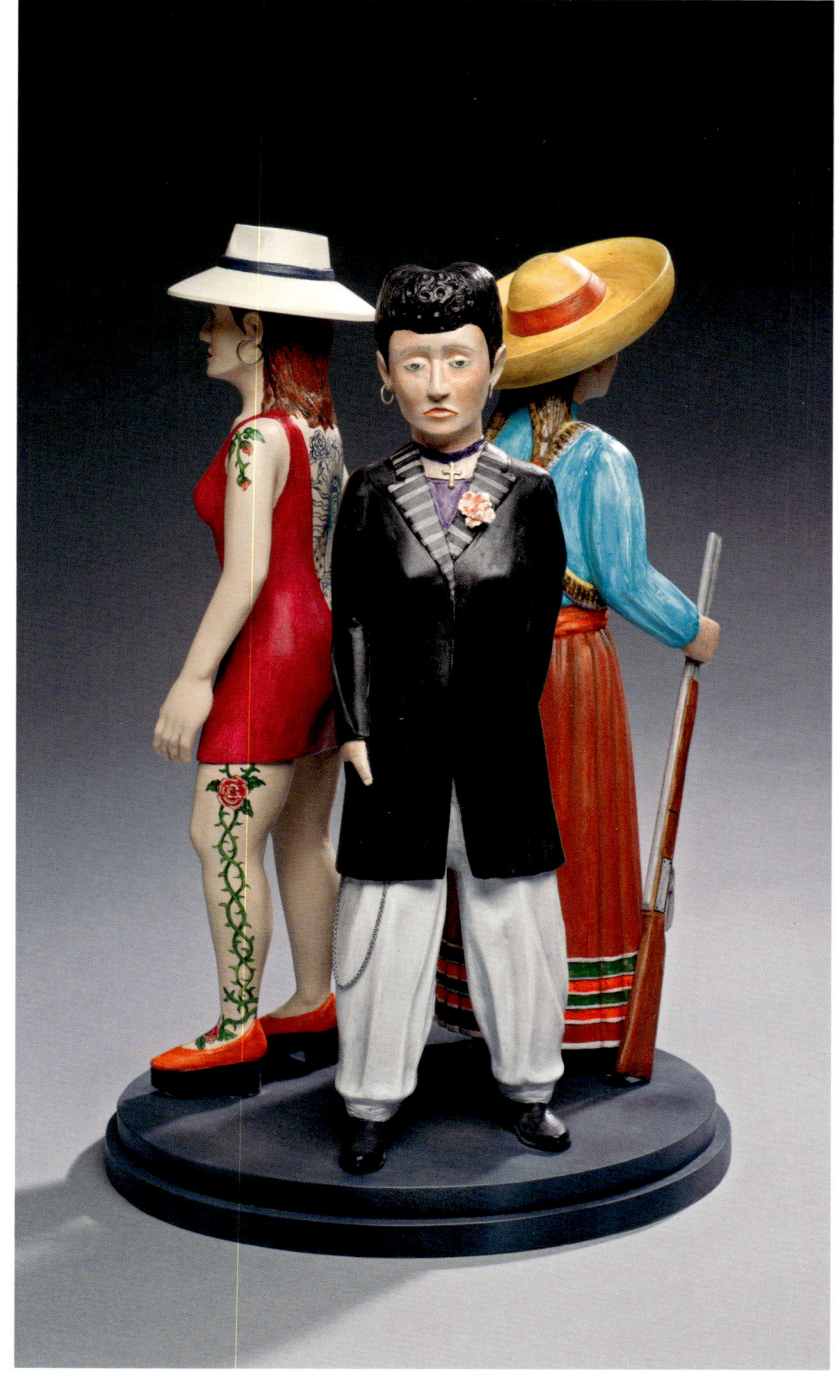

Plate 53. *The Three Graces*, 2016. Carved and painted wood, 22 ½ x 16 ½ x 15 in.
Collection of Kathryn Minette and Stan Biderman. Photo © James Hart.

FOLLOWING SPREAD
Plate 54. *Virgen del camino de sueños*, 2016. Carved and painted wood, 15 ¾ x 13 x 10 ¼ in.
Collection of Curt, Christina, and Jonah Nonomaque. Photo © James Hart.

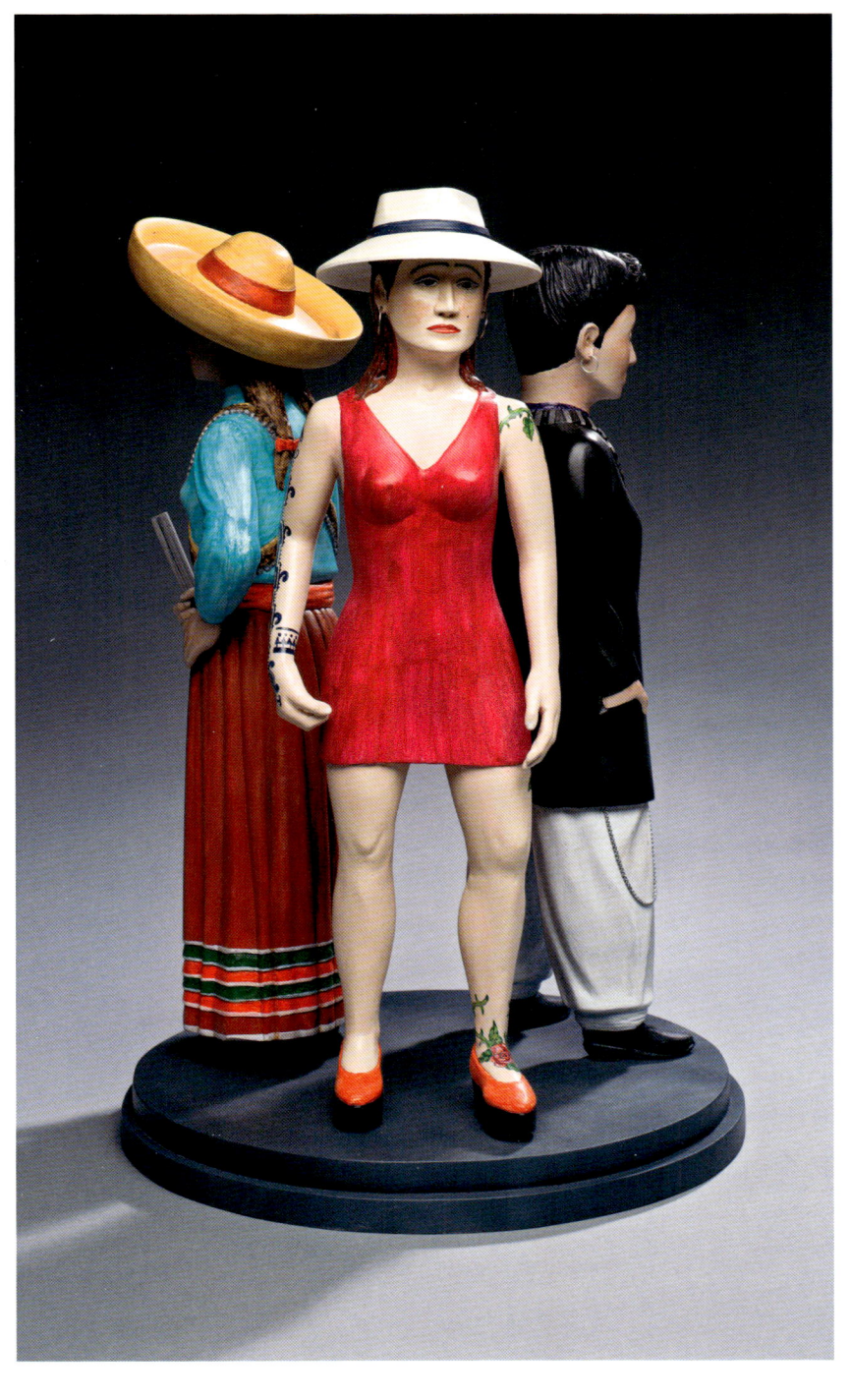

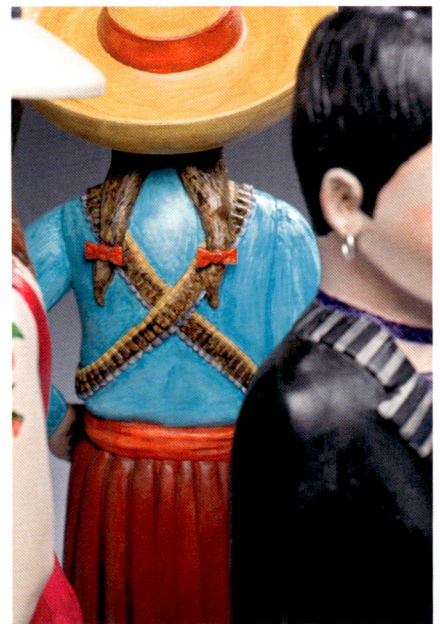

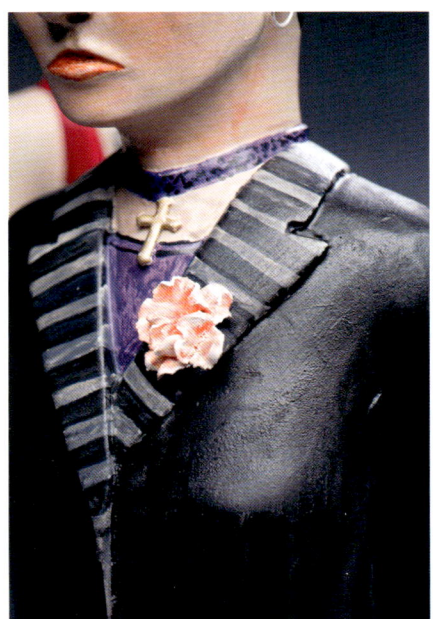

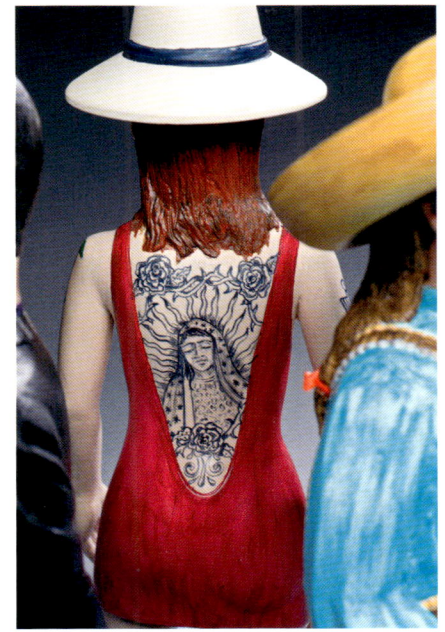

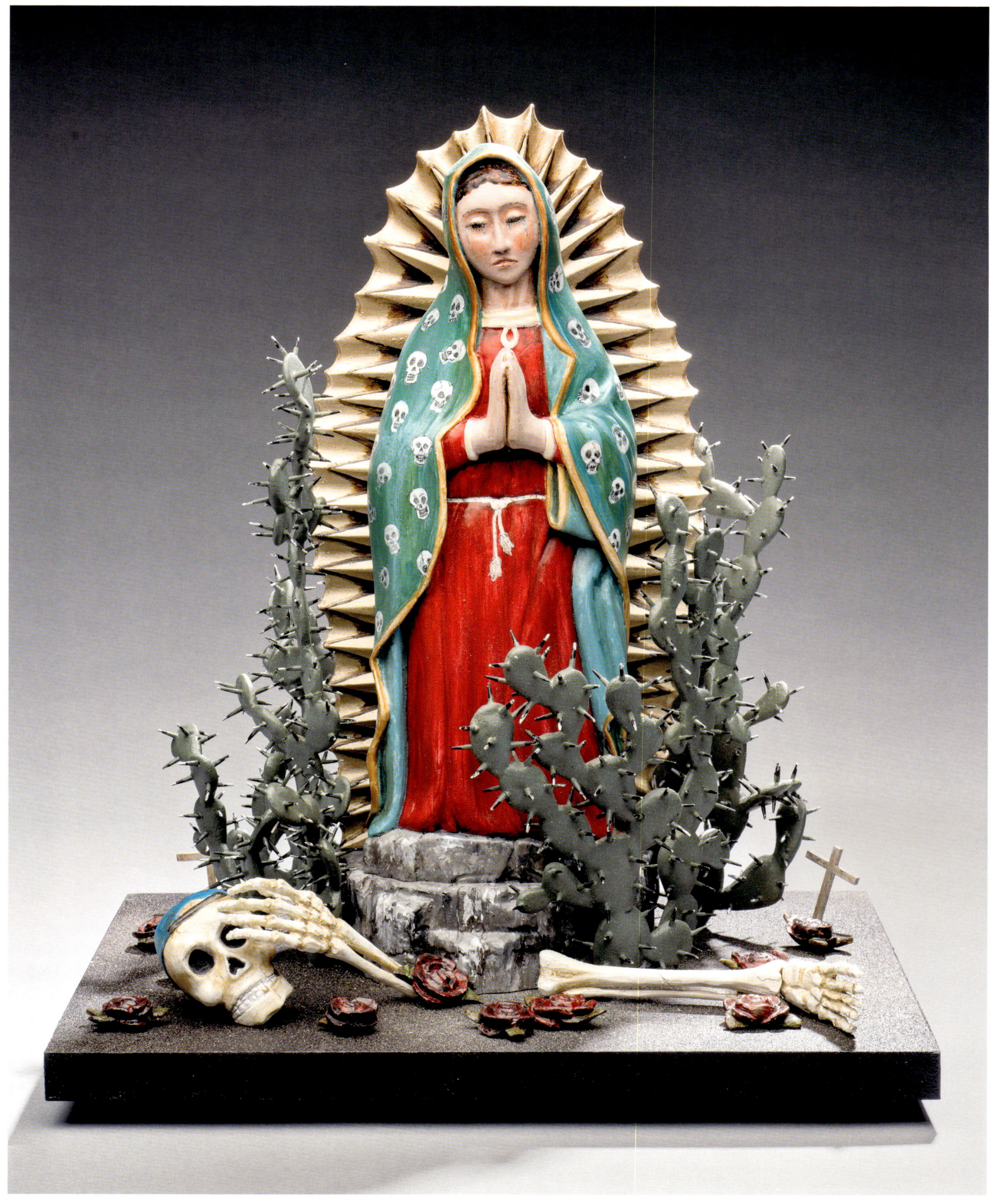

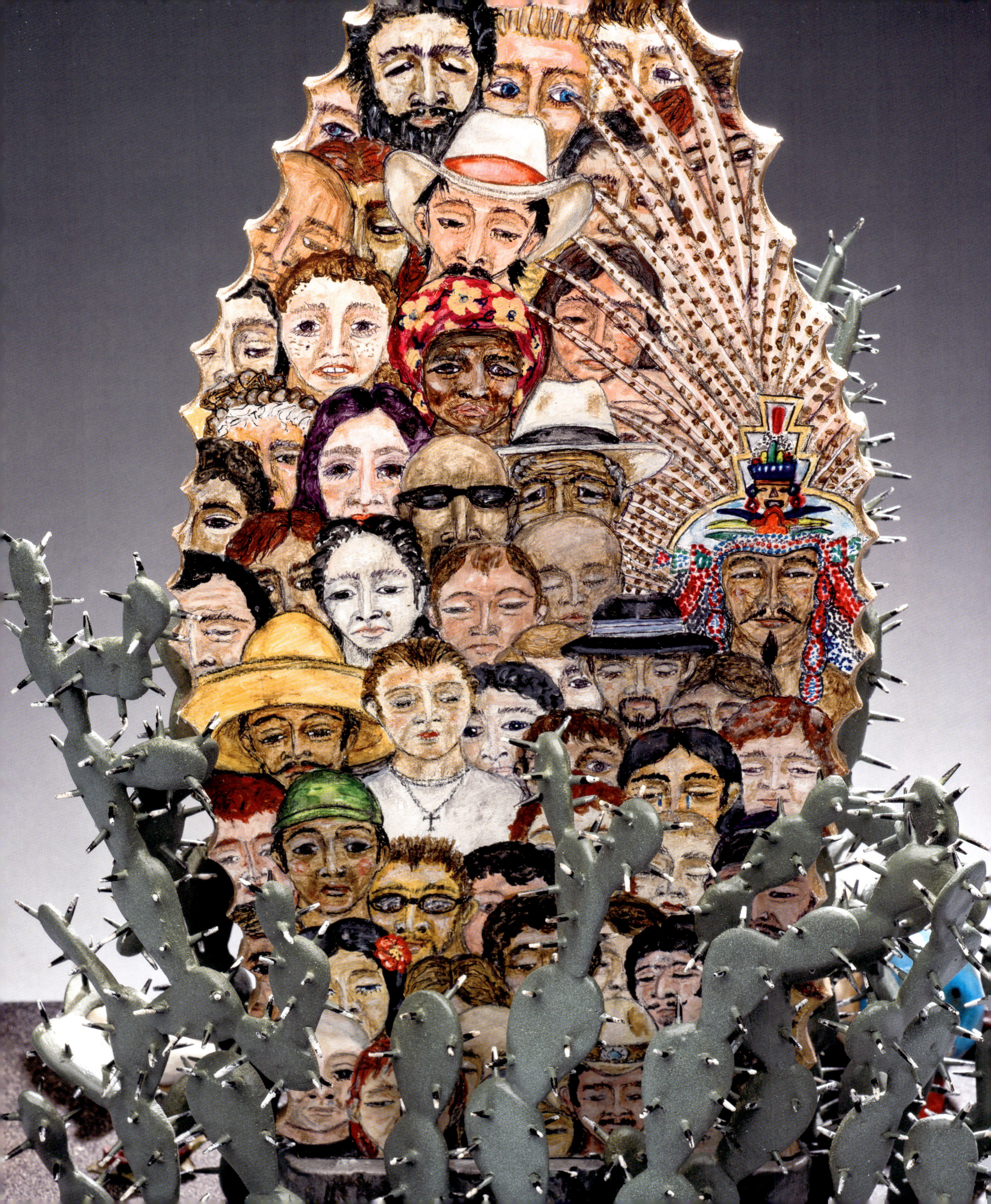

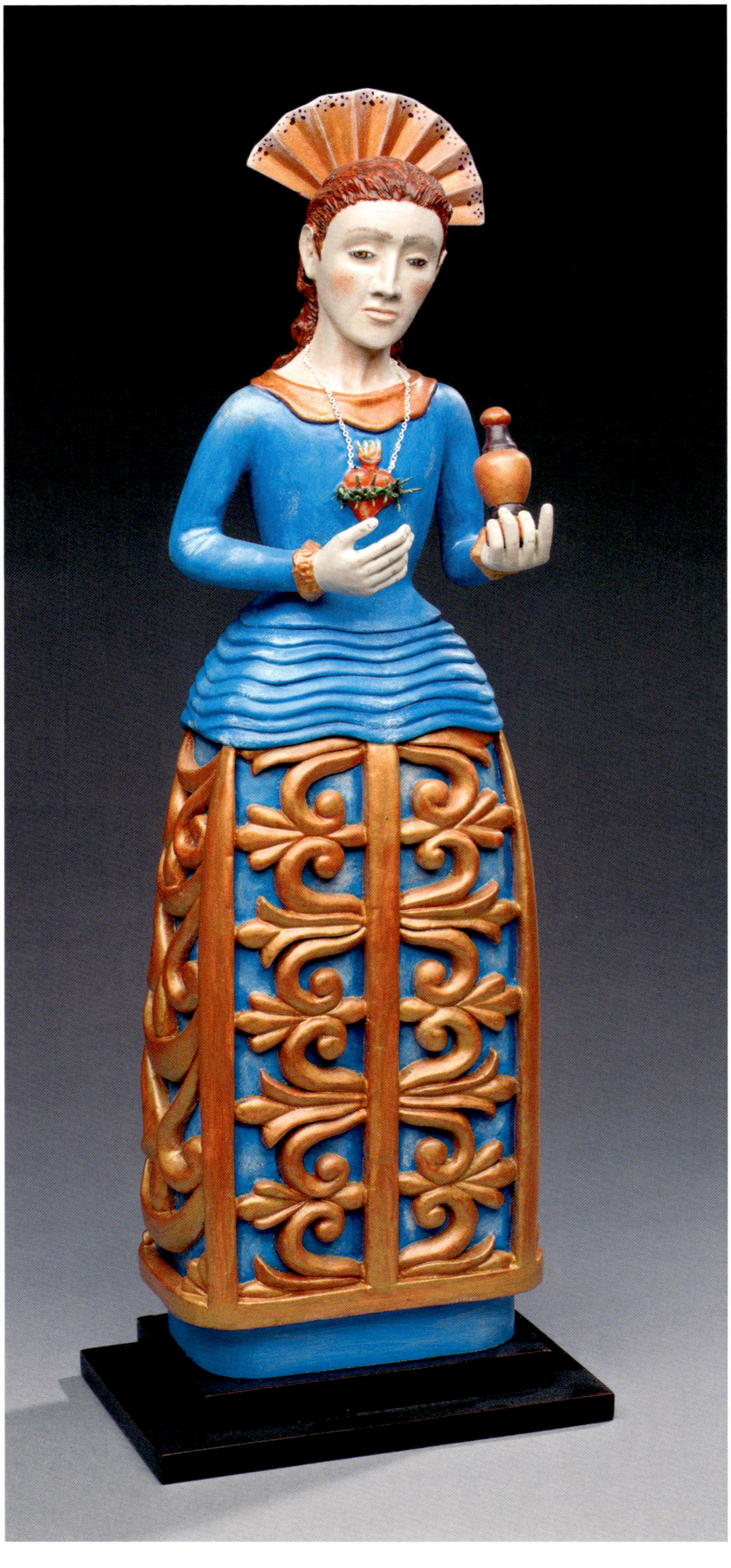

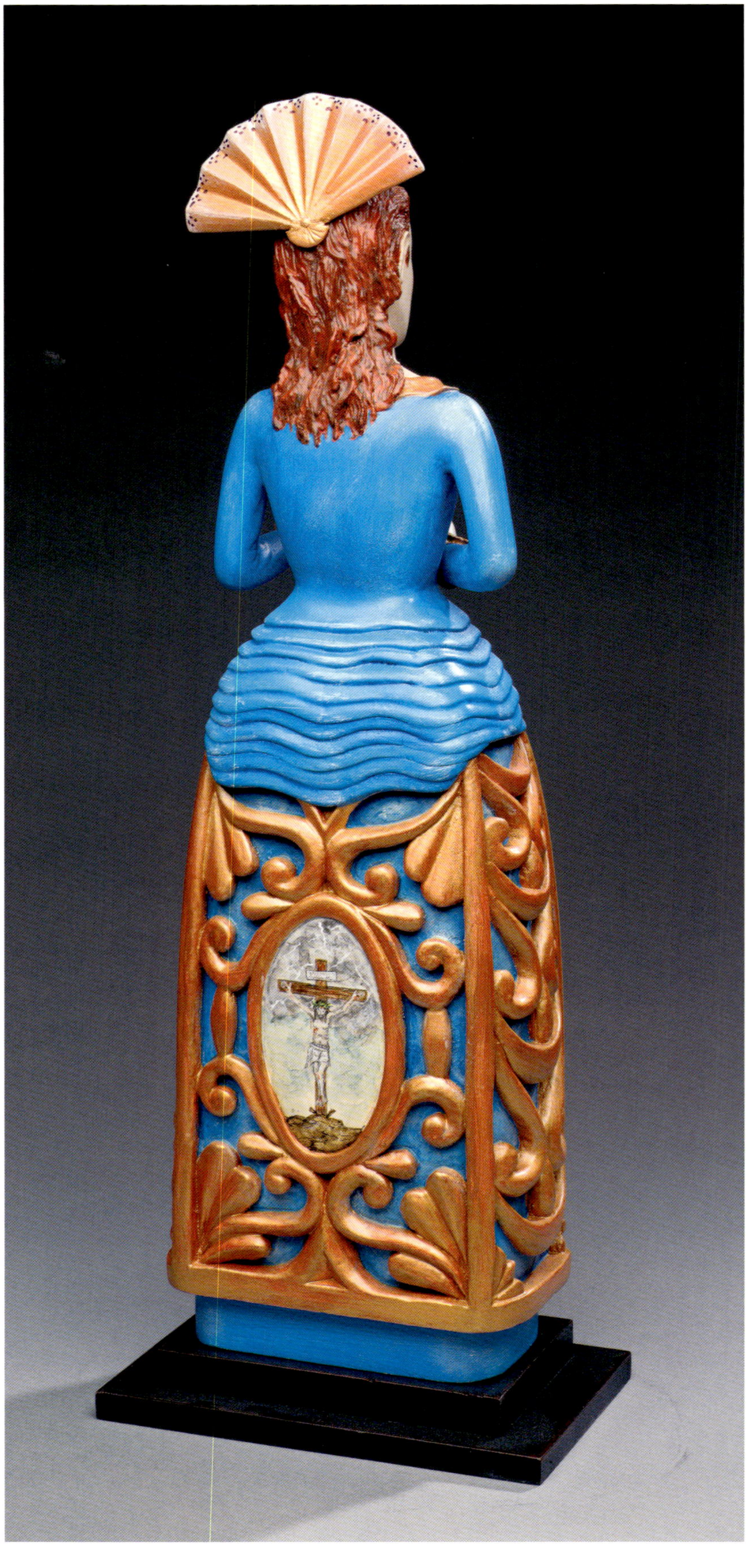

Plate 55. *Mary Magdalene*, 2016. Carved and painted wood, 23¼ x 9 x 8 in. Collection of the artist.
Photo © James Hart.

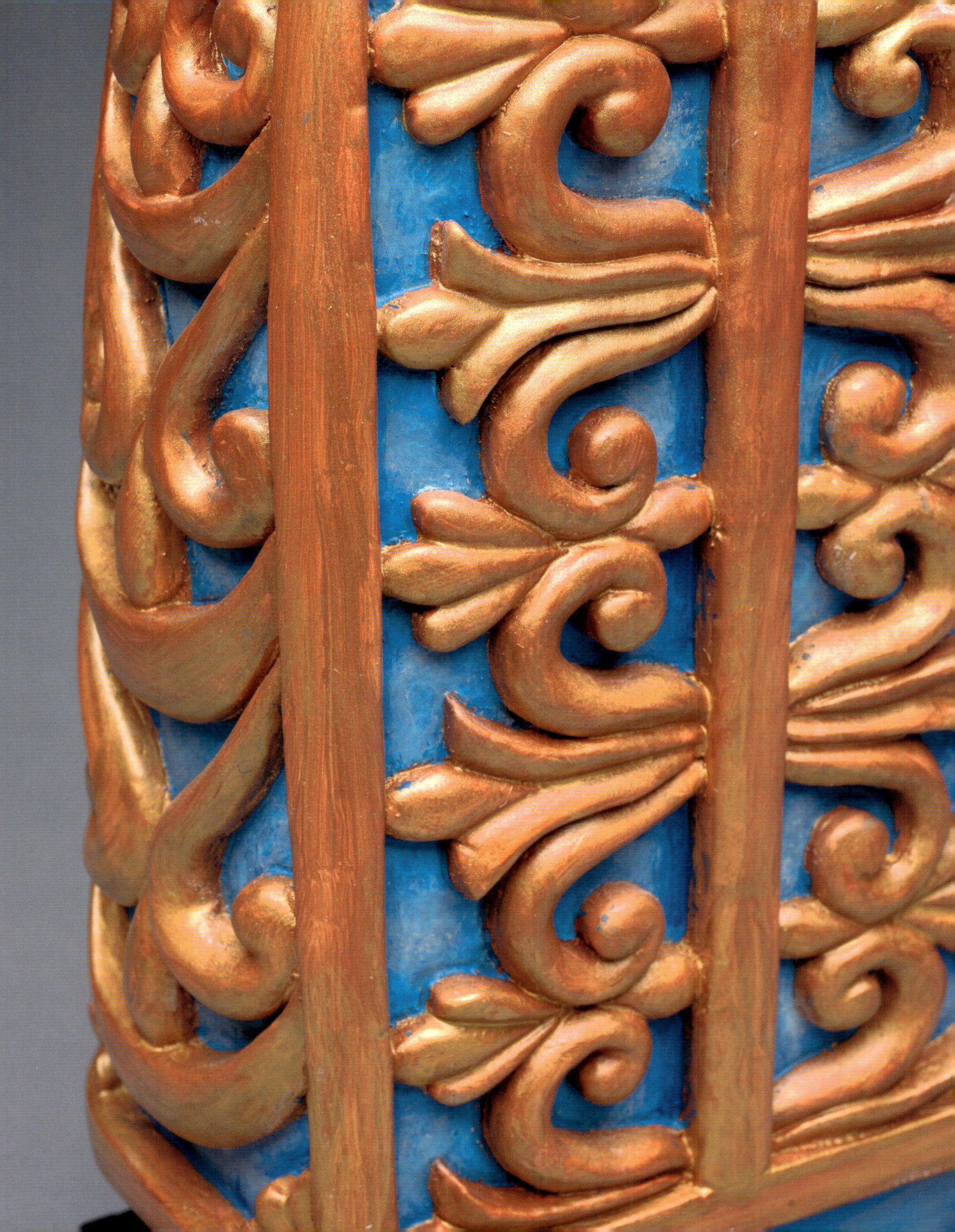

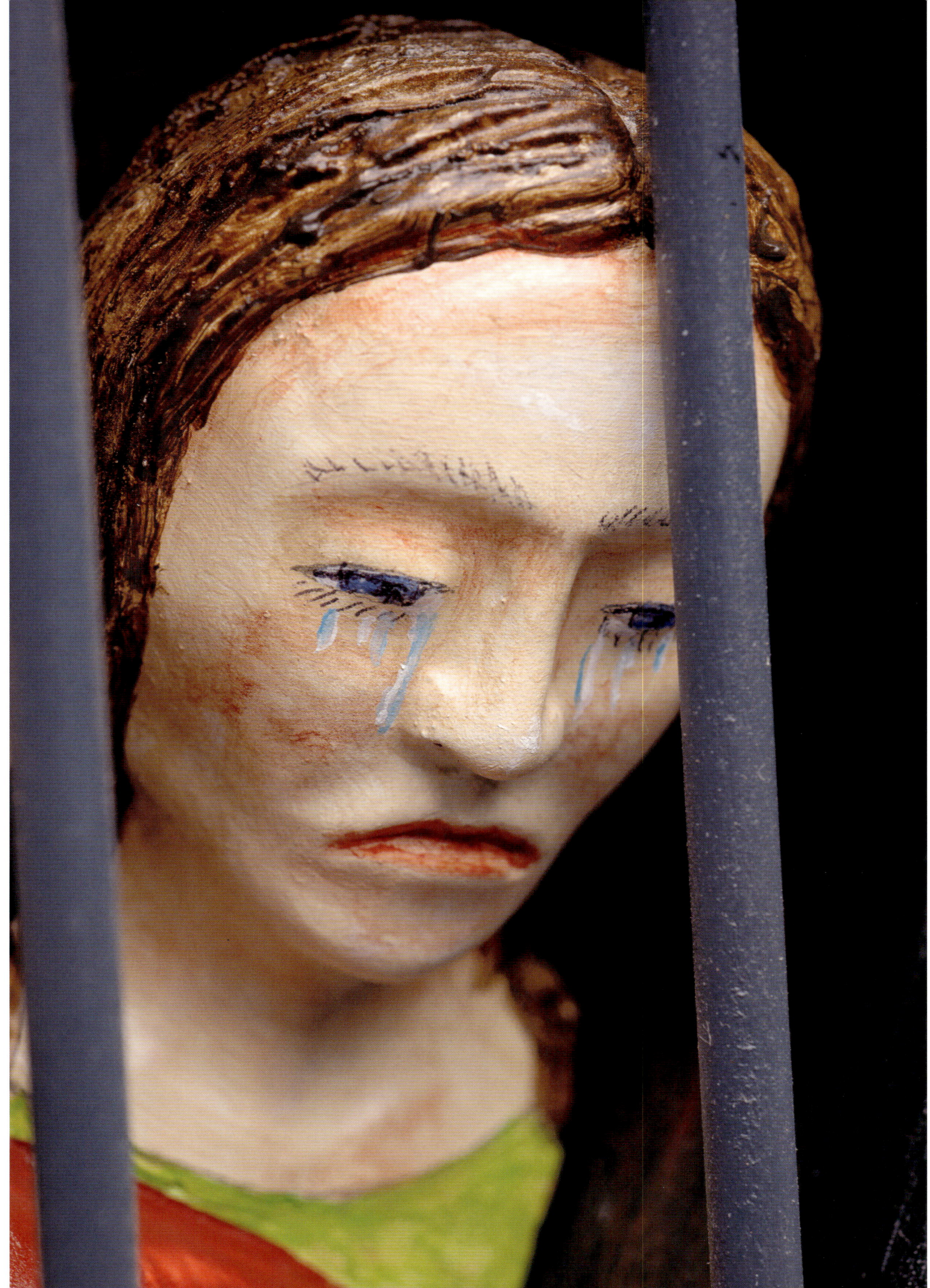

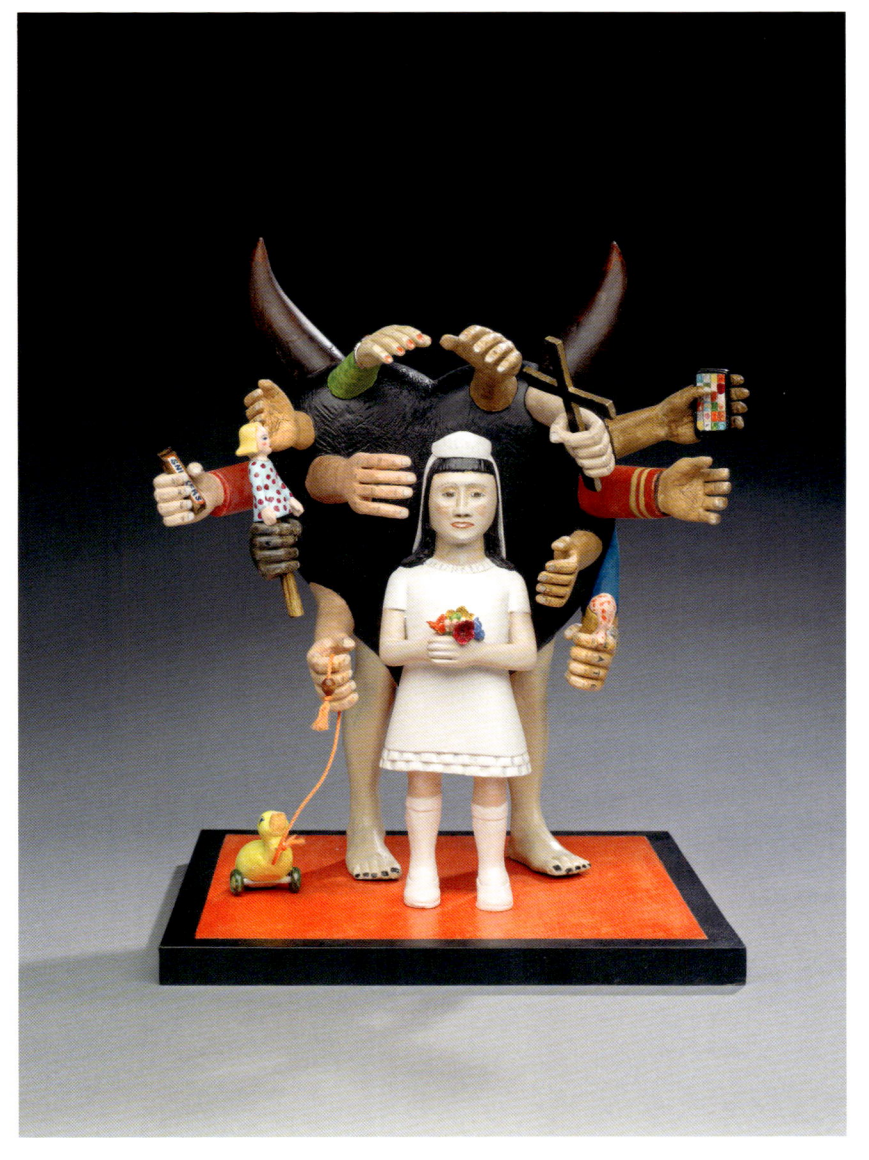

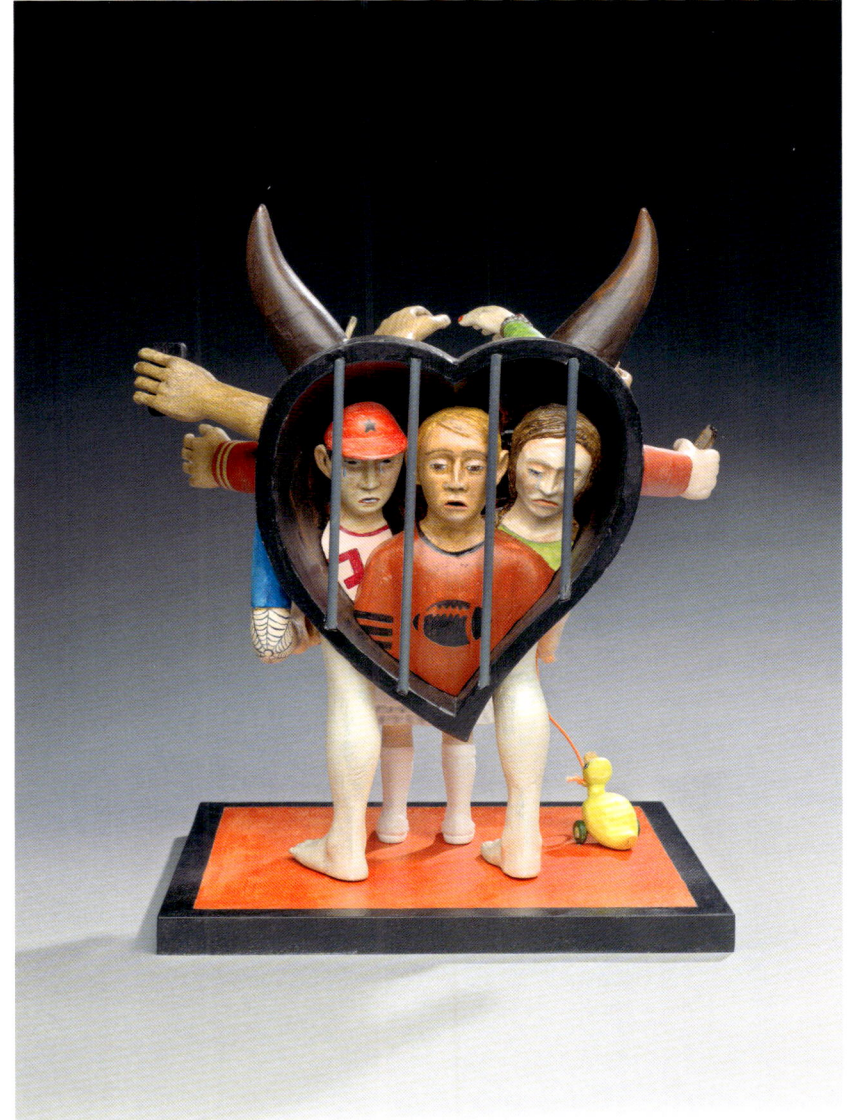

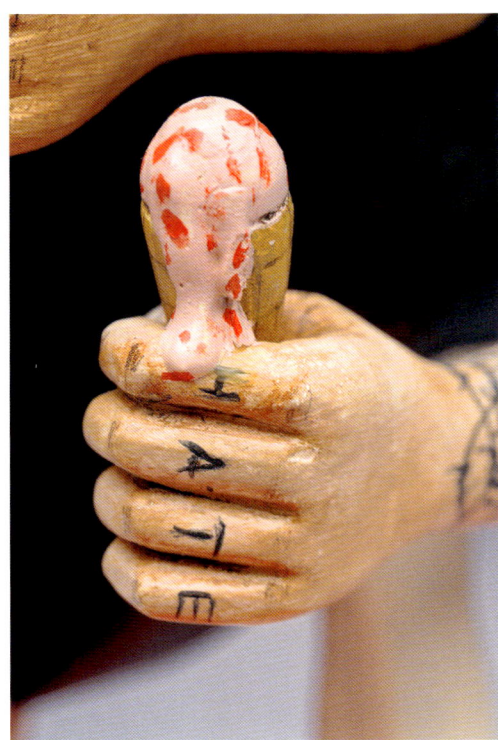

Plate 56. *Corazón negro*, 2016. Carved and painted wood, 14 ¼ x 11 ⅝ x 10 ¼ in. Collection of the artist. Photo © James Hart.

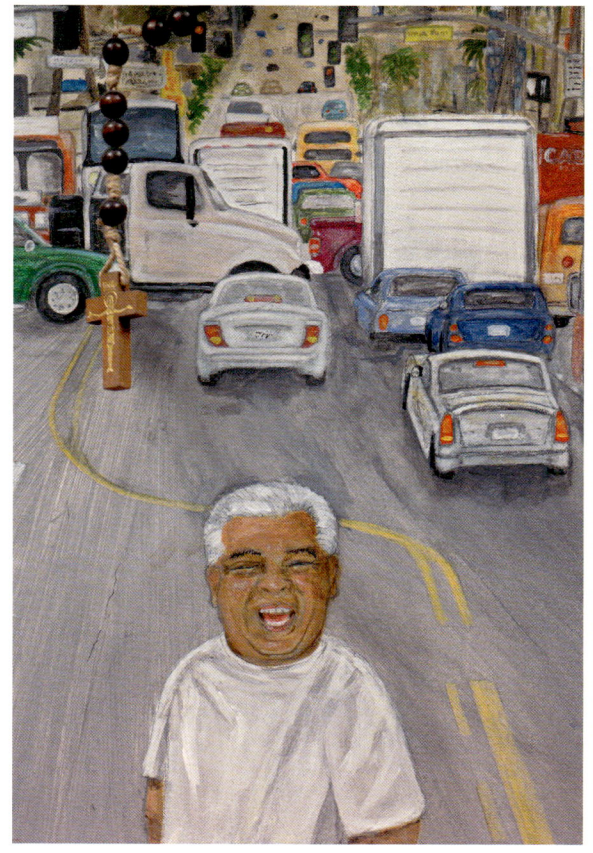

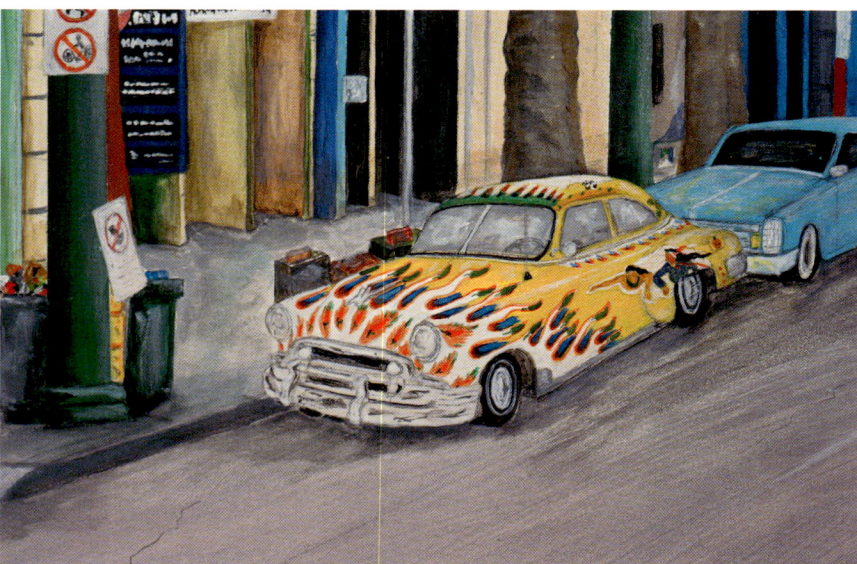

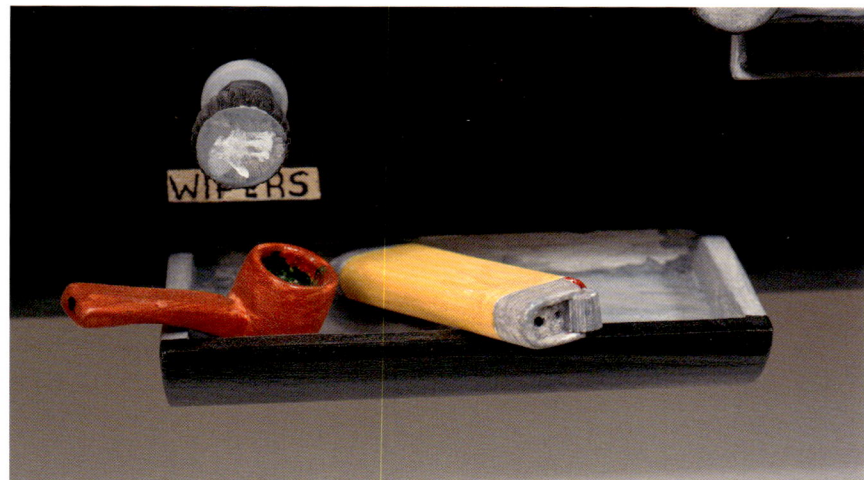

Plate 57. *Cruising Hollywood: Homage to Magu*, 2016. Carved and painted wood, 37 x 58 x 12 in.
Collection of the artist. Photo © James Hart.

FOLLOWING SPREAD
Plate 58. *¡Ay! Qué milagro*, 2017. Carved and painted wood, 24 x 12 x 8 in.
Collection of Curt, Christina, and Jonah Nonomaque. Photo © Addison Doty.

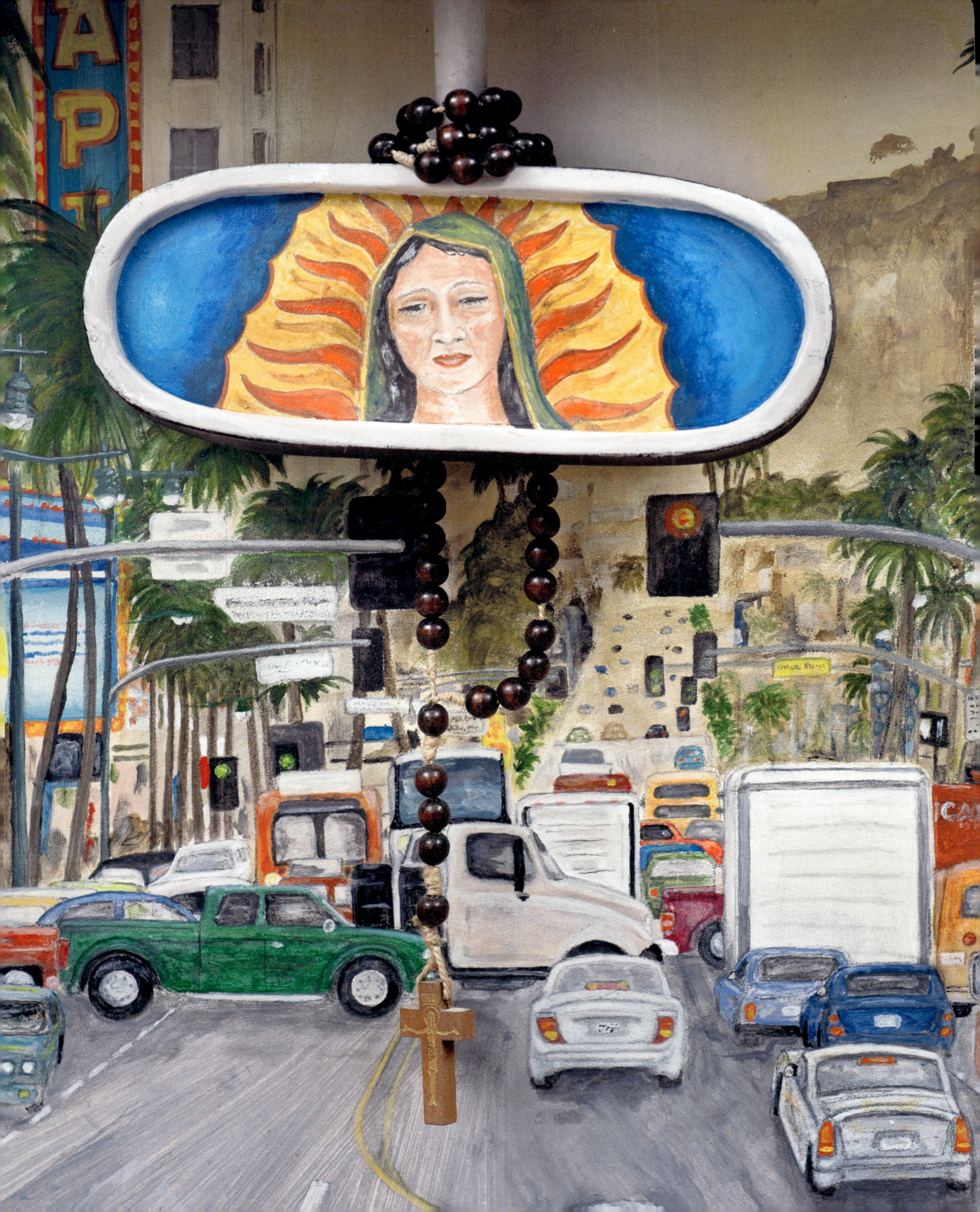

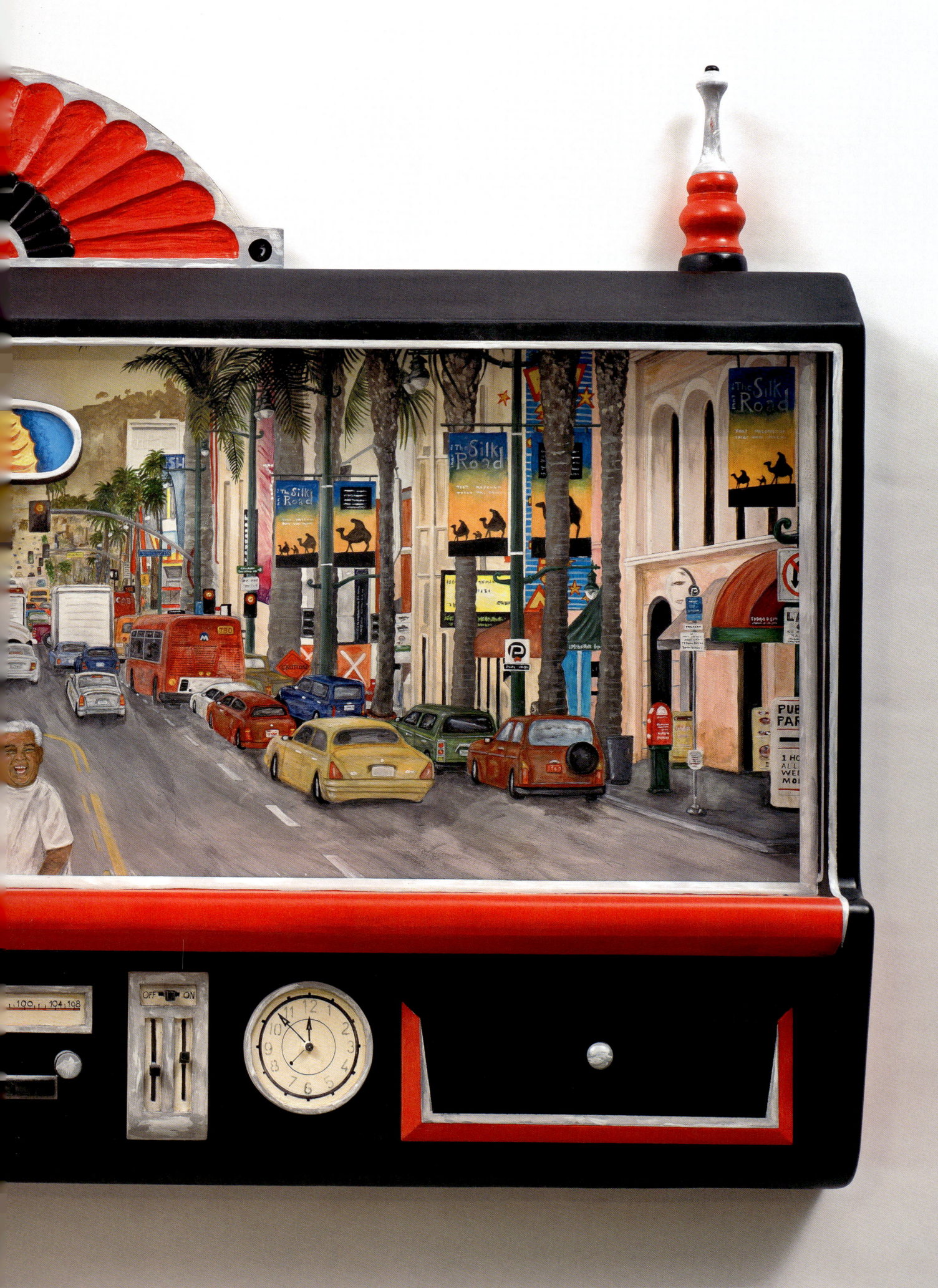

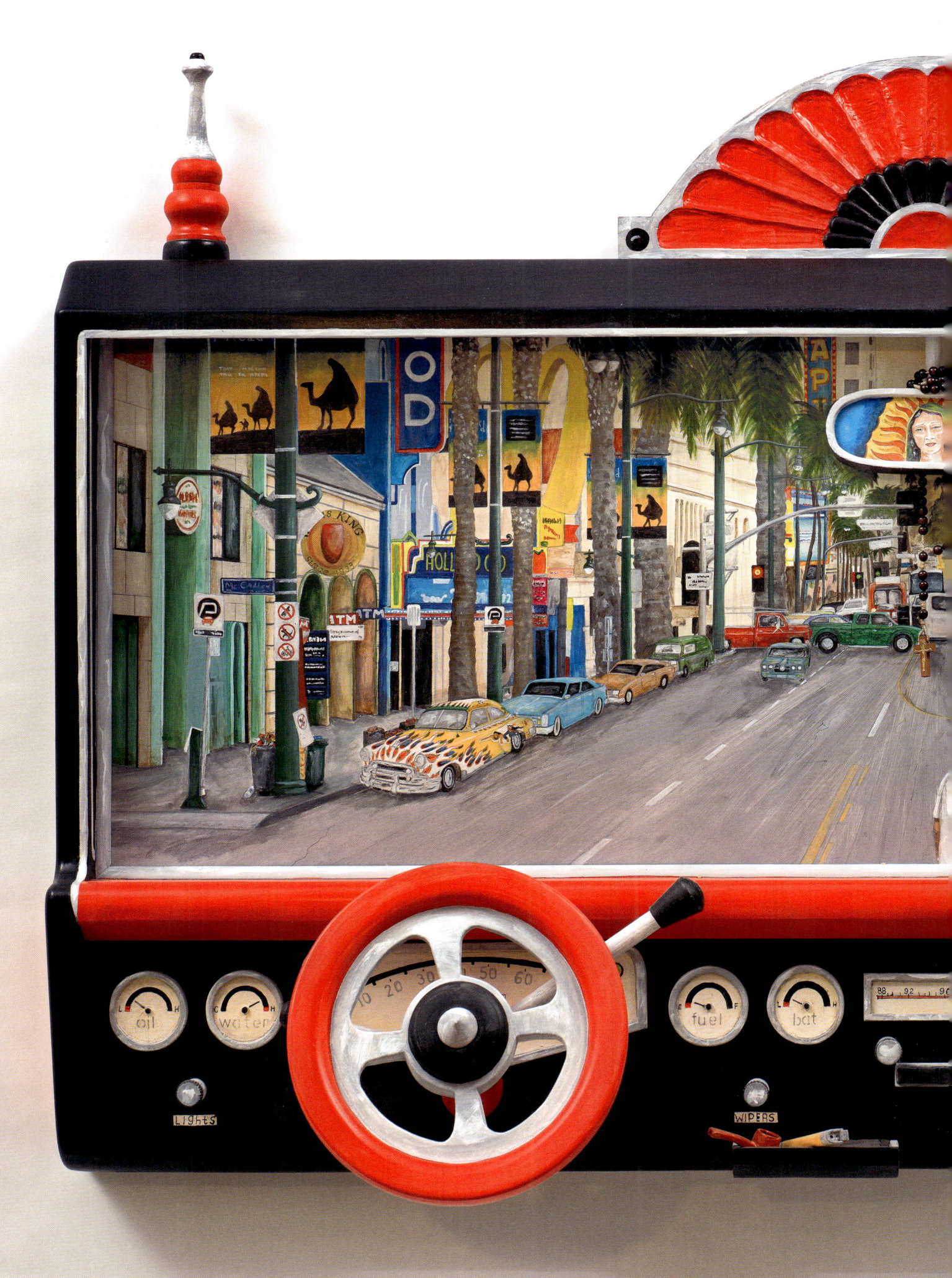

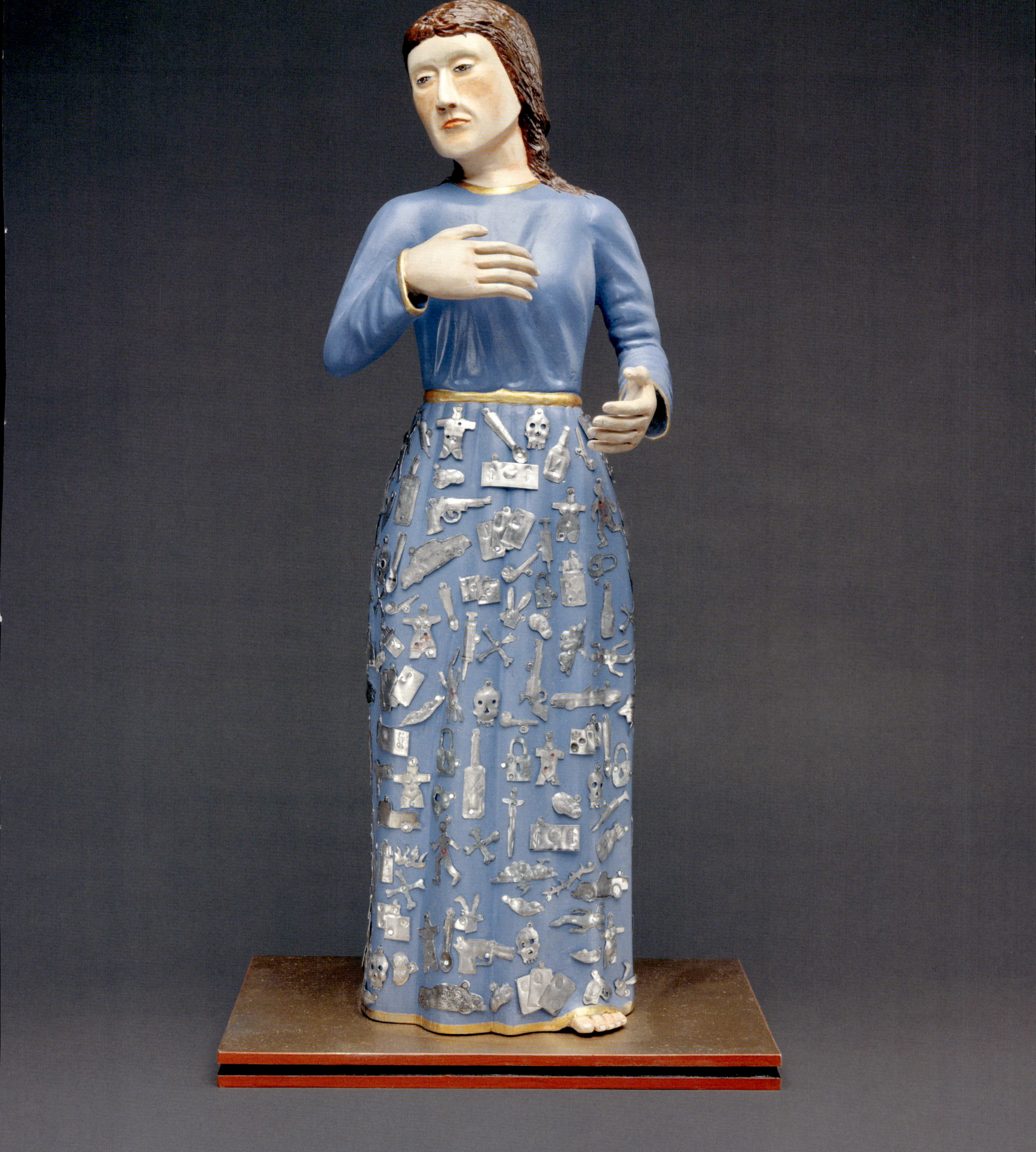

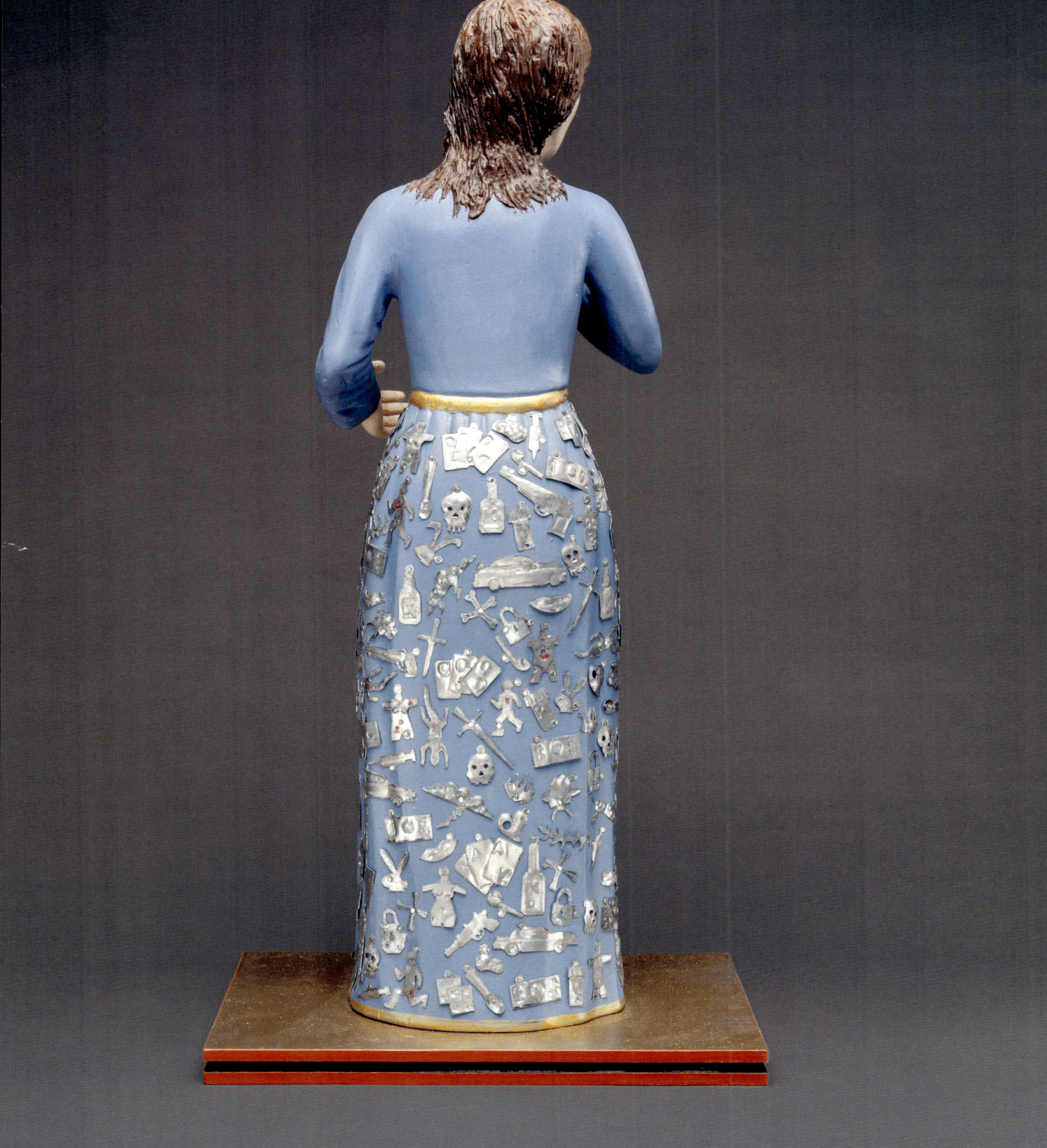

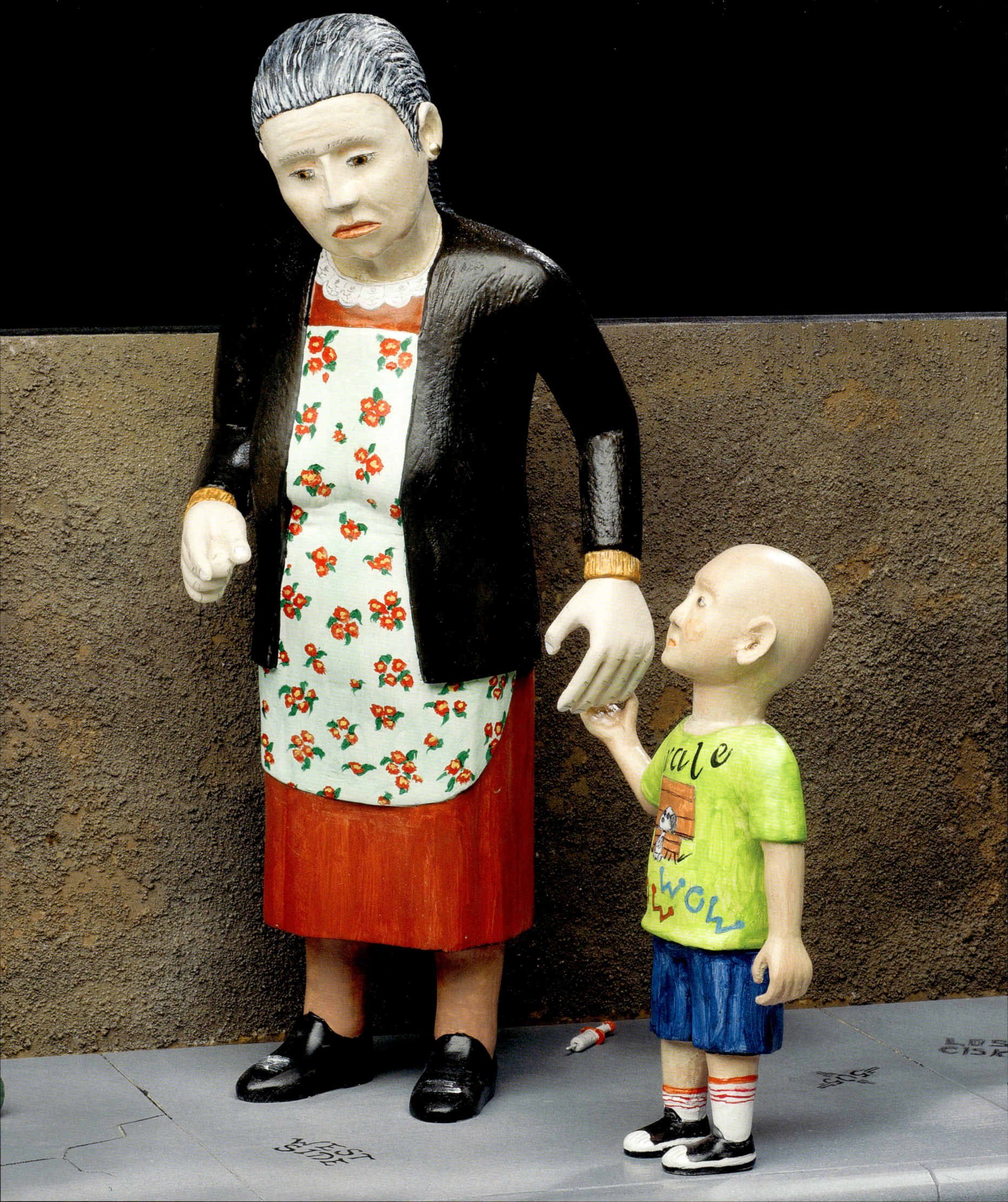

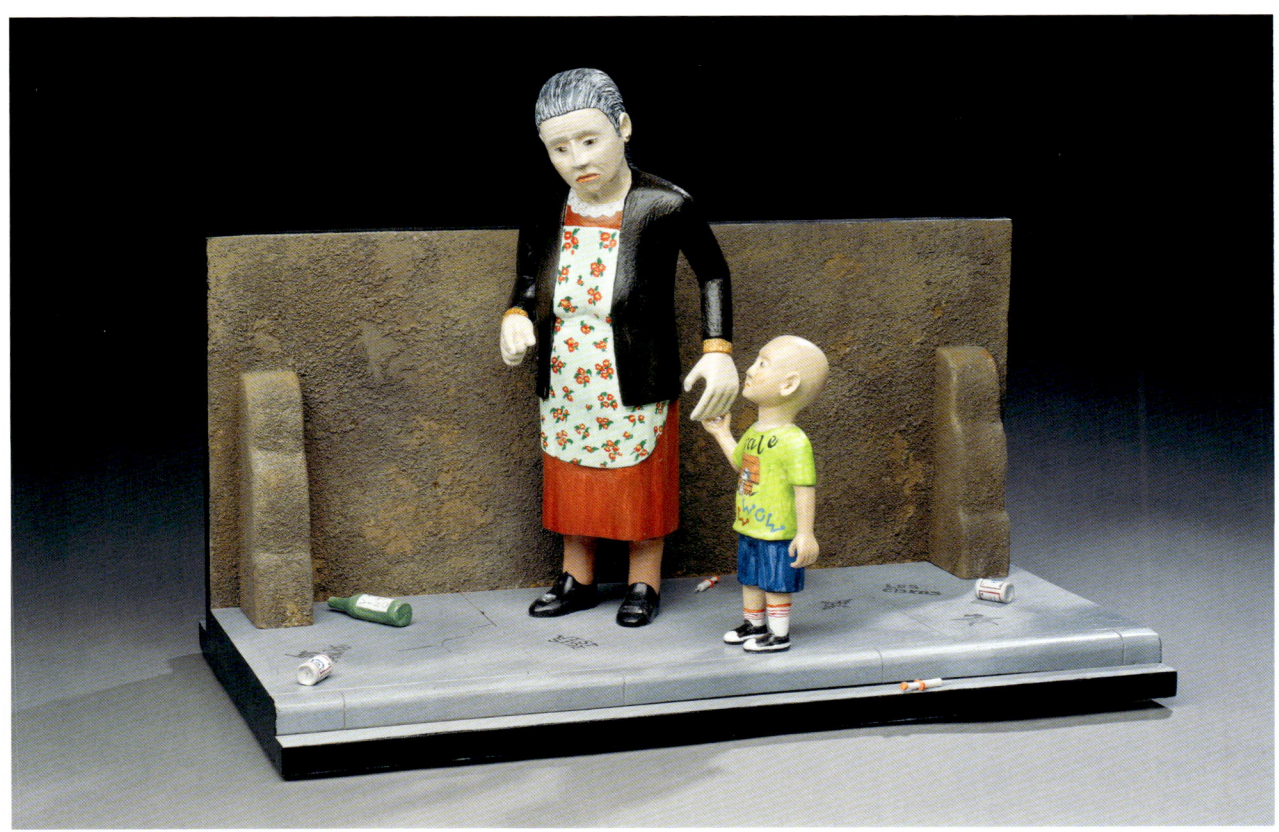

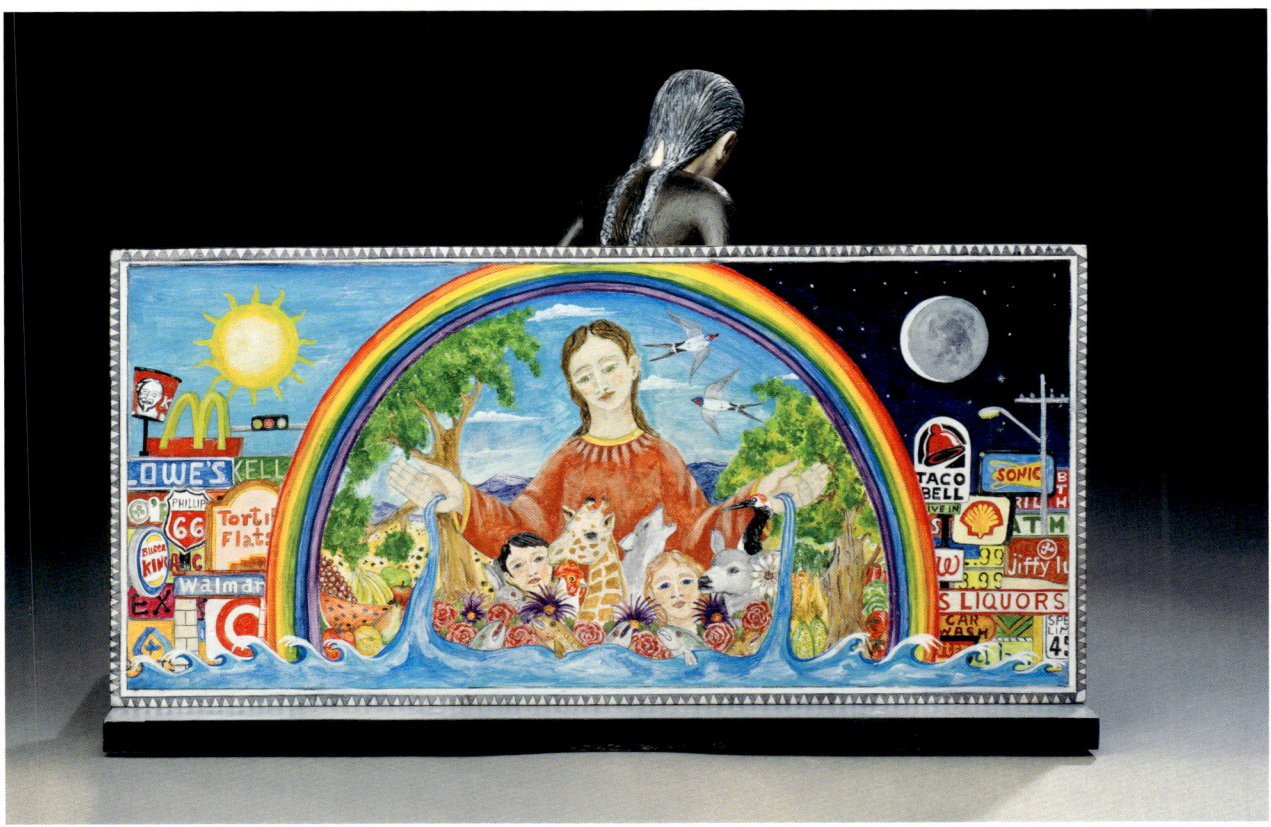

Plate 59. *Abuela*, 2017. Carved and painted wood, 15¾ x 22¼ x 12 in. Collection of the artist.
Photo © James Hart.

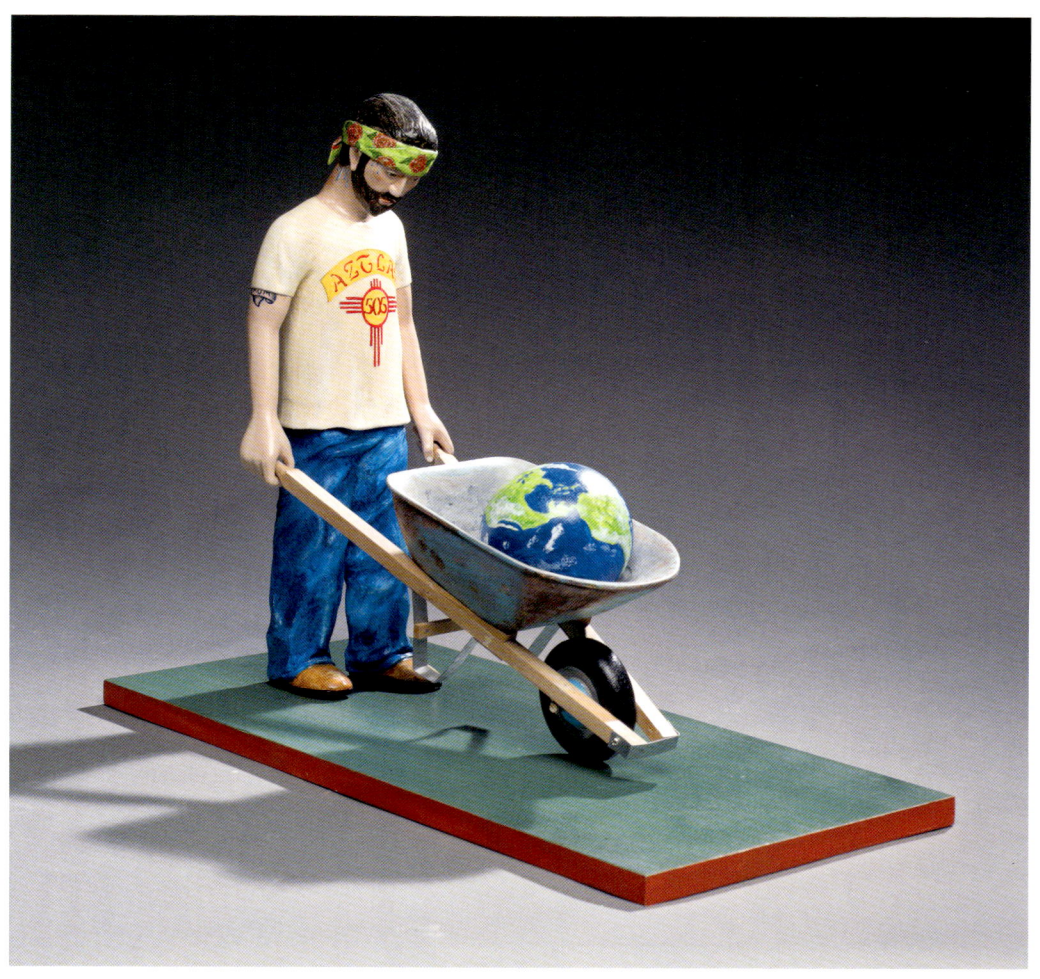

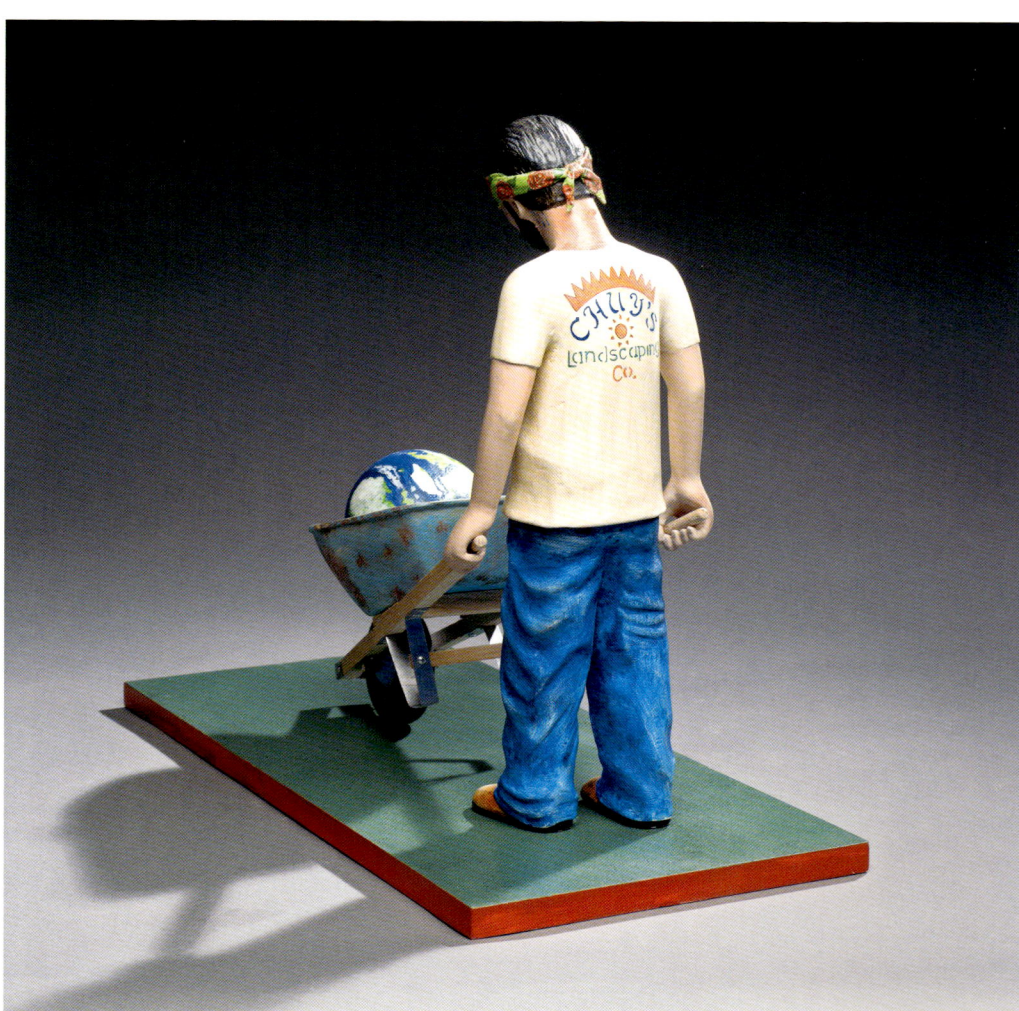

Plate 60. *Chuy con su carga*, 2017. Carved and painted wood, 18¾ x 23 x 10½ in. Collection of Kathryn Minette and Stan Biderman. Photo © James Hart.

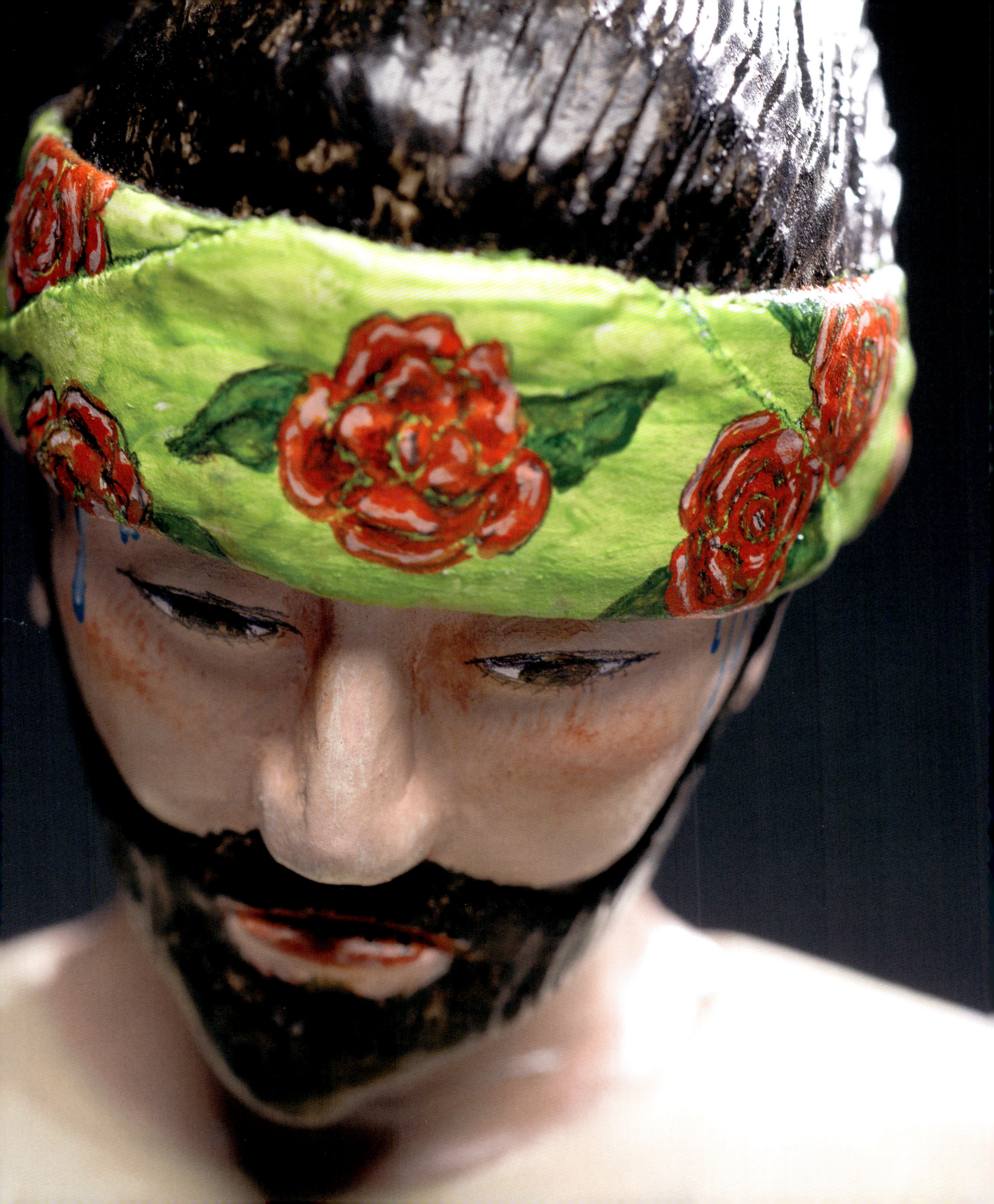

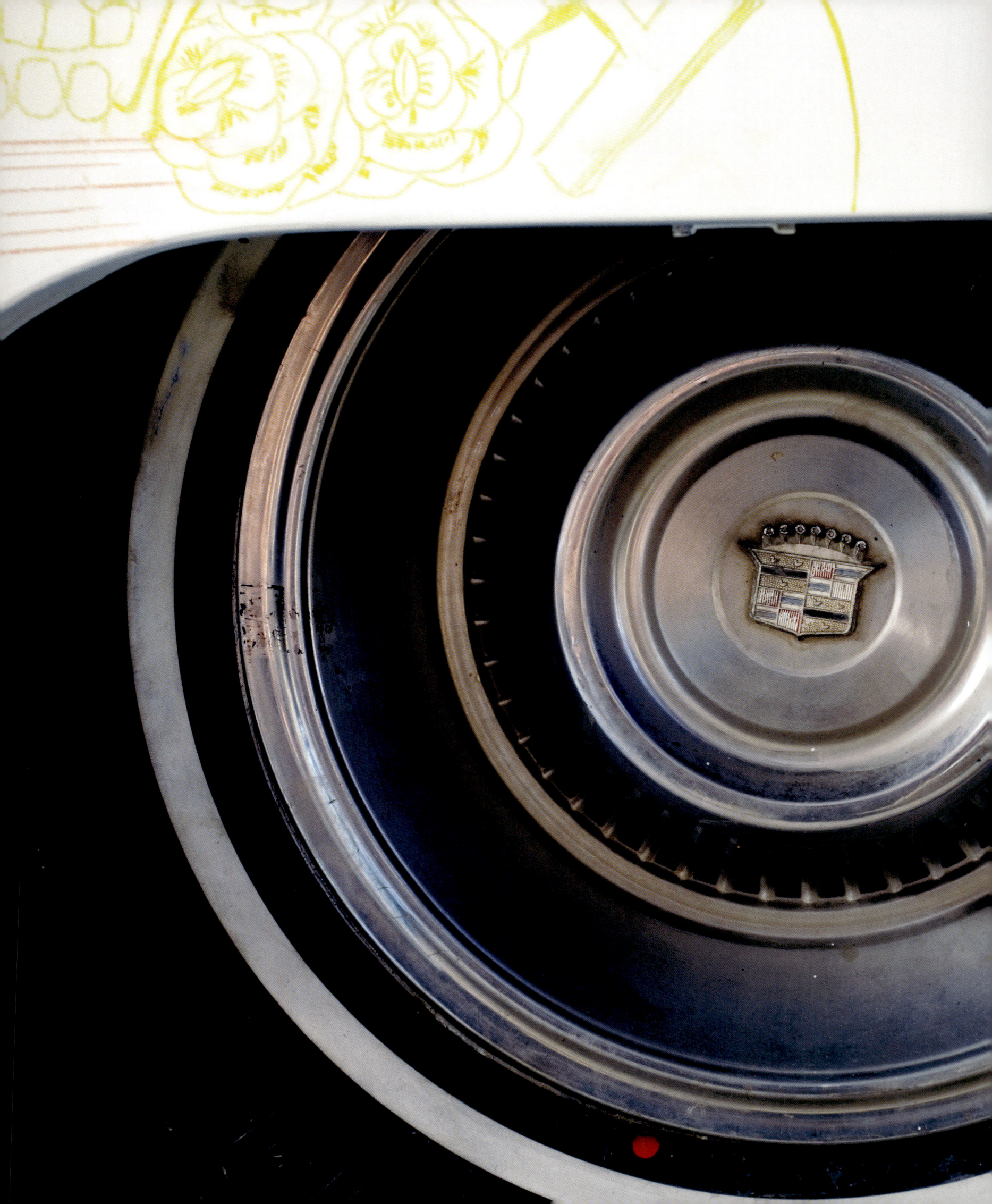

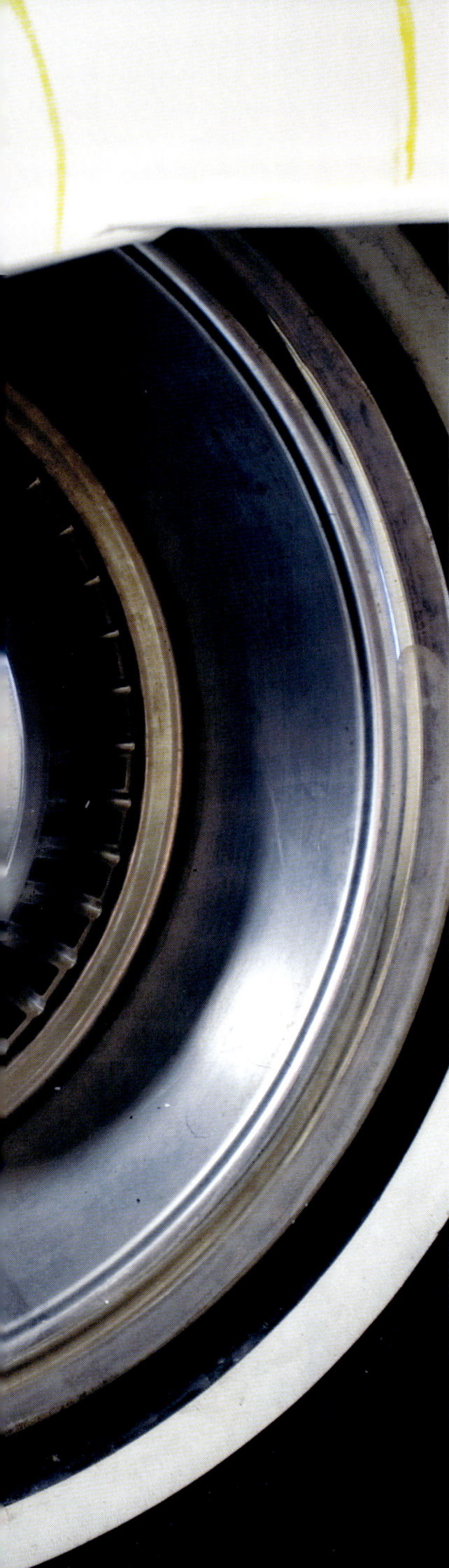

Cada mente es un mundo
A Day in the World of Luis Tapia

EDWARD HAYES

On November 15, 2016, I travel to Santa Fe to spend a day with Luis Tapia as he prepares for an exhibition of twenty-five sculptures, *Luis Tapia: Cada mente es un mundo,* to be held at the Museum of Latin American Art in Long Beach, California, from June 10 to September 3, 2017. Luis picks me up at the home of Stuart Ashman, executive director of Santa Fe's Center for Contemporary Arts, who first introduced us. We head out in the artist's Ford F-150 for a daylong drive and conversation as easy, enlightening, and meandering as the New Mexico landscape. Luis explains that the title for his upcoming exhibition is an old New Mexican *dicho* (saying), "Cada mente es en mundo," or "Every mind is its own world." Before the day is over, our talks will traverse the complex world of Luis's New Mexican Hispano heritage, his political commitment rooted in Chicanismo, and his creative process and technique.

First stop: El Comal, a traditional New Mexican strip mall café on busy Cerrillos Road, where most of the staff and many patrons know the artist as a regular. Here I have the pleasure of tasting my first blue corn enchiladas with a side of crunchy *chicharrones* and hearing Luis's story for the first time. As we are getting to know each other, a patron asks if Luis is available to teach art at a nearby community center. Our conversation on pause, I get a sense of his humility and approachability. Luis kindly declines the invitation, and we get on with coffee and conversation.

EDWARD HAYES: Tell me a bit about where you grew up.

LUIS TAPIA: I'm a Santa Feo, man. I'm a true blood Santa Feo. [*Feo,* meaning "ugly," is Luis's humorously self-deprecating play on *Santa Fean,* the common term for a Santa Fe resident.] I was born in Santa Fe in 1950, in an area called Agua Fría, which in those days was the village of Agua Fría. Today the village is incorporated into Santa Fe, so it's just a street now. I was born with chickens and goats and cows in the backyard, a very rural area, and spent most of my life in Santa Fe, through grade school and high school. I went to college for a year at Las Cruces at New Mexico State University but didn't last there very long. I spent more time in Juárez [then a college party destination just over the Mexican border] than I did in school [laughs]. That was my life until my twenties.

HAYES: What changed in your twenties?

TAPIA: We're talking late sixties, early seventies . . . and that's when all the Chican-ismo really came to life. Cesár Chávez was doing his marches [in California]; Reies [López] Tijerina was doing his marches in New Mexico. So I got involved in all that and started thinking one day, you know, there I was on the streets chanting *"¡Viva la raza!, ¡Viva la raza!"* And I come to realize that I really didn't know anything about *mi raza* . . . even though I was living the life of *mi raza*. So I started to research my own culture. And that's when I fell upon the *santero* tradition, and music, and that's how it all began.

I mean, who was I? I was calling myself, at that time, Spanish American, but what did that mean? It was confusing for me because I didn't really have the knowledge. I think . . . the thing that brought me to where I am now is finding out, getting that knowledge, and then doing something with that knowledge. And even today, my work comes from a Hispanic and Chicano background and logic, but all the issues I deal with in my work are everybody's issues. I mean, if I'm doing a piece that deals with gangs, there are gangs in every culture.

HAYES: What does the term *Chicano* mean to you, in New Mexico?

TAPIA: Many people here don't understand the terminology of being called a Chicano. They've always been called Spanish because of the historical background of New Mexico. Being an isolated area, where the Spaniards came and retained a lot of their culture . . . even though there is a *mezcla* [mixture] with the Native Americans . . . they tried to keep their roots in the Spanish line. When we grew up, we called ourselves Spanish American. And then as I grew older and educated myself to the historical aspects of what happened here . . . the Mexican flag flew over New Mexico for twenty-five years . . . I realized we're so *mezclados*, man.

So *Chicano* is the right term for sure, for me anyway. . . . It's a political statement and also a generational one. . . . But there are still a lot of people that consider themselves Spanish American. And the art is starting to change. The younger generation is push-ing through and is not identifying as Chicano. In some ways, it seems like Chicanismo is dying. It's dying with me and people like me—Magu and Luis Jiménez and other artists that have passed on.

HAYES: You are hinting at an end of an era, but there is renewed interest in Chicano art and Chicano studies. At least in southern California, 2017 is turning out to be the year of the Los Four Chicano art collective. LACMA [Los Angeles County Museum of Art] is organizing a Carlos Almaraz retrospective. At MOLAA [Museum of Latin American Art] we organized a Frank Romero retrospective. A Gilbert "Magu" Luján survey is being held at UC–Irvine, and Beto de la Rocha's work will be included in several of these exhi-bitions. I understand you are also honoring Magu in a painting. What was your relation-ship with Magu?

TAPIA: We were very close. We met during the [1987] *Hispanic Art in the United States* exhibition, and we bonded immediately. In *Hispanic,* we would travel to the different venues, so in New York and Houston and L.A. I would meet up with Magu and Luis Jiménez, Rudy Fernandez, and others. Then they brought *Hispanic* to Santa Fe, so I told him, "Stay with me, man." So he did, him and [wife] Marty and the kids, and he just fell in love with New Mexico.

He was one of those people that's like booze. The more you get, the more you need, no? And then before you know it, "Andas bien borracho con Magu," you know! He was a very intoxicating kind of guy. I introduced him to many of the *santeros* here, and they were very intrigued by him. I think he felt at home here and didn't realize what was here. He hung out here for a long time. He even discovered he had relatives here!

And then I would visit him in L.A. Then I got a commission in Santa Margarita [California] for a church, so I decided to go. Magu was living on Hollywood [Boulevard], and he said, "Come work out of my studio." I went over and stayed with him for a year. We were tight. He loved arguing, and we would get into it all the time, but it was *all good,* you know?

HAYES: What did Magu connect with in your work?

TAPIA: He liked the connection to the historical and how I was carrying the historical pieces out. . . . He liked that a lot. Then of course I started to do a lot of social commentary, which he loved.

Talk of Magu, who savored countless *comidas* at El Comal with Luis, trails as our breakfast ticket arrives. We drip honey over our fresh *sopaipillas,* drain our water glasses, say our good-byes, and head out to Luis's truck. We drive another ten miles southwest to his chapel-like studio garage in La Ciéneguilla to see new works in progress for the *Cada mente es un mundo* exhibition.

HAYES: Looking at your studio, you have a poster of Homies [plastic cholo figurines] pinned to the wall and other images from popular culture, like Mexican calendar art. Tell me about your source material.

TAPIA: I was doing something similar before the Homie toy culture came out, but I was calling them Josés y Marías. If you look at my early work, from the early nineties, I took José y María, which means Joseph and Mary [the biblical couple], and I put them on the streets [Figure 31]. So they became this gang guy with his *chava* with big hair, tattooed. You know, they're portraits.

HAYES: What about the backyard scenes, like that poster on the wall of one of your clothesline sculptures [*Northern New Mexico Clothesline (Two Weeks of Laundry);* Figure 35]?

TAPIA: My mom washed our clothes in a tub, and we'd go hang them on the clothesline. Even at a young age, I realized you could tell the history of a family by just looking at their clothesline . . . if they had fancy sheets or whatever. Somehow that came back to me as I hung clothes out to dry one day because my dryer went out. To this day I have this clothesline at my house. Haven't used it since then, but I started thinking how that was telling a story, because I used to wear these T-shirts with imagery, and it came to me that that was *my* portrait. I had T-shirts with Guadalupanas, with Catrinas, with Budweiser on them, so that's what I incorporated. And as a joke, just one pair of *chones*. Hopefully nobody believes I have just one pair!

HAYES: Is there something particular about your northern New Mexican culture that you identify with, beyond the *santero* influence?

TAPIA: There is a real strong spiritual connection, maybe even more so than in any other Latino community. I guess because we're such a small area and sort of socially . . . how do I put it? . . . socially isolated . . . that the religion really stuck close. So there is this really strong spiritual aspect to northern New Mexico, especially in the Latino and Chicano culture, that I think comes out in my work. And there is a unity, maybe not so much today as there used to be when I was growing up, but we always stuck together because most of these places were ranchos, so you had to take care of your neighbor, and your neighbor took care of you, and if somebody needed help, we all came out to help. Today, very seldom do you see that happening, so that's a part of it too.

Growing up on a rancho, it's all still imbedded in me, to this day. I still chop my wood for heat for the house every year. I've been doing it since I was a child. So I still keep a lot of our tradition of daily living within myself, and I think that tradition comes through in my work.

HAYES: There's an undeniable connection here. You are a sculptor making wood carvings, and you've been chopping wood all your life.

TAPIA: Yeah, it's kind of sad sometimes because there is a piece of wood there that you could probably carve, and you need it for heat!

HAYES: I notice, in the work you are creating here for the exhibition, the homage to Magu [*Cruising Hollywood: Homage to Magu*; Plate 57]. There is a radio carved into the center of the dash. It makes we wonder if music is a part of your work at all. What kind of music do you listen to?

TAPIA: Oh yeah, I have the radio on all day, a variety of types of music. I like the Chicano music a lot. They have a program on Saturdays that plays on KUNM, the University [of New Mexico] station. I like everything. You know, I'm a sixties guy. But I like the Americana music more than anything anymore. . . . Something I wish I would have caught onto when I was younger was music. Learned something about it, right? But I never did.

HAYES: This carving also has a good amount of two-dimensional painting, perhaps more painting than carving. How did you develop both skills?

TAPIA: Well, I don't consider myself a painter, to be honest with you, man. I mean, it's a very difficult thing for me to do. I am dyslexic, and so sculpting really works well for me because of that three-dimensional contact. Then, when we get into the painting skills, I work really hard. Obviously, I paint my sculptures, but I shy from two-dimensional painting.

I call myself a sculptor primarily. I think it's the choice of other people to decide whether you are an artist or not, and everybody has an idea about what an artist should be, right? But I think that if you have that specific [artistic] talent, that you can do any medium you want so long as you learn to control the medium.

With that, Luis turns off the lights and locks up the shop. We hop back into his Ford, wind down a few back roads, and before I know it, we are headed south on Interstate 25 to Albuquerque. Luis informs me that we are going to the National Hispanic Cultural Center to view a major sculpture recently purchased with State of New Mexico public art funds for the permanent collection of the center's art museum.

HAYES: What are we going to see now?

TAPIA: We're going to show you the Cadillac [*A Slice of American Pie* Plate 32]. I think you'll enjoy it. It took me about a year to make, and it's an actual '63 Cadillac. It was kind of crazy, because I always thought that somehow I wanted to bring lowrider imagery into the household. I do wood carvings of cars, but I wanted something that was more full scale.

So I was sitting one day with a welder friend of mine, Bill Van De Valde, having a couple of beers, and I asked Bill what he thought about cutting a car in half. I guess he'd had a few too many, and he started thinking, "I could do that!" So we went to take a look at a '63 Cadillac four-door out in a junkyard . . . and it was trashed, man. I ended up buying the car without realizing it was over seventeen and a half feet long! It took about a whole year to complete the project by the time we cut it down and did the bodywork, and we had to rebuild the frame because it rolls. And then I had to do the mural painting. A year into the project, it was one of those things like, "Whose idea was this?"

HAYES: You had made wooden cars before?

TAPIA: Yes, I had made a few Cadillacs out of wood, and they were pretty popular, right, and they were fun to do. I'm sort of a car guy myself, and I was really intrigued by the lowrider theme, especially in New Mexico, because they use a lot of religious iconography on the cars. Historically, that's right in line with when the Spaniards came. They had images of the Virgin Mary on the *conchas* [silver adornments] on the horses and the decorative parts on their saddles. So it's translating that tradition from one moving object to another, right? One hundred years later, we're doing the same thing, decorating our rides.

HAYES: Other Chicano artists have made lowriders out of wood, such as Frank Romero or Magu. How are yours different?

TAPIA: I think mine are more realistic. I really try to make the car look like a real car. If it's a '63 Cadillac, it looks like a '63 Cadillac, but with New Mexican details. With Frank or

Magu, they change up the car. You get the image, but you don't specifically get the model or make.

HAYES: What's your process?

TAPIA: My cars are made in a traditional method. You have the wood, and you prime it with gesso, which also fills in the cracks. You know, with a lot of my work, especially if you look closely, I'm not shy about leaving marks behind. I don't sand everything so it's totally cherried out. I like leaving chisel marks, or grass marks, because that gives the viewer the idea that this thing is actually handmade. It's not from a mold. Texture is really important to me. I love adding extra texture, even though you can't tell from a distance. It's something you experience closer to the work. It gives the work more depth.

HAYES: When did figures come into your work?

TAPIA: I was self-taught, right, so everything was trial and error. There was nobody to show me how to do the traditional *santos*. I knew they were carved, and then I found out they were gessoed, and being . . . in the learning process, I stuck pretty close to the tradition of religious art and just dealing with *santos*. I didn't last there very long. The transition almost started immediately because I started getting more involved with the color. Back then, the religious pieces were more muted, or completely unpainted, and I started to brighten up my color. And then I got tired of doing Saint Francis over and over again. Man, how many Guadalupanas can you make in one year?

So I started to think of other images and how to change those images, but I still stayed within the realm of religious art. I did Noah's Ark, which was a big step out of that [traditional] world, because that was never done. Then I started doing research on other saints not done by northern New Mexico historical artists. I started doing those saints because that presented more of a challenge. Then, after years of development, and as I would research the saints, I found that all the stories or subjects of these images have social commentary involved.

HAYES: For example?

TAPIA: The Passion of Christ was a whole political movement. Although we celebrate it as a religious experience, it was a political *movida*. So I started to incorporate today's political and social issues and feelings into the work. If you look at my work today, there is a lot of reference to religion, especially Christianity. And in the tradition of the *santos,* there are religious figures, but I always place them in a contemporary environment or give them some kind of contemporary commentary or iconography. I haven't done straight-up religious work in a long, long time.

HAYES: In what other ways have you changed or expanded tradition? Are you still using the same kind of wood that historic *santos* were made from?

TAPIA: No, I used to use New Mexico aspen and cottonwood, make my own paints and all that sort of stuff, but I stopped doing that. I like this wood that I'm using now. It's a soft wood, but it has a lot of strength, and I can manipulate it a lot easier than other woods. And I can trust it more, because sometimes when you collect aspen, you have to make sure it's totally dry by the time you start painting. If you don't, it's going to crack.

It's the same issue with paints. I'm using acrylic paints. I like the brilliance of commercial paints. Some people have made a big deal out of that. But I say sometimes it's better to go to the store. I think that if there had been a paint store around in Spanish colonial New Mexico, the early *santeros* would have agreed.

We wrap up the day at Luis's home south of Santa Fe. It's situated, perhaps not so coincidentally, on a historic rancho that is more than three hundred years old. We turn onto a dirt road, and suddenly, like a scene from one of Luis's classic "dashboard altar" sculptures, a valley landscape fills the windshield.

HAYES: Look at this view! Where are we now?

TAPIA: This is La Ciénega. I've been here for nearly thirty years. You hit this valley, and it's all *ciénegas.* It's all marshland. See all the willows, and there are natural ponds. And look, there's that tree I was telling you about earlier that still has yellow leaves. It's a cottonwood, and like this home, it's probably about two hundred years old.

So here we are. Carmella's home. *¡Bienvenido!*

The massive cottonwood towers over the front yard as we pull into the drive. Just beyond, I see the clothesline that Luis referred to earlier in the day. Instead of Luis's *chones*, a mop and a bird feeder hang from the line. We step out of the truck, and I marvel at the front porch of the old adobe home. It's covered, floor to ceiling, with a perfectly sculptural stack of firewood, collected and cut by Luis for the winter ahead. I see three vintage cars parked in the front drive.

TAPIA: This is my car collection: a '53 Studebaker Champion, sea-foam green; a '64 Falcon convertible; and a '51 Chevy stand delivery wagon. Carmella calls it my Chicano apartment complex!

HAYES: Are these cars that will be made into sculptures?

TAPIA: No, these are supposed to run! Let's say they are the projects I haven't gotten to yet.

Notes

Introduction (Page 15)

1. See Laura E. Pérez, *Chicana Art: The Politics of Spiritual and Aesthetic Altarities* (Durham, NC: Duke University Press, 2007), 44.

2. Miguel León-Portilla, *Endangered Cultures,* trans. Julie Goodson-Lawes (Dallas: Southern Methodist University Press, 1990), 10–11. León-Portilla's explanation of *nepantla* derives from sixteenth-century Native testimony as recorded by friars Diego Durán and Bernardino de Sahagún.

3. Gloria Anzaldúa, "Border Arte: Nepantla, el Lugar de la Frontera," in *The Gloria Anzaldúa Reader,* ed. AnaLouise Keating (Durham, NC: Duke University Press, 2009), 180.

4. Gloria Anzaldúa, "(Un)natural Bridges, (Un)safe Spaces," in *The Gloria Anzaldúa Reader,* 243.

5. Néstor García Canclini, "Modernity after Postmodernity," in *Beyond the Fantastic: Contemporary Art Criticism from Latin America,* ed. Gerardo Mosquera (London: Institute of International Visual Arts, 1995), 27–28. García Canclini is also the author of *Hybrid Cultures,* where this idea forms a major thread. See *Hybrid Cultures: Strategies for Entering and Leaving Modernity,* trans. Christopher L. Chiappari and Silvia L. López (Minneapolis: University of Minnesota Press, 1995).

6. Pérez, *Chicana Art,* 44.

Nobody's Perfect (Page 19)

1. John Beardsley, "And/Or: Hispanic Art, American Culture," in *Hispanic Art in the United States* (Houston: Museum of Fine Arts, 1987), 45.

2. Unattributed quotations are from an interview with Tapia by the author in September 2016.

3. John Beardsley, *Hispanic Art in the United States* (Houston: Museum of Fine Arts, 1987), 244.

¡ÓRALE! (Page 37)

1. Quotations are from an interview with Tapia by the author in August 2016.

2. The author intentionally and strategically uses different identifying terms throughout this essay.

3. For more information on the history of Spanish Market, its artists, and the collections of the Spanish Colonial Arts Society and the Museum of Spanish Colonial Art in Santa Fe, see Donna Pierce and Marta Weigle, eds., *Spanish New Mexico: The Spanish Colonial Arts Society Collection.* 2 vols. (Santa Fe: Museum of New Mexico Press, 1996). See also Carmella Padilla and Donna Pierce, *Conexiones: Connections in Spanish Colonial Art* (Santa Fe: Museum of Spanish Colonial Art, 2002). Better yet, visit New Mexico and meet the artists of Spanish Market and Contemporary Hispanic Market, held annually the last weekend of July in and around the Santa Fe Plaza.

4. In 1992 the United States observed the five-hundredth anniversary of Christopher Columbus's "discovery" of America. The quincentennial was a significant marker for the inclusion of Hispanics and Latinos in many things, including museum exhibitions and American art history.

5. Diana Pardue, "Luis," Santa Fe Rotary Foundation Distinguished Artist Award catalog, 1994, 3.

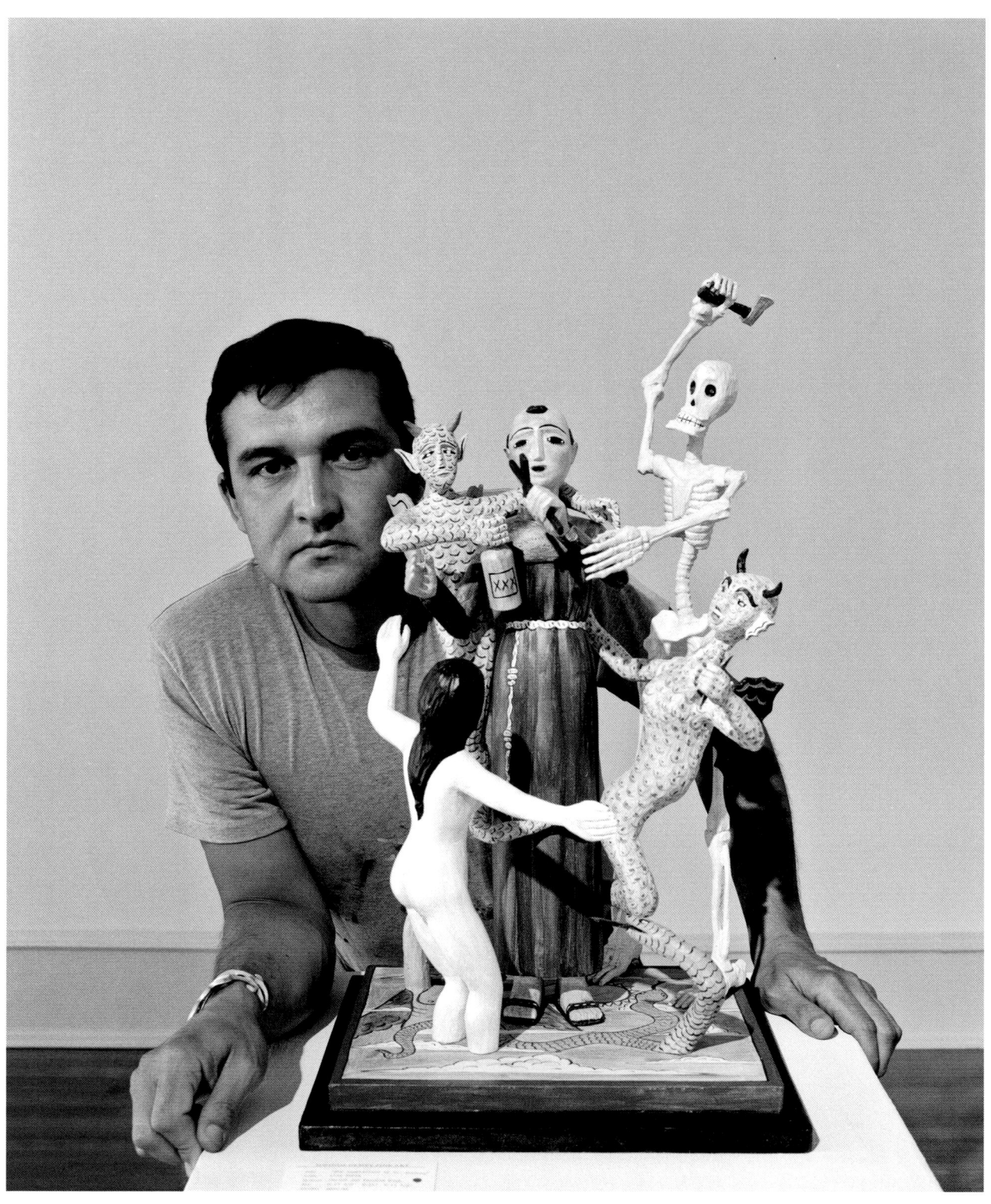

200

Selected Collections

Albuquerque International Sunport Collection, Albuquerque

Albuquerque Museum, Albuquerque

Arizona State University Art Museum, Tempe

Autry National Center of the American West, Los Angeles

Bent's Old Fort, La Junta, Colorado

Colorado Springs Fine Arts Center Museum, Colorado Springs

Craft and Folk Art Museum, Los Angeles

Denver Art Museum, Denver

El Museo del Barrio, New York

Harwood Museum of Art, Taos

Heard Museum, Phoenix

Hemphill Collection, New York

Maxwell Museum of Anthropology, University of New Mexico, Albuquerque

Millicent Rogers Museum, Taos

Museum of American Folk Art, New York

Museum of International Folk Art, Santa Fe

Museum of Spanish Colonial Art, Santa Fe

National Hispanic Cultural Center Art Museum, Albuquerque

National Museum of American Art, Smithsonian Institution, Washington, D.C.

National Museum of American History, Smithsonian Institution, Washington, D.C.

New Mexico Capitol Art Collection, Santa Fe

New Mexico Museum of Art, Santa Fe

Qwest Corporation, Denver

Rockwell Museum of Western Art, Corning, New York

Roswell Museum and Art Center, Roswell, New Mexico

The Tia Collection, Santa Fe

University of Colorado Art Museum, Boulder

University of New Mexico Art Museum, Albuquerque

Church Commissions and Collections

Church of the Nativity, Rancho Santa Fe, California

Our Lady of Guadalupe Church, Pojoaque, New Mexico

Our Lady of the Most Holy Rosary, Albuquerque

Sacred Heart Catholic Church, Durango, Colorado

San Francisco de Asís Mission Church, Ranchos de Taos, New Mexico

San Francisco Solano Catholic Church, Rancho Santa Margarita, California

San Ildefonso Church, San Ildefonso Pueblo, New Mexico

San Isidro Catholic Church, Agua Fría Village, New Mexico

Selected Exhibitions

2017   *Luis Tapia: Cada mente es un mundo*
         Museum of Latin American Art, Long Beach, California

2017   *The High Art of Riding Low: Ranflas, Corazón e Inspiración*
         Petersen Automotive Museum, Los Angeles, California

2017   *The World in New Mexico/New Mexico in the World: Bridging Continental
         Traditions at the Museum of International Folk Art*
         Governor's Gallery, New Mexico State Capitol, Santa Fe

2016   *Con Cariño: Artists Inspired by Lowriders*
         New Mexico Museum of Art, Santa Fe

2015   *La Muerte Niña: Day of the Dead Exhibition*
         National Museum of Mexican Art, Chicago

2014–   *Between Two Worlds: Folk Artists Reflect on the Immigrant Experience*
2016   Museum of International Folk Art, Santa Fe

2014   *New Art/New Mexico*
         Ross Art Museum, Ohio Wesleyan University, Delaware, Ohio

2013   *The Arts: Grounded in Region, Second Triennial of International
         Kogei in Kanazawa*
         Twenty-First Century Museum of Contemporary Art, Kanazawa, Japan

2013   *Art of the West*
         Autry National Center of the American West, Los Angeles

2012–   *It's About Time: 14,000 Years of Art in New Mexico*
2013   New Mexico Museum of Art, Santa Fe

2012–   *Wooden Menagerie: Made in New Mexico*
2013   Museum of International Folk Art, Santa Fe

2008–   *Maverick Art*
2009   Autry National Center of the American West, Los Angeles

2008   *Luis Tapia: ¡Órale!*
Owings-Dewey Fine Art, Santa Fe

2008   *Three New Mexican Innovators: Celso Gallegos, Horacio Valdez and Luis Tapia*
Museum of Spanish Colonial Art, Santa Fe

2008   *Caminos Distintos: Patrocino Barela and Edward Gonzales in New Mexico*
National Hispanic Cultural Center Art Museum, Albuquerque

2008   *Santeros*
De Paul University Art Museum, Chicago

2007   *Out West: The Great American Landscape*
Meridian International Center, Washington, D.C., and the National Art
Museum of China, Beijing

2004   *Voces y Visiones*
El Museo del Barrio, New York

2003–   *Arte y Amistad: Selections from the Diane and Sandy Besser Collection*
2004   Museum of International Folk Art, Santa Fe

2003   *Re-Presenting Representation VI*
Arnot Art Museum, Elmira, New York, with the Rockwell Museum of
Western Art, Corning, New York

2002   *¡Ahora! New Mexican Hispanic Art*
National Hispanic Cultural Center Art Museum, Albuquerque

2002   *Conexiones: Connections in Spanish Colonial Art*
Museum of Spanish Colonial Art, Santa Fe

2002   *Luis Tapia: ¡Ay, Qué Vida!*
Owings-Dewey Fine Art, Santa Fe

2001   *Earth*
Owings-Dewey Fine Art, Santa Fe

2001   *Voices from Our Communities: Perspectives on a Decade of Collecting
at El Museo del Barrio*
El Museo del Barrio, New York

2000–   *Arte Latino: Treasures from the Smithsonian American Art Museum*
2002   Smithsonian Institution traveling exhibition: El Paso Museum of Art; Orlando
Museum of Art; Palm Springs Desert Museum; Museum of Fine Arts, Santa Fe;
Oakland Museum

2000   *La Luz: Contemporary Latino Art in the United States*
National Hispanic Cultural Center Art Museum, Albuquerque

2000	*Con Sentimiento desde Nuevo México* Ministerio de Educación, Cultura y Deporte, Museo de América, Madrid
2000	*New Art of the West 7* Eiteljorg Museum of American Indians and Western Art, Indianapolis
1999	*Luis Tapia: Recent Work* Owings-Dewey Fine Art, Santa Fe
1999	*Patrocino Barela: Recordando un Pueblo* Millicent Rogers Museum, Taos
1999	*Day of the Dead* Buddy Holly Museum, Amarillo, Texas
1999- 1998	*The Saint Makers: Contemporary Santeras y Santeros* Owensboro Museum of Fine Arts, Owensboro, Kentucky
1998	*Reencuentro de Tres Culturas* Museo de América, Madrid
1997	*O'Keeffe's New Mexico* Museum of Fine Arts, Santa Fe
1997	*La Guadalupana* Tacoma Art Museum, Tacoma, Washington
1997	*Water* Owings-Dewey Fine Art, Santa Fe
1996	*Visiones de la Vida, Tierra y Agua* Millicent Rogers Museum, Taos
1996	*Luis Tapia: Recent Works* Owings-Dewey Fine Art, Santa Fe
1996	*Valley Light* Arte Américas, Casa de la Cultura, Fresno
1995	*Cuando Hablan Los Santos: Contemporary Santero Traditions from Northern New Mexico* Maxwell Museum of Anthropology, University of New Mexico, Albuquerque
1994	*Crafting Devotions: Tradition in Contemporary New Mexico Santos* Gene Autry Western Heritage Museum, Los Angeles
1994	*Guadalajara International Book Fair Art Exhibition* Guadalajara, Mexico
1994	*Seis Santeros* Millicent Rogers Museum and the Harwood Foundation, Taos

1993 *Luis Tapia: New Work*
   Owings-Dewey Fine Art, Santa Fe

1993 *Borderless Art: Sculpture North and South of the Río Grande*
   Red Mesa Art Center, Gallup, New Mexico, and Mexico City

1992 *Chispas! Cultural Warriors of New Mexico*
   Heard Museum, Phoenix

1992 *Luis Tapia and Bernadette Vigil*
   Albuquerque Museum, Albuquerque

1992 *Ventanas Visiones Culturales*
   Plains Art Museum, Moorhead, Minnesota

1991 *Miniatures 91*
   Albuquerque Museum, Albuquerque

1991 *Tamarind Invites: Lithographs by Six New Mexican Santeros*
   Museum of International Folk Art, Santa Fe

1991 *Santeros: Lithographs from Tamarind*
   Grove Gallery, University of California at San Diego Crafts Center, San Diego

1990 *Shrine Exhibition*
   Armory for the Arts, Santa Fe

1990 *Second Annual Invitational*
   Center for Contemporary Arts, Santa Fe

1990 *Easter Exhibition*
   Owings-Dewey Fine Art, Santa Fe

1989 *Luis Tapia: Contemporary Hispanic Woodcarving*
   Owings-Dewey Fine Art, Santa Fe

1989 *Encuentros: Recordando La Cofradía*
   Millicent Rogers Museum, Taos

1989 *Invitational Exhibition*
   Roswell Museum and Art Center, Roswell, New Mexico

1989– *Hispanic Art in the United States: Thirty Contemporary Painters and Sculptors*
1988 Museum of Fine Arts, Houston

1988 *Santos, Statues and Sculpture: Contemporary Woodcarving from New Mexico*
   Craft and Folk Art Museum, Los Angeles

1988 *New Mexico Images Past and Present*
   Owings-Dewey Fine Art, Santa Fe

1982 *Luis Tapia: One-Man Exhibition*
   Governor's Gallery, New Mexico State Capitol, Santa Fe

1982   *Santa Fe Festival of the Arts*
        Santa Fe

1980   *Santa Fe Festival of the Arts*
        Santa Fe

1980   *Luis Tapia: Solo Exhibition*
        Institute of American Indian Arts, Santa Fe

1979   *Wood in Art Invitational*
        Arizona State University, Tempe

1979   *Contemporary Hispanic Art*
        Santa Fe Council for the Arts, Santa Fe

1979   *Luis Tapia and Star Tapia*
        El Santuario de Guadalupe, Santa Fe

1979   *Hispanic Heritage Festival*
        Santa Fe Council for the Arts and La Cofradía de los Artes y Artesanos
        Hispánicos, Santa Fe

1979   *Cultura '79*
        La Cofradía de los Artes y Artesanos Hispánicos, El Santuario de Guadalupe,
        Santa Fe

1979   *Folk Art*
        Governor's Gallery, New Mexico State Capitol, Santa Fe

1979   *Border Folk Festival*
        Chamizal National Memorial, El Paso

1978   *One Space, Three Visions*
        Albuquerque Museum, Albuquerque

1977   *Hispanic Crafts of the Southwest*
        Taylor Museum, Colorado Springs Fine Arts Center, Colorado Springs

1977   *Festival of American Folklife*
        Smithsonian Institution, Washington, D.C.

1976   *Festival of American Folklife*
        Smithsonian Institution, Washington, D.C.

1976   *Día de Más, Días de los Muertos*
        Museum of International Folk Art, Santa Fe

Selected Bibliography

Adlmann, Jan, and Barbara McIntyre. *Contemporary Art in New Mexico.* Roseville East, New South Wales, Australia: Craftsman House, 1996.

Ahlborn, Richard A. "Spanish Crafts in the American Southwest." In *1977 Festival of American Folklife.* Washington, DC: Smithsonian Institution, 1977.

Baca, Elmo. *Santa Fe Fantasy: The Quest for the Golden City.* Santa Fe: Clear Light Publishers, 1994.

Baugh, Scott L., and Victor A. Sorrell. *Born of Resistance: Cara a Cara Encounters with Chicana/o Visual Culture.* Tucson: University of Arizona Press, 2015.

Beardsley, John, and Jane Livingston. *Hispanic Art in the United States: Thirty Contemporary Painters and Sculptors.* New York: Abbeville Press with Museum of Fine Arts, Houston, 1987.

Boss, Gayle. *Santo Making in New Mexico: Way of Sorrow, Way of Light.* Washington, DC: Potters House Press, 1991.

Bowman, Russell, ed. *Common Ground, Uncommon Vision: The Michael and Julie Hall Collection of American Folk Art.* Milwaukee: Milwaukee Art Museum, 1993.

Briggs, Charles L. *The Woodcarvers of Córdova, New Mexico.* Knoxville: University of Tennessee Press, 1986.

Bullis, Douglas. *One Hundred Artists of the Southwest.* Atglen, PA: Schiffer Publishing, 2006.

Cirillo, Dexter, Nancy Pletka Benkof, and Eric Swanson. *Across Frontiers: Hispanic Crafts of New Mexico.* San Francisco: Chronicle Books, 1998.

Connors, Andrew. "Luis Tapia: Inside and Out." *Luis Tapia ¡Ay, Qué vida!* Santa Fe: Owings-Dewey Fine Art, 2002.

Flores, Lauro, ed. *The Floating Borderlands: Twenty-Five Years of U.S. Hispanic Literature.* Seattle: University of Washington Press, 1998.

Haggerty, Donald J. *Leading the West: One Hundred Contemporary Painters and Sculptors.* Flagstaff: Northland Publishing Company, 1997.

Ice, Joyce, ed. *On Collecting: From Public to Private, Featuring Folk and Tribal Art from the Diane and Sandy Besser Collection*. Seattle: University of Washington Press, 2009.

Kalb, Laurie Beth. *Crafting Devotions: Tradition in Contemporary New Mexico Santos*. Albuquerque: University of New Mexico Press, 1994.

———. *Santos, Statues, and Sculpture: Contemporary Woodcarving from New Mexico*. Los Angeles: Craft and Folk Art Museum of Los Angeles, 1988.

Keller, Gary D., Mary Erickson, Kaytie Johnson, and Joaquín Alvarado. *Contemporary Chicana and Chicano Art: Artists, Works, Culture, and Education*. Tempe: Bilingual Press/ Editorial Bilingüe, Arizona State University, 2002.

Latino Art and Culture. Washington, DC: National Museum of American Art, Smithsonian Institution, 1996.

Lewthwaite, Stephanie. *A Contested Art: Modernism and Mestizaje in New Mexico*. Norman: University of Oklahoma Press, 2015.

———. "Reworking the Spanish Colonial Paradigm: Mestizaje and Spirituality in Contemporary New Mexican Art." *Journal of American Studies* 47, no. 2 (May 2013): 339–362.

Lippard, Lucy R. "Bodywork, Sacred and Profane." *Luis Tapia: ¡Órale!* Santa Fe: Owings-Dewey Fine Art, 2008.

Mather, Christine, and Jack Parsons. *True West: Arts, Traditions and Celebrations*. New York: Clarkson Potter, 1992.

Mather, Christine, and Sharon Woods. *Santa Fe Style*. New York: Rizzoli International Publications, 1980.

Montaño, Mary. *Tradiciones Nuevomexicanas: Hispano Arts and Culture of New Mexico*. Albuquerque: University of New Mexico Press, 2001.

Moore, James. "Luis Eligio Tapia." *Luis Tapia*. Santa Fe: Owings-Dewey Fine Art, 1991.

Newmann, Dana, and Jack Parsons. *New Mexico Artists at Work*. Santa Fe: Museum of New Mexico Press, 2005.

Olivares, Julian, ed. "About the Artist: Luis Eligio Tapia." *Americas Review: A Review of Hispanic Literature and Art of the USA* (Arte Público Press, University of Houston) 21, no. 2 (Summer 1993).

———. "Luis Tapia." *Americas Review: A Review of Hispanic Literature and Art of the USA* (Arte Público Press, University of Houston) 17, no. 2 (Summer 1989).

Padilla, Carmella, and Donna Pierce. *Conexiones: Connections in Spanish Colonial Art*. Santa Fe: Museum of Spanish Colonial Art, 2002.

Pardue, Diana. *Chispas! Cultural Warriors of New Mexico*. Phoenix: Heard Museum, 1992.

Pierce, Donna, and Marta Weigle, eds. *Spanish New Mexico: The Spanish Colonial Arts Society Collection*. Santa Fe: Museum of New Mexico Press, 1996.

Quirarte, Jacinto, "Luis Eligio Tapia." *Luis Tapia: ¡Ay, Qué Vida!* Santa Fe: Owings-Dewey Fine Art, 2002.

Re-presenting Representation VI. Elmira, NY: Arnot Art Museum, 1993.

Rosenak, Chuck, and Jan Rosenak. *Museum of American Folk Art Encyclopedia of Twentieth-Century Folk Art and Artists*. New York: Abbeville Press, 1991.

———. *The Saint Makers: Contemporary Santeras y Santeros*. Flagstaff: Northland Publishing, 1998.

Rudnick, Lois Palken, and Malin Wilson-Powell, eds. *Mabel Dodge Luhan and Company: American Moderns and the West*. Albuquerque: University of New Mexico Press, 2016.

Salvador, Mari Lyn C. *Cuando Hablan Los Santos: Contemporary Santero Traditions from Northern New Mexico*. Albuquerque: Maxwell Museum of Anthropology, University of New Mexico Press, 1995.

Salvador, Mari Lyn C., et al. *Con Sentimiento desde Nuevo México*. Madrid: Museo de América, Ministerio de Educación, Cultura y Deporte, 2000.

Spitta, Sylvia. *Misplaced Objects: Migrating Collections and Recollections in Europe and the Americas*. Austin: University of Texas Press, 2009.

Traugott, Joseph. *The Art of New Mexico: How the West Is One*. Santa Fe: Museum of New Mexico Press, 2007.

———. *New Mexico Art through Time: Prehistory to the Present*. Santa Fe: Museum of New Mexico Press, 2012.

Ventanas: Visiones Culturales. Fargo: Plains Art Museum, 1992.

Voices from Our Communities: Perspectives on a Decade of Collecting at El Museo del Barrio. New York: El Museo del Barrio, 2001.

Walch, Peter. *University of New Mexico Art Museum: Highlights of the Collections*. Albuquerque: University of New Mexico Art Museum, 2001.

Wertkin, Gerard C., ed. *Encyclopedia of American Folk Art*. New York: Routledge with the American Folk Art Museum, 2004.

Wroth, William, ed. *Hispanic Crafts of the Southwest*. Colorado Springs: Taylor Museum, Colorado Springs Fine Arts Center, 1977.

Yorba, Jonathan. *Arte Latino: Treasures from the Smithsonian American Art Museum*. New York: Watson-Guptill Publications with the Smithsonian American Art Museum, 2001.

SELECTED FILMS

De Colores: The Work of Luis Tapia. Santa Fe: Santa Fe Rotary Foundation, 1994.

Diverse Roots, Diverse Forms: Six Latino Artists in the United States. New York: Philip Morris, 1993.

Los Santeros. Santa Fe: Blue Sky Productions, 1978.

Santero. Colores! Albuquerque: KNME-TV, 1991.

SELECTED HONORS

2007 Phoenix Home and Garden Masters of the Southwest Award, Phoenix.

1996 New Mexico Governor's Award for Excellence in the Arts, Santa Fe.

1994 Distinguished Artist Award, Santa Fe Rotary Foundation, Santa Fe.

Acknowledgments

This book is bound by a community of professional colleagues, personal friends, and loved ones who shared expertise, creativity, encouragement, and advice. My deepest gratitude goes to all who assisted me in valuable and visionary ways.

My dear friend and colleague David Skolkin, who has been an enthusiastic voice in discussing this book for a decade, brought his comprehensive understanding of design, sophisticated aesthetic sensibility, and patient way of being to create a powerful testament to Luis's life in art. Joanna Hurley, another steadfast friend and colleague, helped determine the partnerships to ensure the book's publication and its life beyond. In that regard, I am sincerely grateful to the Museum of Latin American Art (MOLAA), especially Eddie Hayes, Christopher Gordon, and former MOLAA director Stuart Ashman, for their collaboration. I'm also grateful to Dale Bennie and the University of Oklahoma Press for eagerly signing on as distribution partner.

It was my great fortune to assemble the diverse and gifted writers and photographers who crafted the words and images, insights and impressions that illuminate Luis's creative journey. Lucy Lippard, Tey Marianna Nunn, Denise Chávez, and Dana Gioia are longtime friends, while Eddie Hayes and Charlene Villaseñor Black are new friends I'm delighted to know because of this book. I offer each of you my esteem, admiration, and heartfelt thanks. I'm also indebted to the photographers—especially James Hart, Dan Morse, Jack Parsons, and Addison Doty—whose images bring Luis's sculptures to life on the page. Each of these photographers has helped document and preserve Luis's work for more than forty years. My special thanks to James Hart and Addison Doty, who went to great lengths to shoot new works and to fill gaps in the photographic record, often with limited time.

The Owings Gallery, which has played a pivotal role in exhibiting and archiving Luis's work through time, generously provided images and collections information. *Mil gracias* to Laura Widmar, Kristin Graham, and Nat Owings for patiently fielding countless image queries and other requests, as well as to Mark Mulholland and Robert Stanfield for their assistance in providing a record of Luis's career and collections history.

In word and deed, a host of other friends and colleagues kindly pitched in to help. Peg Goldstein, who has been a cherished partner on many books, brought her detailed copyediting fluency and easygoing energy. Donna Pierce offered scholarly and editorial expertise and imagination (in addition to sisterly support). Cynthia Baughman lent her thorough and curious editorial eye. Alejandro López, a longtime *amigo del norte*, brought a perfectionist touch and a knowledge of New Mexican vernacular to the Spanish-language copyediting. And Clare Hertel and Joanna Hurley provided dynamic ideas and strategy for book promotion.

Many thanks to Barbara Anderson for enthusiastic feedback and her kind introduction to Charlene Villaseñor Black. Nancy Benkof gave helpful tips gleaned through her own book project. Laura Addison of the Museum of International Folk Art was a valuable sounding board, while others at the folk art museum, including Nicolasa Chávez, Ruth LaNore, Polina Smutko, and Khristaan Villela, generously provided access to their collections of Luis's work. Julie Wilson at the Denver Art Museum, Robin Farwell Gavin and Tannis Eberts at the Museum of Spanish Colonial Art, and Amy Scott and Marilyn Van Winkle at the Autry Museum also contributed collections information and assistance. Tey Marianna Nunn and David Gabel of the National Hispanic Cultural Center went above and beyond to assist in photography of important works. Finally, Jim Moore and Andrew Connors, both longtime Luis advocates, shared words of support, while Charles Rushton presented a lovely portrait.

This book would never have gotten out of the starting blocks—or to the finish line—if not for Curt, Christina, and Jonah Nonomaque, whose high regard for Luis and confidence in me propelled it forward. The New Mexico Community Foundation, especially Linda Milbourn and MaryAnn Lucero, as well as a caring group of collectors, lenders, and donors, further rooted this project in community to represent the true meaning of the word.

It is probably no surprise that most artists would rather spend time making art than looking back at the art they've made. Since he first took blade to wood, Luis has been carving a consciously consistent path forward, looking ahead to the next day in the studio, to the next piece that asks to be shaped. My inestimable thanks to Luis, my creative role model (who happens to be my husband), for trusting me to look back on his behalf. It was my honor to finally help make the book that celebrates his extraordinary imagination and dedication.

—Carmella Padilla

About the Contributors

DANA GIOIA is the Poet Laureate of California. He is the author of five collections of poetry, including *Interrogations at Noon* (2001), which won the American Book Award, and *99 Poems: New & Selected* (2016). His three critical collections include *Can Poetry Matter?* (1992), which was a finalist for the National Book Critics Award. Gioia has written three opera libretti and edited twenty literary anthologies. He served as chairman of the National Endowment for the Arts from 2003 to 2009. He holds the Judge Widney Chair of Poetry and Public Culture at the University of Southern California.

CHARLENE VILLASEÑOR BLACK is a professor of art history and Chicana/o Studies at the University of California, Los Angeles. She recently edited *Tradition and Transformation: Chicana/o Art from the 1970s to the 1990s* and a dossier on teaching Latina/Latino art in *Aztlán: A Journal of Chicano Studies*. Her 2006 book *Creating the Cult of St. Joseph: Art and Gender in the Spanish Empire* was awarded a College Art Association Millard Meiss Subvention. She is associate director of UCLA's Chicano Studies Research Center and the editor of *Aztlán*. In 2016 she was awarded UCLA's Gold Shield Faculty Prize for Academic Excellence.

LUCY R. LIPPARD is a writer, activist, sometime curator, and author of twenty-four books on contemporary art and cultural criticism, including *Undermining: A Wild Ride through Land Use, Politics and Art in the Changing West* (2014), *Down Country: The Tano of the Galisteo Basin, 1250–1782* (2010), *Mixed Blessings: New Art in a Multicultural America* (1990), and *The Lure of the Local: Senses of Place in a Multicentered Society* (1997). Recipient of nine honorary degrees, a Guggenheim fellowship, and a Lannan grant, among other awards, she lives off the grid in rural New Mexico, where she edits the monthly community newsletter *El Puente de Galisteo*.

TEY MARIANNA NUNN is director and chief curator of the art museum and the visual arts program at the National Hispanic Cultural Center. She previously spent a decade as curator of the contemporary Hispano and Latino collections at the Museum of International Folk Art. Nunn is active in issues concerning Latinos, the arts, and museums and has published numerous articles and books on these topics, including *Sin Nombre: Hispana and Hispano Artists of the New Deal Era* (2001). She has served on the board of directors of the American Alliance of Museums and the Western States Arts Federation and has received several awards and research fellowships. In 2016 President Barack Obama appointed her to the National Museum and Library Services Board.

Denise Chávez is a performance writer, novelist, and teacher whose work celebrates the border corridor of southern New Mexico, West Texas, and northern Mexico. Her novel *Face of an Angel* (1994) won the American Book Award, and her *The King and Queen of Comezón* (2014) won the 2015 International Latino Book Award and the New Mexico–Arizona Award for fiction. Her other books include *Loving Pedro Infante* (2001) and *A Taco Testimony: Meditations on Family, Food and Culture* (2006). Chávez is director of Casa Camino Real, a cultural center, bookstore, and art gallery on the historic Camino Real in Las Cruces, New Mexico.

Edward Hayes is curator of exhibitions at the Museum of Latin American Art (MOLAA), a position he began in 2013 after working at the McNay Art Museum in San Antonio. Hayes curated MOLAA's *Luis Tapia: Cada mente es un mundo* (2017) and has coordinated numerous other MOLAA exhibitions, including *Dreamland: A Frank Romero Retrospective* (2017), *Korda: Revolutionary Photographer* (2015), *Frida Kahlo, Her Photos* (2014), and *Neomexicanism* (2014). Hayes is author of *Dreamland: A Frank Romero Retrospective* (2017) and has supported several McNay publications, including *Andy Warhol: Fame and Misfortune* (2012) and *Estampas de la Raza: Contemporary Prints from the Romo Collection* (2012).

Carmella Padilla (editor) is a Santa Fe journalist, author, and editor who explores intersections in art, history, and culture in New Mexico and beyond. Padilla co-edited and contributed to *A Red Like No Other: How Cochineal Colored the World* (Skira Rizzoli, 2015), winner of the 2017 Alfred H. Barr Jr. Award for distinguished scholarship in art history. Her books include *The Work of Art: Folk Artists in the 21st Century* (2013), *El Rancho de las Golondrinas: Living History in New Mexico's La Ciénega Valley* (2009), and *Low 'n Slow: Lowriding in New Mexico* (1999), and her articles have appeared in the *Wall Street Journal*, the *Dallas Morning News*, *American Craft*, and elsewhere. In 2009 Padilla received the New Mexico Governor's Award for Excellence in the Arts.

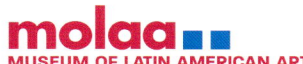

Published in 2017 by the Museum of Latin American Art
628 Alamitos Avenue
Long Beach, CA 90802

Distributed by University of Oklahoma Press, Norman, Oklahoma

Editor and project manager: Carmella Padilla
Design and production: David Skolkin
English copy editor: Peg Goldstein
Spanish copy editor: Alejandro López
Pre-press: John Vokoun, Fire Dragon Color
Printed in Singapore by Pristone Pte. Ltd.

ISBN: 978-0-9801080-8-8
Library of Congress Control Number: 2017938000

Page 1: *Santa cruz* (detail), 2006. Carved and painted wood, 30 x 58 x 15 in. Collection of Curt, Christina, and Jonah Nonomaque. Photo © Addison Doty, courtesy of The Owings Gallery.

Pages 2–3: *Gangster Crossing* (detail), 2008. Carved and painted wood, 30 x 20⅜ x 8¾ in. Collection of John Robertshaw. Photo © Addison Doty, courtesy of The Owings Gallery.

Pages 3–4: Worn work gloves line a wall of Luis Tapia's studio. Photo © Addison Doty.

Pages 6–7: Luis Tapia's studio. Photo © Addison Doty.

Pages 8–9: *Man without a Heart* (detail), 2007. Carved and painted wood, 30 x 20½ x 9 in. Private collection. Photo © Addison Doty, courtesy of The Owings Gallery.

Pages 10–11: Luis Tapia at work on *A Slice of American Pie*, 2007. Photo © Addison Doty.